UNIX® Desktop Guide to X/Motif™

Nabajyoti Barkakati

Consulting Editors: Stephen G. Kochan and Patrick H. Wood

HAYDEN BOOKS

A Division of Macmillan Computer Publishing
11711 North College, Carmel, Indiana 46032 USA

To Leba, Ivy, Emily, and Ashley

©1991 by Hayden Books

Library of Congress Catalog No: 91-61708

ISBN: 0-672-22836-X

94 93 92 91   8 7 6 5 4 3 2 1

Interpretation of the printing code: the rightmost double-digit number is the year of the book's printing; the rightmost single-digit number, the number of the book's printing. For example, a printing code of 91-1 shows that the first printing of the book occurred in 1991.

This book covers X Window System Version 11 Release 4 (X11R4) and OSF/Motif Version 1.1.

Overview

Contents

Part III   OSF/Motif Quick Reference

Preface

Using UNIX typically means typing commands at a text terminal. Whereas UNIX includes excellent mechanisms, such as the `termcap` and `terminfo` files for device-independent text output, it lacked a similar support for graphics output. Happily for UNIX users, this situation changed in 1987 when the X Window System (X) became widely available. X is essentially a mechanism for displaying device-independent bit-mapped graphics. It is also a windowing system so that applications can organize output in separate windows. Whereas X provides the mechanisms for windowed output, it does not offer any specific *look-and-feel* for applications. The look-and-feel comes from graphical user interfaces (GUIs), such as OSF/Motif and OPEN LOOK, based on X. Both GUIs are popular among UNIX users, with OPEN LOOK favored by Sun Microsystems and AT&T and OSF/Motif backed by the members of the Open Software Foundation. This foundation includes Hewlett-Packard, Digital Equipment Corporation, and IBM. Additionally, UNIX vendors, such as Santa Cruz Operations and Interactive Systems Corporation, include OSF/Motif in their offering.

The increasing availability of X and OSF/Motif is good news for UNIX, but UNIX users and programmers are now faced with the dilemma of understanding and using the Motif GUI. Most users are perplexed by the workings of X-based GUIs. Unlike Apple Macintosh and Microsoft Windows, the OSF/Motif environment does not appear as a monolithic entity to the user. Because Motif is based on X, the user has to contend with the concepts of an X server and one or more client applications displaying at the server. For example, the users have to know that the window manager that helps them move and resize windows is an X client just like any other X application. The situation is further complicated by X's capability for working across the network; it is often difficult to grasp the details of running an X application at a remote machine and having the output appear at a local workstation's screen. What UNIX users need is a practical guide that explains the basic concepts of X and OSF/Motif and describes how to customize and use the Motif environment.

UNIX Desktop Guide to X/Motif is a tutorial reference designed to address these needs. It introduces UNIX users and programmers to X and OSF/Motif, explains how to customize the Motif Window Manager (mwm), and shows how to use various X utilities for routine chores such as accessing the UNIX shell and taking snapshots of the screen. The book also includes chapters on creating applications using the OSF/Motif toolkit. The latter half of the book is a quick reference guide to the Motif Window Manager, OSF/Motif widgets, Xt Intrinsics, and X events. The information in the reference section will help you set up the Motif graphical environment and write Motif toolkit-based programs. Because this is a guide to a GUI, the book includes many screen shots illustrating how the interface looks and how it works.

In summary, the book features

- Concise overviews of X and OSF/Motif

- Step-by-step instructions for starting X and the Motif Window Manager

- Description for customizing the look-and-feel of the Motif environment

- Explanation for using the standard X clients, such as xterm, xwd, and xman

- Introduction to programming with the OSF/Motif toolkit

- Quick Reference Guides to the Motif Widgets, Xt Intrinsics, and X Events

Even if you have already seen X and Motif in action, this guide can provide the background that you need to understand how X works and see how X provides the foundation for the OSF/Motif graphical user interface. This guide is not a complete reference manual to X and OSF/Motif. The idea behind the guide is to familiarize you with the concepts underlying X and get you started with some simple programming exercises using the Motif widget set. For detailed information on Xlib and Motif functions, consult one or more of the books listed at the end of Chapter 1.

Acknowledgments

I am grateful to Linda Sanning of Macmillan Computer Publishing for initiating the *UNIX Desktop Guide Series* and for giving me the opportunity to work on this desktop guide. Thanks to Ella Davis for subsequently taking care of the project and seeing it through to its successful completion. Barbara LoFranco of The Santa Cruz Operations helped me immensely by providing copies of Open Desktop Personal System and Open Desktop Development System so that I could use the X Window System and OSF/Motif and develop the examples for this book. Finally, I am thankful for the love and support of my wife Leha and my daughters Ivy, Emily, and Ashley as I spent my evenings working on yet another book.

Nabajyoti Barkakati

Trademark Acknowledgments

All terms mentioned in this book that are known to be trademarks or service marks are listed here. In addition, terms suspected of being trademarks or service marks have been appropriately capitalized. SAMS cannot attest to the accuracy of this information. Use of a term in this book should not be regarded as affecting the validity of any trademark or service mark.

AT&T is a registered trademark of American Telephone and Telegraph Company.

Apple and Macintosh are registered trademarks of Apple Computer, Inc.

BSD is a trademark of University of California, Berkeley.

CompuServe is a registered trademark of CompuServe, Inc.

DEC is a registered trademark of Digital Equipment Corporation.

DECnet, Ultrix, VAX, VAXstation II/GPX, VAX/VMS, and VMS are trademarks of Digital Equipment Corporation.

Ethernet is a trademark of Xerox Corporation.

Helvetica and Times are trademarks of Linotype Company.

Hewlett-Packard and HP are registered trademarks of Hewlett-Packard Company.

IBM, IBM PC, IBM XT, and IBM AT are registered trademarks of the International Business Machines Corporation.

Intel is a registered trademark and Intel 8088, 8086, 80186, 80286, 80386, 80486, i860, 8087, 80287, and 80387 are trademarks of Intel Corporation.

Microsoft and MS-DOS are registered trademarks of Microsoft Corporation.

Motif, OSF, and OSF/Motif are trademarks of Open Software Foundation, Inc.

Motorola MC68000 is a trademark of Motorola, Inc.

Open Desktop and SCO are registered trademarks of The Santa Cruz Operation, Inc.

OPEN LOOK and System V are trademarks of AT&T.

OS/2 and Presentation Manager are trademarks of International Business Machines.

PostScript is a registered trademark of Adobe Systems, Inc.

Sun Workstation and Sun Microsystems are registered trademarks of Sun Microsystems, Inc.

TEKTRONIX is a registered trademark of Tektronix, Inc.

The Santa Cruz Operation is a trademark of The Santa Cruz Operation, Inc.

Times Roman is a trademark of Monotype Corporation.

UNIX is a registered trademark of UNIX System Laboratories.

X Window System is a trademark of The Massachusetts Institute of Technology.

Introduction

What This Book Is About

UNIX Desktop Guide to X/Motif is an intermediate level book that introduces the basic concepts of X and OSF/Motif and shows how to write programs using the Motif toolkit. This book assumes that you already know the C programming language. The goal is to get you, the UNIX user and C programmer, started so that you can make productive use of an X toolkit such as OSF/Motif in your programs. To this end, the book focuses on the basic concepts of X, using X applications, and configuring the Motif Window Manager (mwm). It also covers programming with the Xt Intrinsics and shows how to use the OSF/Motif widget set. Examples and screen snapshots are used to show the result of using a function or a widget. The idea is to get you to say, "Oh, I see! *That's* what this function does." Once you reach this point, it is a simple matter to use that function or widget when you need it.

Although *UNIX Desktop Guide to X/Motif* includes reference pages on the Xt Intrinsics and the Motif widgets, it is not a complete reference for the Xt Intrinsics or the OSF/Motif toolkit. This book's goal is to introduce these tools, not simply to duplicate the wealth of information available in the official OSF/Motif reference manuals. However, once you are familiar with a function or a widget, you can use this guide to look up quickly the calling syntax for a function or to verify the name of a widget's resource. In this way, the guide can be handy for experienced X and Motif programmers as well.

What You Need

To make the best use of this book, you need access to a graphics workstation with the X Window System or an X terminal connected to a host that runs X. That way you can test the examples as you progress through the book.

For those who want to explore X on their own, a reasonable "workstation" would include an Intel 80386-based PC with a VGA monitor, at least 8MB of memory, a 150MB hard disk running one of the commercially available

UNIX System V implementations and, of course, X and OSF/Motif. All examples in this book were tested on such an Intel 80386-based workstation running SCO Open Desktop (which includes UNIX System V/386 Release 3.2, X Version 11 Release 3, and OSF/Motif version 1.0). The examples should compile and link on most UNIX systems without any change. They do assume an ANSI-standard C compiler because two features of standard C are used: function prototypes and the variable-length arguments.

Although the examples were tested under X version 11 Release 3 (X11R3) and OSF/Motif version 1.0, the reference material conforms fully to X11R4 and OSF/Motif version 1.1.

Conventions Used in This Book

UNIX Desktop Guide to X/Motif uses a simple notational style. All listings are typeset in a monospace font for ease of reading. All file names, function names, variable names, and keywords appearing in text are also in the monospace font. The first occurrence of new terms and concepts are in *italic*. Text that has to be entered by the user appears in **bold monospace**.

How to Use This Book

This book has three parts. The first two are tutorials with a total of seven chapters. Part One includes three chapters that explain the basic concepts of X and OSF/Motif and show how to configure the Motif Window Manager (mwm). Part Two has four chapters that describe how to use standard X applications and how to get started as a Motif programmer. Part Three consists of four chapters meant to serve as quick reference guides to mwm, the Motif Widgets, Xt Intrinsics, and X Events.

If you are a newcomer to X and Motif, read Chapters 1 through 7 in sequence. If you already know enough about using X applications and specifying color and font names and you want to get started with Motif programming, read Chapters 6 and 7. These two chapters explain the basic architecture of the Xt Intrinsics and show some sample programs using Xt Intrinsics and Motif widgets. For experienced X and Motif programmers, Chapters 8 through 11 are a handy source of information on the calling syntax of Motif and Xt Intrinsics functions.

How to Contact the Author

If you have any questions, suggestions, or errors to report, please contact me by mail or electronic mail. Here is how:

- Write to LNB Software, Inc.
  2005 Aventurine Way
  Silver Spring, MD 20904

- If you have access to an Internet node, send e-mail to

  naba@grebyn.com

- If you use CompuServe, specify the following as SEND TO

  >INTERNET:naba@grebyn.com

- From MCIMAIL, specify the following when sending mail:

  EMS: INTERNET
  MBX: naba@grebyn.com

Please do not phone, even if you happen to come across my telephone number. Send a letter or an e-mail message. You are guaranteed a prompt reply.

Part

I

Introducing X and OSM/Motif

## Chapter 1

Learning the Basics
of X and OSF/Motif

The X Window System (X) is a device-independent, network-transparent, graphics windowing system for raster displays. Chapter 1 expands this terse definition of X, describes how X works, and explains how the OSF/Motif graphical user interface (GUI) fits into the picture.

It starts with a comparison of the X Window System with graphics terminals. This should help you understand how X is essentially like a graphics terminal with greater graphics and communications capabilities. Next, the chapter describes the components of X, explains how they support user interaction, and indicates where X fits in a computing environment. The latter part of the chapter provides a general definition of graphical user interfaces and describes the components of the OSF/Motif graphical user interface including a summary of the tools you can use to create Motif applications.

1

Terminology

Bit-Mapped or Raster Graphics Displays

Graphics displays have two distinct components:

- Video monitor, the terminal where the output appears

- Video controller, the circuitry that causes the output to appear by sending the appropriate signals to the monitor

In a bit-mapped graphics display system, the monitor displays an array of dots (*pixels*), and the appearance of each pixel corresponds to the contents of a memory location in the video controller. For a black-and-white display where each pixel is either bright or dim, a single bit of memory can store the state of a pixel. The term *bit mapped* refers to this correspondence between each bit in memory and a pixel on the screen.

Raster graphics is another name for bit-mapped graphics because the graphics appearing on the monitor are constructed from a large number of horizontal lines known as *raster lines.* An electron beam generates these raster lines by sweeping back and forth on a phosphor-coated screen. Because each dot of phosphor, corresponding to a pixel, glows in proportion to the intensity of the beam, each line of the image can be generated by controlling the beam's intensity as it scans the screen. Drawing the raster lines repeatedly creates the illusion of a steady image.

Process

In most operating systems, the term *process* refers to a program executing in memory and its associated environment. The environment usually includes the input and output files belonging to the program and a collection of variables known as *environment variables.* You create a process whenever you execute a program. The command interpreter of the operating system (called a *shell* in UNIX) is also a process—one that creates processes at your command.

Traditional Approach to Graphics Versus the X Window System

To understand how X works, you must compare it with the conventional approach to graphics output. Until workstations came along, graphics terminals were the only way to get graphics output from a computer program. For the sake of concreteness, consider how a terminal such as the Tektronix 4107 is used and programmed. Typically, this terminal is connected to a computer through a serial RS-232 connection. Application programs that have to display graphics output do so by calling the appropriate functions from a graphics library. These functions do their job by sending a stream of bytes to the terminal, which interprets these bytes and produces graphics output. Figure 1.1 illustrates this approach to graphics output. The following are the salient points of the traditional approach to graphics output:

- A graphics terminal usually displays output from one system at a time.

- The graphics library is tied to a specific type of terminal; it is device-dependent.

Graphics with X (see Figure 1.2) are similar to graphics done in the traditional way, but X improves on the traditional approach in a number of important ways:

- An X-based application program is partitioned into two distinct components: an *X server* controlling the graphics workstation and an *X client* program that sends the drawing commands to the server.

- The X server uses a standard protocol called the *X protocol* to interpret the data stream sent by the X clients and to perform the tasks requested by client applications.

- The client applications send graphics requests to the server via an 8-bit communication link such as TCP/IP, DECnet, or AppleTalk. This allows the X clients running on a computer to display their output on an X server elsewhere in a network.

The X protocol is similar to the byte sequences necessary to program a graphics terminal like the Tektronix 4107. Just as bytes sent from the application control the Tektronix 4107 terminal, the X protocol byte stream controls the X display server.

1

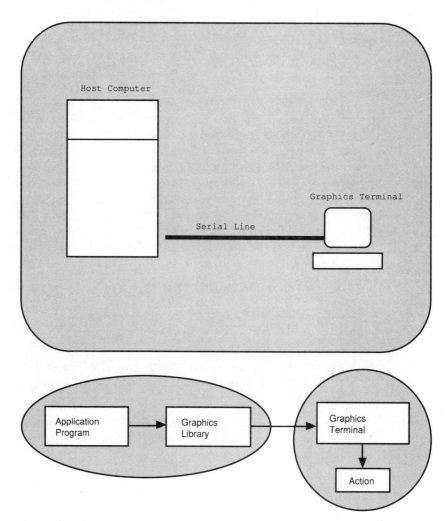

Fig. 1.1. Traditional host-based graphics.

However, the differences between terminals like the Tektronix 4107 and X are crucial. Whereas the Tektronix 4107 is typically configured as a terminal that works over a serial connection, the X protocol will work over any 8-bit network connection. This means X can work over many different types of communication links, including many types of local area networks as well as serial communication links over modems. Also, the X protocol defines a more powerful set of capabilities than the 4107. For example, X supports a hierarchy of windows and conceptual models of hardware display devices to achieve device independence.

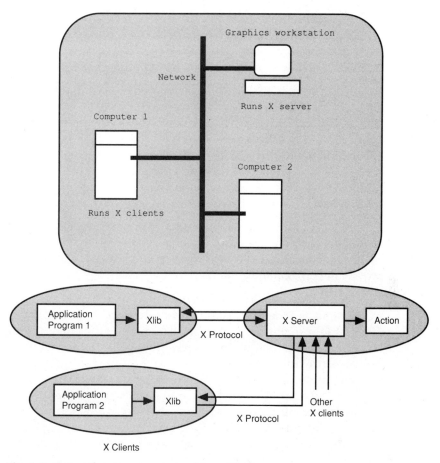

Fig. 1.2. Network-transparent graphics with X.

Components of X

Even after reading through the comparison of X and a graphics terminal, if you are not sure how to describe X concisely, you are not alone. Defining X is like defining UNIX. If you are willing to accept the definition that UNIX is an operating system, you can settle for the definition that X is a windowing system. However, if you want to know exactly what a windowing system means, you would have to read the entire chapter before you arrive at your own definition of X.

1

Essentially, the term *X Window System* is loosely applied to a number of components that facilitate window-based graphics output on a variety of bit-mapped displays. Although you will learn about the components of X in detail in the following sections, here is a summary description of X.

At the heart of X is the *X server*—a process (a computer program) running on a computer system with a bit-mapped display, a keyboard. Applications—*X clients*—that need to display output do so by communicating with the X server by one of several possible interprocess communication mechanisms. The communication between the X clients and the server follows a well-defined protocol—the *X protocol*. In addition to the X server, the clients, and the X protocol, the term *X* also encompasses a library of routines known as *Xlib* that constitutes the C language interface to the facilities of the X server.

As you can see from the brief comparison of X to traditional graphics, X has several components: the X server, X clients, and the X protocol used by clients and servers to exchange messages. Additionally, the Xlib routines provide the programming interface to X.

In a typical scenario, your workstation is connected to several other workstations and computers through a local area network. As shown in Figure 1.3, with X running at your workstation, you can interact with several processes, each displaying in its own window on the screen. Some of the processes may run locally at the workstation (provided your workstation's operating system is capable of handling multiple processes), and some may be executing on another system. For example, in Figure 1.3, window 1 is where you are interacting with your workstation. This window appears as a terminal to the workstation. Window 2 shows the output of an X application also running in the workstation. Window 3 is another terminal window where you may be interacting with computer A, while the output of another X application executing in computer B appears in the fourth window.

Clients and Servers

Behind the scenes in Figure 1.3, the X server is running in your workstation, listening to the network connection at a specific port, and acting on the commands sent by X clients (applications that use the workstation's display).

This arrangement, shown in Figure 1.4, is known as the *client-server model*. As the name implies, the server provides a service requested by the client. Usually, clients communicate with the server through a network, and client and server exchange data using a protocol understood by both. You may have seen this model in action. For example, a *file server* stores files and allows clients to access and manipulate them. Another common application, the *database server,* provides a centralized database from which clients can retrieve data by sending queries. Similarly, as illustrated in Figure 1.4, the X display server offers graphics display services to clients that send X protocol requests to the server.

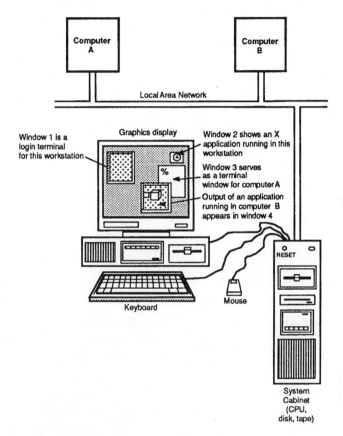

Fig. 1.3. A workstation with the X Window System.

Whereas file servers and database servers are usually processes executing in remote machines, the X server is a process executing in your workstation while serving clients that may be running locally or on remote systems.

X Server

The functionality of the X Window System is in the X server—the process executing in your workstation and managing the graphics output and the inputs from the keyboard and mouse. Figure 1.5 provides a simplistic representation of what goes on in an X display server. It shows modules that read X protocol requests from clients over a network connection and processes requests from each client. If a request is for graphics output, a device-dependent graphics module takes care of generating the output on your workstation's display.

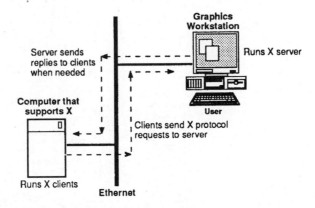

Fig. 1.4. Client-Server Model.

Hierarchy of Windows

Creating a window is one of the basic X protocol requests the X server handles. An X application often appears to have a single output window, yet most X applications use many windows to construct the user interface.

Consider the sample X application shown in Figure 1.6. This text editor has a text entry area and two scrollbars to examine text that may not be visible in the window. Even at this basic level in the application, two windows are on-screen: the *root window,* which occupies the entire display screen, and the *editor window*, which is inside the root window. On closer examination, the editor window turns out to be a frame that holds three other windows: the document window where the text appears and the two scrollbar windows. Looking further, each scrollbar window contains three smaller windows (see Figure 1.7): the thumbwheel in the middle and two arrows at the ends.

This arrangement of windows in a parent-child hierarchy is the norm in X. Figure 1.6 shows the editor window as a child of the root. The editor window has three children: the document window and two scrollbar windows. Each scrollbar window, in turn, has three children: two arrow windows and a thumbwheel window. This results in a tree-like hierarchy of windows for the text editor (see Figure 1.8).

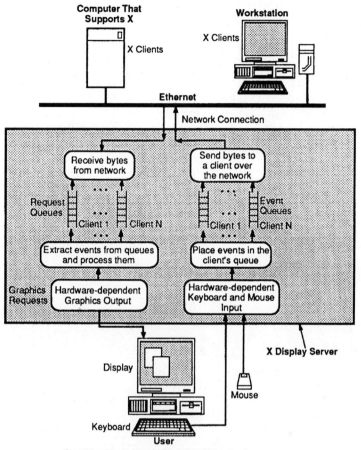

Fig. 1.5. Simplified view of the X server.

Event Delivery

The X server considers anything you do with the keyboard and the mouse as events to be reported to the clients. Typically, you move the mouse, and a small graphics shape (the *mouse pointer)* follows the motion on the screen. When you run X applications, everything on the screen appears in windows, and each window is associated with a specific client. When you press and release a mouse button, the X server sends these *mouse events* to the client that originally created the window containing the mouse pointer. For *keyboard events,* the keystroke always belongs to a designated window—the window that receives the keyboard events is said to have the *input focus.* As you will learn in Chapter 3, the user can control, via the window manager, which window gets the input focus.

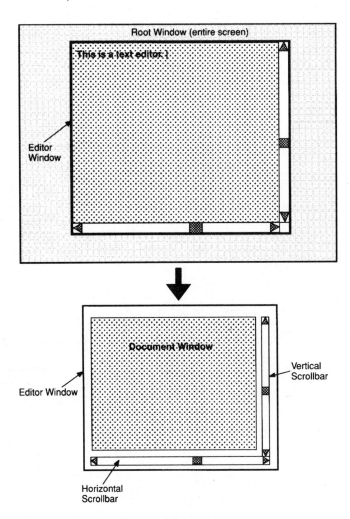

Fig. 1.6. The text editor window and its components.

In addition to mouse and keyboard events, the X server sends *expose events* to clients. These inform a client when something happens to its window. For example, previously obscured parts of a window may reappear when you move the overlapping windows around. In this case, the server sends an expose event to the client application, which is responsible for redrawing the exposed area of the window. In X applications, as with standard Macintosh displays and the PC screen under Microsoft Windows, the burden of maintaining the appearance of a window rests with the application that owns it, not with the X server. This is one aspect of X server that usually surprises newcomers: If an application's code does not handle expose events, nothing will be drawn in the window.

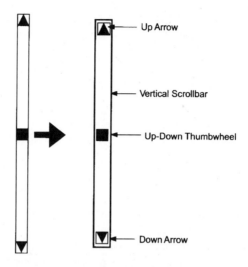

Fig. 1.7. Components of the scrollbar window.

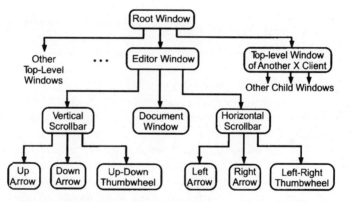

Fig. 1.8. Hierarchy of windows in the editor.

X Protocol: The Machine Language of X

Because X clients communicate with display servers using the X protocol, X protocol defines exactly what can be achieved with the X Window System. A *protocol* is an agreement between the server and the client regarding how they exchange information and how that information is interpreted. Using the X protocol, clients and the server exchange data through some form of inter-process communication mechanism. The X protocol defines the meaning of the data exchanged between the clients and the server. By drawing an analogy with a microprocessor, you might say that the X protocol is the machine

1

language of the X Window System. Just as the logic circuitry in a microprocessor interprets the bit-patterns in instruction bytes and performs some simple task, the X display server interprets the X protocol byte stream and generates graphics output. Thus, the X protocol completely defines the capabilities of the X Window System.

Xlib: The Assembly Language of X

You can write an application that uses the X display server by directly sending bytes that conform to the X protocol. Doing so, however, is tedious—like programming a microprocessor using only machine language. Fortunately, the X Window System comes with a library of C routines known as Xlib. Xlib gives you access to the X protocol through more than 300 utility routines. If the X protocol is the machine language of X, then Xlib is its assembly language. Programming in assembly language is not easy, but it is much easier than using machine language.

X Toolkits: The High-Level Languages of X

Although the Xlib is convenient, its capabilities are basic. For example, Xlib does not have a function that displays a menu with a selected list of entries. You can create a menu by calling a number of Xlib routines, but that takes some work. To solve this problem, you need another set of routines that implements objects such as buttons, lists, and menus, which can be used to build a GUI. This idea has been pursued by several groups. The X Window System comes with the *X Toolkit Intrinsics* (also known as *Xt Intrinsics)*, which uses an object-oriented approach to implement basic building blocks called *widgets.* Some other toolkits, such as the Motif toolkit from Open Software Foundation, use a still higher level of abstraction. The Motif toolkit is built on the X Toolkit Intrinsics. Continuing with our analogy of microprocessor programming, these are the high-level languages of the X Window System.

X Protocol, Xlib, or Toolkit?

You may be wondering whether anyone ever uses the X protocol directly. You need to worry about X protocol only when implementing an X display server or when writing a library of routines for use in X applications as a programming interface to the X protocol. Of course, just as all C programs are ultimately translated to machine code, all calls to Xlib or X toolkit routines eventually get converted to X protocol requests.

1

If you plan to begin programming in X, Xlib is a good place to start. You'll learn what X can do and how to perform basic tasks such as opening a window, handling a keystroke or button press, and drawing text and graphics in a window. When developing complete applications, you will find it more productive to use a toolkit. The penalty for using a toolkit is that toolkit-based applications generally require more memory than those based on bare-bones Xlib routines.

Most meaningful X applications cannot be written using routines from a toolkit alone. The toolkit developers try to build a repertoire of widgets that are most likely to be used in a user interface, but they cannot guess the exact purpose of an application. For example, many of the application-dependent tasks involve drawing inside a window. The same user interface may be used in a text editor and a drawing program, but each program behaves differently when you press a mouse button inside the application's display area. The text editor may move a cursor, whereas the drawing program may draw a line in response to the same button press. To handle these tasks, the application calls Xlib routines. This is why knowledge of Xlib is essential for X application developers.

Figure 1.9 shows the general structure of an X application. The application calls routines primarily from a toolkit. The toolkit may call routines from the Xt Intrinsics, which, in turn, calls Xlib. The application may also make direct calls to some Xlib routines for generating text and graphics output in a window.

Graphical User Interfaces

If you are familiar with other window systems such as the Macintosh Operating System and Microsoft Windows, you may be surprised to learn that the X Window System does not offer any specific on-screen appearance. This is because the designers of X refrained from imposing any requirements on how the windows are laid out. All X provides is a way to create a hierarchy of windows, draw in them, and determine whether any key or mouse button is pressed. With X, programmers are free to create any appearance and behavior they like. The actual look-and-feel issues are left to the programmers of GUIs such as OSF/Motif and OPEN LOOK, which are based on the X Window System.

An application's user interface determines its appearance (look) and behavior (feel). When the user interface makes use of graphical objects such as windows and menus, it's called a *graphical user interface* (GUI). You might call it a *point and click* user interface because users generally interact with a GUI

1

by moving the mouse pointer on the screen and clicking it. For example, to indicate consent to closing a file, the user may click the mouse button with the pointer inside a box labeled OK.

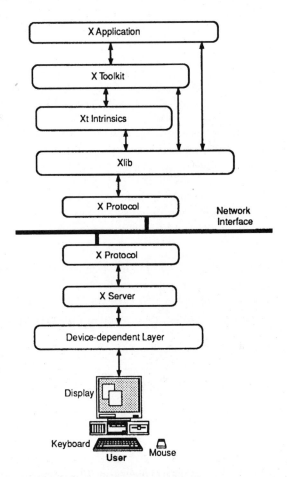

Fig. 1.9. General structure of an X application.

GUIs were pioneered at the Xerox Palo Alto Research Center (PARC). Subsequently such interfaces were made popular by Apple Computer in their Lisa and Macintosh systems. Now GUIs are available for most systems. Microsoft Windows is available for MS-DOS PCs, Presentation Manager is available for OS/2, and several interfaces built on X are available for UNIX.

Components of a GUI

A GUI has four components, which are discussed in detail later in this book.

- A graphical *window system* that organizes graphics output on the display screen and performs the basic text and graphics drawing functions.

- A *window manager* that provides a mechanism by which, when several windows are on the screen, users can indicate the window with which they intend to interact. This is referred to as giving the input focus to a window. The window manager also lets the user move windows around and resize them. A window manager is also partly responsible for the appearance of the windows because it usually adds a decorative frame to the windows.

- A *toolkit,* which is a library of routines with a well-defined programming interface. This toolkit allows programmers to write applications that make use of the facilities of the window system and have a consistent look and feel.

- A *style guide* that specifies the appearance and behavior of the user interface of an application. This component is necessary to guarantee the consistent look and feel of applications built with a GUI.

You may think that following a style guide hinders creativity, but it applies only to the common elements of the applications' user interface. The GUI does not impose any restrictions on the specific functions that an application performs. Programmers have ample opportunity to be creative in designing these application-specific parts.

Optionally, a GUI may also include, as a fifth component, a high-level language to describe the layout of a user interface. For example, the OSF/Motif GUI includes the User Interface Language (UIL) that developers can use to describe the user interface of an application in a plain text file. A compiler for the UIL converts the text file to a binary one that is read by the application's main program during start-up. If you define an interface in UIL, you can change its look by merely editing and recompiling the UIL file.

GUI Construction with X

The window system provides graphics facilities necessary to build any GUI. Because X is a window system, you can build a GUI using the facilities of X.

1

The basic capabilities of X are primitive. You can define a hierarchy of windows, draw in them, and determine when a key or a mouse button is pressed. An application with a graphical interface, on the other hand, typically allows users to interact by selecting items from menus and clicking buttons. The GUI toolkit must provide routines that programmers can use to create items such as menus and buttons, display them, and handle mouse clicks in them. Although the primitive operations in X do not include these capabilities, you can build the toolkit for a GUI by writing higher-level routines that in turn call Xlib functions to do their job. For example, you may want to use an object-oriented approach and create a hypothetical `StaticButton` object that displays some text or a bit map image in a window. You can then create a `CommandButton` out of this `StaticButton` by assigning a function that will be called whenever the user clicks a mouse button inside the `StaticButton`'s window. Finally, a more complex `Menu` object can be constructed out of a number of `CommandButtons`.

To say that a GUI is built from X means that the GUI's toolkit is based on Xlib, the low-level C language interface to the X protocol. Many GUI toolkits are based on another set of routines called the Xt Intrinsics, which can be thought of as a library of utility functions for building other toolkits. The Xt Intrinsics is not an exclusive standard, but it is distributed with the X software from M.I.T., so several GUI toolkits use it.

X Toolkits

Xlib, the standard C language interface to X, does not include routines to create menus and buttons. Although you can use a number of Xlib routines to create an application with menus and buttons, it is much more productive to use a well-designed library of routines to create a user interface for any application. The Xt Intrinsics, included with the X software, is such a library. These routines are collectively called the Intrinsics because they can serve as the basis for other toolkits, such as the one for the OSF/Motif GUI.

The Intrinsics do not dictate any specific look and feel, which is why they can be used as the basis for any GUI. Instead, the Xt Intrinsics are a set of utility routines that programmers can use to build user-interface components such as labels, menus, dialog boxes, forms, and scrollbars. You can think of each user-interface component, or widget, as a hierarchy of X windows together with some functions that operate in the window. The toolkit of a GUI refers to a collection of such widgets. That is why toolkits are sometimes called *widget sets*. Chapter 6 describes the Xt Intrinsics and the Motif widget sets and shows you how to write application programs using these widgets.

OSF/Motif

OSF/Motif is the common user environment chosen by the Open Software Foundation (OSF), which was formed in 1988 by a group of major hardware vendors including IBM, DEC, and Hewlett-Packard. Instead of building a GUI from scratch, OSF solicited submissions from various organizations for existing X-based user interfaces. After reviewing more than 30 submissions, OSF decided on a hybrid GUI built from parts of other user interface systems. The new GUI, named OSF/Motif, uses X as the underlying window system. It includes DEC's toolkit (API), technology from DEC's X User Interface (XUI) Intrinsics-based toolkit, a window manager and widgets with a three-dimensional look derived from work done by Hewlett-Packard and Microsoft, and provides the look and feel of Microsoft's Presentation Manager (the successor to Microsoft Windows). The member companies of OSF expect this heritage of OSF/Motif to ease its acceptance among the large number of PC users who are familiar with Microsoft Windows and Presentation Manager.

The Motif Window Manager (mwm)

The Motif Window Manager (mwm) allows the user to move and resize windows. You can designate which window gets the keyboard input. And mwm provides a configurable menu through which you can start X client applications (Chapter 3 explains how to set up this menu). As shown in Figure 1.10, it also adds a frame around the top-level window of an application. This frame, with an optional three-dimensional bevelled look, has room for a title and gives you the ability to move and resize the window by pressing mouse buttons in the frame. The Motif window manager also adds a menu that can be activated by clicking in the button to the left of the title area (see Figure 1.10). The title area and the other boxes (collectively known as *gadgets*) added to the frame have been taken from Microsoft's Presentation Manager and Windows.

OSF/Motif Toolkit

The OSF/Motif toolkit (widget set and convenience routines) is based on the Xt Intrinsics. The toolkit includes a large number of widgets. *Shell widgets* are used as the top-level window of an application and as containers for pop-up menus and dialogs. The *text widget* is available for editing text, and a variety of Label, ArrowButton, ScrollBar, and List widgets are useful for constructing other customized components of an application's user interface.

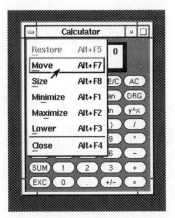

Fig. 1.10. Frame and menu added by mwm.

The first thing you will notice about the Motif widgets is their three-dimensional appearance. The appearance of a raised button is achieved by shading the boundary of the button's rectangle. The magnified version of the upper right corner of a Motif window frame, shown in Figure 1.11, illustrates the type of shading used to achieve this effect. Reversing the shading of the top and bottom areas creates the illusion of a button being pressed down.

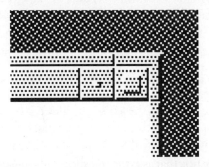

Fig. 1.11. Magnified version of Motif window frame showing three-dimensional shading.

Another interesting feature of the Motif widgets is that you can specify the size of objects in several different units. By default, the Motif toolkit assumes that all sizes are specified in pixels, but you can set the unit type to a device-independent one such as 1/100 of a millimeter, 1/1000 of an inch, 1/100 of a point, or 1/100 of a font size.

OSF/Motif Style Guide

The OSF/Motif style guide specifies the way an application should interact with the user. The style guide states how to indicate that a particular window (the focus window) is to receive all future keystrokes, how to move around on-screen, and how to perform common tasks such as selecting one or more objects for an operation.

The primary goal of these specifications is to promote consistency. All applications with similar menus and dialog boxes should act in a similar manner. The menu selections for an application should be presented to the user in an orderly manner.

The secondary goal is to allow the user to perform tasks by manipulating graphical representations of objects displayed on the screen. Examples of such direct manipulations include pushing a button to start some action and dragging a slider to scroll the display.

Flexibility is another key concern of the style guide. The user should be able to perform a task many ways. There should be ways of performing actions through a menu selection or by pressing a special combination of keys (this requirement comes from Motif's Presentation Manager heritage). Users should be able to specify parameters such as colors, fonts, and key bindings through resource files (resource files are described in Chapter 5). This means that applications should make use of the X resource manager to access these user-specified resources.

The Motif style guide also requires applications to provide as much help information for the user as possible. The information should depend on the context. For example, if the user asks for help as he or she tries to print a document, the information displayed should pertain to printing. Applications are also expected to request confirmation from the user whenever an action may irreversibly destroy something. For example, if the user selects the `Quit` option from the menu while working on a drawing, the application must display a dialog box that asks the question, `Do you want to save this drawing?`

Because the window manager determines part of the look and feel of a GUI, the style guide also specifies the requirements to be met by any window manager meant for the OSF/Motif environment. However, the style guidelines for window managers should not concern you unless you plan to write a new window manager.

Next to the Motif toolkit, the style guide is the most important document for application developers. You can learn most of the stylistic requirements by using existing Motif applications. For detailed information, consult the documentation that comes with the OSF/Motif software development package.

1

Summary

The X Window System is a network-transparent windowing system based on the client-server model. The X server process, running on a workstation with a bit-mapped graphics display, manages regions of the screen known as windows, where the output from X client applications appears. The X clients, whether running locally or on a remote computer, send requests to the server using a communication channel. The bytes exchanged between a client and the server conform to the X protocol. X version 11 (X11) consists of the X server, X protocol, and Xlib—the library of C routines that programmers use to access the server. The designers of X sought to provide only the primitive building capabilities necessary to support user interaction. They refrained from dictating how a user interface should look and feel. Thus, X can be used to build a variety of user interfaces.

By offering a standard window system, X allows clients and servers to interoperate: An X client on a system can display its output on any X server without regard to the display hardware or the operating system. A workstation can become an integral part of an environment as long as it supports X and it can be networked with the rest of the system. X servers are available even for MS-DOS PCs and Macintoshes.

The concept of X is much like that of a graphics terminal, except for X's network connection and better input and output capabilities. This similarity is exploited in a new type of terminal—the X terminal—which is a stripped-down workstation running an X server and having a network connection.

The term *graphical user interface* (GUI) describes a user interface that makes use of windows, menus, and other graphical objects and that, to a large extent, is an interface with which users interact by pointing and clicking mouse buttons. From an application developer's point of view, a GUI is a combination of a window manager, style guide, and library of routines (toolkit) that can be used to build the user interface.

By design, X provides the basic functions that can be used to build a GUI, but does not require the programmer to follow any specific style. Because of this, X itself is not a GUI, but many GUIs are built on X. OSF/Motif and OPEN LOOK are examples of such GUIs. Each of these GUIs has its own unique style and terminology, but neither offers substantial benefits over the other. Both OSF/Motif and OPEN LOOK provide adequate facilities for building user interfaces for applications and are the two dominant GUIs in UNIX systems.

Further Reading

1

If you want detailed information on using and programming the X Window System, you will find this author's recent book (Barkakati, 1991) handy. You may also want a copy of the book by Scheifler and Gettys (Scheifler and Gettys 1990) for the same reason C programmers need Kernighan and Ritchie—to get the official word on X from the architects of X. In addition to this book, the article by Scheifler and Gettys (Scheifler and Gettys, 1986) gives a good overview of the basic design philosophy of X. This article, the first to describe X in a journal, is based on version 10 of X, but much of the overview applies to X11 as well. Another good source of information on Xlib is the book by Oliver Jones (Jones, 1989) who provides many tips and techniques that you may not find in the standard manuals on X.

Of all X books, the ones from O'Reilly & Associates (O'Reilly, 1988–1990) were the first to appear and are the most widely used by programmers. Many workstation vendors have used these books as their manual for X.

The books by Young (Young, 1989, 1990) were the first available resources on X toolkit programming. Young's first book (Young, 1989) covers the X toolkit intrinsics; the second one (Young, 1990) is based on the OSF/Motif toolkit. More recently, Paul Asente and Ralph Swick (Asente and Swick, 1990) have documented the X Toolkit extensively. Their book is a complete reference to the X Toolkit.

For the official word on all aspects of OSF/Motif, you may want to get the five-volume set (Open Software Foundation, 1990) recently published by Prentice-Hall. Randi Rost's reference guide (Rost, 1990) to Motif is also a good source of information, but it does not include a tutorial.

Magazines such as UNIX Review and UNIX World are also a good source of information on X. David Rosenthal's recent article (Rosenthal, 1989) on interoperability of X clients and servers is an example of an article that covers a topic relevant to X programmers. Another notable article (Lee, 1988) is by Ed Lee who gives a good overview of X.

To learn more about various aspects of UNIX systems, consult the books (Kochan and Wood, 1989) by Kochan and Wood. Their compendium on UNIX networking has a chapter devoted to explaining how the X protocol works over a network.

Asente, Paul J., and Swick, Ralph R., *X Window System Toolkit*, Digital Press, 1990, 1002 pages.

Barkakati, Naba, *X Window System Programming*, SAMS, Carmel, IN, 1991, 778 pages.

Jones, Oliver, *Introduction to the X Window System*, Prentice-Hall, 1989, 525 pages.

Kochan, Stephen G., and Wood, Patrick H., *Exploring the UNIX System*, Second Edition, Hayden Books, Indianapolis, IN, 1989, 390 pages.

Kochan, Stephen G., and Wood, Patrick H., Editors, *UNIX Networking*, Hayden Books, Indianapolis, IN, 1989, 408 pages.

Lee, Ed, "Window of Opportunity," *UNIX Review* 6, No. 6, June 1988, pp.47–61.

Open Software Foundation, *OSF/Motif Style Guide*, 1990, 128 pages. *OSF/Motif Programmer's Guide*, 1990, 672 pages. *OSF/Motif Programmer's Reference*, 1990, 960 pages. *OSF/Motif User's Guide*, 1990, 96 pages, *Application Environment Specification (AES) User Environment Volume*, 1990, 854 pages, Prentice-Hall, Englewood-Cliffs, NJ.

O'Reilly & Associates, 6 volumes on the X Window System: *Volume 0: X Protocol Reference Manual*, 1989, 414 pages. *Volume 1: Xlib Programming Manual*, 1988, 664 pages. *Volume 2: Xlib Reference Manual*, 1988, 723 pages. *Volume 3: X Window System User's Guide*, 1989, 450 pages. *Volume 4: X Toolkit Intrinsics Programming Manual*, 1990, 574 pages. *Volume 5: X Toolkit Intrinsics Reference Manual*, 1990, 565 pages. O'Reilly & Associates, Petaluma, CA.

Rosenthal, David, S., "Window Exchange," *UNIX Review* 7, No. 12 (December 1989), pp. 59–64.

Rost, Randi J., *X and Motif Quick Reference Guide*, Digital Press, 1990, 376 pages.

Scheifler, Robert W., and Gettys, Jim, *X Window System: The Complete Reference to Xlib, X Protocol, ICCCM, XLFD*, Second Edition, Digital Press, 1990, 875 pages.

Scheifler, Robert W., and Gettys, Jim, "The X Window System," *ACM Transactions on Graphics* 5, No. 2, April 1986, pp. 79–109.

Young, Douglas A., *X Window Systems Programming and Applications With Xt*, Prentice-Hall, Englewood Cliffs, NJ, 1989, 478 pages.

Young, Douglas A., *Introduction to the X Window System: Programming and Applications with Xt, OSF/Motif Edition*, Prentice-Hall, Englewood Cliffs, NJ, 1990, 543 pages.

Up and Running

with X and Motif

Chapter 1 provided an overview of the X Window System and the OSF/Motif GUI. Now you have an opportunity to get acquainted with C as a user. Suppose that you have been given a UNIX workstation with X, and your assignment is to learn X well enough to implement an X-based user interface for an application. Chapter 2 helps you get started by showing you how to run X on your workstation.

Terminology

Shell Script. A file containing commands for the UNIX shell.

Environment Variables. A way to associate a name to an arbitrary string. In UNIX, the environment of a process consists of an array of strings, each string defining an environment variable of the form `VARIABLE=value`.

Starting X

2

Chapter 1 explained that an X server must be running in your workstation before you can display output from X applications. Thus, starting X involves running the X server, followed by running the X applications you want. If you also want to run applications on remote machines, follow the additional steps of logging onto the remote system, starting the application, and making sure the application knows where to send the output. The exact steps for doing this differs from one workstation vendor to another. Workstations that also have their own windowing system may require you to manually start the X server followed by the applications. Before you do any of this, however, you have to learn how to name displays in X.

Naming X Displays and Screens

The X Window System display consists of one or more screens, a keyboard, and a mouse. A system may have several displays, and each display may, in turn, have more than one screen. Each display has exactly one server process controlling all its input and output. Therefore, the terms *display* and *server* are used synonymously in X.

When an X client runs, it has to open a connection to a display. To do this, you have to identify the display by a name and cause the output to appear in a specific display. You can choose to specify the screen as well. Because the display can be anywhere in the network, you have to provide the network name of the system to which the display is connected in order to identify a display. Moreover, because more than one display can be in a system, you must also give the display number.

In X the displays in a system are numbered starting with zero. The name of a display is constructed by appending the display number to the system name, with a colon (:) as the separator. Thus, as shown in Figure 2.1, the first display in the system, lnbsys, will be named lnbsys:0; the second one will be named lnbsys:1. In UNIX System V, you can use the **uname -n** command to find the network name of your system. In BSD UNIX, the equivalent command is **hostname**.

In X, the screens within a display are numbered starting with zero also. To specify a screen, you append the screen number to a display's name with a period (.) as the separator. The first screen in Figure 2.1, display lnbsys:0, is named lnbsys:0.0. Because display 0 has two screens, the second one will be referred to as lnbsys:0.1. When the screen is not specified, the server assumes that you want screen 0, which is the default screen. Some displays may have only one physical CRT but support a number of logical screens. For example, an X display with a color monitor may provide a monochrome screen as well as a color one, each with its own screen number.

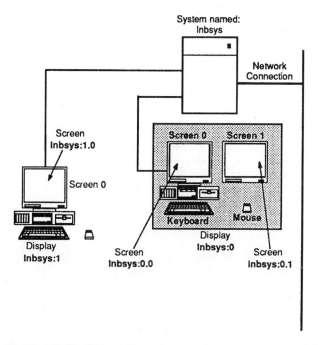

Fig. 2.1. Naming X displays and screens.

Environment Variables

Environment variables provide a convenient way to pass information to processes. For example, whenever you type the name of a program to be executed, the UNIX shell searches a list of directories given by the PATH environment variable, which is always set to a string containing a list of directory names separated by colons (:). You can examine the current setting of PATH with the shell command **echo $PATH**. A typical setting might appear as

```
/bin:/usr/bin:/etc:/usr/bin/X11:
```

With this setting for PATH, when you enter the name of a program, the shell will search the directories /bin, /usr/bin, /etc, /usr/bin/X11, and the current directory, in that order. When you use X, be sure the PATH environment

2

variable includes the directory that contains the X server and the X utility programs, usually /usr/bin/X11.

Environment variables are used not only by the shell but also by many application programs, including X applications, that use the DISPLAY environment variable to determine which server receives the output of a client. Accordingly, on the machine where you start an X client, you have to set DISPLAY to the name of the server where you want that client's output to appear. If you are going to run X applications locally in your workstation, you have to set DISPLAY variable on this system also. For example, if the system's name is lnbsys, DISPLAY should be set to lnbsys:0.0 to get the output on the first screen of the first display.

In the Bourne shell, use the command **DISPLAY=*sysname*:0.0; export DISPLAY** to set up the DISPLAY variable for output on a workstation named *sysname*. In C shell, use **setenv DISPLAY *sysname*:0.0**. You can see a list of your current environment variables by typing **printenv** at the shell prompt.

Starting the X Server

Now that you know how to name an X display and set the DISPLAY variable, you are ready to start the X server and run some X applications. After making sure that the PATH environment variable contains the /usr/bin/X11 directory, you can start X by typing the command **xinit**.

This executes the xinit program that comes with the standard X software distribution. The xinit script looks for a shell script named .xinitrc in the login directory. As you will see later, the .xinitrc file contains commands to be executed by xinit. If there is no such script file, xinit starts the X server and an application named xterm that behaves like a terminal. Figure 2.2 shows the appearance of the screen after running xinit in the absence of the .xinitrc file in your login directory. Once you have the X server and xterm running, you can start other X applications by typing commands in the xterm window. For example, you can start the xclock application and place its window at the lower right corner of the screen by typing the command:

```
xclock -digital -geometry -10-10&
```

Figure 2.3 shows the screen layout after xclock starts. The -digital option is for displaying the clock in a digital format. The -geometry option is for specifying the size and placement of xclock's window (see Chapter 5 for further details).

Fig. 2.2. The display screen after running `xinit`.

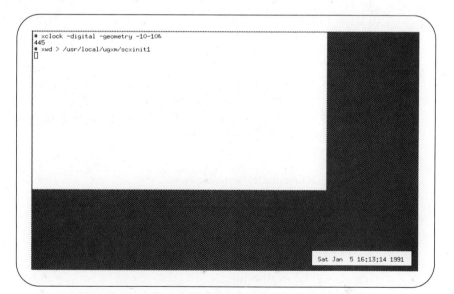

Fig. 2.3. The display screen after running `xclock`.

At this point, you do not have any way of resizing or moving the windows belonging to `xterm` and `xclock`. For that, you have to run a window manager. With OSF/Motif, the window manager is named `mwm` (Motif Window Manager). You can start this window manager by typing **mwm&** in the `xterm` window. The & ensures that `mwm` runs in the background, enabling you to use the `xterm` window for other tasks.

When you do this, the cursor will temporarily change to an hourglass, and soon the screen will appear as shown in Figure 2.4. Note that the window manager adds frames to the windows already on the screen. The Motif Window Manager also creates a window labeled `Icons` in which it displays a number of icons—one for each application connected to that X server.

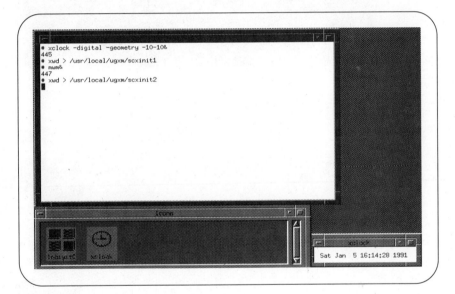

Fig. 2.4. Screen layout after starting mwm.

.xinitrc Start-Up Script

Because xinit automatically executes the shell script `.xinitrc` in your login directory, you can start a number of applications by specifying them in the `.xinitrc` file. For example, you can get a screen layout similar to the one shown in Figure 2.4 by placing the following commands in a file named `.xinitrc` in your login directory:

```
#  Clients started by xinit
#  Last client should not be in background
xterm -sb 2> /dev/null &
xclock -digital -geometry -10-10 2> /dev/null &
mwm 2> /dev/null
```

This will start xterm (the -sb option will enable the scrollbar), xclock, and the OSF/Motif Window Manager (mwm), with all error messages discarded (because of the redirection to the null device, indicated by 2> /dev/null).

In summary, this is how you can start the X server and selected X applications:

1. Make sure PATH contains /usr/bin/X11 so that the shell can find the X server program. If your vendor provides the server in a file with a name different than X, make a copy of that file to /usr/bin/X11/X.

2. Set the DISPLAY environment variable to your workstation's screen and prepare an .xinitrc file with the applications you want to run. Make sure that all applications except the last one are started in the background.

3. Start X by typing **xinit** at the shell prompt.

The startx Shell Script

Using xinit is simpler than starting the server and the applications manually; however, it is still complicated for X newcomers. For this reason, most system administrators and vendors of workstations provide a shell script, appropriately named startx, to perform all of the tasks that start the server and other applications. In its simplest form, the script typically starts off by setting the environment variables: the DISPLAY variable to identify the X server to X clients and PATH to include the directory where the X server program resides. Then the script invokes xinit to get the X server and applications going.

Most sites, however, have many more requirements. For example, a site may have a mix of X workstations and X terminals. Workstations may run local X clients, but X terminals will run only remote clients. The site administrator may want to have X terminal users log automatically into a specific remote system. Site administrators can meet these requirements by writing a site-specific startx script file. If your site uses startx to start an X session, you should consult its documentation or ask the system administrator for information on the site-specific features.

2

Running Remote X Clients

You learned how to start the X server and local clients by using `xinit` or the `startx` script file. Now how do you run remote X clients and have their output appear at your workstation's screen? Follow this basic process:

1. Log on the remote system.

2. Set the `DISPLAY` environment variable on that system to your screen.

3. Execute the client application.

For an X terminal displaying the login window from a remote `xdm` process, simply enter your name and password to get to the remote host. Otherwise, you will have to log into the remote system from an `xterm` window on your workstation.

Logging onto Remote Systems from `xterm`

To access a remote system from `xterm`, a network connection must exist between your workstation and that system. If there is a TCP/IP connection, you can log onto the remote system with the **rlogin *rname*** command, where **rname** is the name of the remote system. If you have an account on that system with the user name under which you have logged onto the workstation, you will immediately get the shell prompt from the remote system. Otherwise, you will be prompted for user name and password. Once you are logged onto the remote system, you can set the `DISPLAY` variable to your workstation and run the X clients of your choice. Consult Chapter 4 for a full description of the `xterm` terminal emulator.

Controlling Access to Your Workstation

When you are running a remote X client, a typical problem is that your workstation may refuse connection to the client; the remote client fails with an error message. If this happens, examine the contents of the file `/etc/X0.hosts` (assuming that your workstation has only one display). This file is used as an *access list* for display 0. It should contain the names of remote systems that are allowed to establish a connection with your workstation's X server. If you want clients running in two remote systems named `remote1` and `remote2` to display on your workstation, your workstation's `/etc/X0.hosts` file should contain

```
# List of authorized foreign hosts
#
remote1
remote2
```

Alternatively, while logged onto your workstation, you can give the command `xhost +remote1` to add the name `remote1` to the access list of your display.

Summary

2

Because X can work across a network connection, an X application has to open a connection to the display where its output appears. In X the display is synonymous with the X server and is identified by a name of the form `sysname:m.n`, where m and n are integers identifying the display number and the screen within a display. Because most workstations have only one display with a single screen, the name is `sysname:0.0`, where `sysname` is the network name of the workstation. Some workstations have a single physical screen but support several logical screens. For example, a single color monitor might provide color as well as monochrome logical screens. An X server's documentation would indicate whether it supports multiple screens.

Once you know how to name an X display, you can start X by setting the `DISPLAY` environment variable and running the `xinit` utility. Many sites also have a custom shell script, usually called `startx`, to start X and some selected clients. A utility named `xdm` is also available to manage sessions on X terminals.

Configuring the Motif

Environment

I n Chapter 2 you learned how to start X. This chapter focuses on the window manager, which is an X client designed to manage the layout of windows being displayed by an X server. Window managers impose policies on how windows are moved and resized, and how keyboard events are delivered, which controls much of the look and feel of applications. Chapter 3 briefly describes how to customize much of the Motif environment by configuring mwm. (Chapter 8 has a detailed reference guide to the many configurable parameters and options mwm supports.)

Terminology

Resource. In X, the meaning of this term depends on the context in which it is used. In the context of X's client-server architecture and in Xlib routines, *resource* refers to data items such as windows, fonts, colormaps, and bit maps that are created and maintained in the X server. These resources are accessed by clients through a resource identification (ID).

3

From a user's point of view, a resource is any feature of an X application that can be specified by the user. This includes the window's size, placement, foreground, and background colors, the font used to display text, and so on. Resources are used to customize the look and feel of X applications.

Resource File. A file containing values of resources for an X application. The entries in the resource file are of the form

```
resource_name: value
```

Typical resource files are .Xdefaults and .mwmrc in your login directory. See Chapter 5 for further details on resource file formats.

Click and Drag. Describes the user's interactions with the mouse. Clicking involves pressing and releasing a mouse button while the pointer is in a particular area of the screen. Dragging, on the other hand, means that the user has pressed a mouse button and is moving the mouse while keeping that button pressed.

Using mwm

A *window manager* is a special X client that allows you, at a bare minimum, to move and resize windows. For a closer look at a full-fledged window manager, consider mwm, the window manager for the OSF/Motif environment.

The executable file for the Motif Window Manager is named mwm; it usually resides in the directory /usr/bin/X11 along with the other X clients. Typically, you start it from a shell script that is used by xinit or a site-specific shell script named startx. For example, you can run mwm by placing the following command at the end of the startx script:

```
mwm 2> /dev/null
```

Once started, mwm adds a frame to all on-screen client windows. This frame allows users to move windows, resize them, change a window to an icon, and change the input focus. It also adds a menu to each window that enables you to kill that application by closing the window. Additionally, mwm provides a menu for the root window. This root menu allows you to launch new applications.

The following discussion assumes that the default settings of mwm as defined by the resource file /usr/lib/X11/system.mwmrc. Like most X applications, mwm is highly configurable. Therefore, do not be surprised if you find that mwm in your system does not behave exactly as described here.

Motif Window Frame

Under mwm, users can perform a variety of window management functions via the components built into the window frame that mwm adds to a client's window. As shown in Figure 3.1, the OSF/Motif window frame includes the following distinct components:

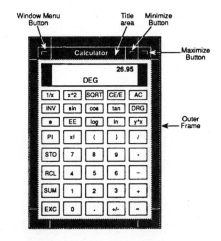

Fig. 3.1. Components of window frame in OSF/Motif.

Title Area. Displays the title of the window and enables you to move the window. Press the left mouse button while the pointer is in the title area. Move the mouse while you keep the button pressed. You will see an outline that follows the mouse movements. Select the new location and release the mouse button to indicate the new position of the window to mwm.

Minimize Button. The button to the right of the title area helps you to reduce the window to an *icon*—a small rectangle with the window's title in it. To activate this button, click the left button of the mouse while the pointer is in the button.

Maximize Button. The maximize button, located next to the minimize button, is used to enlarge the window to the full screen (or to the largest size allowed by the application). Activate the maximize button by clicking it once.

Window Menu Button. The window menu button appears to the left of the title area. When you press the left mouse button with the pointer in this area, mwm displays a menu from which you can select window resizing and placement functions. Use the Close option in the menu to kill a client.

Outer Frame. By dragging a corner, you can enlarge or shrink the window. Additionally, you can resize the window by dragging any of the four straight line segments of the frame. The window manager changes the cursor when you are in the border and draws an outline of the window to provide feedback as you drag the mouse.

Motif Icon Box

The mwm manager can be configured to start with an *icon box*—a window for storing icons. As shown in Figure 3.2, each application has an iconic representation in the icon box. When you click on the minimize button of an application, a border appears around its icon in the icon box. For example, in Figure 3.2 the border around the icon of the calculator (note how the title is truncated) indicates that it has been reduced to an icon. Absence of a border implies that the application is running in its window.

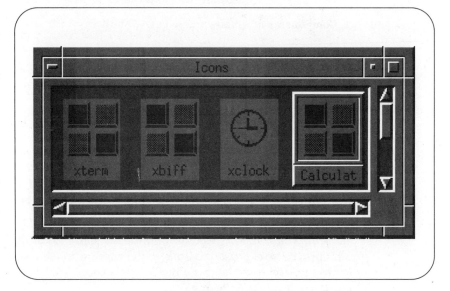

Fig. 3.2. The icon box under the Motif window manager.

Root Menu

Under mwm, when you press the left mouse button anywhere in the root window, you will get a menu (often called the root menu). This menu is configurable by the user. Typically it lists items that start an application when selected. The menu may even include choices for rearranging windows. You can configure the root menu so that a selected item pops up a submenu with further selections. For example, in the root menu shown in Figure 3.3, pressing the mouse button with the pointer in the Clients item brings up a submenu with a list of clients. To start any of these clients, simply move the pointer to the client's name and release the mouse button. The following discussions briefly describe how to customize mwm. Consult Chapter 8 for further details on configuring the Motif window manager.

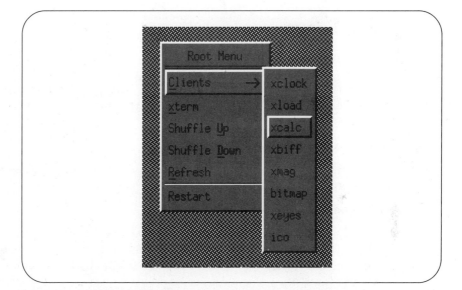

Fig. 3.3. A typical root menu in mwm.

Customizing mwm

You can customize mwm in two ways:

- Through a resource file that provides values for resources in a general format used by all Xt-based applications (see Chapter 5)

- Through a configuration file that specifies settings in a format accepted by mwm

If you start mwm without any command-line options, by default it reads resource settings from a file named /usr/lib/X11/app-defaults/Mwm. In this file, a resource named configFile gives the name of the configuration file that specifies menus and bindings for mouse buttons and keys. If this resource is not found, mwm looks for a file named .mwmrc in the user's home directory, which is specified by the HOME environment variable. If no .mwmrc file is found in that directory, mwm uses the contents of the file /usr/lib/X11/system.mwmrc to configure its menus and bind the keys and mouse buttons to specific actions.

It is easy to get confused by the variety of ways in which you can customize X applications. For the mwm, a good approach is to create a file named .mwmrc in your home directory and place all configuration options in that file. Chapter 5 discusses other ways of specifying resources.

Input Focus

You can control the style of input focus through a resource named keyboardFocusPolicy. The window with the input focus receives all keyboard events. For example, to achieve a Macintosh-style behavior where you explicitly indicate which window has the focus, place the following line in your .mwmrc file:

```
Mwm*keyboardFocusPolicy:        explicit
```

On the other hand, if you want the focus to follow the mouse pointer, set this resource as follows:

```
Mwm*keyboardFocusPolicy:        pointer
```

This is the format for specifying resources, which Chapter 5 further explains. The mwm has a large number of configurable resources, including background and foreground colors, which are tabulated in Chapter 8.

Defining Menus for mwm

The configuration file is a text file whose format is best understood by looking at a sample, such as the configuration file generating the menu in Figure 3.3. The lines in the system.mwmrc file defining this menu are as follows:

```
#   This is a comment. Comments and blank lines are ignored.
#   Define the root menu for mwm

Menu RootMenu
{
    "Root Menu"            f.title
    "Clients"        _C    f.menu ClientsSubMenu
```

```
    "xterm"              _x      f.exec "xterm -sb  &"
    "Shuffle Up"         _U      f.circle_up
    "Shuffle Down"       _D      f.circle_down
    "Refresh"            _R      f.refresh
    no-label                     f.separator
    "Restart"                    f.restart
}

# Now the submenu of clients . . .
Menu ClientsSubMenu
{
    "xclock"              f.exec "xclock &"
    "xload"               f.exec "xload &"
    "xcalc"               f.exec "xcalc &"
    "xbiff"               f.exec "xbiff &"
    "xmag"                f.exec "xmag &"
    "bitmap"              f.exec "bitmap $HOME/TEMP.bitmap &"
    "xeyes"               f.exec "xeyes &"
    "ico"                 f.exec "ico &"
}
```

Customizing a Menu

Chapter 8 explains the format of the menu specifications. Here is an example of customizing the root menu. First, make a local copy of the system-wide configuration file in your home directory by entering the following commands at the shell prompt:

cd
cp /usr/lib/X11/system.mwmrc .mwmrc
chmod +w .mwmrc

Because system.mwmrc is usually read-only, .mwmrc, its copy, will be read-only also. You may want to alter it, so you should use the chmod command to allow overwriting the file. Now use your favorite text editor and change the ClientsSubMenu to the following:

```
Menu ClientsSubMenu
{
    "CLIENTS"                            f.title
    "xclock"                             f.exec "xclock &"
    "xload"                              f.exec "xload &"
    "xcalc"                              f.exec "xcalc &"
    @/usr/include/X11/bitmaps/flagdown   f.exec "xbiff &"
    "xmag"                               f.exec "xmag &"
    "bitmap"                     f.exec "bitmap $HOME/TEMP.bitmap &"
    "xeyes"                              f.exec "xeyes &"
    "ico"                                f.exec "ico &"
}
```

We are adding a title to this menu and replacing the old entry, xbiff, with the mailbox icon (whose bit map is in the file named /usr/include/X11/ bitmaps/flagdown). After saving the changes to .mwmrc, select Restart from the root menu of mwm (see Figure 3.3). This restarts the mwm, forcing it to read the altered configuration file. Now press the left mouse button with the pointer anywhere in the root window. When the root menu appears, select the Clients item. The resulting Clients menu is shown in Figure 3.4. Notice the menu now has a title and the mailbox icon appears in place of xbiff.

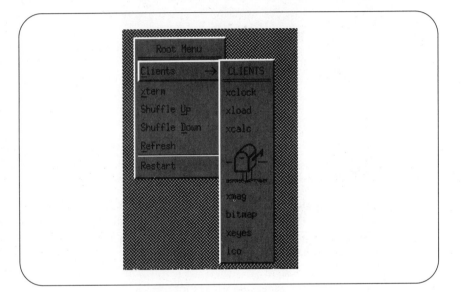

Fig. 3.4. The new customized root menu in mwm.

Key and Button Bindings

With a window manager you can specify what happens when certain keys or mouse buttons are pressed. This is referred to as *key and button bindings*. You can specify these bindings in the same configuration file (either .mwmrc in your home directory or system.mwmrc in /usr/lib/X11) where the menus are defined.

Key Bindings

The syntax for defining key bindings is similar to that for defining menus. For example, the default key bindings are specified by a table named DefaultKeyBindings. A typical definition of the default key bindings may be as follows:

```
# A short list of default key bindings

Keys DefaultKeyBindings
{
    Shift<Key>Escape        icon¦window       f.post_wmenu
    Meta<Key>space          icon¦window       f.post_wmenu
    Meta<Key>Tab            root¦icon¦window  f.next_key
    Meta Shift<Key>Tab      root¦icon¦window  f.prev_key
}
```

Here is how you read the first line of the list: if the user presses the Shift and Esc keys together while in an icon or a window, execute the function f.post_wmenu. From the list of mwm functions shown in Chapter 8, you can determine that f.post_wmenu will cause the window menu to pop up. Similarly, the second line also performs the same action when the user presses the Meta key (this is usually the key labeled Alt or Extend on most keyboards) and the space bar. Note that you have to use the keyword Meta in the configuration file even though the key is labeled Alt or Extend on your keyboard. Chapter 8 provides further information on key and button bindings in the OSF/Motif environment.

Button Bindings

Button bindings indicate what happens when a mouse button is pressed, particularly when pressed in combination with modifier keys such as Alt, Ctrl, or Shift. Note that X provides for a mouse with up to five buttons (although in practice most workstations have mice with one, two, or three buttons). By default, the buttons are numbered one through five from left to right, but this can be changed through configuration files.

The syntax for specifying button bindings is identical to that for key bindings. Here is a short list of default button bindings:

```
# A few default button bindings for mwm

Buttons DefaultButtonBindings
{
    <Btn1Down>          root         f.menu   RootMenu
    <Btn1Down>          frame¦icon   f.raise
    <Btn2Down>          frame¦icon   f.post_wmenu
    <Btn3Down>          frame¦icon   f.post_wmenu
    Meta<Btn1Down>      icon¦window  f.move
}
```

The first line explains the mystery of why the root menu pops up every time you press the left button (button one) in the root window. That line says that whenever button one is down—<Btn1Down> translates to this—with the mouse pointer in the root window (this is because of the context keyword root), mwm should execute the f.menu function with the menu named RootMenu (described earlier).

The second line specifies that if button one is pressed in any frame or icon, that window should be brought to the top of the stacking order. According to the next line, if buttons two and three are pressed in these areas, the window menu pops up. The last line uses a modifier key. It says that if button one is pressed while the pointer is in a window or icon and the Meta (Alt) key is down, then allow the user to interactively move the window.

More on Window Manager Customization

3

Now that you have some idea how configuration files work, you can tap the full potential of the mwm. The trick is to start with a working configuration file—usually you can start with the system-wide file called system.mwmrc in the directory /usr/lib/X11. Copy this file to your home directory under the name .mwmrc. Change its read/write protection (if you have to) and edit it to alter one or two features at a time. You can do this from your xterm window while running X. Once you make some changes, use the Restart option from the default root menu. When mwm restarts, it will accept your changes and you will be able to verify whether your modifications work properly. Following this approach, you can arrive at a configuration file that suits your needs.

If you are a system administrator, you can follow the same steps to build a customized root menu that may allow users to log into specific systems in your local network. When the .mwmrc file is in its final version, you can replace the system.mwmrc file with the .mwmrc from your home directory.

Summary

The window manager is an X client that manages the layout of other clients' windows on the screen. The window manager imparts a certain amount of look and feel to X applications. Several window managers are available for X; the window manager for OSF/Motif is named mwm. Most window managers, including mwm, can be configured through configuration files. Configuration files are text files where, following a specific format, the user can define values of parameters (resources), define menus, and indicate what should happen when certain keys and mouse buttons are pressed. The window manager reads and interprets the configuration file at startup.

Part

II

Using X and Motif

Using the xterm

Terminal Emulator

The one indispensable X application has to be the xterm terminal emulator. The window manager and xterm are the two applications most users run when starting X on a workstation. By default, xterm emulates a VT102 terminal (24 lines by 80 columns). You interact with the UNIX shell in this window, just as you would in any alphanumeric terminal. Character-oriented applications can run directly in this window. You can also start more xterm processes, thus creating several terminals on the same screen.

The VT102 terminal window in xterm is useful also for starting X applications on remote machines. For a networked machine, use the remote login command rlogin to log onto the remote machine. On the remote system, first set the DISPLAY environment variable so that X clients executing there can send output to your workstation. After that, you can start the X applications you want.

In addition to the VT102 terminal, xterm also can emulate the Tektronix 4014 graphics terminal. If you start xterm with the command **xterm -t**, it comes up in the Tektronix 4014 mode. This chapter briefly describes how to use xterm.

Terminology

Signals. UNIX uses signals to notify a process that a specific event has occurred. The SIGKILL and SIGHUP signals terminate a process.

Job Control. Job control enables you to start multiple programs from your terminal and have some control over their execution. It is available in 4.3BSD UNIX.

Main Features of xterm

The xterm application emulates a terminal, but it also has these features not found in a real VT102 or Tektronix 4014 terminal:

- Pop-up menus for switching terminal modes and setting up other characteristics

- Support for cut-and-paste operations

- The option to change the foreground and background colors and the font used to display text

- Support for programmable keys

  This section briefly describes these capabilities.

Main Menu

The main menu in xterm is displayed as xterm X11 (see Figure 4.1a) in X Window System Version 11 Release 3 (X11R3) and Main Options (see Figure 4.1b) in X11R4. To activate it, simultaneously press Ctrl and the extreme left mouse button. This menu is available in both VT102 and Tektronix modes. You can use this menu as follows:

- Select the Secure Keyboard option to ensure that keystrokes are delivered only to the xterm application and not to other X applications displaying at your workstation. If you are prompted for a password, first select the Secure Keyboard option, then type in the password. When selected, a check mark appears beside the option and the xterm window appears in reverse video. This option is a toggle—reselecting the option disables it.

- Select the Logging option in X11R3 xterm (Log to File in X11R4) to save all output in a log file (with a default name XtermLog.*xxxxx*, where the string *xxxxx* varies from one session to another). You can use this feature to capture output appearing in xterm.

- Selecting any one of the last five entries in Figure 4.1a, as well as the corresponding entries in the Main Options menu (Figure 4.1b) in X11R4 version of xterm, terminates xterm. Its window disappears from the screen. The difference among the choices is in the UNIX signal sent to xterm to terminate it.

- On 4.3BSD UNIX systems, you can suspend the current process by pressing Ctrl-Z. Resume it by pressing Ctrl-Y. The Suspend program and Resume program entries of X11R3 xterm (Send STOP Signal and Send CONT Signal in X11R4) provide you the functionality that you get by pressing Ctrl-Z and Ctrl-Y. These menu options dim if your system does not support job control.

The X11R3 version of xterm has another entry labeled Visual Bell. When selected, this option causes xterm to flash the screen instead of sounding the bell. You can see the effect by pressing Ctrl-G. In X11R4, this option appears as Enable Visual Bell in the VT Options menu (see Figure 4.1b).

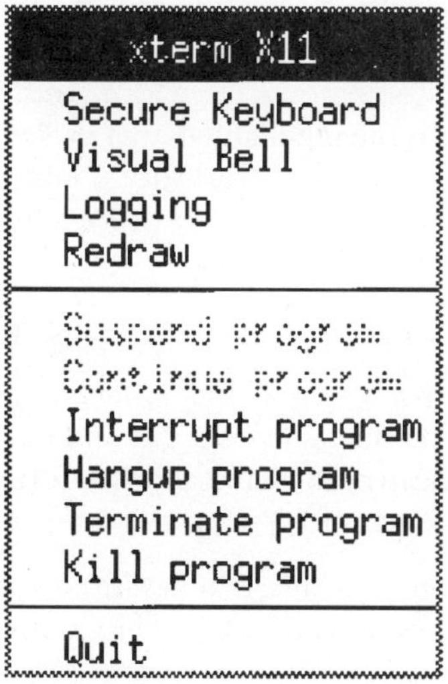

4

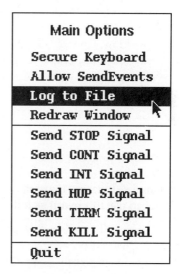

Fig. 4.1a. The xterm X11 menu in X11R3 version of xterm.

Fig. 4.1b. The Main Options menu in X11R4 version of xterm.

VT102 Emulation

In addition to providing a way to interact with the UNIX shell, emulating an alphanumeric terminal in a window has an added benefit: You can scroll back and look at old output, something you cannot do on a real VT102 terminal. For example, if a directory listing displayed in response to the ls command is too long, you can scroll the window's contents down to view the lines that had scrolled off the top of the VT102 window.

Another convenient feature of the VT102 window is that you can cut and paste text. For example, if you type a long command that you need to repeat later, simply select the line and paste it as the new command.

Scrolling the VT102 Window

Scrolling is not enabled by default. To enable scrolling, start xterm with this command:

```
xterm -sb&
```

The -sb option causes xterm to display a scrollbar attached to the left edge of the window.

You can scroll the VT102 window because xterm allocates a 64-line buffer to hold lines sent to the terminal. Of these, only 24 lines usually are visible in the window. The scrollbar indicates the amount of text in this buffer by changing the size of the thumb, which is the highlighted area in the scrollbar. When the buffer is empty, the thumb fills the scrollbar. As text fills the buffer, the thumb gradually becomes smaller. To enlarge the size of the buffer, specify a new value in one of two ways:

1. Use the -sl option when you start xterm. For example, the command xterm -sl 120& will cause xterm to save the last 120 lines that have scrolled off the window.

2. Set the saveLines resource to the number of lines you want saved by placing the following line in a file named XTerm (or in the .Xdefaults file) in your login directory:

```
*saveLines: 120
```

To scroll back and forth and view the rest of the buffer, bring the mouse pointer inside the scrollbar and then click a button. If you have a three-button mouse, pressing the left button (button 1) in the scrollbar causes xterm to scroll the contents of the window up. Clicking the right button scrolls the contents down (you can see older output this way). Pressing the middle button causes the window to scroll to a position that corresponds to the location of the pointer in the scrollbar. In other words, if you press the middle button with the mouse pointer at the top of the scrollbar, the window will show the oldest 24 lines in the buffer. If you move the mouse while the middle button remains pressed, the window's contents will scroll in keeping with the mouse movement.

Cut and Paste

Unlike the real terminal, in xterm's VT102 window you can cut and paste text. X has no explicit cut operation. Instead, you make a selection and then paste the text. When you select text in xterm, it becomes the current selection. You can then paste the text into any application that can accept selections.

In xterm, select text in the following ways:

* Press the left button and drag it across the characters to be selected. As the mouse is dragged, the selected text is highlighted.

* Double-click (in rapid succession) on a word to select it.

* Click the right button (button 3) to select everything between the current location of the pointer and the point where the left button was last clicked.

You can paste a selection into xterm by pressing the middle mouse button.

A common use of cut and paste is to avoid typing long repetitive commands. You can simply select the command and paste it at the command prompt by pressing the middle mouse button. Another use is to start two xterm processes, each running an editor (such as vi). Suppose you are editing two files in the two editor sessions. You can select from the window of one editor and paste into the other by using the paste mechanism of xterm. For this to work, the editor receiving the pasted text has to be in insert mode.

VT102 Menus

If you press Ctrl together with the middle mouse button while the pointer is in the VT102 window, a pop-up menu appears (see Figures 4.2a and 4.2b). This menu enables you to set a number of features of the VT102 emulation. For example, if you had not started xterm with the scrollbar enabled, you can do so by selecting the Scrollbar option (Enable Scrollbar in X11R4) from the menu shown in Figure 4.2a.

The last section of the menu has another important item. You can switch to the Tektronix emulation mode by bringing the pointer into the Select Tek Mode (Switch to Tek Mode in X11R4) item and releasing the mouse button. To get back to the VT102 window, select the Hide Tek Window option from the

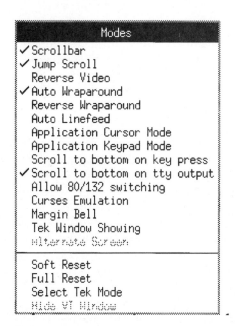
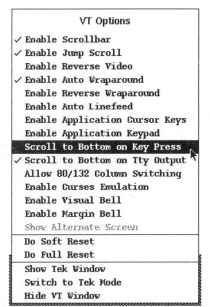

Fig. 4.2a. The Modes menu in the VT mode of X11R3 version of `xterm`.

Fig. 4.2b. The VT Options menu in the X11R4 version of `xterm`.

The X11R4 version of `xterm` provides another menu in the VT102 mode that lets you change the font used in the VT102 window. Press Ctrl along with the right mouse button while the mouse pointer is in the VT102 window. You will see the menu shown in Figure 4.3. Usually, the VT102 window uses the `Default` font. Select another font, such as `Medium`. The VT102 window will resize and its contents will appear in a slightly larger font. This is helpful on large-screen displays where the `Default` font may be too small for practical use.

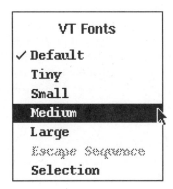

Fig. 4.3. The VT Fonts menu in X11R4 version of `xterm`.

A `termcap` Entry for `xterm`

All alphanumeric terminals support programming that you can use to move the cursor, erase portions of the screen, and occasionally display characters in bold or reverse video. To perform these actions, you have to send the terminal special sequences of characters, which usually start with the Escape character. (That is why these sequences are often called *escape sequences*.)

UNIX uses a clever approach to programming the alphanumeric terminals. The capabilities of the terminals are stored in a file (called `termcap` in 4.3BSD and `terminfo` in System V and located in the `/etc` directory). Each `termcap` entry identifies the terminal by name (for example, `vt100`, `ansi`, and `tek4014`) and specifies the escape sequence necessary to activate each feature of the terminal. With this approach, support for a new terminal can be added by placing an entry for that terminal in the `termcap` file. The `termcap` entry for `xterm`'s VT102 emulation usually appears under the name `xterm`. M.I.T. provides the necessary `termcap` entry in a file named `termcap`, along with the source code for `xterm`.

Most UNIX processes that need to program the terminal extract the `termcap` entry for the terminal specified by the `TERM` environment variable. Thus, when you are using `xterm`, set `TERM` to `xterm`.

Tektronix 4014 Mode

The Tektronix 4014 emulation in `xterm` is useful for displaying output from older graphics programs that require the older Tektronix graphics terminal. If you are developing X applications, you are not likely to use this emulation mode, because X gives you much greater control over the display than the Tektronix 4014 does.

If you do get to the Tektronix 4014 mode, you can interact with `xterm` using one of the menus shown in Figures 4.4a and 4.4b, which pop up when you press Ctrl together with the middle button of the mouse. The most important item in this menu is the one displayed as `Hide Tek Window`. By selecting this item, you can get rid of the `Tektronix` window and revert back to the VT102 emulation.

4

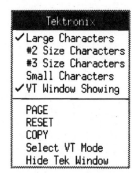   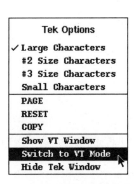

Fig. 4.4a. The Tektronix menu in the   **Fig. 4.4b. The Tek Options**
Tektronix 4014 mode of X11R3 xterm.   **menu in the X11R4** xterm.

Summary

Of all X clients, the xterm terminal emulator and the window manager are special. The xterm application is a popular way to interact with a system through an X display, because it lets you maintain a shell process through which you can start other clients and log into remote systems. You get two terminals in one in xterm—an alphanumeric VT102-compatible terminal and a Tektronix 4014 graphics terminal. You can pop up several menus by pressing mouse buttons in combination with special keys. Using these menus, you can switch between the terminal emulation windows, change font sizes, and alter each terminal's settings.

Like any X application, you can customize xterm through resource files (described in Chapter 5), although the default behavior is adequate for most needs. You can get further information on xterm from the on-line manual pages available on most UNIX systems. Use the command **man xterm** to see this information.

Exploring Other

X Utilities

S o far you have read about two applications: the Motif Window Manager (mwm) and xterm terminal emulator. Both are special X clients—the window manager controls layout of other client's windows, and xterm emulates a terminal in a window. Most X applications are not like xterm or mwm. Before diving into Xlib or Motif programming, take a look at some of the more common X applications to see how they work. Because the X Window System is relatively new, few X-based commercial products are widely used. However, the standard X software distribution includes a number of utilities such as xcalc and xclock, which can serve as adequate examples. Your vendor may also include them with X, or you can get the source code for these utilities from M.I.T.

This chapter guides you through several of these applications and then explains how you can customize X applications using resource files and command-line options.

Desk Accessories

X comes with several popular utilities that fall under the category of desk accessories, a term that became popular with the Apple Macintosh. On the Macintosh, *desk accessories* are small applications devoted to a single task. They are available to the user at any time, just as real-life desk accessories such as clocks and calculators are. In X, the clock (xclock), the calculator (xcalc), and the mail notifier (xbiff) are the most popular desk accessory programs (most software suppliers include these utilities with X but are not required to). You can start these programs from the xterm window. For example, you can start the three accessories and place them in the background with the commands:

```
xclock &
xcalc &
xbiff &
```

This gets each program started with default settings. Typically, you will arrange the xclock, xcalc, and xbiff windows along the edge of the screen, while you continue with your main task in another window (either the xterm window or in another application). The xclock window will always show the current time. While you are working, if you suddenly need the calculator, you can simply move the mouse pointer to the xcalc window and begin using it.

xclock

One of the most common items on any X workstation or terminal is the clock. By default, xclock displays an analog clock (shown in Figure 5.1). You can, however, get a digital clock by starting xclock with the following command:

```
xclock -digital &
```

Figure 5.2 shows the 24-hour format used by the digital clock.

5

Fig. 5.1. The xclock in analog mode.

Fig. 5.2. The xclock in digital mode.

X11R4 added a new twist to the clock—it includes a new analog clock, named oclock, that displays the clock's face as an oval. The oclock application uses an extension to the X protocol, called SHAPE, that is supported by X11R4 server provided by M.I.T. Figure 5.3 shows the result of running oclock with an oclock& command. Figure 5.3 intentionally shows oclock's window without the frame placed by the window manager. The oclock window clearly has an oval shape.

Fig. 5.3. Analog clock with oval face displayed by oclock.

xcalc

The xcalc calculator, by default, displays a calculator styled after Texas Instrument's TI-30 model. The X11R3 version of xcalc has rectangular buttons (Figure 5.4a). In X11R4, xcalc's buttons have rounded corners (Figure 5.4b). You can use the calculator by clicking on the buttons or by pressing the numbers on the keyboard. Of course, for the keystrokes to work, you must make xcalc's window the current focus window. The window manager defines how this is done—usually either by clicking on it once or simply bringing the mouse pointer into the window.

If you prefer the Reverse Polish Notation (RPN) of the Hewlett-Packard calculators, you can get a calculator modeled after the HP-10C with the command xcalc -rpn &. In RPN, the operands precede the operation. For example, on an HP-10C calculator, to add 2.25 to 9.95, press the keys in the following order: **2.25** (press Enter) **9.95** +. Figures 5.5a and 5.5b show the HP-10C look-alike in X11R3 and X11R4.

You can also configure xcalc to work as a slide rule. The slide rule is activated by the command xcalc -analog.

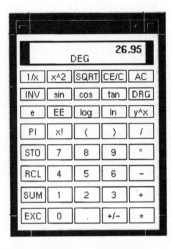

Fig. 5.4a. The TI-30 style calculator in X11R3.

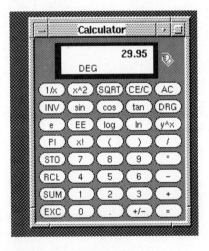

Fig. 5.4b. The same calculator in X11R4.

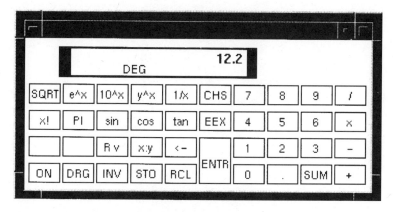

Fig. 5.5a. The HP-10C style calculator in X11R3.

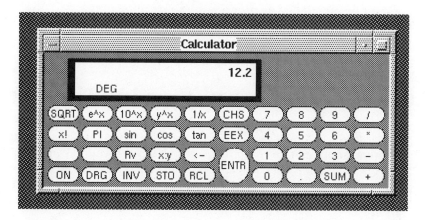

Fig. 5.5b. The HP-10C style calculator with rounded buttons in X11R4.

xbiff

The xbiff mail notifier utility alerts you when you have new mail. It is named after the UNIX biff utility, which serves the same purpose in alphanumeric terminals. The xbiff program displays a mailbox icon in a window. As shown in Figure 5.6, when the flag on the mailbox is down, you have no mail. When mail arrives, xbiff raises the flag on the mailbox and displays its window in reverse video (see Figure 5.7). You can revert the window back to "no mail" status by clicking in it.

Fig. 5.6. The xbiff window when there is no mail.

Fig. 5.7. The xbiff window announcing new mail.

5

Window Capture and Viewing Utilities

The category of X utilities that enables you to capture and view the image of a window is important. You often need to print images of the screen for inclusion in your application's documentation. The pair xwd and xwud are for capturing and viewing images. Additionally, the xpr utility prints images captured by xwd.

Capturing a Window's Image with xwd

The xwd utility is written in the style of many other UNIX utilities. It sends the image of a selected window to the standard output. To get the image into a file, you have to redirect standard output to a file. For example, here is how you can capture the image of a selected window and save it in a file named windump1:

1. Type **xwd > windump1**.

2. The cursor changes to a small cross-hair. Move the cursor to the selected window and press the left mouse button.

3. A single beep warns you that the image is being captured and that you should not change the appearance of the window. Two beeps let you know that the image capture is complete.

Another way to capture the image to a file is to start xwd with the -out option, as follows:

xwd -out windump1&

and follow the sequence outlined previously in steps 1–3.

What can you do with the captured image? You can preview the image using the companion utility xwud. For example, the command xwud <windump1 will display the captured image in another window. Click once in this window to exit xwud.

Capturing Pop-Up Menus with xwd

Capturing the image of a pop-up menu is one problem that often baffles a beginner to X. If you do not mind an image of the entire screen, including the pop-up menu, you can do this easily from your xterm window by following this procedure:

1. Type the command **sleep 10; xwd -root > scdump1 &**.

2. Press the appropriate mouse button to pop up the menu.

3. Wait until you hear the beeps from xwd indicating that the image capture has been completed.

The command sleep 10; before xwd gives you 10 seconds to pop up the menu or bring a specific window to the top of the stack of windows on the screen.

When you enter the **-root** option, xwd interprets it as a request to capture the root window. Therefore, xwd does not prompt for a window to be captured; it saves the entire screen.

5

Formatting a Window Image for a Printer with xpr

The xpr utility enables you to format the image captured by xwd for printing. Unfortunately, xpr is geared toward printing on a few specific printers. Specify the printer by using the -device option. You can specify a generic PostScript printer by using the option -device ps. Suppose you want to create a PostScript file for the image windump1, generated in the earlier example. Type the following command:

xpr -device ps windump1 > windump1.ps

Instead of creating a PostScript file named windump1.ps, this command gives you the following message:

```
xpr: image not in XY format
```

The reason is that xpr can only process images that were saved by xwd in the XYPixmap format. Also, xpr can print images only in black and white—it converts color or grayscale images to black and white by computing an intensity for each pixel and assuming that any pixel with an intensity exceeding a threshold is white; all other pixels are printed as black. To prepare an image for processing with xpr, create the image file from xwd as follows:

xwd -xy > windump1

Utilities to Display Information About X

A few other utilities included with X provide information on windows. The xwininfo utility prints information about a selected window, and xlswins displays the entire hierarchy of windows.

Displaying Information About a Window Using xwininfo

When invoked without any arguments, xwininfo changes the cursor to a crosshair and prints the following message:

```
xwininfo ==> Please select the window about which you
         ==> would like information by clicking the
         ==> mouse in that window.
```

Once you click on the window, xwininfo displays a host of useful information about the window. For example, clicking on the xterm window might generate the following list:

```
xwininfo ==> Window id: 0x30000f (xterm)

         ==> Upper left X: 0
         ==> Upper left Y: 0
         ==> Width: 498
         ==> Height: 316
         ==> Depth: 4
         ==> Border width: 0
         ==> Window class: InputOutput
         ==> Colormap: 0x80066
         ==> Window Bit Gravity State: NorthWestGravity
         ==> Window Window Gravity State: NorthWestGravity
         ==> Window Backing Store State: NotUseful
         ==> Window Save Under State: no
         ==> Window Map State: IsViewable
         ==> Window Override Redirect State: no
         ==> Corners:  +0+0  -142+0  -142-164  +0-164
```

The window location and size are displayed by the first four items in the list. This information is often useful in deciding the default settings for the placement and size of an application's window.

Listing the Window Hierarchy with xlswins

If you invoke xlswins without any argument, it displays the entire tree of windows, starting with the root window and identifying each window with its identification (ID), a hexadecimal number. The list gives you a feeling for the way windows are used in X applications. What will amaze you is that most X applications use a large number of windows; scrollbars, menus, and message boxes are all built out of a hierarchy of windows. Additionally, the frame added by a window manager around an application's main window is also composed of many smaller windows.

Take, for example, the case of xterm running under mwm. The window manager was started with its Icon Box enabled. Here is an annotated printout showing the tree of windows displayed by xlswins for this simple scenario (Figure 3.1 shows the screen that this output describes):

```
0x8006c   ()                        ← The root window
  0x100006   ()
  0x100028   ()
  0x10002d   (mwm)                   ← Motif Window Manager
    0x10002e   ()
```

```
0x10005e  ()
  0x10005f  ()
0x10006b  ()
0x100060  ()                          ← Frame added to icon box
  0x100061  ()                        ← Gadgets added to
  0x100062  ()                          icon box by mwm
  0x100063  ()
  0x100064  ()
  0x100065  ()
  0x100066  ()
  0x100067  ()
  0x100068  ()
  0x100069  ()
  0x10006a  ()
    0x100046  (iconbox)               ← Motif Icon Box
      0x100047  ()                    ← The rest are windows
        0x100048  ()                    internal to the
          0x100049  ()                  icon box
        0x10004a  ()
        0x10004b  ()
          0x10004c  ()
          0x1000bb  ()
0x100072  ()
  0x100073  ()
0x1000b0  ()                          ← xterm's frame
  0x1000b1  ()                        ← These are the
  0x1000b2  ()                          "gadgets" added
  0x1000b3  ()                          by mwm
  0x1000b4  ()
  0x1000b5  ()
  0x1000b6  ()
  0x1000b7  ()
  0x1000b8  ()
  0x1000b9  ()
  0x1000ba  ()
    0x30000f  (xterm)                 ← Main window of xterm
      0x300012  ()                    ← VT102 window
        0x300017  ()                  ← Scrollbar
0x300022  (Xterm Menu)                ← xterm X11 menu
0x300023  (Xterm Menu)                ← VT102 Modes menu
```

The notes next to the arrows explain the major components in the tree of windows that exist for this scenario. The child windows are indicated by an indentation. As expected, there is a root window and windows for each of the following: mwm, the Motif Icon Box, and xterm. What is surprising is that many more windows are in the hierarchy than you might have expected. The additional windows are created by mwm when it provides a frame around the main window of each application. For example, the xterm application has a main window labeled xterm (ID = 0x30000f). Inside that window, xterm has the VT102 window (0x300012) and the scrollbar window (0x300017). The two windows labeled Xterm Menu are for xterm's main menu and the VT102 Modes menu. These windows are created only when you activate them.

Now comes the surprising part. If you use xwininfo to get information on xterm's window by clicking on it, what you get is information on a window whose ID is 0x1000b0 (xterm's frame), not 0x30000f as you might expect after perusing the output of xlswins. This is because mwm attaches the tree of xterm's windows as a subtree of yet another hierarchy of windows that constitutes the frame. The frame's main window (0x1000b0) has 10 child windows (IDs 0x1000b1 through 0x1000ba in the preceding list) that are used to implement the standard Motif gadgets (for example, the title area or minimize and maximize boxes) that adorn the window frame.

If you have trouble identifying windows in the tree, you can find the size and placement of each window by using the command **xlswins -1**. By knowing the size and location of a window, you may be able to identify it on the screen.

Browsing Manual Pages with xman

With the xman application you can browse through formatted versions of manual pages available on your UNIX system—you can think of it as the UNIX man command with a GUI. To start the xman application, type the command **xman&** at the shell prompt in an xterm window. You will be greeted by a small window containing three buttons, labeled Help, Quit, and Manual Page (see Figure 5.8). The Quit button lets you exit xman, whereas Help displays the manual page on xman.

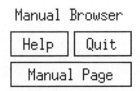

Fig. 5.8. The main window of xman.

When you click on the button labeled Manual Page, a new window appears. As shown in Figure 5.9, this window initially displays the manual page for xman itself. You would have seen the same information if you were to select the Help button from xman's main window.

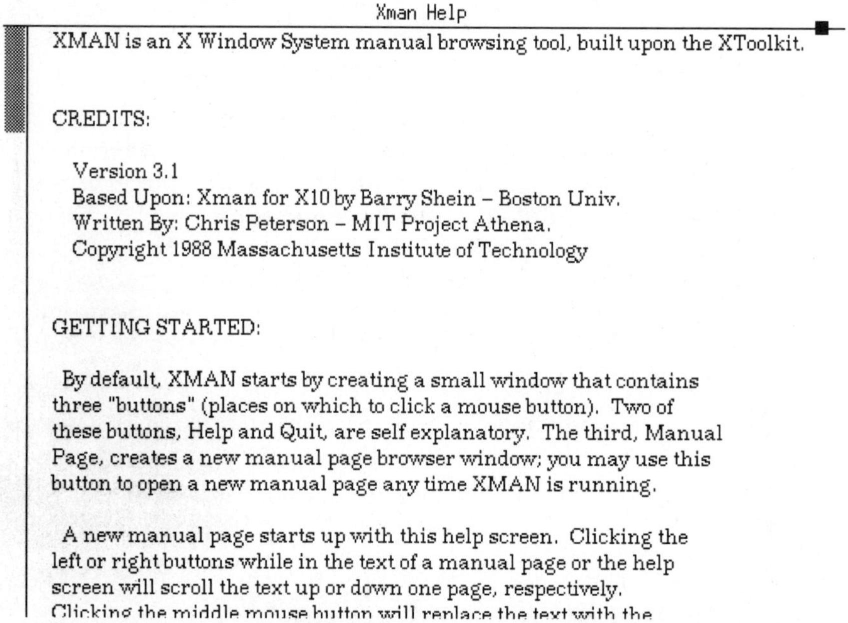

Xman Help

XMAN is an X Window System manual browsing tool, built upon the XToolkit.

CREDITS:

Version 3.1
Based Upon: Xman for X10 by Barry Shein – Boston Univ.
Written By: Chris Peterson – MIT Project Athena.
Copyright 1988 Massachusetts Institute of Technology

GETTING STARTED:

By default, XMAN starts by creating a small window that contains
three "buttons" (places on which to click a mouse button). Two of
these buttons, Help and Quit, are self explanatory. The third, Manual
Page, creates a new manual page browser window; you may use this
button to open a new manual page any time XMAN is running.

A new manual page starts up with this help screen. Clicking the
left or right buttons while in the text of a manual page or the help
screen will scroll the text up or down one page, respectively.
Clicking the middle mouse button will replace the text with the

Fig. 5.9. The window after selecting `Manual Page` from the main window.

From the window shown in Figure 5.9, you can read any available manual
page by following these steps:

1. Move the mouse pointer into the area at the top of the window,
    above the divider (the horizontal line with a small filled rectangle
    near the right edge of the window). Press the extreme left mouse
    button. The Xman Options menu shown in Figure 5.10 pops up.

2. Move the mouse pointer into the button labeled Change Section
    and release it. Another menu pops up (Figure 5.11), which shows
    you the manual pages organized by sections. The menu shown in
    Figure 5.11 happens to be customized for The Santa Cruz
    Operation's SCO Open Desktop 1.0 system. This menu will be
    different on other UNIX systems.

3. Select an appropriate section from the Manual Sections menu
    (Figure 5.11). For example, if you select the button labeled
    `X man pages`, the window displays the directory shown in
    Figure 5.12.

Fig. 5.10. The Xman Options menu in xman.

Manual Sections

Administration	(ADM)
Commands	(C)
Miscellaneous	(M)
File Formats	(F)
Hardware Dependent	(HW)
Subroutines & Libs	(S)
Programming Cmds	(CP)
Streams	(STR)
Network Services	(NSL)
C Subroutines	(K)
Dos Subroutines	(DOS)
TCP/IP (ADMN,ADMP,SFF,TC)	
Networking Commands	
NFS (NADM,NC,NF,NS)	
NFS Dev. Sys.	(NS)
X Library	(XS)
Motif	(Xm)
X Toolkit Intrinsics (Xt)	
X man pages	(X)

Fig. 5.11. Manual Sections menu in xman **under SCO Open Desktop.**

```
              Directory of: X man pages        (X)
X         Xsight     bdftosnf   bitmap    dos       ico       image
lccdm     mkfontdir  mwm        resize    showsnf   xanswer   xbiff
xcalc     xclipboard xclock     xcutsel   xdm       xdpyinfo  xedit
xev       xeyes      xfd        xhost     xinit     xkill     xload
xlogo     xlsfonts   xlswins    xmag      xman      xmodmap   xpr
xprop     xrdb       xrefresh   xset      xsetroot  xterm     xwd
xwininfo  xwud
```

Fig. 5.12. Directory of X man pages in xman under SCO Open Desktop.

4. Select one of the entries from the directory—move the mouse pointer into an item and press the left mouse button. Figure 5.13 shows the contents of the window after you have selected the item labeled xwd. This is the manual page for the xwd application. You can scroll through the manual page by clicking on the text—click the left button to move forward and the right button to move back.

While you are viewing a manual page, you can bring up the Xman Options menu by pressing the left mouse button with the pointer in the area above the divider. From that menu, you can again switch sections and select other manual pages to browse. In particular, on SCO's Open Desktop system you can read the manual pages for the Motif widgets and functions (you will find this handy when you write Motif programs).

```
          The current manual page is: xwd.

   xwd(1)      X Version 11 (24 October 1988)     xwd(1)




   NAME
      xwd – dumps an X window image

   SYNOPSIS
      xwd [–options ...]

   DESCRIPTION
      The xwd utility lets you store window images in a specially
      formatted dump file.  This file can then be read by various
      other X programs for redisplaying, printing, editing,
      formatting, archiving, image processing, and so on.

      You select the target window by clicking the mouse in the
      desired window.  The keyboard bell rings once at the
      beginning of the dump and twice when the dump is completed.

   OPTIONS
      –display display
         Specifies the server.
```

Fig. 5.13. The manual page for xwd.

For example, if you choose the Motif section from the Manual Sections menu, you get the directory shown in Figure 5.14. Selecting the XmForm item from this directory brings up the manual page for the XmForm widget (Figure 5.15).

```
              Directory of: Motif              (Xm)
 Application Composite   Constraint  Core        MrmCloseHie MrmFetchCol MrmFetchIco
 MrmFetchInt MrmFetchLit MrmFetchSet MrmFetchWiA MrmFetchWiB MrmInitiali MrmOpenHier
 MrmRegisteA MrmRegisteB Object      OverrideShe RectObj     Shell       TopLevelShe
 TransientSh Uil         UilDumpSymb VendorShell WMShell     WindowObj   XmActivateP
 XmActivateW XmAddProtoA XmAddProtoB XmAddTabGro XmAddWMProA XmAddWMProB XmArrowButA
 XmArrowButB XmBulletinB XmCascadeBA XmCascadeBB XmCascadeBC XmClipboarA XmClipboarB
 XmClipboarC XmClipboarD XmClipboarE XmClipboarF XmClipboarG XmClipboarH XmClipboarI
 XmClipboarJ XmClipboarK XmClipboarL XmClipboarM XmClipboarN XmClipboarO XmClipboarP
 XmClipboarQ XmCommand   XmCommandAp XmCommandEr XmCommandGe XmCommandSe XmConvertUn
 XmCreateArA XmCreateArB XmCreateBuA XmCreateBuB XmCreateCaA XmCreateCaB XmCreateCom
 XmCreateDia XmCreateDrA XmCreateDrB XmCreateErr XmCreateFiA XmCreateFiB XmCreateFoA
 XmCreateFoB XmCreateFra XmCreateInf XmCreateLaA XmCreateLaB XmCreateLis XmCreateMai
 XmCreateMeA XmCreateMeB XmCreateMeC XmCreateMeD XmCreateOpt XmCreatePan XmCreatePop
 XmCreatePro XmCreatePuA XmCreatePuB XmCreatePul XmCreateQue XmCreateRad XmCreateRow
 XmCreateScA XmCreateScB XmCreateScC XmCreateScD XmCreateSca XmCreateSeA XmCreateSeB
 XmCreateSeC XmCreateSeD XmCreateTex XmCreateToA XmCreateToB XmCreateWar XmCreateWor
 XmCvtString XmDeactivaA XmDeactivaB XmDestroyPi XmDialogShe XmDrawingAr XmDrawnButt
 XmFileSeleA XmFileSeleB XmFileSeleC XmFontListA XmFontListC XmFontListF XmForm
 XmFrame     XmGadget    XmGetAtomNa XmGetMenuCu XmGetPixmap XmInstallIm XmInternAto
 XmIsMotifWM XmLabel     XmLabelGadg XmList      XmListAddIA XmListAddIB XmListDeleA
 XmListDeleB XmListDeseA XmListDeseB XmListDeseC XmListItemE XmListSeleA XmListSeleB
 XmListSetBA XmListSetBB XmListSetHo XmListSetIt XmListSetPo XmMainWindA XmMainWindB
 XmMainWindC XmMainWindD XmManager   XmMenuPosit XmMenuShell XmMessageBA XmMessageBB
 XmOptionBut XmOptionLab XmPanedWind XmPrimitive XmPushButtA XmPushButtB XmRemovePrA
 XmRemovePrB XmRemoveTab XmRemoveWMA XmRemoveWMB XmResolvePa XmRowColumn XmScale
 XmScaleGetV XmScaleSetV XmScrollBaA XmScrollBaB XmScrollBaC XmScrolledA XmScrolledB
 XmSelectioA XmSelectioB XmSeparatoA XmSeparatoB XmSetFontUn XmSetMenuCu XmSetProtoc
 XmSetWMProt XmStringBas XmStringByt XmStringCom XmStringCon XmStringCop XmStringCrA
```

Fig. 5.14. The directory for the Motif section of Manual Sections in SCO Open Desktop.

Figure 5.15 also shows the result of selecting the item labeled Show Both Screens in the Xman Options menu. If you select this option, xman displays the directory and the manual page for the current item in a split window with the directory at the top and the manual page at the bottom.

5

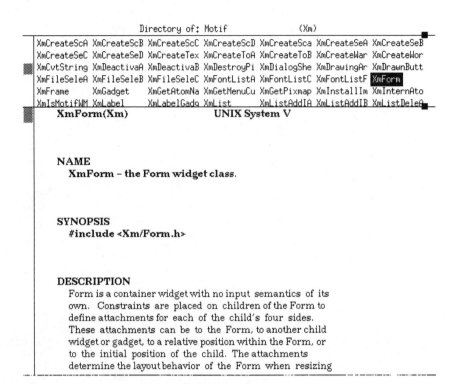

Fig. 5.15. The manual page for the XmForm widget.

Appearance and Behavior of X Applications

By now, you have seen a number of X applications in action. You may have noticed that the text often mentions what an application does by default. If this has prompted you to conclude that there must be ways to alter the behavior of X applications, you're correct.

Most X applications, especially those based on any Xt-based toolkit, are highly configurable. A user can alter the appearance and, to some extent, even the behavior of an application. Applications can accomplish this alteration in two ways:

- Their default values can be changed through options specified in the command line that start the application.

- Their default values can be modified through options specified in a text file. This file is called a *resource file*, after the terminology used by X programmers to refer to any user-configurable options in an application.

Resources in X Applications

Specifying options on the command line works fine for small UNIX utilities, but X applications tend to have a large number of variables that the user can (and should) set. For example, an X application may contain a large number of windows, each of which may have a border, a background color, and a fore-ground color. The user should not have to live with the colors selected by a programmer. The application should provide default values that can be, if desired, overridden by the user.

Similarly, if a window contains several child windows, you may want the user to be able to specify the location and size of each child. Then there are fonts for any text to be displayed. An X application has too many variables to set through the command-line mechanism alone. The authors of X recognized this problem and, starting with X11R2, included utility routines in the Xlib library to manage a database of resources.

The term *resource* has two meanings in X:

- In the context of programming with Xlib, windows, colors, bit maps, and fonts are resources maintained by the X server and accessed by the X client applications through X protocol requests.

- For an X application, a resource is any parameter that affects its behavior or appearance, such as foreground colors, background colors, fonts, window size, and window placement.

A resource does not have to be a parameter related to X. It can be anything that controls the behavior of an application and should be specified by the user. For example, an application might have a variable named debug, which, when set, enables printing of detailed information as it runs. In addition to the application's window size and location, debug also qualifies as a resource of this application.

Resource File and Resource Manager

The resources for an X application are specified in a text file known as a *resource file* or a *resource database*. A set of utility routines (with names having the Xrm prefix), collectively known as the *resource manager*, can read and interpret the resource files. This does not happen automatically. The X application must call the resource manager to retrieve the user's selections for various parameters. Applications built with a toolkit such as Motif have higher-level resource management routines to do the job.

The resource database in X is a simple text file in which you can specify the value of various parameters using a well-defined format. X resource files are not as complicated and sophisticated as a traditional database. The X resource database contains specifications such as "All foreground colors are white," and "xterm's background is light cyan."

The X resource manager extracts the value of precisely identified individual parameters from this rather imprecise database. For example, a query might be "What is the foreground color of the xclock application?" If you have specified the foreground color of xclock in the resource file, the resource manager returns this value. If, however, the only specification for foreground color in the database is the general statement "all foreground colors are white," the value returned for xclock's foreground color will be white.

Resource Naming Convention

How do you specify that xterm's foreground color should be light cyan, for instance? You must learn how to name a resource and how to specify the value for a resource.

The name of a resource depends on the name of the application and the names of its components, which are usually the major child windows. For X toolkit-based applications, the components would be the names of widgets used to build the application. The names of the application and its components can be of two types: class name and instance name. The class name indicates the general category to which the application or the component belongs, whereas each individual copy can have its own instance name.

The definition will be clear if you consider a concrete example: the xterm application. This application is of the class XTerm, whereas the instance goes by the name xterm. The xterm application uses a component named vt100 of class VT100 (yes, it emulates a VT102, but the internal name is VT100), which contains a component named scrollbar of the class Scrollbar. Now consider the following resources: the foreground color of the VT100 window and the visibility of the scrollbar in that window. In xterm, as in most X applications, the foreground color resource has the class name Foreground and instance name foreground. The scrollbar's visibility is controlled by the Boolean variable named on.

Most X applications follow this convention of naming the class of a resource by capitalizing the first letter of its instance name. Names of applications follow this convention, which promotes some consistency among

applications. The naming of the application, its components, and the resources, however, is an issue entirely under the application's control (only
toolkit-based applications are somewhat constrained by the built-in names
of predefined widgets).

Now you are in a position to uniquely name these resources in xterm and
specify values for them. The foreground color of the VT100 window and the on
variable of its scrollbar can be assigned values in the following manner:

```
xterm.vt100.foreground:       light cyan
xterm.vt100.scrollbar.on:     true
```

This illustrates the syntax of naming resources and giving their values.
The name of a resource is constructed by the name of the application followed
by names of the components, each separated from the next by a period (.). The
resource name comes last, and the value of the resource follows a colon (:).
The value is given as text string. It is up to the application to interpret it internally. The resource manager has utility routines to help the programmer with
this task.

The names illustrated so far are full instance names showing the application and all of its components. You can also have full class names, which for
xterm.vt100.foreground is XTerm.VT100.Foreground, obtained by replacing
the instance name of each component with the corresponding class name.
When querying the value of a resource, X applications must use either its full
instance or full class name.

Partial Names for Resources

You have seen how to specify a resource by its full name, but you also read that
the specification can be imprecise. What sort of imprecise entries can you
specify? For example, you might indicate that all components of class VT100
should have a yellow foreground color. You can do this by the following entry
in the resource database:

```
*VT100.Foreground:   yellow
```

Because there is no application name, this specification of the foreground color applies to the VT100 component used in any application.
Similarly, to specify that the background of every component in the xterm
application should be navy, include the following line in the resource file:

```
xterm*background:navy
```

To understand the resource naming scheme, you have to know something about the inner workings of the X resource manager. By now, you
probably guessed that the X resource manager locates a resource's value by

matching a precisely specified resource name against the imprecise entries in the resource database. The search algorithm used by the resource manager follows certain rules when matching a full resource name with the partial names in the resource database. Knowing the following rules can help you understand what kind of specification for a resource is precise enough to suit your needs:

1. An asterisk (*) matches zero or more components in the name. Thus, the query for `xterm.vt100.foreground` will match the entry:

   ```
   xterm*foreground:    yellow
   ```

2. After accounting for the asterisk, the application name, component names, and the resource name (class or instance) must match the items present in the entry. Thus, a query for `XTerm.VT100.Scrollbar.Background` will match the entry:

   ```
   xterm.vt100.scrollbar.background: navy
   ```

   but not

   ```
   xterm.vt100.scrollbar.on: true
   ```

3. More specific resource specifications take precedence over less specific settings. Entries with a period (.) take precedence over ones with an asterisk (*). Thus, if you specify

   ```
   xterm*background: navy
   xterm.vt100.scrollbar.background:   white
   ```

   everything in `xterm` will have the navy background, but the scrollbar will have a white background.

4. Instance names take precedence over class names. Thus, the specific entry `xterm*background` will override the one that uses class names: `XTerm*Background`.

5. An entry with a class name or an instance name takes precedence over one that uses neither. For example, in `xterm`, the value given in the entry `XTerm*Foreground` will override that under the more general entry `*Foreground`.

6. The matching of names is done from left to right, because the hierarchy of components in the name of a resource goes from left to right. In other words, when looking for the resource named xterm.vt100.scrollbar.background, the resource manager will match the entry

   ```
   xterm.vt100*background: white
   ```

instead of

```
xterm*scrollbar.background: navy
```

because vt100 appears to the left of scrollbar.

Resource Placement

Now you know how to specify resources for an X application, but how do you ensure that your resource specifications take effect? An X application must include explicit code to read and interpret a resource file. Most toolkit-based applications do this, but an X application does not have to accept resource specifications from a database. It is, however, not advisable to ignore resources because such applications tend to be unpopular with users. As a user you may never set any resources, but you will take comfort in knowing that the facility is there should you decide to change any aspect of the application.

Most X applications (especially toolkit-based ones) load resource settings from several sources in a specific order. First, they look for a filename with the format /usr/lib/X11/app-defaults/*app_class*, where *app_class* is the class name of the application. Thus, xterm will look for its resources in /usr/lib/X11/app-defaults/XTerm.

Next, the application will look for a string named RESOURCE_MANAGER associated with the root window of the display where the application is sending its output. This is known as a *property* of the root window. You can use the utility routine xprop to see whether this property exists on your display's root window. Simply type **xprop -root** and look for an entry labeled RESOURCE_MANAGER(STRING) in the output. The xprop utility also can read a resource file and load the contents into this property (as a long string).

If the RESOURCE_MANAGER property does not exist, the application reads the resource specifications from the file .Xdefaults in your home directory. Following this, the application will load the resources specified by the file indicated by the environment variable XENVIRONMENT, if any. If this variable is not set, the next source for resources is a file named .Xdefaults-*hostname* in your home directory. Here *hostname* is the system where the application is running.

Applications created with the OSF/Motif toolkit automatically load resources from several sources. Resources from all the sources are merged, and new specifications override older ones encountered earlier. For a Motif application named xmhello of class XMhello, the sequence of loading resources is as follows:

1. Load the file /usr/lib/X11/app-defaults/XMhello.

2. Load data in the RESOURCE_MANAGER property, provided it exists.

5·

3. In the absence of the `RESOURCE_MANAGER` property, load the file `.Xdefaults` in the home directory of the user.

4. Last, load the command-line options (discussed in the next section).

These basic steps are followed by most X toolkits. Because the command-line options are loaded last, the user can always override resources from the command line. In OSF/Motif, the sequence can be further controlled with the environment variables `LANG`, `XAPPRESLANGPATH`, `XAPPRESDIR`, and `XENVIRONMENT`. Consult your toolkit's documentation for exact details.

If you want to see the effect of the resources, here is an example of how you might do it. From your current `xterm` window, create the file `testrm` with the following lines:

```
xterm.vt100.scrollBar.on:          true
*VT100.Foreground:                 yellow
xterm*background:                  navy
xterm.vt100.scrollbar.background:  white
```

Now, use the `xrdb` utility program to load these settings into the `RESOURCE_MANAGER` property under the root window by typing the command:

```
xrdb -load testrm
```

You can verify that the resources are loaded by using **xprop -root**. You will notice how the contents of the resource file are stored internally in the property `RESOURCE_MANAGER` as a long string. Now start another `xterm` session using the command **xterm &**. You will see that the new `xterm` window has yellow characters on a navy background except for the scrollbar, which has a white background.

Common Resources

Some resource names are, by convention, standard in X applications. These include parameters such as foreground and background colors; window size and location (collectively known as *geometry*); and font. Table 5.1 lists some of the common resources.

Command-Line Options in X Applications

You read that, in addition to resource databases, X applications accept command-line arguments as most conventional UNIX applications do. Table 5.1 shows that most common features of an X application can be specified on the command line.

Table 5.1. Standard X Resources.

Instance Name	Class Name	Command Line	Specifies Option
background	Background	-bg -background	Background color
borderColor	BorderColor	-bd -border	Border color
borderWidth pixels	BorderWidth	-bw -borderwidth	Border width in
display	Display	-display -d	Name of display
foreground	Foreground	-fg -foreground	Foreground color
font	Font	-fn -font	Font name
geometry	Geometry	-geometry	Size and location
reverseVideo	ReverseVideo	-rv	Enable reverse video
title	Title	-title	The title string

Display Specification

An important command-line option for X applications is -display, which you use to specify the display where the application's output should appear. This can be used as an alternative to setting the DISPLAY environment variable before starting an application. For example, if you are logged into a remote host and want to run the client xbiff on that system, you can start it with the command:

xbiff -display *yoursys*:0 &

where *yoursys* is the node name of your workstation.

Window Size and Location

Another common option is -geometry, used to specify the size and location of the application's main window. The geometry is specified in the standard format as follows:

*width*x*height*[+-]*xoffset*[+-]*yoffset*

where *width*, *height*, *xoffset*, and *yoffset* are numbers and you pick one of the two signs shown in the square brackets. The *width* and *height* usually specify the size of the window in pixels (for xterm you have to specify these in number of columns and rows of text). The xoffset and yoffset quantities are also in pixels. The meaning of these two numbers depends on the application. In xterm, for example, a positive xoffset indicates the number of pixels that the left side of the window is offset from the left side of the screen. A negative xoffset, on the other hand, specifies the number of pixels that the right edge of the window is offset from the right edge of the screen. Similarly, positive and negative yoffset indicate offsets from the screen edges of the top and bottom edges of the window, respectively. Most toolkit-based X clients interpret xoffset and yoffset in the same way as xterm does.

For example, the following command places a 120-pixel-by-120-pixel clock in the upper right corner of your screen with a 16-pixel gap between the clock's frame and the screen's top and right edges:

```
xclock -geometry 120x120-16+16 &
```

Window Appearance

Most of the other command-line options determine the appearance of an application's window. They specify the foreground color (-fg), the background color (-bg), the border color (-bd), and the border width (-bw) in pixels. The colors are given by names such as white, yellow, red, and blue. For example, to start an xterm session with yellow characters on a navy background, use the command:

```
xterm -bg navy -fg yellow &
```

If a color name includes embedded space, you have to give the name in quotes. For example, to specify light blue as the background for xterm, you would use the following command:

```
xterm -bg "light blue" &
```

Alternative Color Naming in Resource Files

In addition to the descriptive name for a color, you can specify it as a hexadecimal number, usually with six hexadecimal digits, which works out to two digits for each of the three components in a color—red (R), green (G), and blue (B). The digits in a 6-digit hexadecimal RGB value of a color are interpreted from left to right, with the most significant pair of digits assumed to be for R, the middle pair for G, and the least significant pair for B. The character # precedes the hexadecimal digits to signify that this is a color specification in hexadecimal format. Following are some of the common colors expressed in this format:

```
black    #000000
red      #ff0000
green    #00ff00
blue     #0000ff
yellow   #ffff00
cyan     #00ffff
magenta  #ff00ff
white    #ffffff
```

After noticing how the standard colors are specified, you can start experimenting with new colors you want as the background and foreground of a window. For example, you can try a strange color for xterm's background with a line like the following in your resource file:

```
XTerm*Background: #ccb0b0
```

Although RGB values of colors in hexadecimal format are often specified with 6 digits, the X server correctly interprets colors specified by as many as 9 (3 digits per component) or 12 (4 digits per component) hexadecimal digits. Internally, each of R, G, and B components is a 16-bit quantity.

Font Specification

The font resource of an application usually controls how the text outputs look. Like colors, fonts are specified by names. Starting with X11R3, the font names became very descriptive. Here is an example:

```
-adobe-courier-medium-r-normal--12-120-75-75-m-60-iso8859-1
```

For this font, adobe is the maker, courier is the family, and the font is of medium weight (alternatively, you might specify it as bold or another style). The r indicates that the font is roman. An i at this position indicates italic, and o, oblique. The normal is a spacing parameter; it can be condensed, narrow, or double width.

The numbers following the double dash (--) indicate the font's size. The 12 indicates the pixel size of the font, and 120 gives the size in tenths of a printer's point. The next two numbers (75-75) give the horizontal and vertical resolution for which the font is designed. The letter following the resolution (m) is the spacing—this can be m for monospace or p for proportional. The next number (60) is the average width of all characters in this font, measured in tenths of a pixel (in this case it is 6 pixels). The string iso8859-1 identifies the character set of the font as specified by the International Standards Organization (ISO). In this case, the character set is the ISO Latin 1, a superset of the ASCII (American Standard Code for Information Interchange) character set.

5

You do not have to give the entire name when you specify a font in a resource file. You can use asterisks (*) for fields that can be arbitrary. For example, say you want the VT100 window in xterm to use a medium weight 12-point courier font. With a judicious sprinkling of asterisks, you can specify this as follows:

```
*VT100*Font: *courier-medium-r-normal--*120*
```

Resource Specification on Command Line

In addition to the command-line options described so far, an additional option, -xrm, is accepted by most X applications (in particular those based on the X toolkits). It allows the user to pass a string to the resource manager. For example, when starting xterm, you could turn the background to light cyan with the command

```
xterm -xrm "XTerm*Background: light cyan" &
```

Summary

5

This chapter provides a guided tour of some interesting X applications to give you a feel for the appearance and behavior of X applications before you write one of your own. The commonly distributed X applications include the clock (xclock) and calculator (xcalc) desk accessories, utilities to save (xwd) and view (xwud) the image of a window, and xwininfo and xlswins to get information about the windows on the screen. By experimenting with these applications, you will learn that most X applications are built from a large number of windows, organized in a multilevel, single-inheritance hierarchy.

You can customize the appearance and behavior of most X applications by specifying options on the command line or by providing values for parameters in a text file. User-configurable parameters in an X application are commonly referred to as *resources*, and the text file containing the values for parameters is known as the *resource database*. The Xlib library includes a set of utility routines, collectively known as the *X resource manager*, that enables the programmer to retrieve the value of a parameter from the resource database. You must follow a specific syntax when specifying the resources, but once you know the syntax, customizing an X application is straightforward.

Programming with
the Motif Toolkit

I n Chapters 1 through 5, you became acquainted with the X Window System as a user. You saw how to start X on a workstation, run X applications, and customize X applications through resource files. Now you are ready to develop your first X program. The primary programming interface to the X Window System is Xlib, which provides a C programming language interface to X. You can use Xlib functions to build graphical user interfaces with menus and buttons using a hierarchy of windows and display graphics, text, and images in these windows. Although you can do a lot with Xlib, you need careful planning and organization before you build complete programs using Xlib functions alone.

To build user interfaces without getting mired in details, you need utility functions and a collection of prefabricated user-interface components such as buttons, menus, and scrollbars. Luckily, several X toolkits are marketed that provide the tools with which you can build user interfaces easily. The current crop of X toolkits includes Open Software Foundation's OSF/Motif toolkit, AT&T's XT+ OPEN LOOK widget set, Sun's XView, and the Athena Widgets, to name but a few. This book covers the OSF/Motif toolkit.

X toolkits are like the standard C library. In the C library, someone has carefully designed and implemented the functions for many common tasks that you have to handle in a C program. For example, to open a file, all you have to do is call fopen and, regardless of the underlying operating system, the file will be opened. Like the C library, the X toolkit also provides a standard and efficient way to do your job—build a graphical user interface. Aside from keeping the size of the source code manageable, a well-designed X toolkit also makes efficient use of the X protocol requests by sending requests only when necessary. One drawback is the size of toolkit-based applications—they tend to be much larger than comparable applications built using Xlib alone. Another drawback is that there is more than one X toolkit around and each has its own unique programming interface.

Because you are likely to use a toolkit to build your applications, this and the following chapter of this desktop guide provide a brief introduction to the OSF/Motif toolkit, which is based on the Xt Intrinsics. This chapter describes how to create and manipulate widgets through the functions provided by the Xt Intrinsics. The latter part of the chapter gives an overview of the OSF/Motif widget set. Chapter 7 explains how to use the Motif widgets together with Xlib functions to build applications with a Motif *look* and *feel*.

6

> *Note:* The examples in Chapters 6 and 7 assume that you are using Motif 1.0 and X Version 11 Release 3 (X11R3) because these are currently the most widely available Motif and X environments. Certain basic functions have changed in Motif 1.1 and the X11R4 version of the Xt Intrinsics. For instance, in Motif 1.0, you initialize the toolkit by calling XtInitialize; in Motif 1.1, the recommended approach is to call XtAppInitialize. I will point out these changes at the appropriate places in the text. The examples in this book should continue to work in Motif 1.1 because the older versions of the functions will be supported for a while.

Programming with Xt Intrinsics

Xt Intrinsics is a library of functions and data structures layered on top of Xlib. There are two ways of looking at the Xt Intrinsics:

- As a set of utility functions for one-step initialization of an application's main window, for reading and interpreting user-defined resource files, for handling events, and for creating and manipulating widgets. This is the view of Xt Intrinsics that you will see when developing applications.

- As the basis for developing new widgets. For instance, the design of the data structures in Xt Intrinsics is such that you can pick an existing widget and extend its functionality to create a specialized version of the widget. For this widget-writing role, you will have to understand the architecture of the toolkit. Some of this is covered in this chapter.

The following sections explain the Xt programming model and how you use it to build user-interfaces with existing widgets.

X Toolkit Programming Model

When using an Xt Intrinsics-based toolkit, you write your application in a specific manner prescribed by the Xt Intrinsics. The programming model is closely related to that for Xlib, with some crucial differences. As shown in Figure 6.1, your application can make use of functions from Xlib, the Xt Intrinsics layer, and the toolkit itself. The toolkit also calls functions from your application.

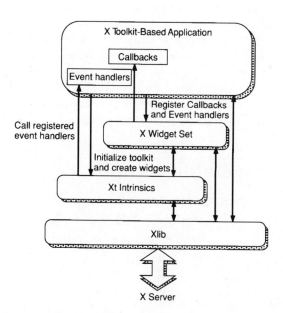

Fig. 6.1. X Toolkit Programming Model.

Event Handlers and Callbacks

With Xlib, you set up your windows and enter a loop where the program continually retrieves events and processes them. With an X toolkit, the event-handling loop is simplified:

1. Initialize the toolkit, create the widgets, and set up their internal parameters (the resources).

2. Write small functions for handling specific events such as a mouse button-press occurring in a push-button widget.

3. Register these event handlers with the toolkit by calling the `XtAddEventHandler` function.

4. Call the `XtMainLoop` function and let the toolkit handle all events. The toolkit, in turn, calls your registered event handlers at the appropriate time.

Callback Functions

Most of the time, you do not have to handle events by installing event handlers. Instead, each widget handles the X events and decides when to call another type of registered function, known as *callback functions*, that are registered by calling `XtAddCallback`. Most of an application's work is done in one or more callback functions. The exact number and type of callback functions depend on the widget. For example, a push-button widget may accept a callback function that will be invoked when the left mouse button is pressed and released with the pointer inside the push-button widget's window. Typically, a widget accepts a list of callback functions so that you can have a number of functions called in response to a single event. The callback functions are called one after another according to the order in which they were registered.

Your First Motif Program

Use the following steps when writing programs that use widgets such as those in OSF/Motif that are built on the Xt Intrinsics:

1. Include the header files. For the OSF/Motif toolkit, this involves using the following:

```
#include <X11/Intrinsic.h>
#include <X11/StringDefs.h>
#include <Xm/Xm.h>
```

6

```
/* Include header file of each widget you plan to use
 * This is for the Form, Label, and PushButton widgets
 */
#include <Xm/Form.h>
#include <Xm/Label.h>
#include <Xm/PushB.h>
```

2. Initialize the toolkit using the **XtInitialize** function. This returns an identifier for the top-level widget. In Motif 1.1, use the **XtAppInitialize** function (instead of **XtInitialize**) to initialize the toolkit.

3. For each widget, set up the argument lists with **XtSetArg**, create the widget using **XtCreateManagedWidget**, add callbacks using **XtAddCallback**, and add event handlers, if any. Usually, all application-specific work is handled in the callbacks.

4. Create the windows for the widgets by calling the **XtRealizeWidget** with the identifier of the top-level widget as the argument.

5. Start the main event-processing loop by calling

   ```
   XtMainLoop();
   ```

   In Motif 1.1, you should start the main event-processing loop by calling

   ```
   XtAppMainLoop(app_context);
   ```

   where **app_context** is a variable of type XtAppContext where the application's context is saved (the XtAppInitialize function will do this).

   Listing 6.1 shows a short example, xmdemo, that illustrates the steps involved in writing a program that uses the OSF/Motif toolkit. You will find a more substantial example at the end of this chapter.

Listing 6.1. `xmdemo.c`—**An example of X Toolkit programming.**

```
/*-------------------------------------------------------------*/
/*  File: xmdemo.c
 *
 *  A sample program that displays a PushButton widget.
 */

/* STEP 1: Include the header files */

#include <X11/Intrinsic.h>
#include <X11/StringDefs.h>
```

continues

Listing 6.1. continued

```c
#include <Xm/Xm.h>
#include <Xm/PushB.h>

/* Label for the push-button. */
static char quit_label[] = "Press here to exit...";

/* Room for setting up arguments passed to widgets. */
static Arg args[10];

/* Prototype of callback function. */

static void button_pushed(Widget w, caddr_t client_data,
                          XmAnyCallbackStruct *call_data);


/*--------------------------------------------------------------*/
void main(int argc, char **argv)
{
    Widget main_widget, quit_button;

/* STEP 2: Initialize toolkit and create the top-level widget.
 *   Use XtAppInitialize in Motif 1.1.
 */
    main_widget = XtInitialize(argv[0], "XMdemo", NULL, 0,
                               &argc, argv);

/* STEP 3: Set up argument list for the push-button widget,
 *   create the push-button, and set up a callback
 *   function. In this case, the argument is a label
 *   for the push-button.
 */
    XtSetArg(args[0], XmNlabelString,
             XmStringCreateLtoR(quit_label,
             XmSTRING_DEFAULT_CHARSET));

    quit_button = XtCreateManagedWidget("Exit",
                     xmPushButtonWidgetClass, main_widget,
                     (ArgList) args, 1);

/* Install the callback function for this pushbutton. */
    XtAddCallback(quit_button, XmNactivateCallback,
                  button_pushed, NULL);

/* STEP 4: Realize the widgets. */
    XtRealizeWidget(main_widget);

/* STEP 5: Start the main event-handling loop.
 *   Use XtAppMainLoop in Motif 1.1
 */
    XtMainLoop();
```

6

```
}
/*--------------------------------------------------------------*/
/* b u t t o n _ p u s h e d
 *
 * Callback Function to be called when user presses and releases
 * button in the "exit" pushbutton.
 */
static void button_pushed(Widget w, caddr_t client_data,
                          XmAnyCallbackStruct *call_data)
{
    XtCloseDisplay(XtDisplay(w));
    exit(0);
}
```

In the callback function, button_pushed, we close the display by calling
XtCloseDisplay. This function requires a pointer to a Display structure as the
argument. We use XtDisplay(w) to obtain a pointer to the Display structure
used by the widget w. Similarly, the ID of a widget w's window is given by
XtWindow(w).

The exact steps for compiling and linking an X toolkit-based application
depends on the toolkit and on your operating system. On a typical Intel 80386-
based PC running SCO UNIX Open Desktop 1.0, the following command line
compiles and links the example shown in Listing 6.1:

```
cc -o xmdemo -DSYSV xmdemo.c -lXm -lXt -lX11 -lsocket -lmalloc
```

The libraries up to the -lX11 are standard on most systems, the rest are
specific to the SCO UNIX system. For your system, these extra libraries may be
different or they may not be needed at all. Note that you will need an ANSI
standard C compiler to compile the examples shown in this book.

After xmdemo has been built, you can run it from the UNIX shell—from an
xterm window, for instance. Figure 6.2 shows the output generated by the
xmdemo program. When you click on the push-button (by pressing and releasing
the left mouse button with the pointer inside the push-button's window), the
program exits.

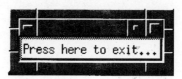

Fig. 6.2. Output of the xmdemo program.

Step-by-Step Toolkit Programming

Now that you have seen the basic structure of a toolkit-based program (Listing 6.1), we'll examine each of the steps in detail. This will introduce you to the convenience functions in Xt Intrinsics that help you create and manipulate widgets.

Including the Header Files

In addition to C header files such as <stdio.h>, programs that use Xt Intrinsics must include the header files <X11/StringDefs.h> and <X11/Intrinsic.h>. These files define symbolic names for standard widget resources (such as foreground and background colors) and structures used to initialize and use widgets.

In addition to <X11/StringDefs.h> and <X11/Intrinsic.h>, the OSF/Motif toolkit requires that you include the header file <Xm/Xm.h>. Following this, comes the header files for each type of widget you use in the program. For example, if a program uses ScrolledWindow, ScrollBar, and PushButton widgets, the sequence of header files is as follows:

```
#include <X11/StringDefs.h>
#include <X11/Intrinsic.h>
#include <Xm/Xm.h>
#include <Xm/PushB.h>
#include <Xm/ScrolledW.h>
#include <Xm/ScrollBar.h>
```

Initializing the Toolkit

Because of the client-server architecture of X, all X applications must start by opening a connection to the X server. Once the connection is established, you have to create a top-level window for your application. This step involves working with the window manager to set up the initial position and size (geometry) of the top-level window. If the user specifies a geometry on the command-line, the application is supposed to use that information to set up the top-level window.

Toolkit Initialization in X11R3

The Xt Intrinsics in X11R3 provides the XtInitialize function to take care of these steps. This function opens a connection to the X display, parses the command-line options, and creates a top-level widget with an associated top-level window (because each widget has a window) that serves as the parent of all other widgets in your application. This top-level widget is known as a *shell widget*.

The XtInitialize function has the following syntax:

```
Widget XtInitialize(app_name, app_class, options, num_options, argc, argv)

String      app_name;             /* Name of application      */
String      app_class;            /* Class name of application */
XrmOptionDescRec options[];       /* List of acceptable options */
Cardinal    num_options;          /* Number of options in list */
Cardinal    *argc;                /* Pointer to number of      */
                                  /* command-line arguments    */
String      argv[];               /* Array of command-line     */
                                  /* arguments to be processed */
```

The data types Cardinal and String are defined in the header file <X11/Intrinsic.h>.

The first argument to XtInitialize is the name of the program. The second argument is supposed to be the name of the class of the application. By convention, Xt-based applications use the name of the application with the first letter capitalized as the class name. When the first letter of the application's name is an X, the next letter is also capitalized in the class-name. Thus, for the xmdemo program shown in Listing 6.1, the application name is xmdemo and the class-name is XMdemo.

The options array of XrmOptionDescRec structures describe the options accepted by the application. You will learn more about the options later in this chapter.

For an application that does not accept any options on the command line, a typical call to XtInitialize is:

```
/* Program's name is "demo"--thus, class-name is "Demo" */

void main(int argc, char **argv)
{
  Widget toplevel;

  toplevel = XtInitialize(argv[0], "Demo", NULL, 0, &argc, argv);

  . . .
}
```

This example uses argv[0] as the name of the program and passes the address of argc as the next-to-last argument to XtInitialize.

Toolkit Initialization in X11R4

In X11R4, the recommended approach to initialize the toolkit is to call `XtAppInitialize`. The Xt Intrinsics (even in X11R3) support the notion of an *application context*, which allows multiple logical applications inside a single physical application; each logical application has its own event-processing loop and connection to the X server. Internally, Xt Intrinsics uses an `XtAppContext` structure to store the information pertinent to each logical application. Most applications use the default application context, maintained as a global variable by the Xt Intrinsics. In fact, when you call `XtInitialize`, it does its job by calling three other functions:

```
XtToolkitInitialize();
XtOpenDisplay(app_context, display_name, application_name,
              class_name, options, numoptions, &argc, argv);
XtAppCreateShell(application_name, class_name, widget_class,
                 display, arglist, numargs);
```

where `app_context` will be the default application context. In X11R4, the Xt Intrinsics provides the `XtAppInitialize` function as a replacement for `XtInitialize`. You use `XtAppInitalize` in a manner similar to `XtInitialize`. For instance, to initialize the toolkit and create the top-level widget for a simple application, you would use `XtAppInitialize` as follows:

```
/* Program's name is "demo"--thus, class-name is "Demo" */

void main(int argc, char **argv)
{
  Widget toplevel;
  XtAppContext this_app;

  toplevel = XtAppInitialize(&this_app, "Demo", NULL, 0,
                             &argc, argv, NULL, NULL, 0);

  . . .
}
```

Consult Chapter 10 for the complete syntax of `XtAppInitialize`.

Creating and Initializing Widgets

You can think of a widget as a window with some relevant data. The latter part of this chapter covers the details of the data structures used by a widget. To get a rough idea of a widget's data structure, consider a `Label` widget that displays some text in a window. Clearly, this widget needs a window to display the label.

Additionally, it needs a text string and a graphics context (GC) to display the string. The window's size must be remembered, and a procedure is needed to draw the label whenever an Expose event is reported for its window. As you will see later in this chapter, Xt Intrinsics provides the necessary data structures to store the information for a widget and the Intrinsics has a standard method of handling tasks such as drawing in response to Expose events.

Setting a Widget's Resources

When using a widget in an application, you need not know the details of the widget's data structure. What you do need is information on the arguments that each widget accepts. These arguments, also known as the widget's *resources*, control its appearance and behavior.

To be useful as a building block of user interfaces, a widget must be highly configurable. For instance, a widget that allows the programmer to pick the foreground and background colors is much more useful than one that hard-wires these values. The best solution is to set a widget's resources from a resource database—a text file that defines values of parameters in a specific syntax. (Chapter 5 describes how you can specify an application's resources in a text file.)

The next best approach to setting a widget's resources is to set them with an argument list. To do this, you first consult the widget's documentation and determine the names of the resources you want to set. The resource names are constants defined in the header file <Xm/Xm.h>. For example, XmNwidth and XmNheight are defined in <Xm/Xm.h> as

```
#define XmNwidth     "width"
#define XmNheight    "height"
```

You use the constants XmNwidth and XmNheight to refer to the width and height resources of a widget. The value of each resource is specified in an Arg structure which is defined in <X11/Intrinsic.h> as

```
typedef struct
{
    String    name;  /* Name of resource */
    XtArgVal  value; /* Its value        */
} Arg, *ArgList;
```

where the value of the named resource is stored as an XtArgVal—a system-dependent data type capable of holding a pointer to any C variable. If the value of a resource is less than the size of XtArgVal, it is stored directly in the value field of Arg. Otherwise, the value field is a pointer to the resource's value.

6

When creating a widget, you can specify an array of `Arg` structures with values of the resources that you wish to set. You can prepare the array of resource values in two ways:

- Use a statically initialized array.

- Assign values at run-time using the `XtSetArg` macro.

To see how to set resources, consider the OSF/Motif `PushButton` widget. Suppose you want to set the push-button's width and height as well as the label to be displayed in it. The documentation of the `XmPushButton` widget in Chapter 9 tells us the names of the resources: `XmNwidth`, `XmNheight`, and `XmNlabelString`. You also have to know that the string for `XmNlabelString` is not a simple C character array—it is a compound string, a special data type that you create by passing the string as an argument to an utility routine (`XmStringCreateLtoR`).

With the information about the resources in hand, you can set the values in the following manner:

```
Arg    args[20];
Cardinal nargs;
.

.

.
XtSetArg(args[nargs], XmNwidth, 300); nargs++;
XtSetArg(args[nargs], XmNheight, 100); nargs++;
XtSetArg(args[nargs], XmNlabelString,
        XmStringCreateLtoR("Press for help",
        XmSTRING_DEFAULT_CHARSET)); nargs++;
```

> There is a reason why `nargs++` is not used in `XtSetArg` to increment the count of arguments—`XtSetArg` is defined as a macro in such a way that it uses the first argument twice. If you use `nargs++` in the first argument, the macro will end up incrementing `nargs` twice in each call. This is why most toolkit applications define the argument list as shown.

Creating a Widget

Once the argument list is ready, you can create a widget and set its resources by calling the `XtCreateManagedWidget` function:

```
Widget   toplevel, /* Previously created top-level shell */
         button1;  /* New push-button               */
```

```
button1 = XtCreateManagedWidget("HelpButton",
                    xmPushButtonWidgetClass, toplevel,
                    (ArgList) args, nargs);
```

This creates a new push-button named HelpButton, whose parent widget is toplevel and whose initial resource settings are in the array args.

The name of the widget is used to retrieve from the resource database any resource meant for this widget. Chapter 5 explains how users can specify the resources of the widgets in the resource database.

Callbacks

Many widgets include a class of resources known as *callbacks* that are pointers to functions. You can set such a resource to point to one of your functions and have the widget call the function in response to one or more events. The *callback functions* are so named because the widget calls them whenever appropriate. A widget may have more than one type of callback resource, with each type pointing to functions to be called under a specific situation. A widget's callback resource is actually a list of functions rather than a single function. The widget calls all the callbacks when the conditions for that callback resource are met. The calling order is the same as the order in which you registered the callbacks.

In Listing 6.1, the function button_pushed is set to be a callback function for the push-button widget's XmNactivateCallback resource. According to the documentation of the XmPushButton widget, the widget calls the functions in the XmNactivateCallback resource when the user presses and releases the left mouse button (this can be changed to another button) with the pointer inside the push-button's window. The XmPushButton widget has two more callback resources:

- XmNarmCallback functions, called when the user presses the button

- XmNdisarmCallback list, called when the user releases the button

As shown in Listing 6.1, you use the XtAddCallback function to add a function to the callback list of a widget. To add the button_pushed function to the callback list XmNactivateCallback of the XmPushButton widget quit_button, you would write the following:

```
XtAddCallback(quit_button, XmNactivateCallback,
              button_pushed, NULL);
```

The last argument to XtAddCallback—defined to be of type caddr_t—is a pointer to data that you want passed to the callback function when the widget calls it. The callback function button_pushed has the following prototype:

```
static void button_pushed(Widget w, caddr_t client_data,
XmAnyCallbackStruct *call_data);
```

When the widget calls this function, the second argument will be whatever data you had passed to XtAddCallback as the last argument. The last argument passed to the callback function is an XmAnyCallbackStruct structure, which is defined in <Xm/Xm.h> as

```
typedef struct
{
    int     reason;    /* Indicates why callback was called   */
    XEvent  *event;    /* Information on event that triggered */
                       /* the callback                        */
} XmAnyCallbackStruct;
```

where the reason field indicates why the widget called the callback function. You have to consult the widget's documentation to interpret the value of this field. The event field is a pointer to an XEvent structure with information on the event that triggered the callback (see Chapter 11 for more information on X events).

What if you want to catch a mouse button-press in a widget's window? The designers of the Xt Intrinsics thoughtfully made provisions for this using a method similar to the callback resources used by widgets. Essentially, you can register your own event handler for selected events on a widget's window. Thereafter, when these events occur, the Xt Intrinsics will call the registered event handler, giving you a chance to take the desired action.

For example, suppose you want to alter the xmdemo program (Listing 6.1) so that when the user presses any mouse button in the push-button window, the label changes. Then on the next button-press, the program terminates. You can do this by adding your own handler for the ButtonPress event. Listing 6.2 shows the modified version of the program.

You use the Intrinsics function XtAddEventHandler to add the handler. To add a function named my_event_handler as the handler for ButtonPress events in the quit_button widget, you would write:

```
XtAddEventHandler(quit_button, ButtonPressMask, FALSE,
                  my_event_handler, NULL);
```

The second argument to XtAddEventHandler is an event mask that determines for which events the handler is invoked. The third argument is a Boolean that should be set to TRUE if you are setting the event handler for one of the events—ClientMessage, MappingNotify, SelectionClear, or SelectionRequest—for which there is no event mask. In this case, set the second argument to NoEventMask.

As in XtAddCallback, the last argument is a pointer to any data that you want passed back to the event handler when it is called.

You have to write the event handler, my_event_handler, according to the following prototype:

```
static void my_event_handler(Widget w, caddr_t client_data,
                             XEvent *p_event);
```

Xt Intrinsics calls the event handler with three arguments. The first argument is the widget's ID, and the second one is the same pointer that you had passed as the last argument of XtAddEventHandler when you registered this event handler. The third argument is a pointer to the XEvent structure (see Chapter 11) that triggered the function call.

In Listing 6.2, the event handler retrieves the current label for the widget, frees it, creates a new label, and sets it with the following code:

```
    static Arg args[10];
    XmString xmlabel;

/* Get the current label and free it */
    XtSetArg(args[0], XmNlabelString, &xmlabel);
    XtGetValues(w, args, 1);
    XmStringFree(xmlabel);

/* Create a new label and set it */
    xmlabel = XmStringCreateLtoR("Press again please",
                                 XmSTRING_DEFAULT_CHARSET);
    XtSetArg(args[0], XmNlabelString, xmlabel);
    XtSetValues(w, args, 1);
```

An interesting point to note is that when you set the XmPushButton widget's label string to a new value by calling XtSetValues, the widget automatically clears its window and generates an expose event which subsequently causes the window to be redrawn with the new label.

Listing 6.2. xmdemo_ev.c—Push-button with event handler.

```
/*---------------------------------------------------------------*/
/*  File: xmdemo_ev.c
 *
 *  A sample program that displays a PushButton widget and
 *  uses an event handler to change the message when user
 *  presses the left mouse button.
 */
#include <X11/Intrinsic.h>
#include <X11/StringDefs.h>
#include <Xm/Xm.h>
#include <Xm/PushB.h>

static int quit_now = 0;
```

continues

Listing 6.2. continued

```c
/* Label for the push-button */
static char quit_label[] = "Press here to exit . . .";

/* Room for setting up arguments passed to widgets */
static Arg args[10];

/* Prototype of callback function */

static void my_event_handler(Widget w, caddr_t client_data,
                             XEvent *p_event);
/*--------------------------------------------------------------*/
void main(int argc, char **argv)
{
    Widget main_widget, quit_button;

    main_widget = XtInitialize(argv[0], "XMdemo", NULL, 0,
                               &argc, argv);

    XtSetArg(args[0], XmNlabelString,
            XmStringCreateLtoR(quit_label,
            XmSTRING_DEFAULT_CHARSET));

    quit_button = XtCreateManagedWidget("Exit",
                    xmPushButtonWidgetClass, main_widget,
                    (ArgList) args, 1);

/* Install an event handler for ButtonPress events */

    XtAddEventHandler(quit_button, ButtonPressMask, FALSE,
                    my_event_handler, NULL);

/* Realize the widgets and start event-processing loop */

    XtRealizeWidget(main_widget);
    XtMainLoop();
}
/*--------------------------------------------------------------*/
/* m y _ e v e n t _ h a n d l e r
 *
 * Function to be called when the user presses a mouse button
 * in the "Exit" pushbutton
 */
static void my_event_handler(Widget w, caddr_t client_data,
                             XEvent *p_event)
{
/* Exit if the quit flag is set */
    if(quit_now)
        exit(0);
    else
    {
        XmString xmlabel;
```

6

```
/* Get the current label and free it */
        XtSetArg(args[0], XmNlabelString, &xmlabel);
        XtGetValues(w, args, 1);
        XmStringFree(xmlabel);

/* Create a new label and set it */
        xmlabel = XmStringCreateLtoR("Press again please",
                        XmSTRING_DEFAULT_CHARSET);
        XtSetArg(args[0], XmNlabelString, xmlabel);
        XtSetValues(w, args, 1);

/* Set flag so that, we quit on next ButtonPress */
        quit_now = 1;
    }
}
```

Realizing the Widgets

After all the widgets are created, you have to display their windows on the screen. You do this by calling the `XtRealizeWidget` function with the top-level widget as the sole argument:

```
Widget top-level;   /* The top-level widget */
.
.
/* Create the widget hierarchy */
.
.
/* Display the windows */
XtRealizeWidget(top_level);
```

Calling `XtRealizeWidget` is similar to calling `XMapWindow` in Xlib programming. Although the widgets are created, they are not visible until `XtRealizeWidget` is called.

The Event-Handling Loop

When programming with Xlib alone, you have to retrieve events and process each event—even if the processing for certain events is to simply ignore them. In fact, much of the complexity of Xlib-based programs comes from the need to process events for a large number of windows in X applications. The Xt Intrinsics greatly simplifies event handling. Each widget in an X toolkit-based application has an associated window and an event-handling function. You can retrieve an event and process it by the following sequence of function calls:

6

```
XEvent theEvent;   /* Structure for retrieving event */

XtNextEvent(&theEvent);
XtDispatchEvent(&theEvent);
```

Because X applications usually work by repeatedly retrieving and processing events, you can code the entire event-handling loop as follows:

```
XEvent theEvent;   /* Structure for retrieving event */
 .
 .
 .
while(1)
{
    XtNextEvent(&theEvent);
    XtDispatchEvent(&theEvent);
}
```

The Xt Intrinsics simplifies event handling even further by providing the function XtMainLoop, which embodies this loop. You call this function without any arguments. Once you call XtMainLoop, you have no way of exiting the application except through a callback function or a registered event handler, as illustrated in Listings 6.1 and 6.2.

In OSF/Motif Version 1.1, the recommended approach to handling events is by calling XtAppMainLoop. Here is a fragment of code showing the new approach:

```
/* Program's name is "demo"--thus, class-name is "Demo"     */

void main(int argc, char **argv)
{
  Widget toplevel;
  XtAppContext this_app;

  toplevel = XtAppInitialize(&this_app, "Demo", NULL, 0,
                             &argc, argv, NULL, NULL, 0);

  ...
  XtRealizeWidget(toplevel);
  XtAppMainLoop(this_app);  /* X11R4 event-processing loop */
}
```

Hello, World! with OSF/Motif Widgets

You have seen the basic functions of Xt Intrinsics and how they are used to create and manage widgets. This section presents a somewhat larger example than the one in Listing 6.1. The example is xmhello, the OSF/Motif version of the classic "Hello, World!" program. In the process of showing how to display Hello, World! using Motif widgets, we will explain how toolkit-based applications can process command-line options and retrieve application-specific resources from the resource files.

Designing xmhello

The xmhello program will, by default, display the Hello, World! message in a window. To provide a convenient way of exiting from xmhello, we include a push-button labelled Quit. The program ends when the user clicks in this button.

Selecting Widgets

We are writing xmhello using the OSF/Motif toolkit, so the first step is to identify appropriate widgets to accomplish the job. We can display the Hello, World! message in an XmLabel widget, and we can use an XmPushButton widget for the Quit button. However, we need some way to position these two widgets in the application's main window. The XmForm widget is a good candidate for this. Thus, our widget hierarchy will be a top-level shell with a form widget as the only child. The form widget will have a label and a push-button as children. Figure 6.3 illustrates the widget tree for xmhello.

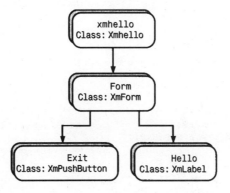

Fig. 6.3. The widget hierarchy in xmhello.

Application-Specific Resources

Widgets in X toolkits retrieve their resources automatically from one or more resource files—usually, a file with the same name as the application's class in the directory /usr/lib/X11/app-defaults or the .Xdefaults file in the user's login directory. Chapter 5 describes how to specify resources in a resource file.

In addition to the resources used by the widgets, you may need additional resources for parameters used by your application. In xmhello, we want to allow the user to specify the message and the label for the Quit button. Accordingly, we use two resources, msg_text and exit_text, which are the strings to be displayed in the label and in the Exit push-button, respectively.

To use application-specific resources, you have to first define a data structure to hold the values of these resources. Then, you create an array of XtResource structures that contains information about the resources and where each resource's value should be loaded. The XtResource structure is defined in <X11/Intrinsic.h> as

```
typedef struct _XtResource
{
    String   resource_name;    /* Name of resource              */
    String   resource_class;   /* Class name of resource        */
    String   resource_type;    /* Type of resource              */
    Cardinal resource_size;    /* Size of its value in bytes    */
    Cardinal resource_offset;  /* Offset from base of structure */
                               /* that will hold resource values */
    String   default_type;     /* Type of default value         */
    caddr_t  default_addr;     /* Address of default value      */
} XtResource;
```

The following sample code from xmhello clarifies the meaning of the different fields in an XtResource structure:

```
typedef struct APP_DATA       /* Application's data            */
{
    char    *mtext;           /* Message string                */
    char    *etext;           /* Label on exit button          */
} APP_DATA, *P_APP_DATA;


/* Resources specific to this application */
static XtResource resources[] =
{
    {"msg_text", "Msg_text", XtRString, sizeof(String),
     XtOffset(P_APP_DATA, mtext), XtRString, "Hello, World!"},

    {"exit_text", "Exit_text", XtRString, sizeof(String),
     XtOffset(P_APP_DATA, etext), XtRString, "Quit"}
};
```

```
Widget      main_widget;        /* Top-level shell widget      */
APP_DATA    data;               /* Application's data structure */
    .
    .
    .
/* Later, in main program . . . Get the resources */

XtGetApplicationResources(main_widget, &data, resources,
                          XtNumber(resources), NULL, 0);
```

This code sets up the `resources` array with two `XtResource` structures initialized with information necessary to retrieve and interpret the values. The type of the resource is specified using the defined constant `XtRString`, defined in `<X11/StringDefs.h>`. Other common representation types such as `XtRInt` for integers and `XtRColor` for colors, are also defined in this header file.

To actually retrieve and load the resources, you call the `XtGetApplicationResources` function as shown in the code. This function converts the value of each resource from a string to the specified type and places the value at a specified offset in the data structure whose address you provide as the second argument (`data` in example). The offset for each resource is indicated in the `resource_offset` field of that resource's `XtResource` structure. Note that the `XtOffset` macro is used to indicate the offset to the location within the structure where the resource's value is to be placed.

Command-Line Options

As explained in Chapter 5, all toolkit-based applications always accept a standard complement of command-line options. The common ones are foreground (`-fg`) and background (`-bg`) colors and the geometry of the top-level window (`-geometry`). Parameters specified in the command-line usually have corresponding resources.

If needed, your application can have command-line options in addition to those already supported by Xt Intrinsics. In `xmhello`, we allow the user to specify the strings for the label and the push-button on the command line. Like the resources, you specify the acceptable command-line options in an array of `XrmOptionDescRec` structures. This structure and its pointer types are defined in `<X11/Xresource.h>` as

```
typedef struct
{
    char    *option;            /* Option string in command line */
    char    *specifier;         /* Corresponding resource name    */
    XrmOptionKind argKind;      /* The "style" of option          */
    caddr_t value;              /* Pointer to value if argKind    */
                                /* is XrmoptionNoArg */
} XrmOptionDescRec, *XrmOptionDescList;
```

The `argKind` field indicates how the value of an option is given on the command line. This can be one of the enumerated constants shown in Table 6.1.

Table 6.1. Argument Styles for Specifying Command-Line Options

Argument Style	Description
XrmoptionIsArg	Value is the option string itself
XrmoptionStickyArg	Value immediately follows option without any intervening space
XrmoptionSepArg	Value is the next argument in command line
XrmoptionResArg	A resource and its value appears in the next argument in the command line
XrmoptionSkipArg	Ignore this option and the next argument in the command line
XrmoptionSkipLine	Ignore this option and the rest of the command line

For `xmhello`, the option strings are `-mtext` and `-etext` and each requires the value to follow the option (`XrmoptionSepArg`). Thus, its `options` array is defined as follows:

```
/* Command-line options specific to this application */

static XrmOptionDescRec options[] =
{
    {"-mtext", "*mtext", XrmoptionSepArg, NULL},
    {"-etext", "*etext", XrmoptionSepArg, NULL}
};
```

Note that each command-line option requires the name of the corresponding resource's name. When you call `XtInitialize` (`XtAppInitialize` in Motif 1.1 and later) to create the top-level shell widget and initialize the toolkit, it loads the value of each option specified in the command line into the structure where its corresponding resource's value is supposed to go. For example, in `xmhello`, the options array is provided to `XtInitialize` as follows:

```
void main(int argc, char **argv)
{
    Widget main_widget;

/* Create and initialize the top-level widget. Also parse
 * the command-line and accept any specified options.
```

```
*/
    main_widget = XtInitialize(argv[0], "XMhello", options,
                    XtNumber(options), &argc, argv);
    .
    .
    .
}
```

Putting Together `xmhello`

Listing 6.3 shows `xmhello.c`—the OSF/Motif application that displays a string in a label and provides a button so that the user can exit the program by clicking on it.

The only part of the program left unexplained so far is how to control the placement of the label and push-button widget inside the form widget. This requires learning about the resources of the `XmForm` widget. The latter part of this chapter describes some of the OSF/Motif widgets including the form widget.

On a typical SCO UNIX Open Desktop 1.0 system (System V/386 Release 3.2), the following command line compiles and links the `xmhello` program:

```
cc -o xmhello -DSYSV xmhello.c -lXm -lXt -lX11 -lsocket -lmalloc
```

Some variation of this command should work on your system. You may need to modify or omit the last two library specifications.

Listing 6.3. `xmhello.c`—Saying "Hello, World!" with OSF/Motif widgets.

```
/*-------------------------------------------------------------*/
/*  File: xmhello.c
 *
 *  Motif version of the "Hello, World!" program
 *  with an exit button. Uses Motif's Form,
 *  PushButton, and Label widgets.
 */
#include <X11/Intrinsic.h>
#include <X11/StringDefs.h>
#include <Xm/Xm.h>
#include <Xm/Form.h>
#include <Xm/Label.h>
#include <Xm/PushB.h>

typedef struct APP_DATA   /* Application's data    */
{
```

6

```c
    char    *msg_text;     /* Message string         */
    char    *exit_text;    /* Label on exit button */
} APP_DATA, *P_APP_DATA;

/* Command-line options specific to this application */

static XrmOptionDescRec options[] =
{
    {"-mtext", "*mtext", XrmoptionSepArg, NULL},
    {"-etext", "*etext", XrmoptionSepArg, NULL}
};

/* Resources specific to this application */

static XtResource resources[] =
{
    {"msg_text", "Msg_text", XtRString, sizeof(String),
     XtOffset(P_APP_DATA, mtext), XtRString, "Hello, World!"},

    {"exit_text", "Exit_text", XtRString, sizeof(String),
     XtOffset(P_APP_DATA, etext), XtRString, "Quit"}
};

/* Room for setting up arguments passed to widgets */
static Arg args[10];

/* Prototype of callback function */

static void quit_action(Widget w, caddr_t client_data,
                        XmAnyCallbackStruct *call_data);

/*--------------------------------------------------------------*/
void main(int argc, char **argv)
{
    APP_DATA data;

    Widget main_widget, form_widget, hello_message, exit_button;

/* Create and initialize the top-level widget */
    main_widget = XtInitialize(argv[0], "XMhello", options,
                    XtNumber(options), &argc, argv);

/* Get the resources from the resource file */
    XtGetApplicationResources(main_widget, &data, resources,
                    XtNumber(resources), NULL, 0);

    printf("mtext = %s\netext = %s\n", data.msg_text,
            data.exit_text);

/* Next, create the Form widget that will hold the exit
 * pushbutton and the label widget.
 */
```

6

```
        form_widget = XtCreateManagedWidget("Form",
                        xmFormWidgetClass, main_widget, NULL, 0);

/* Create the exit button and position it in the form */
    XtSetArg(args[0], XmNtopAttachment, XmATTACH_FORM);
    XtSetArg(args[1], XmNleftAttachment, XmATTACH_FORM);
    XtSetArg(args[2], XmNlabelString,
            XmStringCreateLtoR(data.etext,
                                XmSTRING_DEFAULT_CHARSET));

        exit_button = XtCreateManagedWidget("Exit",
                        xmPushButtonWidgetClass, form_widget,
                                        (ArgList) args, 3);

/* Install the callback function for this pushbutton */
    XtAddCallback(exit_button, XmNactivateCallback,
                quit_action, NULL);

/* Now, create the message label and position it in the form */
    XtSetArg(args[0], XmNtopAttachment, XmATTACH_WIDGET);
    XtSetArg(args[1], XmNtopWidget, exit_button);
    XtSetArg(args[2], XmNleftAttachment, XmATTACH_FORM);
    XtSetArg(args[3], XmNrightAttachment, XmATTACH_FORM);
    XtSetArg(args[4], XmNbottomAttachment, XmATTACH_FORM);
    XtSetArg(args[5], XmNlabelString,
            XmStringCreateLtoR(data.mtext,
                                XmSTRING_DEFAULT_CHARSET));

        hello_message = XtCreateManagedWidget("Hello",
                        xmLabelWidgetClass, form_widget,
                                        (ArgList) args, 6);

/* Realize the widgets and start processing events */
    XtRealizeWidget(main_widget);
    XtMainLoop();
}
/*-------------------------------------------------------------*/
/* q u i t _ a c t i o n
 *
 * Function to be called when user presses and releases button
 * in the "exit" pushbutton
 */
static void quit_action(Widget w, caddr_t client_data,
                        XmAnyCallbackStruct *call_data)
{
    XtCloseDisplay(XtDisplay(w));
    exit(0);
}
```

6

Running `xmhello`

To run `xmhello`, type its name at the shell prompt. You can specify resources for `xmhello` in one of three files:

- `/usr/lib/X11/app-defaults/XMhello`

- `XMhello` in your login directory

- `.Xdefaults` file in your login directory.

For instance, to specify an initial size and position for `xmhello`'s main window and its foreground and background colors, you can place the following lines in the `.Xdefaults` file in your login directory:

```
XMhello*foreground:    black
XMhello*background:    white
XMhello*geometry:      200x100+10+10
```

Figure 6.4 shows the result of running `xmhello` after specifying these resources.

Fig. 6.4. "Hello, World!" from `xmhello`.

6

If you want `xmhello` to display some other message than `Hello, World!` and a different string on the Exit push-button, you can use the command-line options `-mtext` and `-etext`, respectively. An example might be:

```
xmhello -mtext "File creation succeeded!" -etext " OK "
```

Customizing the `xmhello` Program

When you run the `xmhello` program, you might be somewhat surprised to see that resources such as foreground, background, and geometry are automatically handled in a toolkit-based application. In addition to automatically handling certain resources, the Xt Intrinsics includes a *translation manager* that enables users to specify a mapping between the user's actions and the functions provided by a widget. The translation manager provides a powerful mechanism for customizing the behavior of an application without recompiling the program.

Using the Translation Manager

In response to user's actions (a combination of keystrokes and mouse button events), a widget performs an action, either by default or by calling functions in its callback list. You can use the translation manager to specify which callback to activate when certain keystrokes and mouse button events occur.

As an example, consider the push-button widget in xmhello. Normally, when you press the left mouse button (Button1) in this widget, it calls the callbacks registered under the XmNactivateCallback resource. Suppose a user wants the push-button to call these callback functions when the *Control* key is pressed together with Button1. This user can modify the behavior of xmhello by simply adding the following lines to the file /usr/lib/X11/app-defaults/ XMhello (or in the .Xdefaults file):

```
*XmPushButton.translations: #replace\n\
         Ctrl<Btn1Down>: ArmAndActivate()
```

These lines specify the translations resource for the push-button. The exact specification is in a format specified by the translation manager. In this case, the code says that the action ArmAndActivate() should be bound to the event—Button1 of the mouse pressed while the *Control* key is down. The names of the actions are specified by each widget's documentation. After this has been done, users can exit from xmhello only by pressing the left button of the mouse while pressing the Control key.

Adding Your Own Actions

As an application developer, you can also add your own list of actions that the user can bind to a combination of keystrokes and mouse events. To see how this is done, consider adding to xmhello a function that can be invoked by a user-defined sequence of keystrokes. Here are the steps to follow:

1. Define the function that will be called when the user-defined keystrokes occur. Suppose we call this function quit. The function, which must accept four arguments, has the following prototype:

```
static void quit(Widget w, XEvent *ev,  String *params,
                 Cardinal *num_params)
{
    printf("Quit() called\n");

/* Print out the parameters, if any */
    if(num_params)
    {
        int i;
        printf("num_params = %d\n", *num_params);
```

6

```
        for(i = 0; i < *num_params; i++)
                printf("Parameter %d = %s\n", i, params);
    }

    XtCloseDisplay(XtDisplay(w));
    exit(0);
}
```

When this function is called, you exit xmhello. (Soon you will see how parameters are passed to this function.)

2. Prepare an array of XtActionsRec structures in which each structure is initialized with two fields. The first is the name by which you want the user to refer to this action, and the second is the function that performs the action. Here is the table for the quit function:

```
/* Function prototype */
static void quit(Widget w, XEvent *ev,  String *params,
                    Cardinal *num_params);

/* Actions table */
static XtActionsRec actions[] =
{
    {"Quit",  quit}
};
```

The actions table performs the crucial step of binding the name of an action to a function. In this case, the user will refer to this action by the name Quit.

3. Prepare a default binding for the action. This is simply a string that looks just like a resource specification for the translation manager. For example, to bind the letter q to the action Quit, you would write

```
static char default_translation[] = "<Key>q: Quit()";
```

In this case the user types **q** to activate the Quit action.

4. In the program, after the toolkit has been initialized, call XtAddActions to register the new actions and parse the default binding from the string default_translation:

```
XtTranslations translations;
    .
    .
    .
XtAddActions(actions, XtNumber(actions));
translations = XtParseTranslationTable (default_translation);
```

5. After the push-button widget `exit_button` has been created, call `XtAugmentTranslations` to add the default bindings to the translation table for this widget:

```
XtAugmentTranslations(exit_button, translations);
```

6. Rebuild (compile and link) the program.

After these steps are done, you can exit the program by typing the letter **q**. Then the program displays the following:

```
Quit() called
num_params = 0
```

The user can bind a new key to this action. For instance, if the user adds the following to the resource file:

```
*XmPushButton.translations: #replace\n\
              Ctrl<Key>z:  Quit(Goodbye, 10)
```

this binds *Ctrl-Z* (which means press Z while you press the Control key) to the `Quit` action. Additionally, it passes two arguments to the function called to handle this action.

After you do this, you can exit from the modified `xmhello` by either typing **q** or pressing Ctrl-Z. When you exit using Ctrl-Z, the program prints the following on the console:

```
Quit() called
num_params = 2
Parameter 0 = Goodbye
Parameter 1 = 10
```

As you can see, the arguments specified in the resource file are passed to the `quit` function (which is bound to the action named `Quit`). These arguments appear like command-line arguments, each as a string. How you use them in the function is up to you.

OSF/Motif Widget Set

The previous sections show you how to use the facilities of the Xt Intrinsics to build user interfaces with widgets. However, to make productive use of the widgets, you need to know what widgets are available, what they do, and what are their configurable resources. Accordingly, discussions in this remaining section of the chapter describe the widgets available in the OSF/Motif toolkit. Because of limited space, this chapter does not cover every available widget in the toolkit; it focuses on the general features of the OSF/Motif widget set—the widgets' object-oriented architecture and the way they are implemented. Then it describes the major categories of widgets and presents short examples that illustrate how to create and use some of the widgets.

Basic Architecture of
Xt Intrinsics-Based Widgets

You can use the OSF/Motif widgets without knowing the internal details of any of the widgets. All you need to know is the functionality provided by a widget and how to configure the widget's parameters—the resources. However, you will find it very helpful to know the basic architecture of the widgets. For example, knowing the object-oriented design of the widgets helps you understand what it means to say, for instance, that the XmPushButton inherits from the XmLabel widget or that XmNwidth is a part of the Core resource set. The following sections describe the object-oriented nature of Xt Intrinsics-based widgets and explains how a widget inherits from its parent.

Xt Intrinsics and Object-Oriented
Programming (OOP)

Xt Intrinsics provides the basic data structures on which all OSF/Motif widgets are built. The designers of the Xt Intrinsics used an *object-oriented programming* (OOP) model for the widgets. In particular, the widgets are designed so as to support the concepts of data abstraction and inheritance.

Objects and Data Abstraction

To understand data abstraction, consider the file I/O routines in the C run-time library. These routines help you to view the file as a stream of bytes and perform various operations on this stream. For example, you can open a file (fopen), close it (fclose), read a character from it (getc), write a character to it (putc), and so on. This abstract model of a file is implemented by defining the FILE data type using C's typedef facility.

To use the FILE data type, you do not have to know the C data structure that defines the FILE data type. In fact, FILE's underlying data structure can vary from one system to another. Yet, the C file I/O routines work in the same manner on all systems. This is what is known as *data hiding* or *information hiding*.

Data abstraction is the combination of defining a data type and data hiding. Thus, C's FILE data type is an example of data abstraction.

You can use the idea of data abstraction to create an object by defining a block of data together with the functions necessary to operate on that data. The data represents the information contained in the object; the functions define the operations that can be performed on that object.

In C, you can represent an object by a structure. Because an object's data is not accessible to the outside world, a basic tenet of OOP is that you must access and manipulate the object's data by calling functions provided by that object. Although object-oriented languages such as C++ enforce this principle, implementing object-oriented techniques in a C program requires discipline on the part of the programmer because C does not prohibit code that directly accesses members of a object's data structure.

Classes and Methods

In OOP terminology, the template defining an object's data type is usually called a *class*—the term may differ from one object-oriented programming language to another. Thus, each object is an *instance* of a class. In C, a class can be implemented by defining a new data type (based on a struct) with typedef.

The functions that operate on an object have a special name. They are known as *methods*, because that was the name used in the object-oriented language Smalltalk. The methods define the behavior of an object. When applying OOP techniques in C, the methods are usually pointers to functions.

Another important concept of OOP, also from Smalltalk, is the idea of sending messages to an object to perform an action by invoking one of its methods. In C, this is done by calling a function through the pointer stored in the object's class.

Inheritance

We often describe a real-world object by pointing out how it differs from an existing one. For example, we might say that a square is a rectangle whose sides are all equal. OOP uses the term *inheritance* for this concept because you can think of one object inheriting the properties from another. Inheritance imposes a parent-child hierarchical relationship among classes where a child inherits from its parent. The parent class is often called the *super class* (or *base class* in C++).

6

Widgets as Objects

Widgets based on the Xt Intrinsics implement OOP techniques in C using `structs` and `typedefs`. The approach is to define two types of data structures for a specific type (class) of widget:

- Class structure

- Instance structure

The methods of the widget are represented by pointers to functions. These are stored in the class data structure. Also included in the class structure are variables common to all widgets of this type as well as a pointer to the parent or super class.

The instance data structure contains information that is unique to each copy of the widget. By design, each widget has a window. The ID of this window is stored in the widget's instance data structure, because each copy of the widget must have its own window. Also, because X supports a hierarchy of windows, the widgets are also used in a hierarchy. The widget's instance record stores the ID of its parent. When you create a widget, the Xt Intrinsics allocates a new copy of the instance structure and initializes it.

The information in a widget's class data structure is the same for all widgets in that class. Thus, only one copy of the class structure is needed for each type of widget. Figure 6.5 shows a widget class with several instances.

Inheritance in Widgets

A widget can employ inheritance to use, extend, or replace all or part of another widget's characteristics and functions. Inheritance involves altering the class and instance data structures. Figure 6.6 illustrates the technique used in the Xt Intrinsics. Here a newly defined class of widgets (class B) inherits data and functions from class A. B's class structure is defined by appending B's new data to a copy A's structure. The instance structure is defined similarly. Later, if a class C inherits from B, the same process is repeated for C's new data structures.

The structures shown in Figure 6.6 are only meant to illustrate how Xt Intrinsics implements inheritance. They are not the actual data structures used in Xt Intrinsics.

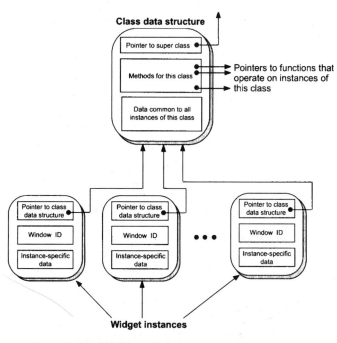

Fig. 6.5. A widget class with several instances.

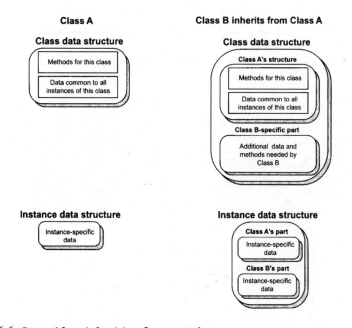

Fig. 6.6. One widget inheriting from another.

Widget Hierarchy Versus Class Hierarchy

The parent-child relationship among widget classes controls the inheritance of properties; the widget instances have their own parent-child hierarchy. This hierarchy is similar to the hierarchy of windows in the X Window System. In fact, because each widget in Xt Intrinsics has an associated window, the widget hierarchy is the same as the window hierarchy.

Keep in mind this notion of two distinct hierarchies. The *class hierarchy* defines the properties of a widget, whereas the *widget hierarchy* controls the placement of its window and handling of the events. The class hierarchy is necessary because of the object-oriented design of the widgets and the widget hierarchy is there to take advantage of the hierarchical arrangement of windows supported by the X Window System.

By design, the Xt Intrinsics provides a fixed class hierarchy. The widget hierarchy, on the other hand, can be anything you want. Each application has its own unique hierarchy of widgets that defines the unique screen layout of the widget's windows.

Basic Widgets in Xt Intrinsics

Xt Intrinsics does not define a complete hierarchy of widget classes; it defines several basic classes. Widget sets such as the OSF/Motif toolkit and the Athena widgets build new classes by inheriting from these basic classes. In fact, you will rarely have to directly use the widgets provided by Xt Intrinsics. These widgets are used only as the foundation of other widgets.

Class and Instance Records

As outlined earlier, the Xt Intrinsics uses two C structures for each widget class: one for the class information and the other for data specific to each instance of that class. The class structure is commonly referred to as the *class record*, whereas the other structure is called the *instance record*. The class record is allocated as static data and most of its members are initialized at compile-time. The instance record, on the other hand, has to be allocated dynamically whenever a widget of that class is created.

The class record contains pointers to the methods—functions for all operations that can be performed by the widget including creating, initializing, and destroying the widget.

The `Core` Widget

The Xt Intrinsics defines the `Core` class as the basis of all widgets in a toolkit. Thus, the class record of the `Core` class embodies information common to all widgets. You need to know the members of `Core`'s class record only when you are writing a new widget.

The resources of the `Core` widget are important to programmers because every widget in a toolkit inherits these resources. In fact, when you want to use a new widget, you have to know what types of resources (parameters) are used by the widget. Because all widgets are derived from the `Core` widget, its resources are available in every widget. Chapter 9 lists the resources for the `Core` widget.

The `Composite` Widget

Xt Intrinsics includes only a few basic widgets besides `Core`. The `Composite` widget inherits directly from `Core` and is meant to be used as a container for other widgets. Because many user-interface components consist of a number of widgets contained in an outer shell, the `Composite` class comes in handy when you have to build a widget that manages the positions of several child widgets. Any widget class that manages the layout of a number of child widgets is a subclass of the `Composite` class.

Because a child widget is managed by its parent, the child cannot resize or move itself. To change its geometry, the child makes a request to its parent by calling `XtMakeGeometryRequest`. The parent widget decides what to do depending on its policy.

In addition to the resources inherited from `Core`, the `Composite` class includes a new resource named `XmNinsertPosition`, which is of type `XmRFunction`, a pointer to a function that decides the position where a child is inserted. Because application programmers do not create `Composite` widgets directly, this information is only of interest to widget writers.

Other Widgets in Xt Intrinsics

Another basic widget in the Xt Intrinsics is the *Shell widget*. You have to take special care when setting up the top-level window of an X application. Because the X display is shared among different applications, your application has to work with a window manager to establish the position and size of the top-level window. In the Xt Intrinsics, the `Shell` class takes care of setting up the top-level window of an application.

6

The Constraint widget inherits from the subclass of Composite. Whereas the Composite class uses a fixed management policy to lay out the child widgets, the Constraint class handles the layout of child widgets based on information associated with each child. The name of the class comes from the fact that the layout information is specified in the form of constraints, such as

"The OK button is to the left of the Cancel button with both below the message area."

The Constraint class attaches extra information to each child widget's instance record to store the layout constraints. The xmhello program shown in Listing 6.3 uses the OSF/Motif XmForm widget, a class that inherits from Constraint. In that example you can see how certain resources in each child of the XmForm widget are set to indicate its layout inside the form widget.

OSF/Motif Class Hierarchy

As an application programmer, you cannot do much with the widgets defined in the Xt Intrinsics. These widgets provide the framework for writing other widgets that can be directly used in your application. Many widget sets are built on the Xt Intrinsics' widget architecture. Of these, the OSF/Motif widget set is a good example. Another popular widget set is M.I.T.'s Athena widgets. The following sections describe the OSF/Motif widgets.

All OSF/Motif widget classes are subclasses of the Core, Composite, and Shell widgets of the Xt Intrinsics. As you can see from Figure 6.7, OSF/Motif adds some more scaffolding to the class tree before defining the classes that you use directly in your applications. Specifically, it adds the class XmPrimitive under Core and XmManager under Composite. There are new additions under the Shell class also. As such, the Xt Intrinsics also defines several subclasses of Shell (which will be explained soon).

A widget set is like any toolbox—before using the tools you have to know what each tool does. The key to understanding and using the OSF/Motif widgets is to study the class hierarchy (see Figure 6.7), identify the broad categories, and learn what each category can do. After that you should learn about the individual widgets in each category. Then you can pick the widgets that meet your needs and set up the instance hierarchy for your application. To see what resources (parameters) of a widget you should set, you should look up the detailed documentation of the widget in the back of this book. Finally, you can use your knowledge of Xt Intrinsics to create and realize the widgets and use them in your application.

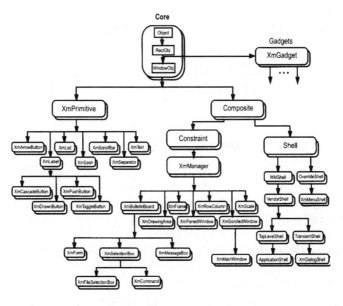

Fig. 6.7. The class hierarchy of OSF/Motif widgets.

Figure 6.7 features three distinct categories of widgets:

- *Shell widgets* are meant for creating widgets whose window is a child of the root window. In other words, these widgets are for creating top-level windows. An example of a shell widget is the top-level widget that you create in any toolkit-based application by calling `XtInitialize` (see example programs earlier in this chapter). Other examples include pop-up menus like the ones that you get when you press the Control key and the left mouse button together in the `xterm` terminal emulator.

- *Primitive widgets* include all stand-alone widgets such as labels, push-buttons, and scrollbars.

- *Manager widgets* include the widgets that manage the layout of several child widgets. In this category you will find forms, lists, and menus.

Shell Widgets

`Shell` widgets are a special subclass of the `Composite` widgets. Their primary purpose is to set up the top-level window of an application. A shell widget manages only one child. The Xt Intrinsics provide several classes of shell widgets, the important ones being: `TopLevelShell`, `OverrideShell`, and `TransientShell`.

When you call `XtInitialize`, the Xt Intrinsics create an instance of `ApplicationShell` widget, a subclass of `TopLevelShell`. The `ApplicationShell` and `TopLevelShell` widgets are used for normal top-level windows of applications. These windows interact with the window manager.

`TransientShell` Widgets

The `TransientShell` class is used for top-level windows that can be manipulated via the window manager but that cannot be reduced to an icon. Pop-up dialog boxes use this type of shells. OSF/Motif provides a subclass, `XmDialogShell`, just for this purpose. In fact, there are a number of convenience functions in the Motif toolkit that create a `XmDialogShell` widget and place another widget such as a selection box or a message box inside it. These functions have names that start with `XmCreate` and end with `Dialog`. You will see examples of these functions in the latter sections.

`OverrideShell` Widgets

The `OverrideShell` widget, derived from the `Shell` widget, completely bypasses the window manager. It does so by setting the `override_redirect` attribute of its window to `True`. This causes the window manager to ignore the window and not attempt to put frames around it or position it by prompting the user. The `OverrideShell` is primarily used to display pop-up menus. OSF/Motif defines a subclass, `XmMenuShell`, for this purpose. As you will see in the following sections, you can use the function `XmCreatePopupMenu` to create a `XmMenuShell` with a menu inside it.

Primitive Widgets

All OSF/Motif primitive widgets are derived from the `XmPrimitive` class, which is defined as a subclass of the `Core` class. You never create an instance of the `XmPrimitive` class. It is there to define a standard set of resources that are inherited by all primitive widgets. In particular, the `XmPrimitive` class is responsible for the three-dimensional shadowing effect of OSF/Motif widgets. This class also provides support for keyboard traversal—the concept of transferring keyboard focus from one widget to another.

Six widgets are derived directly from the `XmPrimitive` class:

- `XmArrowButton`

- `XmLabel`

- XmList

- XmScrollBar

- XmSeparator

- XmText

The functionality of the XmLabel class is further specialized by the following subclasses:

- XmCascadeButton

- XmDrawnButton

- XmPushButton

- XmToggleButton

The following sections describe some of these widget classes. In general, the primitive widgets appear as components inside other manager widgets that are described later in this chapter.

The XmPrimitive Class

Because all primitive widgets inherit the resources of the XmPrimitive class, you should be familiar with the resources of this class. Chapter 9 lists the resources for the XmPrimitive class. You will notice that several resources are for controlling the three-dimensional look of the Motif widgets. The colors used for the shading that imparts the three-dimensional look are set at run-time, depending on the type of display (monochrome or color).

One of the resources, XmNuserData, can store a pointer to any data that you may want to associate with a primitive widget. This pointer is not used internally by the widgets—its sole purpose is to enable you to store your own data in a widget.

Another innovative idea in the Motif widget set is the use of a help callback resource. By setting the XmNhelpCallback resource, you can have your help function called by the toolkit whenever the user presses the help key sequence. The user specifies the key sequence through a translation table.

Labels and Push-Buttons

The XmLabel widget is one of the simplest widgets: it displays a string or a pixmap inside a window. You have seen the label widget used earlier in this chapter. As the name implies, labels are used to display a fixed text string or a pixmap. Nothing happens when you click on a label widget.

Another class of widgets, derived from the XmLabel class, invokes a callback function when the user presses a mouse button inside the widget. The XmPushButton widget is one such widget.

As explained earlier in this chapter, the push-button widget calls any registered callback with three arguments:

- The widget's ID

- A pointer you had previously passed when registering the callback

- A pointer to an XmAnyCallbackStruct structure

The reason field of the XmAnyCallbackStruct structure indicates why the callback was invoked. The XmPushButton class supports three callback resources:

- XmNarmCallback is a list of callback functions that are called when the button is *armed*—when the user presses the mouse button while the pointer is inside the push-button's window. The reason field of the XmAnyCallbackStruct is set to the constant XmCR_ARM. Also, the button is inverted if the XmNinvertOnArm resource (a Boolean) is set to True.

- XmNactivateCallback is the list of functions called (with XmCR_ACTIVATE as the reason) as the button is activated when the user releases the mouse button with the pointer inside the window.

- XmNdisarmCallback lists the functions that are called when the push-button is disarmed by releasing the mouse button (not necessarily inside the widget). In this case, the reason field of the XmAnyCallbackStruct structure is set to XmCR_DISARM.

Of course, in addition to these callback resources, XmPushButton inherits the label string and the pixmap from its super class, XmLabel. Figure 6.8 shows a typical instance of a push-button widget. You can create this push-button with the following code:

```
#include    <Xm/PushB.h> /* Include file for XmPushButton    */

Arg         args[20];    /* Array for setting up widgets     */
Cardinal    argcount;    /* Number of arguments              */
Widget      main_widget, /* Widget where push-button appears */
            button1;     /* Push button widget's id          */

/* Set up arguments and create the widget */
argcount = 0;
XtSetArg(args[argcount], XmNx, 50); argcount++;
XtSetArg(args[argcount], XmNy, 20); argcount++;
```

```
button1 = XmCreatePushButton(main_widget, "Push Here",
                              args, argcount);
/* Now manage this widget */
XtManageChild(button1);
```

```
Push Here
```

Fig. 6.8. XmPushButton widget.

This code creates and manages widgets by two separate functions—XmCreatePushButton and XtManageChild—instead of using XtCreateManagedWidget alone, as in the earlier examples of this chapter. The XmCreatePushButton function is a convenience function of the OSF/Motif toolkit, specifically intended for creating push-buttons. Note that, in this example, you could have replaced the call to XmCreatePushButton with the following equivalent general-purpose function from Xt Intrinsics:

```
button1 = XtCreateWidget("Push Here", main_widget,
               xmPushButtonWidgetClass, args, argcount);
```

This function requires you to pass the class pointer (xmPushButtonClassWidget), and it expects the first two arguments in a different order from XmCreatePushButton.

Toggle Buttons

The XmToggleButton class is also derived from XmLabel. It displays a string or a pixmap next to a small button. The button represents a state with two values—selected or unselected—that you can interpret as being on or off. When selected, the button is highlighted. As the name indicates, the state of the button toggles from one value to the other with every press of the mouse button on the widget.

By default the toggle buttons are square. If you set the XmNindicatorType resource to XmONE_OF_MANY, the shape changes to a diamond, which is ostensibly for use in situations where only one toggle button out of a group can be set. However, the task of enforcing this is left to the parent widget that manages the toggle buttons.

Toggle buttons are used in dialogs. Figure 6.9 shows three toggle buttons (after the user has clicked on the second button) created by the following code:

```
#include  <Xm/ToggleB.h>

Arg       args[20];
Cardinal  argcount;
Widget    main_widget, button1, button2, button3;

/* Create and manage three toggle button widgets */

argcount = 0;
XtSetArg(args[argcount], XmNx, 50); argcount++;
XtSetArg(args[argcount], XmNy, 10); argcount++;
button1 = XmCreateToggleButton(main_widget, "Xlib",
                               args, argcount);
XtManageChild(button1);

argcount = 0;
XtSetArg(args[argcount], XmNx, 50); argcount++;
XtSetArg(args[argcount], XmNy, 30); argcount++;
button2 = XmCreateToggleButton(main_widget, "OSF/Motif",
                               args, argcount);
XtManageChild(button2);

argcount = 0;
XtSetArg(args[argcount], XmNx, 50); argcount++;
XtSetArg(args[argcount], XmNy, 50); argcount++;
button3 = XmCreateToggleButton(main_widget, "OPEN LOOK",
                               args, argcount);
XtManageChild(button3);
```

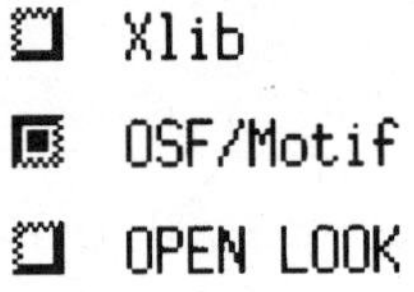

☐ Xlib

▣ OSF/Motif

☐ OPEN LOOK

Fig. 6.9. Three XmToggleButton widgets.

Separator

The XmSeparator widget is a special type of label that draws a line whose orientation is specified by the XmNorientation resource. The default value is XmHORIZONTAL for a horizontal line. You can set this resource to XmVERTICAL for a vertical separator. Separators are used to separate items in a display, particularly to delineate different groups of items in a menu. Figure 6.10 shows a separator drawn between two labels. The code used for this example is as follows:

```
#include  <Xm/Label.h>
#include  <Xm/Separator.h>
```

```
Arg      args[20];
Cardinal argcount;
Widget   label1, label2, separator1;

/* Create and manage two labels */

argcount = 0;
XtSetArg(args[argcount], XmNx, 20); argcount++;
XtSetArg(args[argcount], XmNy, 15); argcount++;
label1 = XmCreateLabel(main_widget, "Item 1", args, argcount);
XtManageChild(label1);


argcount = 0;
XtSetArg(args[argcount], XmNx, 20); argcount++;
XtSetArg(args[argcount], XmNy, 50); argcount++;
label2 = XmCreateLabel(main_widget,
            "Item 2 is below a separator", args, argcount);
XtManageChild (label2);

/* Now place a separator widget between the two labels */

argcount = 0;
XtSetArg(args[argcount], XmNx, 20);       argcount++;
XtSetArg(args[argcount], XmNy, 42);       argcount++;
XtSetArg(args[argcount], XmNwidth, 165); argcount++;
XtSetArg(args[argcount], XmNheight, 2);  argcount++;
XtSetArg(args[argcount], XmNorientation, XmHORIZONTAL);
argcount++;
XtSetArg(args[argcount], XmNseparatorType, XmSHADOW_ETCHED_OUT);
argcount++;
separator1 = XmCreateSeparator(main_widget, "Separator",
                                    args, argcount);
XtManageChild(separator1);
```

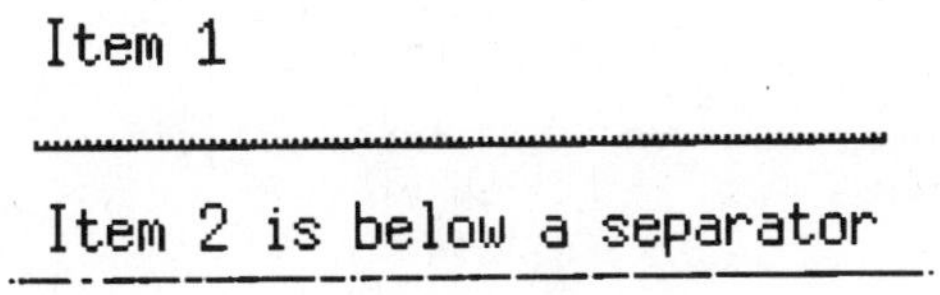

Item 1

Item 2 is below a separator

Fig. 6.10. An XmSeparator widget.

Scrollbars

The XmScrollBar widget, derived from the XmPrimitive class, lets users view data that extends beyond the limits of a widget's window. The scrollbar is usually attached to a widget displaying the data. Through the use of callback functions, you can scroll the data as the user interacts with the scrollbar.

As shown in Figure 6.11, scrollbars can be horizontal or vertical. The orientation is controlled by the `XmNorientation` resource, which can be either `XmHORIZONTAL` or `XmVERTICAL`. The scrollbar consists of a elongated rectangle with an arrow at each end. Another rectangle, called the *slider*, appears inside the larger rectangle. The slider is meant to indicate how much of the total data is visible in the widget being controlled by the scrollbar. For example, if 50 percent of available data is visible, the slider should be half the size of the larger rectangle. The position of the slider indicates which portion of the available data appears in the window.

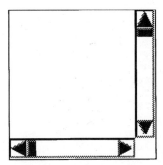

Fig. 6.11. `XmScrollBar` widgets attached to a window.

The following code shows a typical way of using scrollbars. After creating the scrollbars, you attach them to a window that is to be controlled by the scrollbars. In this case, the scrollbars are specified as resources to a `XmScrolledWindow` widget. You can use the OSF/Motif convenience function `XmCreateScrolledWindow` to create the scrolled window. The scrollbars are created by the `XmCreateScrollBar` function. Figure 6.11 displays the result of this code.

```
/* Define names of widgets and their dimensions */

#define SCROLLED_WINDOW_NAME    "SWindowWidget"
#define SB1_NAME                "Sbar1"
#define SB2_NAME                "Sbar2"

#define SB1_X           145
#define SB1_Y           10
#define SB1_WIDTH       20
#define SB1_HEIGHT      130

#define SB2_X           15
#define SB2_Y           140
#define SB2_WIDTH       130
#define SB2_HEIGHT      20
```

```
#define WIN_X        15
#define WIN_Y        10
#define WIN_WIDTH    150
#define WIN_HEIGHT   150


#include  <Xm/ScrollBar.h>
#include  <Xm/ScrolledW.h>

Arg       args[20];
Cardinal  argcount;
Widget    main_widget, scroll1, scroll2, swindow;

/* First create a vertical scrollbar */
argcount = 0;
XtSetArg(args[argcount], XmNorientation, XmVERTICAL); argcount++;
XtSetArg(args[argcount], XmNx, SB1_X);              argcount++;
XtSetArg(args[argcount], XmNy, SB1_Y);              argcount++;
XtSetArg(args[argcount], XmNwidth, SB1_WIDTH);      argcount++;
XtSetArg(args[argcount], XmNheight, SB1_HEIGHT);    argcount++;
XtSetArg(args[argcount], XmNshowArrows, True);      argcount++;
scroll1 = XmCreateScrollBar(main_widget, SB1_NAME,
                            args, argcount);


/* Next, a horizontal scrollbar */

argcount = 0;
XtSetArg(args[argcount], XmNorientation, XmHORIZONTAL);
argcount++;
XtSetArg(args[argcount], XmNx, SB2_X);              argcount++;
XtSetArg(args[argcount], XmNy, SB2_Y);              argcount++;
XtSetArg(args[argcount], XmNwidth, SB2_WIDTH);      argcount++;
XtSetArg(args[argcount], XmNheight, SB2_HEIGHT);    argcount++;
XtSetArg(args[argcount], XmNshowArrows, True);      argcount++;
scroll2 = XmCreateScrollBar(main_widget, SB2_NAME,
                            args, argcount);


/* Attach the scrollbars to a viewing window using the
 * XmCreateScrolledWindow function
 */
argcount = 0;
XtSetArg(args[argcount], XmNx, WIN_X);              argcount++;
XtSetArg(args[argcount], XmNy, WIN_Y);              argcount++;
XtSetArg(args[argcount], XmNwidth, WIN_WIDTH);      argcount++;
XtSetArg(args[argcount], XmNheight, WIN_HEIGHT);    argcount++;
XtSetArg(args[argcount], XmNborderWidth, 1);        argcount++;
XtSetArg(args[argcount], XmNverticalScrollBar, scroll1);
argcount++;
XtSetArg(args[argcount], XmNhorizontalScrollBar, scroll2);
argcount++;
XtSetArg(args[argcount], XmNscrollBarDisplayPolicy, XmSTATIC);
```

6

```
argcount++;
XtSetArg(args[argcount], XmNscrollBarPlacement, XmBOTTOM_RIGHT);
argcount++;
swindow = XmCreateScrolledWindow(main_widget,
                 SCROLLED_WINDOW_NAME, args, argcount);

/* Manage the windows */

XtManageChild(swindow);
XtManageChild(scroll1);
XtManageChild(scroll2);
```

List Widgets

The XmList widget is another primitive widget that displays a list of items in a window and lets the user pick one or more items from the list. The list widget is most useful when combined with a XmScrolledWindow widget. OSF/Motif provides a convenience function XmCreateScrolledList to do exactly this. As shown in Figure 6.12, this allows you to display a list with more elements than will fit in a viewing area. The user can use an attached scrollbar to scroll through the list. The following code shows how the scrolled list of Figure 6.12 is generated:

```
#include   <Xm/List.h>

#define NUMITEMS            6     /* Number of items */
#define VISITEMS            4     /* Number visible  */
#define LIST_MARGIN_WIDTH  30
#define LIST_SPACING        5

/* List entries */
static char *list_items[NUMITEMS] =
{
    "Ada", "BASIC", "C", "FORTRAN", "Pascal", "Lisp"
};

XmString    compound_strings[NUMITEMS];
int         item_count;
Arg         args[20];
Cardinal    argcount;
Widget      main_widget, scrolled_list;
.
.
.
/* Convert the array of strings into compound strings */

item_count = 0;
while(item_count < NUMITEMS)
{
```

```
      compound_strings[item_count] =
          XmStringLtoRCreate(list_items[item_count],
                             XmSTRING_DEFAULT_CHARSET);
      item_count++;
}

/* Set up arguments for list and create list inside scrolled window
 * using the XmCreateScrolledList function.
 */
argcount = 0;
XtSetArg(args[argcount], XmNx, 80);                      argcount++;
XtSetArg(args[argcount], XmNy, 20);                      argcount++;
XtSetArg(args[argcount], XmNlistSpacing, LIST_SPACING);
                                                         argcount++;
XtSetArg(args[argcount], XmNmarginWidth, LIST_MARGIN_WIDTH);
                                                         argcount++;
XtSetArg(args[argcount], XmNitemCount, NUMITEMS); argcount++;
XtSetArg(args[argcount], XmNvisibleItemCount, VISITEMS);
                                                         argcount++;
XtSetArg(args[argcount], XmNitems, compound_strings);
                                                         argcount++;
XtSetArg(args[argcount], XmNscrollBarPlacement, XmBOTTOM_RIGHT);
                                                         argcount++;
scrolled_list = XmCreateScrolledList(main_widget,
                         "ScrolledList", args, argcount);
XtManageChild(scrolled_list);
```

Fig. 6.12. A list widget inside a scrolled window.

Text Widget

The XmText widget is another powerful and useful widget in the OSF/Motif repertoire. The XmText widget is essentially a self-contained text editor that you can use to accept keyboard input. You can use the XmNeditMode resource to configure the XmText widget for editing single or multiple lines. The default value of this resource is XmSINGLE_LINE_EDIT, which indicates that the text widget should accept a single line only. For multiline editing, set this resource to the constant XmMULTI_LINE_EDIT.

A convenient way to use the XmText widget, like the XmList widget, is to use it as a child of a scrolled window. You can do this with the XmCreateScrolledText function. Figure 6.13 shows an XmText widget inside a scrolled window after some text has been typed into it. The code that creates this widget is as follows:

```
#include     <Xm/Text.h>

Arg          args[20];
Cardinal     argcount;
Widget main_widget, scrolled_text;

/* Set up a text widget inside a scrolled window. Make room
 * for 5 rows of text with 23 columns (characters).
 */
argcount = 0;
XtSetArg(args[argcount], XmNeditable, True);            argcount++;
XtSetArg(args[argcount], XmNeditMode, XmMULTI_LINE_EDIT);
                                                        argcount++;
XtSetArg(args[argcount], XmNcolumns, 23);               argcount++;
XtSetArg(args[argcount], XmNrows, 5);                   argcount++;
XtSetArg(args[argcount], XmNx, 15);                     argcount++;
XtSetArg(args[argcount], XmNy, 15);                     argcount++;
XtSetArg(args[argcount], XmNscrollVertical, True);      argcount++;
XtSetArg(args[argcount], XmNscrollHorizontal, True);    argcount++;
XtSetArg(args[argcount], XmNscrollLeftSide, False);     argcount++;
XtSetArg(args[argcount], XmNscrollTopSide, False);      argcount++;
scrolled_text = XmCreateScrolledText(main_widget,
                            "ScrolledText", args, argcount);

/* Manage the new widget to display it */
XtManageChild(scrolled_text);
```

Fig. 6.13. A text widget inside a scrolled window widget.

If you are using a text widget to read a string entered by the user, you need a way to retrieve the string. The OSF/Motif toolkit includes a number of utility functions for manipulating the text displayed in an XmText widget (see Table 6.2). The XmTextGetString function, in particular, returns the contents of the text buffer maintained by the XmText widget. This sample code retrieves the string:

```
Widget   scrolled_text;
char    *contents;

contents = XmTextGetString(scrolled_text);
.
.
.
/* Use "contents" as needed */
.
/* You are responsible for freeing the storage */
XtFree(contents);
```

It is straightforward to get the text string. The only important point is that the text widget allocates storage for the string, copies its contents to that space, and returns a pointer to that location. After you are finished with the string, you are responsible for freeing the memory by calling the XtFree function.

Table 6.2. Functions for Manipulating the Contents of XmText Widgets

Function	Purpose
XmTextClearSelection	Clear the PRIMARY selection.
XmTextGetEditable	Determine if contents can be edited.
XmTextGetInsertPosition	Returns current text insertion position.
XmTextGetMaxLength	Returns maximum length of text string accepted by the widget.
XmTextGetSelection	Retrieves the value of the PRIMARY selection.
XmTextGetString	Retrieves contents of text widget.
XmTextReplace	Replace text between two positions with a new string
XmTextScroll	Scroll the contents by a number of lines.
XmTextSetEditable	Set widget's mode to "editable" or "not editable."
XmTextSetInsertPosition	Moves insertion point to new location.
XmTextSetMaxLength	Set maximum allowable length of string.
XmTextSetSelection	Make the selected text the PRIMARY selection.
XmTextSetString	Stores a string in text widget.

6

Gadgets

In addition to the widgets, OSF/Motif also includes another type of user-interface component called *gadgets*. As shown earlier in Figure 6.7, the gadgets inherit from two components of the Core class—the Object and the RectObj. The difference between widgets and gadgets is that every widget has a window, whereas gadgets do not have any window of their own. A gadget must have a parent widget so that it can display its output in the parent widget's window.

As a programmer, you can use gadgets just as you do widgets. You use the XtCreateManagedWidget function, providing the widget's class pointer as an argument. For example, to create a label gadget whose class pointer is xmLabelGadgetClass, you can write:

```
Widget main_widget, label_gadget;
.
.
.
label_gadget = XtCreateManagedWidget("label_1",
                    xmLabelGadgetClass, main_widget, NULL, 0);
```

Gadgets are included for situations where you may not want to have many windows. Because of its lack of a window, a gadget does not support event handlers, key translations, and pop-up child windows. Gadgets do support callback functions. OSF/Motif includes gadget versions of several primitive widgets. Table 6.3 shows the supported gadgets and the equivalent widget for each gadget and indicates the header file that you have to include when using the gadget. The gadgets have the same appearance as the corresponding widgets.

Table 6.3. OSF/Motif Gadgets

Gadget Name	*Equivalent Widget Name*	*Header File for Gadget*
XmArrowButtonGadget	XmArrowButton	\<Xm/ArrowBG.h>
XmCascadeButtonGadget	XmCascadeButton	\<Xm/CascadeBG.h>
XmLabelGadget	XmLabel	\<Xm/LabelG.h>
XmPushButtonGadget	XmPushButton	\<Xm/PushBG.h>
XmSeparatorGadget	XmSeparator	\<Xm/SeparatoG.h>
XmToggleButtonGadget	XmToggleButton	\<Xm/ToggleBG.h>

> You can derive the name of a widget or gadget's class pointer
> from their names shown in Figure 6.7. For widgets, simply change
> the Xm prefix to xm and append the string WidgetClass to the widget's
> name. For a gadget, change the first letter to lowercase and append
> the string Class. Thus, the class pointer for the XmLabel widget
> is xmLabelWidgetClass, and for XmLabelGadget the class pointer is
> xmLabelGadgetClass.

Manager Widgets

All OSF/Motif manager widgets are derived from the XmManager class, which is
a subclass of Constraint and which, in turn, inherits from the Composite class.
These widgets are meant to be containers for other widgets, and they manage
the layout of their children according to specified constraints. You have already
seen a manager widget—the list and text widgets of Figures 6.12 and 6.13 are
contained in XmScrolledWindow widgets, a manager class. This section describes several other interesting manager widgets.

Selection Box Widget

The XmSelectionBox widget is meant to display a list of items in a scrollable box
and provide an area where the current selection is displayed. The widget
contains three buttons labeled OK, Cancel, and Help. A fourth button, labelled
Apply, can be optionally turned on or off. A typical setup and display is shown
in the following code. The resulting selection box is shown in Figure 6.14.

```
#include   <Xm/SelectioB.h>

#define    NUMITEMS 8

XmString   compound_str[NUMITEMS];
Arg        args[20];
Cardinal   argcount;
int        item_count;

extern void HandleCancel();

/* List of items to be displayed in selection box */
static char *list_items[NUMITEMS] =
{
    "X Protocol", "Xlib", "Xt Intrinsics", "Athena Widgets",
    "OSF/Motif", "OPEN LOOK", "XView", "XT+"
```

6

```
};
    .
    .
    .
/* Convert C strings to Motif compound strings */

for(item_count = 0; item_count < NUMITEMS; item_count++)
{
    compound_str[item_count] = XmStringLtoRCreate(
                                    list_items[item_count],
                                    XmSTRING_DEFAULT_CHARSET);
}

/*  Create an XmSelectionBox widget */

argcount = 0;
XtSetArg(args[argcount], XmNlistVisibleItemCount, VISIBLE_ITEMS);
                                                    argcount++;
XtSetArg(args[argcount], XmNlistItems, compound_str); argcount++;
XtSetArg(args[argcount], XmNlistItemCount, NUMITEMS); argcount++;
XtSetArg(args[argcount], XmNdialogType, XmDIALOG_SELECTION);
                                                    argcount++;
selection_box = XmCreateSelectionBox(main_widget,
                                "SelectionBox", args, argcount);

/* Add callbacks to the OK, Cancel, and Help, as needed;
 * for example, to call the function HandleCancel when the
 * Cancel button is pressed, you can use:
 */

XtAddCallback(selection_box, XmNcancelCallback, HandleCancel,
              (caddr_t)selection_box);
XtManageChild(selection_box);
```

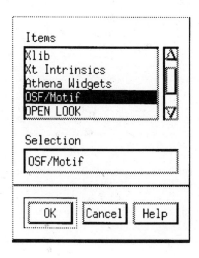

Fig. 6.14. `XmSelectionBox` **widget.**

If you want to display a selection box widget in a pop-up dialog shell, you can use the XmCreateSelectionDialog function to do the job. You call XmCreateSelectionDialog the same way as you call XmCreateSelectionBox.

File Selection Box

A special type of selection box is the file selection box widget represented by the XmFileSelection class in OSF/Motif. This widget is similar to the selection box, except that it is used to display a list of files in a list box. There is an area where the user can enter a file filter, which is a search string used to locate the files of interest (use ***.c** to see all files ending with .c). The user's current selection is displayed in another box. At the bottom of the widget, there are four buttons labeled OK, Filter, Cancel, and Help. Figure 6.15 shows a typical file selection box. You can use the XmCreateFileSelectionBox function to create this widget.

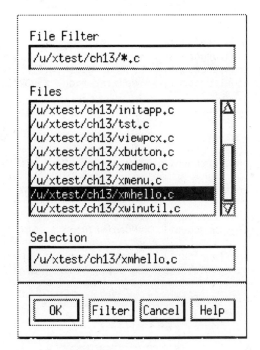

Fig. 6.15. xmFileSelectionBox **widget.**

6

Scale Widget

The XmScale widget displays an elongated rectangle with a slider that the user alters to enter a numerical value. You can set the minimum and maximum values for the scale, and—for floating-point values—specify the number of digits to follow the decimal point. Figure 6.16 shows a scale capable of displaying values between 0.0 and 10.0, in steps of 0.1. As shown in the following code, you can create a scale widget by calling the XmCreateScale function.

```c
#include  <Xm/Scale.h>

/* Minimum and maximum values for scale */
#define SCALE_MIN_VALUE        0
#define SCALE_MAX_VALUE        100
#define SCALE_DECIMAL_POINTS   1

Widget dialog_box, scale;

argcount = 0;
XtSetArg(args[argcount], XmNx, 20);             argcount++;
XtSetArg(args[argcount], XmNy, 20);             argcount++;
XtSetArg(args[argcount], XmNborderWidth, 1);  argcount++;
XtSetArg(args[argcount], XmNorientation, XmHORIZONTAL);
                                                argcount++;
XtSetArg(args[argcount], XmNprocessingDirection, XmMAX_ON_RIGHT);
                                                argcount++;
XtSetArg(args[argcount], XmNscaleWidth, 25);  argcount++;
XtSetArg(args[argcount], XmNscaleHeight, 10); argcount++;
XtSetArg(args[argcount], XmNminimum, SCALE_MIN_VALUE);
                                                argcount++;
XtSetArg(args[argcount], XmNmaximum, SCALE_MAX_VALUE);
                                                argcount++;
XtSetArg(args[argcount], XmNshowValue, True); argcount++;
XtSetArg(args[argcount], XmNdecimalPoints, SCALE_DECIMAL_POINTS);
                                                argcount++;
XtSetArg(args[argcount], XmNtitle, title);    argcount++;
scale = XmCreateScale(dialog_box, "Scale", args, argcount);

XtManageChild(scale);
```

Fig. 6.16. XmScale **widget.**

The Command Widget

The XmCommand widget is a subclass of XmSelectionBox widget. Its purpose is to provide a command history mechanism. There is a command entry area where the user can type in commands. Once a command is entered by pressing the Enter key, that command string is saved in a history buffer, which is displayed in a scrollable list area. You can use the command widget to accept user's inputs for your command-driven applications. Figure 6.17 shows a typical XmCommand widget.

Fig. 6.17. XmCommand widget.

The OSF/Motif Command widget is very much different from the widget with the same name that appears in the Athena Widgets. Athena's Command widget is actually similar to OSF/Motif's PushButton widget.

Message Boxes and Message Dialogs

The OSF/Motif toolkit includes a XmMessageBox widget that you can use to display messages. For your convenience, there are special-purpose functions that create a XmDialogShell widget and display the message box in that shell. Figure 6.18 shows a generic message box created by the XmCreateMessageDialog function.

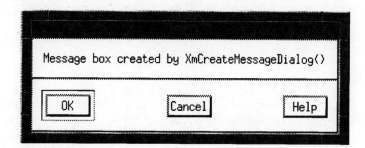

Fig. 6.18. A pop-up message box created by XmCreateMessageDialog.

Creating a message dialog is very straightforward. For instance, the dialog box of Figure 6.18 is generated by the following code:

```
#include   <Xm/Xm.h>
#include   <Xm/DialogS.h>
#include   <Xm/MessageB.h>

#define MESSAGE_BOX_NAME    "Popup Message Box"
#define MESSAGE_BOX_MESSAGE "Message box created \
by XmCreateMessageDialog()"

/* Prototype of a callback */

void HandleCancel(Widget w, caddr_t client_data,
                  XmAnyCallbackStruct *call_data);

Widget   main_widget, message_box;

XmString comp_text;
Argargs[10];
Cardinal argcount;
.
.
.
/* Convert message string to a compound string a la Motif */

comp_text = XmStringLtoRCreate(MESSAGE_BOX_MESSAGE,
                               XmSTRING_DEFAULT_CHARSET);

/* Set up arguments and create the message box dialog */

argcount = 0;
XtSetArg(args[argcount], XmNmessageString, text);  argcount++;
message_box = XmCreateMessageDialog(main_widget,
                MESSAGE_BOX_NAME, args, argcount);

/* Add callbacks for OK, Cancel, and Help buttons. Here is
 * an example of adding a callback for the Cancel button.
 */

XtAddCallback(message_box, XmNcancelCallback, HandleCancel,
              (caddr_t) message_box);

XtManageChild (message_box);
```

Each of the OK, Cancel, and Help buttons can have lists of callbacks that are invoked when the button is pressed. The HandleCancel function, installed in the sample code, is an example of a callback function. Suppose you want the message dialog to disappear when the user clicks the Cancel button. In this case, you might define HandleCancel as follows:

```
/*-------------------------------------------------------------*/
/* H a n d l e C a n c e l
 *
 * Callback that unmanages widget whose ID is passed in
 * the client_data. The unmanaged widget and its ancestors
 * will no longer be displayed on the screen.
 */
void HandleCancel(Widget w, caddr_t client_data,
                  XmAnyCallbackStruct *call_data)
{
    XtUnmanageChild ((Widget) client_data);
}
```

You can hide a widget and its children by calling XtUnmanageChild with the widget's ID as the argument.

In addition to the generic message dialog, the OSF/Motif toolkit provides several styles of message boxes meant for specific situations. Figure 6.19 shows a warning dialog created by calling the XmCreateWarningDialog function. The appearance of this dialog is similar to that of the standard message dialog except for the exclamation mark preceding the message. As the name implies, this dialog is meant for displaying warnings and cautions.

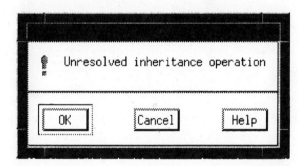

Fig. 6.19. Message dialog created by the XmCreateWarningDialog function.

Figure 6.20 shows an information dialog—with an *i*-shaped icon in the message area. You can use this dialog box to display informative messages. The function that creates this dialog is XmCreateInformationDialog.

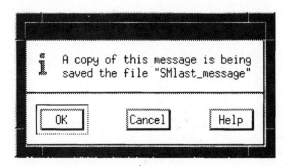

Fig. 6.20. Message dialog created by the `XmCreateInformationDialog` function.

The `XmCreateWorkingDialog` function creates a dialog box of the style shown in Figure 6.21. This dialog, with an hourglass icon, is meant for displaying messages that tell the user that a lengthy operation is in progress.

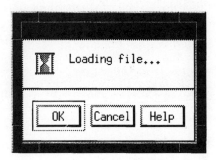

Fig. 6.21. Message dialog created by the `XmCreateWorkingDialog` function.

Menus

Menus play a prominent role in all graphical user interfaces. GUIs use a wide variety of menus from a simple array of push-buttons to the more elaborate ones with a menubar incorporating cascading pull-down submenus. The OSF/ Motif toolkit supports a number of widgets for creating and displaying menus.

You create the basic menu pane (a number of menu entries arranged in column or row) with a `XmRowColumn` widget (see Figure 6.7 for its position in the hierarchy). Menu entries are buttons—either `XmPushButton` or `XmToggleButton` widgets. You can use the `XmCascadeButton` widget for buttons that trigger a submenu. `XmLabel` widgets are used to display nonselectable text or pixmap in a menu and the `XmSeparator` widget draws the lines delineating groups of items.

Figure 6.22 shows a simple menu—a set of *radio buttons*. These are a number of toggle buttons, usually arranged in a column. The user can select one item from the group by pressing a button.

Fig. 6.22. Radio buttons implemented by three toggle buttons inside a RowColumn widget.

To create the radio buttons, you start with a XmRowColumn widget. Next you add the XmToggleButtons as children of the RowColumn widget. The following code illustrates the process of creating the radio buttons shown in Figure 6.22:

```
#include <Xm/RowColumn.h>
#include <Xm/ToggleB.h>

/* Labels for the radio buttons */

#define RADIO_BUTTON1    "Xlib"
#define RADIO_BUTTON2    "OSF/Motif"
#define RADIO_BUTTON3    "OPEN LOOK"

Widget    main_widget;    /* The "parent" widget */
Widget    radio_box;      /* The radio box       */
Widget    entry1;         /* First radio button  */
Widget    entry2;         /* Second radio button */
Widget    entry3;         /* Third radio button  */
Argargs[20];              /* Room for arguments  */
Cardinal argcount;        /* Number of arguments */

/* First, create a RowColumn widget */

argcount = 0;
XtSetArg(args[argcount], XmNx, 70);                       argcount++;
XtSetArg(args[argcount], XmNy, 30);                       argcount++;
XtSetArg(args[argcount], XmNradioBehavior, True);         argcount++;
XtSetArg(args[argcount], XmNorientation, XmVERTICAL);     argcount++;
XtSetArg(args[argcount], XmNpacking, XmPACK_COLUMN);      argcount++;
radio_box = XmCreateRowColumn(main_widget, "RadioBox",
                              args, argcount);

/* Create the Toggle Buttons for the radio box */

entry1 = XmCreateToggleButton(radio_box, RADIO_BUTTON1, NULL, 0);
XtManageChild(entry1);
```

6

```
entry2 = XmCreateToggleButton(radio_box, RADIO_BUTTON2, NULL, 0);
XtManageChild(entry2);

entry3 = XmCreateToggleButton(radio_box, RADIO_BUTTON3, NULL, 0);
XtManageChild(entry3);

/* Display the radio box with the buttons */

XtManageChild(radio_box);
```

Another type of menu you can create is the option menu. As shown in Figure 6.23, this consists of a menu title followed by a box in which the current selection is displayed. If you press the left mouse button with the pointer in the box, a pull-down menu is displayed. You can pick another item from this menu by moving the pointer to the selected item and releasing the mouse button.

Fig. 6.23. An option menu showing the selections in its associated pull-down menu.

You create option menus using the XmCreateOptionMenu function. Before you call this function, you have to prepare a pull-down menu using the XmCreatePulldownMenu function. The pull-down menu, in turn, requires a number of push-buttons that serve as the menu items. Here is the code to generate the option menu of Figure 6.23:

```
#include   <Xm/BulletinB.h>
#include   <Xm/RowColumn.h>
#include   <Xm/PushB.h>

/* Option menu entries */

#define ENTRY1   "None"
#define ENTRY2   "White"
#define ENTRY3   "Black"

Widget    parent;
Widget    dialog_box;
Widget    option_menu;
Widget    sub_menu;
Widget    entry1;
Widget    entry2;
Widget    entry3;
```

```
XmString option_menu_title;
Arg      args[20];
Cardinal argcount;
.
.
.
/* First create a BulletinBoard dialog wherein the option
 * menu will be displayed
 */

argcount = 0;
XtSetArg(args[argcount], XmNdialogStyle, XmDIALOG_MODELESS);
                                            argcount++;
XtSetArg(args[argcount], XmNwidth, 200);   argcount++;
XtSetArg(args[argcount], XmNheight, 180);  argcount++;
dialog_box = XmCreateBulletinBoardDialog(parent, "Options",
                                    args, argcount);
/* Now create the pull-down menu to be displayed by option menu */

argcount = 0;
sub_menu = XmCreatePulldownMenu(dialog_box, "pull-down",
                                args, argcount);

/* Pull-down menu entries—implemented by push-buttons */

entry1 = XmCreatePushButton(sub_menu, ENTRY1, NULL, 0);
XtManageChild(entry1);

entry2 = XmCreatePushButton(sub_menu, ENTRY2, NULL, 0);
XtManageChild(entry2);

entry3 = XmCreatePushButton(sub_menu, ENTRY3, NULL, 0);
XtManageChild(entry3);

/* Now we create the actual option menu */

option_menu_title = XmStringLtoRCreate("Fill Color",
                                XmSTRING_DEFAULT_CHARSET);

argcount = 0;
XtSetArg(args[argcount], XmNy, 30);                    argcount++;
XtSetArg(args[argcount], XmNlabelString, option_menu_title);
                                                       argcount++;
XtSetArg(args[argcount], XmNsubMenuId, sub_menu);  argcount++;
XtSetArg(args[argcount], XmNmenuHistory, entry1);  argcount++;
option_menu = XmCreateOptionMenu(dialog_box, "Options",
                                args, argcount);
XtManageChild(option_menu);

/* Finally, we display everything by managing the dialog */

XtManageChild(dialog_box);
```

6

OSF/Motif also provides functions to create menus with a menubar and cascading panes such as the one shown in Figure 6.24. As you might expect, the steps you follow to create such a menu is considerably more detailed than that for a simple option menu or for radio buttons. Still, with the power of a toolkit, generating such a menu is only a matter of following the steps.

The first step is to create a main window and a menu bar. Here is that part of the code:

```
#include <Xm/RowColumn.h>
#include <Xm/MainW.h>
#include <Xm/PushB.h>
#include <Xm/CascadeB.h>

Widget   top_level, main_window, menu_bar;
Arg      args[20];
Cardinal argcount;
.
.
.
/* Assume that "top_level" widget created by XtInitialize */
.
.
.
/* Create the main window widget */

argcount = 0;
XtSetArg(args[argcount], XmNwidth, 300);   argcount++;
XtSetArg(args[argcount], XmNheight, 200);  argcount++;
main_window = XmCreateMainWindow(top_level, "main",
                                    args, argcount);
XtManageChild(main_window);

/* Create the menu bar */
menu_bar = XmCreateMenuBar(main_window, "MenuBar", NULL, 0);
XtManageChild(menu_bar);

/* Add the menu bar to the main window */
XmMainWindowSetAreas(main_window, menu_bar, NULL, NULL,NULL, NULL);
```

The menu bar is created by the utility function XmCreateMenuBar. You add entries to the menu bar after it has been created. Each entry must be a XmCascadeButton widget. In Figure 6.24, there are two items labeled File and Settings. Each cascade button requires a pull-down menu ID that is to be displayed when the user presses on the cascade button. Because the buttons in the pull-down menu can also be cascade buttons, requiring further pull-down menus, you have to prepare all the menus before adding entries to the menu bar. Figure 6.25 shows the hierarchy of cascade buttons and menus in the example shown in Figure 6.24.

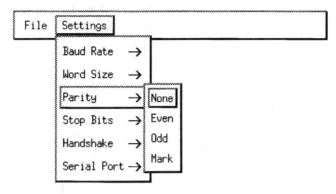

Fig. 6.24. Menu bar with cascading menus

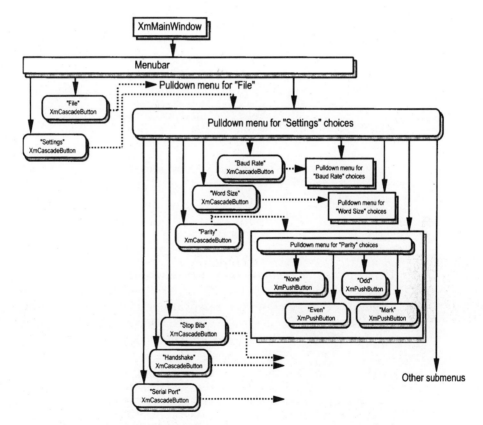

Fig. 6.25. Widget hierarchy for the menu shown in Figure 6.24.

It is convenient to store the menu definitions in a data structure so that you can create all the submenus mechanically. Here are the data structures used in this example:

```
#define MAX_ENTRIES  16

/* Information on individual menu items */
typedef struct ITEM_ACTION
{
    char            *label;     /* Label for the item      */
    XtCallbackProc  callbacks;  /* Callbacks for the item  */
} ITEM_ACTION;

/* Data structure to hold pull-down menu information */
typedef struct PULLDOWN_MENU_INFO
{
    int   size;                     /* Number of entries in menu */
    char  *name;                    /* Name of menu              */
    ITEM_ACTION items[MAX_ENTRIES];
}  PULLDOWN_MENU_INFO;

/* Information for cascade buttons */
typedef struct CASCADE_ITEM
{
    char                 *label;    /* Cascade button's label  */
    PULLDOWN_MENU_INFO *submenu;  /* Menu to be pulled down  */
} CASCADE_ITEM;

/* Structure to hold cascade menu information */
typedef struct CASCADE_MENU_INFO
{
    int     size;                   /* Number of entries in menu */
    char    *name;                  /* Name of cascade menu      */
    CASCADE_ITEM  items[MAX_ENTRIES];
}  CASCADE_MENU_INFO;
```

The term *cascade menu* refers to a pull-down menu whose items are all XmCascadeButton widgets, each capable of displaying another pull-down menu. Figure 6.24 shows a cascade menu (with entries Baud Rate, Word Size, Parity, and so on) with a pull-down menu displayed by an activated cascade button. For these two menus, the entries are defined as follows:

```
/* Define prototypes for callbacks */
void parity_none(Widget, caddr_t, XmAnyCallbackStruct *);
void parity_even(Widget, caddr_t, XmAnyCallbackStruct *);
void parity_odd(Widget, caddr_t, XmAnyCallbackStruct *);
void parity_mark(Widget, caddr_t, XmAnyCallbackStruct *);

/* Submenu 1 */
/* Menu pulled down by "Baud Rate" cascade button */
```

```
.
.
.
/* Submenu 2 */
/* Menu pulled down by "Word Size" cascade button */
.
.
.
/* Submenu 3 */

static PULLDOWN_MENU_INFO sub_menu3_data =
{
    4,  "Parity",
    {
        { "None", parity_none}, { "Even",  parity_even},
        { "Odd",  parity_odd},  { "Mark",  parity_mark}
    }
};

/* Continue with other submenus */
.
.
.
/* Define the Cascade Menu (for second button on menu bar) */

static CASCADE_MENU_INFO menu2_data =
{
    6, "Settings",
    {
  {"Baud Rate",   &sub_menu1_data},
  {"Word Size",   &sub_menu2_data},
  {"Parity",      &sub_menu3_data},
  {"Stop Bits",   &sub_menu4_data},
  {"Handshake",    &sub_menu5_data},
  {"Serial Port", &sub_menu6_data}
    }
};
```

Next, you have to prepare the cascading menu panes—each as a pull-down menu with XmCascadeButton widgets as menu items. Assume that menu1 and menu2 are the pull-down menus attached to the two menu bar entries, File and Settings, respectively. Here is how you can prepare menu2:

```
int                 count=0, subcount;
Widget              menu2, menu_tmp, button, cbutton;
PULLDOWN_MENU_INFO *menu_data;
.
.
.
/* Start with a pull-down menu which is a child of the menu bar */
menu2 = XmCreatePulldownMenu(menu_bar, "Settings", NULL, 0);
```

```
/* Now create the entries that will activate further
 * submenus
 */
for(count = 0; count < menu2_data.size; count++)
{
/* Build the submenu to be attached to each cascade button */
    menu_tmp = XmCreatePulldownMenu(menu2,
                    menu2_data.items[count].label, NULL, 0);

/* Add entries (push-buttons) to this submenu */

    menu_data =  menu2_data.items[count].submenu;
    for(subcount = 0; subcount < menu_data->size; subcount++)
    {
/* Create an entry (can be a push-button, toggle button, label,
 * or a separator. Here we use push-buttons.
 */
        button = XmCreatePushButton(menu_tmp,
                    menu_data->items[subcount].label, NULL, 0);
        XtAddCallback(button, XmNactivateCallback,
                    menu_data->items[subcount].callbacks,
                    NULL);
        XtManageChild (button);
    }

/* Now create the cascade button and attach the sub menu */
    argcount = 0;
    XtSetArg(args[argcount], XmNsubMenuId, menu_tmp);
    argcount++;
    cbutton = XmCreateCascadeButton(menu2,
                menu2_data.items[count].label, args, argcount);
    XtManageChild(cbutton);
}
```

After you have all the submenus ready, you can create the cascade buttons for the menu bar and attach the appropriate menus to each button. For the menu structure shown in Figure 6.24, the code for this step follows:

```
Widget mbar_cbutton1, mbar_cbutton2;

/* Create the cascade buttons on the menu header */
argcount = 0;
XtSetArg(args[argcount], XmNsubMenuId, menu1);   argcount++;
mbar_cbutton1 = XmCreateCascadeButton(menu_bar, "File",
                    args, argcount);

argcount = 0;
XtSetArg(args[argcount], XmNsubMenuId, menu2);   argcount++;
mbar_cbutton2 = XmCreateCascadeButton (menu_bar, "Settings",
                    args, argcount);
```

```
/* Display the widgets by managing them */
XtManageChild (mbar_cbutton1);
XtManageChild (mbar_cbutton2);

/* Go on to XtRealizeWidgets(top_level) and XtMainLoop() */
.
.
.
```

With a few utility functions, you can create menus in a simpler way than this example makes it appear. Listing 7.1 in the next chapter shows some utility functions for easier menu creation.

Summary

Although you can develop applications using Xlib alone, it is much more productive to do so with an X toolkit. Even if you work with Xlib only, you need a set of utility routines and a way of managing the complexity arising from the need to handle events occurring in the windows in the application. The toolkits include these facilities. They provide widgets which can be thought of as predefined software components used to construct user interfaces. Examples of widgets are labels, push-buttons, and dialog boxes.

There are several popular toolkits available. The most prominent ones are the OSF/Motif toolkit from the Open Software Foundation, AT&T's XT+, Sun's XView, and MIT's Athena Widget set. Most of these widget sets are layered on top of the Xt Intrinsics, which is a set of utility routines and data structures that helps you create and manage widgets. This chapter describes how this is done through several small examples. The examples use the widgets provided by the OSF/Motif toolkit and illustrate the use of callbacks, event handlers, and the translation manager.

The Xt Intrinsics not only reduces the event-handling loop to a single function call, it also provides many ways for the user to customize an application. Users can specify values for configurable parameters, known as resources, in a text file using a specific format. The Xt Intrinsics automatically loads these resources during initialization. Additionally, applications can call functions from the Xt Intrinsics to load new resources and accept values specified through the command line.

Effective use of widgets requires that you know the widget set. To build Motif applications, you would use the OSF/Motif widget set. All Xt Intrinsics-based toolkits, including OSF/Motif and the Athena Widgets, share a common object-oriented structure. Instead of working with individual windows, as Xlib

6

does, the toolkits define higher-level objects such as labels and push-buttons, called widgets, that are used as components to build user interfaces for applications. Each widget encapsulates one or more windows with other data and includes functions that provide some predefined functionality.

An Xt Intrinsics-based widget has a class and an instance data structure. There is only one class structure for each class, whereas each copy of a widget has its own private instance data. The class data structure includes data common to all instances and provides the functions that draws the widget and handles events occurring in the window associated with that widget. The widget class is organized in a hierarchy so that child widgets can share data and functions with their parents—this is known as *inheritance*. The widget instances also have their hierarchy which is similar to the hierarchy of windows in X.

The class hierarchy of the OSF/Motif widget set is built on a basic set of widgets defined in the Xt Intrinsics. This base set consist of the `Core`, `Composite`, `Constraint`, and the `Shell` widgets. Motif adds a few more base classes such as `XmPrimitive` and `XmManager`. All other Motif widgets are derived from these base widgets. You can broadly classify the Motif widgets into three categories

- The stand-alone primitive *widgets*, such as labels and push-buttons

- The *manager widgets*, such as `SelectionBox` and `RowColumn` that can contain other widgets

- The *shell widgets* for setting up the top-level windows of applications

This chapter describes several representative members of each class of widget. It includes example code to create these widgets and corresponding figures to illustrate their visual appearance.

6

Building Motif Applications

A toolkit-based X application can use that toolkit's widget set to build most of its user interface, but some parts of the application cannot be constructed from the widgets alone. For example, if your application is a utility for browsing through text files, you can use various widgets to prompt for the file name and prepare a scrollable viewing area to display the contents of the file. But the file browser also has to manage the file's contents in memory and display the text in a window. For these tasks, you have to design your own data structures, open and load the file, and use Xlib functions to draw the text strings in the viewing area provided by the widgets.

No matter how versatile the toolkit, most real applications require you to mix Xlib calls with the toolkit functions. This chapter illustrates how you can use Xlib functions for graphics and text output in widgets based on the OSF/Motif toolkit. First we present two example programs—a simple drawing program and a file viewer—to show how you can do this. The latter part of the chapter describes facilities such as *WorkProcs* and *input callbacks* that can be useful in X applications.

Mixing Xlib and Xt Intrinsics

The approach for mixing Xlib functions with those in an X toolkit is the same for all toolkits based on the Xt Intrinsics. To use Xlib functions in any application, you need the *Display pointer*, the *window ID*, and, for drawing functions, a *Graphics Context* (GC).

Xt Intrinsics provide macros and functions to get these parameters for any widget. This section describes how you can use these macros and functions.

Identifying the Display and Windows

Xt Intrinsics and toolkits based on the Intrinsics work with widgets, but most Xlib functions require a pointer to the Display structure and a window identifier as arguments. Given a widget ID, you can get the pointer to its Display structure with the XtDisplay function. Similarly, the XtWindow function returns the ID of the window associated with a widget. As an example, suppose you want to use the Xlib function XClearWindow to clear a widget's window. Given the widget w, you can do this as follows:

```
#include <X11/Intrinsics.h>
    .
    .
    .

Widget    w;
Display   *p_disp;      /* Display pointer */
Window    win;          /* Window ID */

p_disp = XtDisplay(w);
win = XtWindow(w);
XClearWindow(p_disp, win);
```

Note that the window ID returned by XtWindow will be NULL if the widget has not been realized. The Display pointer, however, is valid immediately after the widget is created by calling XtCreateWidget or another equivalent function.

Creating a Graphics Context

In X, the appearance of text and graphics is controlled by attributes stored in a graphics context (GC). When you program using a toolkit, one of the common tasks is to draw text and graphics in a widget's window. You have to create GCs for this. When using Xlib alone, you use functions such as XCreateGC, XCopyGC, and XChangeGC to create and manipulate GCs. The Xt Intrinsics provides the function XtGetGC for creating GCs. This function tries to minimize the number of GC creations by keeping track of the GCs created by all the widgets in an application. Intrinsics creates a new GC only when none of the existing ones has attributes matching those you request in the XtGetGC call.

When creating a GC for a widget, you should get the foreground and background pixel values from the widget's resources. That way, you will be using the foreground and background colors that the user might have specified for that widget in a resource file.

You get the value of a widget's resources by calling XtGetValues. The steps are similar to those involved in setting resource values. For example, suppose you want the foreground and background colors for the widget drawing_area. Here is how you can get the resource values and set up a GC with these attributes:

```
    Arg         args[20];
    Cardinal    argcount;
    Widget      drawing_area;
    XGCValues   xgcv;
    GC          theGC;
    int         fg, bg;

/* Retrieve the background and foreground
 * colors from the widget's resources.
 */
    argcount = 0;
    XtSetArg(args[argcount], XmNforeground, &fg); argcount++;
    XtSetArg(args[argcount], XmNbackground, &bg); argcount++;
    XtGetValues(drawing_area, args, argcount);

/* Now, define a GC with these colors */
    xgcv.foreground = fg;
    xgcv.background = bg;
    theGC = XtGetGC(drawing_area, GCForeground | GCBackground,
                    &xgcv);
```

Note that when you retrieve a resource's value, you provide the address of a variable in which XtGetValues places the value.

After you have created the GC, you can manipulate it with Xlib functions such as XChangeGC. Note, however, that the GC returned by XtGetGC is read-only; you cannot change it. Use XCreateGC instead of XtGetGC if you need a GC that you can change.

An OSF/Motif Drawing Program: xmfigures

The following sections show how to build xmfigures—a simple OSF/Motif drawing program. The xmfigures program displays a menubar with two cascade buttons (File and Figures) and provides a drawing area underneath the menubar. As shown in Figure 7.1, when the user clicks on the Figures item, a pull-down menu appears. This menu lists five types of figures—line, rectangle, ellipse, filled rectangle, and filled ellipse—that the program can draw. To draw a figure, the user selects the type of figure and starts drawing in the drawing area. The program can draw "rubber-band figures." This means that when the user first clicks the left mouse button in the drawing area, that marks one corner of the figure. As the user moves the mouse (keeping the button pressed), the figure appears, grows, and shrinks in keeping with the mouse movement, like a stretched and released rubber band. The final figure is drawn when the user releases the button.

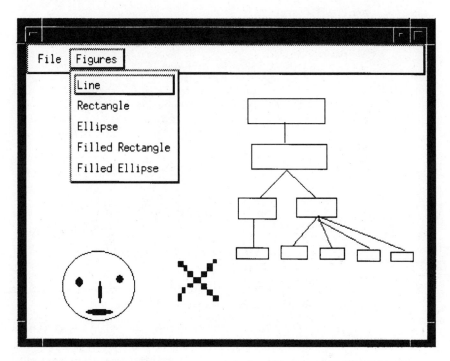

Fig. 7.1. Output from `xmfigures`—**a simple drawing program based on the OSF/Motif toolkit.**

Selecting the Widgets

Selecting the appropriate widgets is the first step in implementing the drawing program with the OSF/Motif toolkit. A good candidate is the `XmMainWindow` widget. This is a composite widget that allows for a menubar, a drawing area, and scrollbars. You have to individually create the component widgets and the components are optional. For `xmfigures`, we will use an `XmMainWindow` with a menubar and a drawing area.

To create the widgets, you have to start with a call to `XtInitialize` (`XtAppInitialize` in Motif version 1.1 and later) to set up a top-level shell widget. Then, you call the convenience function `XmCreateMainWindow` to create the main window. This window is a child of the top-level shell.

The menubar is actually an XmRowColumn widget of type XmMENU_BAR (a constant defined in <Xm/Xm.h>) configured to hold the XmCascadeButton widgets that control the pull-down menus. You can call another convenience function, XmCreateMenuBar, to create the menubar.

Setting Up Menus

To set up the menubar, you have to create a pull-down menu for a cascade button and then attach that menu to the cascade button. Because these steps tend to be repetitive, these are prime candidates for a utility function. We have set up the functions MakeMenuPane and AttachToCascade to create a menu pane and attach it to a cascade button. Listing 7.1 shows the file xmutil.c, which contains these two functions. Note that the menu pane is constructed by laying out a number of push-button widgets, one after another. Each push-button has a callback function that is called when that menu item is selected.

With these two utility functions, setting up menus becomes very easy. For instance, to create the Figures menu in xmfigures, all we have to do is write the following:

```
/* "figure_select" is a callback. zero, one, two, . . . are
 *  integers indicating figure to be drawn.
 */

    Widget menu_bar, new_menu;
    .
    .
/* Create the "Figures" menu ---------------------------------*/
    new_menu = MakeMenuPane("Figures", menu_bar,
            "Line",             figure_select, (caddr_t)&zero,
            "Rectangle",        figure_select, (caddr_t)&one,
            "Ellipse",          figure_select, (caddr_t)&two,
            "Filled Rectangle", figure_select, (caddr_t)&three,
            "Filled Ellipse",   figure_select, (caddr_t)&four,
            NULL);

/* Now create the cascade button and attach this submenu to it */
    AttachToCascade(menu_bar, "Figures", new_menu);
```

Setting Up the Main Window

When the menubar is ready, create an XmDrawingArea widget that will be used as the drawing area. You can use the XmCreateDrawingArea function to set up this widget. The last step in setting up the interface is to attach the menubar and the drawing area to the main window. You can do this by calling XmMainWindowSetAreas as follows:

```
        Widget main_window, menu_bar, drawing_area;

/* Attach the menu bar and the drawing area to main window */
        XmMainWindowSetAreas(main_window, menu_bar, NULL, NULL,
                                NULL, drawing_area);
```

Listing 7.1. `xmutil.c`—Utility functions for OSF/Motif programming.

```
/*-------------------------------------------------------------*/
/*  File: xmutil.c
 *
 *  Utility functions for building menus with the OSF/Motif
 *  toolkit.
 *
 */
/*-------------------------------------------------------------*/
#include <stdio.h>
#include <stdarg.h>   /* ANSI-standard variable argument macros */

#include <X11/Intrinsic.h>
#include <Xm/Xm.h>
#include <Xm/RowColumn.h>
#include <Xm/PushB.h>
#include <Xm/CascadeB.h>

typedef void    (*P_FUNC)();
typedef char    *P_CHAR;

/*-------------------------------------------------------------*/
/* M a k e M e n u P a n e
 *
 * Make a menu pane (uses variable number of arguments) in which
 * each menu entry is a pair of the form label, action_proc;
 * a NULL marks the end
 */
Widget MakeMenuPane(char *name, Widget parent, ...)
{
    va_list  argp;          /* Used to access arguments */
    Widget new_menu;
    char     *item_label;
    Widget   button;
    P_FUNC   item_action;
    caddr_t  action_args;

    new_menu = XmCreatePulldownMenu(parent, name, NULL, 0);

/* Add entries (push-buttons) to this submenu */
/* Get the first optional parameter using "va_start" */
    va_start(argp, parent);

/* Get items one by one and prepare the push-buttons */
    while((item_label = va_arg(argp, P_CHAR)) != NULL)
    {
```

```
/* Create an entry (can be a push-button, toggle button, label,
 * or a separator. Here we use push-buttons
 */
        button = XmCreatePushButton(new_menu, item_label,
                                    NULL, 0);

/* Register callback for this menu button */

        item_action = va_arg(argp, P_FUNC);
        action_args = va_arg(argp, caddr_t);

        XtAddCallback(button, XmNactivateCallback,
                      item_action, action_args);
        XtManageChild (button);
    }
    va_end(argp);
    return(new_menu);
}
/*----------------------------------------------------------------*/
/* A t t a c h T o C a s c a d e
 *
 * Attach a pull-down menu to a cascade button
 */
void AttachToCascade(Widget parent, char *label, Widget sub_menu)
{
    Arg      args[10];
    Cardinal argcount;
    Widget   cbutton;

/* Create the cascade button and attach the sub menu to it */
    argcount = 0;
    XtSetArg(args[argcount], XmNsubMenuId, sub_menu);
    argcount++;
    cbutton = XmCreateCascadeButton(parent, label,
                                    args, argcount);
    XtManageChild(cbutton);
}
```

7

Building xmfigures

The source code for the application, xmfigures.c, appears in Listing 7.2. You can use the following makefile to compile and link xmfigures:

```
# Some common definitions . . .

RM = rm -f
CC = cc

# Compiler flags, paths for include files and libraries
```

```
CFLAGS = -Ox
DEFINES = -DSYSV
INCLUDES = -I/usr/include
LIBS = -lXm -lXt -lX11 -lsocket -lmalloc

# Rule to create .o files from .c files
.c.o:
        $(RM) $@
        $(CC) -c $(CFLAGS) $(DEFINES) $(INCLUDES) $*.c

# Targets...

all::  xmfigures

xmfigures: xmfigures.o xmutil.o
        $(RM) $@
        $(CC) -o $@ $(CFLAGS) xmfigures.o xmutil.o $(LIBS)
```

This *makefile* should work as is in systems running Santa Cruz Operation's SCO Open Desktop System. For other UNIX systems, the compile and link commands should be substantially similar.

Listing 7.2. An OSF/Motif-based drawing program: `xmfigures.c`.

```
/*----------------------------------------------------------------*/
/*  File: xmfigures.c
 *
 *  OSF/Motif version of simple drawing program.
 *
 */
/*----------------------------------------------------------------*/
#include <stdio.h>

#include <X11/Xlib.h>
#include <X11/Xutil.h>
#include <X11/cursorfont.h>

#include <X11/Intrinsic.h>
#include <Xm/Xm.h>
#include <Xm/RowColumn.h>
#include <Xm/MainW.h>
#include <Xm/DrawingA.h>

#define MAXARGS      20
#define MAXFIGURES  100

#define WIDTH       400
#define HEIGHT      300

typedef struct FIGURE
{
    short    type;       /* What type of figure        */
```

```
#define LINE          0
#define RECT          1
#define ELLIPSE       2
#define FILLRECT      3
#define FILLELLIPSE   4
    short   x1, y1;   /* Corners of bounding rectangle */
    short   x2, y2;   /* or end-points of line         */
} FIGURE;

/* Array of figures */

FIGURE  figures[MAXFIGURES];
int     numfigures = 0;
int     curfig = 0,
        figtype = 0;

static int zero=0, one=1, two=2, three=3, four=4;

GC   theGC;     /* GC for regular drawing */
GC   xorGC;     /* GC used for rubber-band drawing */

Cursor xhair_cursor;

/* Function prototypes */

/* These are callbacks */
void start_rubberband(Widget w, caddr_t data, XEvent *p_event);
void continue_rubberband(Widget w, caddr_t data,
                    XEvent *p_event);
void end_rubberband(Widget w, caddr_t data, XEvent *p_event);

void figure_select(Widget w, caddr_t data,
            XmAnyCallbackStruct *call_data);

void handle_expose(Widget w, caddr_t client_data,
            XmDrawingAreaCallbackStruct *call_data);

void quit_action(Widget w, caddr_t client_data,
            XmAnyCallbackStruct *call_data);

/* This function draws the figures */
static void draw_figure(Display *d, Window w, GC gc, int fig);

/* This function, defined in file "xmutil.c," prepares menus */
Widget MakeMenuPane(char *name, Widget parent, ...);

/* This function, also in xmutil.c, attaches a menu to a
 * cascade button
 */
void AttachToCascade(Widget parent, char *label,
                Widget sub_menu);
/*-------------------------------------------------------------*/
void main(int argc, char **argv)
```

continues

Listing 7.2. continued

```
{
    Widget     top_level, main_window, menu_bar, drawing_area,
               new_menu;
    Arg        args[MAXARGS];
    Cardinal   argcount;
    int        fg, bg;
    XGCValues  xgcv;

/* Create the top-level shell widget and initialize the toolkit */
    top_level = XtInitialize(argv[0], "XMfigures", NULL, 0,
                             &argc, argv);

/* Next, the main window widget */
    argcount = 0;
    XtSetArg(args[argcount], XmNwidth, WIDTH);   argcount++;
    XtSetArg(args[argcount], XmNheight, HEIGHT); argcount++;
    main_window = XmCreateMainWindow(top_level, "Main",
                                     args, argcount);
    XtManageChild(main_window);

/* Create the menubar */
    menu_bar = XmCreateMenuBar(main_window, "Menubar", NULL, 0);
    XtManageChild(menu_bar);

/* Create the drawing area */
    argcount = 0;
    XtSetArg(args[argcount], XmNresizePolicy, XmRESIZE_ANY);
    argcount++;
    drawing_area = XmCreateDrawingArea(main_window,
                              "drawing_area", args, argcount);
    XtManageChild(drawing_area);

/* Attach the menubar and the drawing area to main window */
    XmMainWindowSetAreas(main_window, menu_bar, NULL, NULL,
                         NULL, drawing_area);

/* Create the GCs. First retrieve the background and foreground
 * colors from the widget's resources
 */
    argcount = 0;
    XtSetArg(args[argcount], XmNforeground, &fg); argcount++;
    XtSetArg(args[argcount], XmNbackground, &bg); argcount++;
    XtGetValues(drawing_area, args, argcount);

/* Define a GC with these colors */
    xgcv.foreground = fg;
    xgcv.background = bg;
    theGC = XtGetGC(drawing_area, GCForeground | GCBackground,
                    &xgcv);
```

7

```
/* Set up a GC with exclusive-OR mode (for rubber-band drawing)*/
   xgcv.foreground = fg ^ bg;
   xgcv.background = bg;
   xgcv.function = GXxor;
   xorGC = XtGetGC(drawing_area, GCForeground |
                   GCBackground | GCFunction, &xgcv);

/* Add callback to handle expose events for the drawing area */
   XtAddCallback(drawing_area, XmNexposeCallback, handle_expose,
                 &drawing_area);

/* Create the "File" menu ----------------------------------*/
   new_menu = MakeMenuPane("File", menu_bar,
                           "Quit", quit_action, NULL,
                           NULL);
/* Create the "File" cascade button and attach new_menu to it */
   AttachToCascade(menu_bar, "File", new_menu);

/* Create the "Figures" menu -------------------------------*/
   new_menu = MakeMenuPane("Figures", menu_bar,
               "Line",             figure_select, (caddr_t)&zero,
               "Rectangle",        figure_select, (caddr_t)&one,
               "Ellipse",          figure_select, (caddr_t)&two,
               "Filled Rectangle", figure_select, (caddr_t)&three,
               "Filled Ellipse",   figure_select, (caddr_t)&four,
               NULL);

/* Now create the cascade button and attach this submenu to it */
   AttachToCascade(menu_bar, "Figures", new_menu);

/* Create a cross-hair cursor for the drawing area */
   xhair_cursor = XCreateFontCursor(XtDisplay(drawing_area),
                                    XC_crosshair);

/* Add event handlers for button events to handle the drawing */
   XtAddEventHandler(drawing_area, ButtonPressMask, False,
                     start_rubberband, NULL);
   XtAddEventHandler(drawing_area, ButtonMotionMask, False,
                     continue_rubberband, NULL);
   XtAddEventHandler(drawing_area, ButtonReleaseMask, False,
                     end_rubberband, NULL);

/* Realize all widgets */
   XtRealizeWidget(top_level);

/* Set up things so that the cursor changes to a cross-hair and
 * is confined to the drawing_area while the mouse button is
 * pressed. This is done through what is known as a "grab"
 */
```

7

continues

Listing 7.2. continued

```
        XGrabButton(XtDisplay(drawing_area), AnyButton, AnyModifier,
                XtWindow(drawing_area), True, ButtonPressMask|
                ButtonMotionMask | ButtonReleaseMask,
                GrabModeAsync, GrabModeAsync,
                XtWindow(drawing_area), xhair_cursor);

/* Start the main event-handling loop */
    XtMainLoop();
}
/*-----------------------------------------------------------------*/
/* q u i t _ a c t i o n
 *
 * This routine is called when the "Quit" item is selected from
 * the "File" menu
 */
void quit_action(Widget w, caddr_t client_data,
                XmAnyCallbackStruct *call_data)
{
    XtCloseDisplay(XtDisplay(w));
    exit(0);
}
/*-----------------------------------------------------------------*/
/* s t a r t _ r u b b e r b a n d
 *
 * Start of rubber-band figure
 */
void start_rubberband(Widget w, caddr_t data, XEvent *p_event)
{
    int x = p_event->xbutton.x,
        y = p_event->xbutton.y;

/* Crude check to ensure that we don't exceed array's capacity */
    if(numfigures > MAXFIGURES-1)
        numfigures = MAXFIGURES-1;
    curfig = numfigures;
    numfigures++;

    figures[curfig].type = figtype;
    figures[curfig].x1 = x;
    figures[curfig].y1 = y;
    figures[curfig].x2 = x;
    figures[curfig].y2 = y;
    draw_figure(XtDisplay(w), XtWindow(w), xorGC, curfig);
}
/*-----------------------------------------------------------------*/
/* c o n t i n u e _ r u b b e r b a n d
 *
 * Handle mouse movement while drawing a rubber-band figure
 */
void continue_rubberband(Widget w, caddr_t data, XEvent *p_event)
{
```

```
        int x = p_event->xbutton.x,
            y = p_event->xbutton.y;

/* Draw once at old location (to erase figure) */
        draw_figure(XtDisplay(w), XtWindow(w), xorGC, curfig);

/* Now update end-point and redraw */
        figures[curfig].x2 = x;
        figures[curfig].y2 = y;
        draw_figure(XtDisplay(w), XtWindow(w), xorGC, curfig);
}
/*----------------------------------------------------------------*/
/* e n d _ r u b b e r b a n d
 *
 * End of rubber-band drawing
 */
void end_rubberband(Widget w, caddr_t data, XEvent *p_event)
{
        int x = p_event->xbutton.x,
            y = p_event->xbutton.y;

/* Draw once at old location (to erase figure) */
        draw_figure(XtDisplay(w), XtWindow(w), xorGC, curfig);

/* Now update end-point and redraw in normal GC */
        figures[curfig].x2 = x;
        figures[curfig].y2 = y;
        draw_figure(XtDisplay(w), XtWindow(w), theGC, curfig);
}
/*----------------------------------------------------------------*/
/* f i g u r e _ s e l e c t
 *
 * Callback for "Figure" menu
 */
void figure_select(Widget w, caddr_t data,
                    XmAnyCallbackStruct *call_data)
{
/* Set figure type and return */
        figtype = *((int *)data);
}
/*----------------------------------------------------------------*/
/* h a n d l e _ e x p o s e
 *
 * Expose event handler for the drawing area
 */
void handle_expose(Widget w, caddr_t client_data,
        XmDrawingAreaCallbackStruct *call_data)
{
        XEvent *p_event = call_data->event;
        Window win = call_data->window;
        Display *p_display = XtDisplay(w);
```

7

continues

Listing 7.2. continued

```
    if(p_event->xexpose.count == 0)
    {
        int i;
/* Clear the window and draw the figures in the "figures" array*/
        XClearWindow(p_display, win);

        if(numfigures > 0)
        {
            for(i=0; i<numfigures; i++)
            {
                draw_figure(p_display, win, theGC, i);
            }
        }
    }
}
/*--------------------------------------------------------------*/
/* d r a w _ f i g u r e
 *
 * Draw a specified figure
 */
static void draw_figure(Display *d, Window w, GC gc, int curfig)
{
    int x1 = figures[curfig].x1, y1 = figures[curfig].y1,
        x2 = figures[curfig].x2, y2 = figures[curfig].y2, t;

/* Make sure x2 >= x1 and y2 >= y1 */
    if(figures[curfig].type != LINE && x1 > x2)
    {
        t = x1;
        x1 = x2;
        x2 = t;
    }
    if(figures[curfig].type != LINE && y1 > y2)
    {
        t = y1;
        y1 = y2;
        y2 = t;
    }
    switch(figures[curfig].type)
    {
        case LINE:
            XDrawLine(d, w, gc, x1, y1, x2, y2);
            break;
        case RECT:
            XDrawRectangle(d, w, gc, x1, y1, x2-x1, y2-y1);
            break;
```

```
        case ELLIPSE:
            XDrawArc(d, w, gc, x1, y1, x2-x1, y2-y1, 0, 360*64);
            break;
        case FILLRECT:
            XFillRectangle(d, w, gc, x1, y1, x2-x1, y2-y1);
            break;
        case FILLELLIPSE:
            XFillArc(d, w, gc, x1, y1, x2-x1, y2-y1, 0, 360*64);
            break;
    }
}
```

Specifying Resources

Like any toolkit-based application, you can specify resources for xmfigures. Because the class-name of this program is XMfigures (specified in the XtInitialize call), you can provide the resources in the file /usr/lib/X11/appdefaults/XMfigures or in a file named XMfigures in your login directory. For instance, you can specify an initial geometry and the foreground and background colors as follows:

```
#### XMfigures: Resources for the xmfigures program      ####
*foreground:            black
*background:            white
*geometry:              400x300+10+10
```

Consult Chapter 5 for more information on specifying resources.

An OSF/Motif File Browser: xmbrowse

As a second example of an OSF/Motif-based application, we will write a program that lets you open a text file and browse through its contents. As shown in Figure 7.2, xmbrowse sports a menubar, a text display area, and a scrollbar. The text is drawn in a user-selected font of specific size and weight. The user selects these items from pull-down menus. These menus are created in the same way as we did the menus for xmfigures in Listing 7.2.

Like xmfigures, xmbrowse also uses a main window widget for the text display. However, in addition to the menubar and the text display area, it also uses a vertical scrollbar to allow the user to scroll through the file.

7

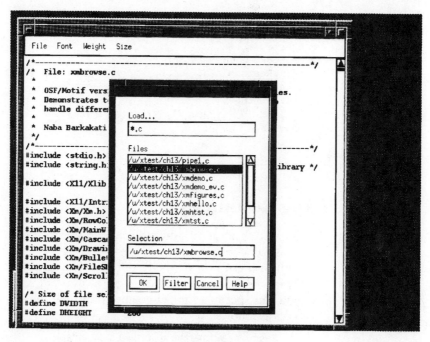

Fig. 7.2. Browsing `xmbrowse.c` **in 12 point Courier Bold.**

File Selection Dialog

The `xmbrowse` program displays a file selection dialog box when the user selects `Open` from the File menu. This is possible because the OSF/Motif toolkit provides the `XmFileSelectionBox` widget that displays a list of files and lets the user select one (see Figure 7.2 above).

The function `open_file`, shown later in Listing 7.3, shows how the file selection box is created. The filename is extracted in the callback `fs_ok`, which is called when the user presses the OK button in the dialog. As shown in `fs_ok`, the filename is provided as a compound string in the `value` field of a `XmSelectionBoxCallbackStruct` structure. You can convert this into a null-terminated C string by using the `XmStringGetLtoR` utility function. Here is an outline of the `fs_ok` callback:

```
/***************** f s _ o k *********************/
char *file_name;

void fs_ok(Widget w, caddr_t client_data,
                XmSelectionBoxCallbackStruct *call_data)
{
```

```
/* Get file name from user's selection */
   if(XmStringGetLtoR(call_data->value,
                      XmSTRING_DEFAULT_CHARSET, &file_name))
/* Open and load file */
   .
   .
   .
}
```

Building `xmbrowse`

Listing 7.3 shows `xmbrowse.c`, the complete source file for the `xmbrowse`
application. You will also need the file `xmutil.c` from Listing 7.1. You can build
`xmbrowse` using the same makefile as the one used to build `xmfigures` (just
change all occurrences of the string `xmfigures` to `xmbrowse`). You need to
compile `xmbrowse.c` and `xmutil.c`, and link them, at a minimum, with the
libraries, `1Xm -1Xt -1X11`. Additional libraries may be necessary for interprocess
communication between the X server and the program.

Listing 7.3. OSF/Motif-based file browser: `xmbrowse.c`.

```
/*------------------------------------------------------------------*/
/*  File: xmbrowse.c
 *
 *  OSF/Motif version of a program for browsing text files.
 *  Demonstrates text drawing functions and shows how to
 *  handle different fonts.
 *
 */
/*------------------------------------------------------------------*/
#include <stdio.h>
#include <string.h>                 /* ANSI standard string library */

#include <X11/Xlib.h>

#include <X11/Intrinsic.h>
#include <Xm/Xm.h>
#include <Xm/RowColumn.h>
#include <Xm/MainW.h>
#include <Xm/CascadeB.h>
#include <Xm/DrawingA.h>
#include <Xm/BulletinB.h>
#include <Xm/FileSB.h>
#include <Xm/ScrollBar.h>

/* Size of file selection dialog box */
#define DWIDTH          180
#define DHEIGHT         200
#define MAXARGS         20
```

continues

Listing 7.3. continued

```
#define LEFT_MARGIN    4        /* Leave a 4-pixel margin    */

#define SCROLL_UP    0
#define SCROLL_DOWN  1

#define MAXCHARS    512         /* Maximum length of a line  */

typedef struct D_LINE           /* Holds info on each line   */
{
    struct D_LINE *prev;        /* Pointer to previous line  */
    struct D_LINE *next;        /* Pointer to next line      */
    char         *line;         /* Null-terminated line      */
    short        length;        /* Number of characters in line */
    short        lbearing;      /* Left and right edges of   */
    short        rbearing;      /* rectangle covered by line */
    short        height;        /* Height of text string     */
} D_LINE;

typedef struct D_LBUF           /* Info on entire buffer     */
{
    D_LINE       *lines;        /* First line in buffer      */
    D_LINE       *lstart;       /* First line in window      */
    GC           gc;            /* GC used to display text    */
    Region       rexp;          /* Current exposed region    */
    XFontStruct  *fstruct;      /* Info on current font      */
    int          font;          /* Currently selected font   */
    int          weight;        /* weight and                */
    int          size;          /* size                      */
    Dimension    dwidth;        /* Width of text display area  */
    Dimension    dheight;       /* Height of text display area */
    long         count;         /* How many lines in buffer  */
} D_LBUF;

static D_LBUF fbuf = { NULL,NULL, None, None, None, 0, 0, 0,
                       0, 0, 0};

static int zero=0, one=1, two=2, three=3, four=4;

static  GC     theGC;   /* GC used for text output */

/* Information necessary to construct X11R3 font names */
static char *fontname[] =
{
  "courier", "helvetica", "new century schoolbook", "times"
};
static char *weight[] = { "medium", "bold" };
static char *size[] = {"100", "120", "140", "180", "240"};

/* File to be opened */
char *file_name = NULL;
```

```
/* Window ID of text area */
static Window  dWin;

/* Dialog box that displays a file selection box */
static Widget file_dialog = (Widget)0, file_sel_box,
               vsbar, text_area;

/* Name of application */
static char *theAppName;

static int last_slider_pos = 0;
static int file_not_loaded = True;

/* Variables for setting resources */
static Arg        args[MAXARGS];
static Cardinal argcount;

/* Function prototypes */

void handle_expose(Widget w, caddr_t client_data,
                   XmDrawingAreaCallbackStruct *call_data);

void quit_action(Widget w, caddr_t client_data,
                   XmAnyCallbackStruct *call_data);

void font_select(Widget w, caddr_t data,
                   XmAnyCallbackStruct *call_data);
void wt_select(Widget w, caddr_t data,
                   XmAnyCallbackStruct *call_data);
void size_select(Widget w, caddr_t data,
                   XmAnyCallbackStruct *call_data);

void open_file(Widget w, caddr_t client_data,
                   XmAnyCallbackStruct *call_data);

void fs_ok(Widget w, caddr_t client_data,
                   XmSelectionBoxCallbackStruct *call_data);

void fs_cancel(Widget w, caddr_t client_data,
                   XmSelectionBoxCallbackStruct *call_data);

void scroll_text(Widget w, caddr_t client_data,
                   XmScrollBarCallbackStruct *call_data);

void resize_text(Widget w, caddr_t client_data,
                   XmAnyCallbackStruct *call_data);

static void load_file(char *filename);
static void apply_font(Widget w);
```

continues

Listing 7.3. continued

```c
static void display_lines(Widget w);
static void scroll_lines(Widget w, int direction, int numlines);

/* This function, defined in file xmutil.c, prepares menus */
Widget MakeMenuPane(char *name, Widget parent, ...);

/* This function, also in xmutil.c, attaches a menu to a
 * cascade button
 */
void AttachToCascade(Widget parent, char *label,
                     Widget sub_menu);
/*------------------------------------------------------------------*/
void main(int argc, char **argv)
{
    Widget    top_level, main_window, menu_bar, new_menu;
    int       fg, bg;
    XGCValues xgcv;

/* Create the top-level shell widget and initialize the toolkit*/
    top_level = XtInitialize(argv[0], "XMbrowse", NULL, 0,
                                  &argc, argv);
    theAppName = argv[0];

/* Next, the main window widget */
    argcount = 0;
    XtSetArg(args[argcount], XmNwidth, DWIDTH);   argcount++;
    XtSetArg(args[argcount], XmNheight, DHEIGHT); argcount++;
    main_window = XmCreateMainWindow(top_level, "Main",
                                          args, argcount);
    XtManageChild(main_window);

/* Create the menubar */
    menu_bar = XmCreateMenuBar(main_window, "Menubar", NULL, 0);
    XtManageChild(menu_bar);

/* Create the text area */
    argcount = 0;
    XtSetArg(args [argcount], XmNresizePolicy, XmRESIZE_ANY);
    argcount++;
    text_area = XmCreateDrawingArea(main_window,
                                     "text_area", args, argcount);
    XtManageChild(text_area);

/* Create a vertical scrollbar for controlling the text area */
    vsbar = XmCreateScrollBar(main_window, "scroll_bar",
                                    NULL, 0);
    XtManageChild(vsbar);

/* Add callbacks to the scrollbar to handle button presses
 * in the arrows and the slider
 */
```

```
    XtAddCallback(vsbar, XmNvalueChangedCallback,
                scroll_text, NULL);
    XtAddCallback(vsbar, XmNdragCallback,
                scroll_text, NULL);

/* Attach the menubar, the text area, and the scrollbar
 * to main window
 */
    XmMainWindowSetAreas(main_window, menu_bar, NULL, NULL,
                    vsbar, text_area);

/* Add callback to handle expose events for the drawing area */
    XtAddCallback(text_area, XmNexposeCallback, handle_expose,
                NULL);

/* Another to handle any resizes . . . */
    XtAddCallback(text_area, XmNresizeCallback, resize_text,
                NULL);

/* Create the "File" menu ------------------------------------*/
    new_menu = MakeMenuPane("File", menu_bar,
                    "Open", open_file, (caddr_t)top_level,
                    "Quit", quit_action, NULL,
                    NULL);
    AttachToCascade(menu_bar, "File", new_menu);

/* Create the "Font" menu ------------------------------------*/
    new_menu = MakeMenuPane("Font", menu_bar,
                "Courier",      font_select, (caddr_t)&zero,
                "Helvetica",    font_select, (caddr_t)&one,
                "New Century Schoolbook",
                                font_select, (caddr_t)&two,
                "Times",        font_select, (caddr_t)&three,
                NULL);

    AttachToCascade(menu_bar, "Font", new_menu);

/* Create the "Weight" menu ------------------------------------*/
    new_menu = MakeMenuPane("Weight", menu_bar,
                "Medium",  wt_select, (caddr_t)&zero,
                "Bold",    wt_select, (caddr_t)&one,
                NULL);
    AttachToCascade(menu_bar, "Weight", new_menu);

/* Create the "Size" menu ------------------------------------*/
    new_menu = MakeMenuPane("Size", menu_bar,
                " 10pt",        size_select, (caddr_t)&zero,
                " 12pt",        size_select, (caddr_t)&one,
                " 14pt",        size_select, (caddr_t)&two,
                " 18pt",        size_select, (caddr_t)&three,
                " 24pt",        size_select, (caddr_t)&four,
                NULL);
    AttachToCascade(menu_bar, "Size", new_menu);
```

7

continues

Listing 7.3. continued

```
/* Set up a GC to display text. First retrieve the background
 * and foreground colors from the widget's resources
 */
    argcount = 0;
    XtSetArg(args [argcount], XmNforeground, &fg); argcount++;
    XtSetArg(args [argcount], XmNbackground, &bg); argcount++;
    XtGetValues(text_area, args, argcount);

/* Define a GC with these colors */
    xgcv.foreground = fg;
    xgcv.background = bg;
    fbuf.gc = XtGetGC(text_area, GCForeground | GCBackground,
                      &xgcv);
/* Realize all widgets */
    XtRealizeWidget(top_level);

/* dWin is a global variable that holds the Window ID of
 * the text display area
 */
    dWin = XtWindow(text_area);

/* Event handling loop—keep processing events until done */
    XtMainLoop();
}
/*------------------------------------------------------------*/
/* h a n d l e _ e x p o s e
 *
 * Expose event handler for the text display area
 */
void handle_expose(Widget w, caddr_t client_data,
    XmDrawingAreaCallbackStruct *call_data)
{
    XRectangle r;

/* Do nothing, if no file has been loaded */
    if(file_not_loaded) return;

/* Accumulate exposed areas in a region */
    r.x = call_data->event->xexpose.x;
    r.y = call_data->event->xexpose.y;
    r.width = call_data->event->xexpose.width;
    r.height = call_data->event->xexpose.height;
    XUnionRectWithRegion(&r, fbuf.rexp, fbuf.rexp);

/* Handle the expose event only if 'count' is 0 */
    if(call_data->event->xexpose.count == 0) display_lines(w);
}
/*------------------------------------------------------------*/
/* q u i t _ a c t i o n
 *
```

```
 * This routine is called when the "Quit" item is selected from
 * the "File" menu
 */
void quit_action(Widget w, caddr_t client_data,
                XmAnyCallbackStruct *call_data)
{
    XtCloseDisplay(XtDisplay(w));
    exit(0);
}
/*----------------------------------------------------------------*/
/* f o n t _ s e l e c t
 *
 * Handle font selection
 *
 */
void font_select(Widget w, caddr_t data,
                XmAnyCallbackStruct *call_data)
{
    int font = *((int *)data);

    if(font != fbuf.font)
    {
        fbuf.font = font;
        apply_font(w);
/* Clear the display window so that text is displayed again */
        XClearArea(XtDisplay(w), dWin, 0, 0, 0, 0, True);
/* Reset the scrollbar variables */
        resize_text(text_area, NULL, NULL);
    }
}
/*----------------------------------------------------------------*/
/* w t _ s e l e c t
 *
 * Font weight changed.
 *
 */
void wt_select(Widget w, caddr_t data,
                XmAnyCallbackStruct *call_data)
{
    int weight = *((int *)data);

    if(weight != fbuf.weight)
    {
        fbuf.weight = weight;
        apply_font(w);
/* Clear the display window so that text is displayed again */
        XClearArea(XtDisplay(w), dWin, 0, 0, 0, 0, True);
/* Reset the scrollbar variables */
        resize_text(text_area, NULL, NULL);
    }
}
```

7

continues

Listing 7.3. continued

```c
/*----------------------------------------------------------------*/
/* s i z e _ s e l e c t
 *
 * New size font selected
 *
 */
void size_select(Widget w, caddr_t data,
                 XmAnyCallbackStruct *call_data)
{
    int size = *((int *)data);

    if(size != fbuf.size)
    {
        fbuf.size = size;
        apply_font(w);
/* Clear the display window so that text is displayed again */
        XClearArea(XtDisplay(w), dWin, 0, 0, 0, 0, True);
/* Reset the scrollbar variables */
        resize_text(text_area, NULL, NULL);
    }
}
/*----------------------------------------------------------------*/
/* l o a d _ f i l e
 *
 * Read in file to be displayed
 *
 */
static void load_file(char *filename)
{
    FILE   *fp;
    D_LINE *p_l = NULL, *p_l_prev = NULL, *p_l_next;
    char   buf[MAXCHARS];

/* If a file was already loaded, first release all memory */
    if(fbuf.lines != NULL)
    {
        p_l = fbuf.lines;
        while (p_l != NULL)
        {
            XtFree(p_l->line);
            XtFree(p_l);
            p_l_next = p_l->next;
            p_l = p_l_next;
        }
        fbuf.count = 0;
        fbuf.lines = NULL;
        fbuf.lstart = NULL;
        fbuf.rexp = NULL;
        file_not_loaded = True;
    }
```

7

```
/* Open the file */
    if((fp = fopen(filename, "r")) == NULL)
    {
        fprintf(stderr, "Cannot open: %s\n", filename);
        exit(1);
    }

/* Read each line and store in linked list of D_LINE structs */
    while((fgets(buf, MAXCHARS, fp)) != NULL)
    {
        if((p_l = (D_LINE *) XtCalloc(1, sizeof(D_LINE)))
                                                    != NULL)
        {
            if(fbuf.lines == NULL)
            {
                fbuf.lines = p_l;
            }
            else
            {
                p_l_prev->next = p_l;
                p_l->prev = p_l_prev;
            }
        }
        else
        {
/* Allocation failed . . . */
            fprintf(stderr, "Failed to allocate memory for\
line data structure...\n");
            exit(1);
        }
        p_l->length = strlen(buf) - 1; /* Exclude newline */
        buf[p_l->length] = '\0';
        if((p_l->line = XtMalloc(p_l->length+1)) == NULL)
        {
            fprintf(stderr, "Failed to allocate memory for\
line:\n%s\n", buf);
            exit(1);
        }
        strcpy(p_l->line, buf);
        p_l_prev = p_l;
        fbuf.count++;
    }
    printf("%d lines loaded from %s\n", fbuf.count, filename);
    file_not_loaded = False;

/* Close the file */
    fclose(fp);
}
/*----------------------------------------------------------------*/
/* a p p l y _ f o n t
 *
```

continues

Listing 7.3. continued

```
* Set up a new font for use. Also compute screen areas
 * occupied by each line
 */
static void apply_font(Widget w)
{
    D_LINE      *p_l;
    int         dir, ascent, descent;
    char        fname[120];       /* Room for font's name */
    XCharStruct cinfo;
    int         font = fbuf.font,
                wt = fbuf.weight,
                sz = fbuf.size;
/* Construct font's name */
    sprintf(fname, "*adobe-%s-%s-r*%s*", fontname[font],
            weight[wt], size[sz]);

    printf("Font = %s\n", fname);

/* Free the font, if necessary */
    if(fbuf.fstruct != NULL)
        XFreeFont(XtDisplay(w), fbuf.fstruct);

/* Load the new font */
    if ((fbuf.fstruct = XLoadQueryFont(XtDisplay(w), fname))
        == NULL)
    {
        fprintf(stderr, "%s: display %s cannot load font: %s\n",
            theAppName, DisplayString(XtDisplay(w)), fname);

/* Set fbuf.fstruct to the "fixed" font */
        if ((fbuf.fstruct = XLoadQueryFont(XtDisplay(w),
                                "fixed")) == NULL)
        {
            fprintf(stderr, "%s: display %s cannot load \
\"fixed\" font\n", theAppName, DisplayString(XtDisplay(w)));
            exit(1);
        }
    }

/* Compute bounding box of each line in the buffer */
    for(p_l = fbuf.lines; p_l != NULL; p_l = p_l->next)
    {
        XTextExtents(fbuf.fstruct, p_l->line, p_l->length,
            &dir, &ascent, &descent, &cinfo);
        p_l->lbearing = cinfo.lbearing;
        p_l->rbearing = cinfo.rbearing;
        p_l->height = ascent + descent;
    }

/* Set the font in the GC */
    XSetFont(XtDisplay(w), fbuf.gc, fbuf.fstruct->fid);
}
```

```
/*-------------------------------------------------------------------*/
/* d i s p l a y _ l i n e s
 *
 * Displays the lines in the text window
 */
static void display_lines(Widget w)
{
    int    xpos, ypos = 0, width;
    D_LINE *p_l;

/* Set the accumulated exposed regions as the clip mask */
    XSetRegion(XtDisplay(w), fbuf.gc, fbuf.rexp);

/* Display the lines starting with the first one. Draw
 * a string ONLY if it falls in the exposed region
 */

    for(p_l = fbuf.lstart; p_l != NULL && ypos < fbuf.dheight;
        p_l = p_l->next)
    {
        xpos = LEFT_MARGIN - p_l->lbearing;
        ypos += p_l->height;
        if(XRectInRegion(fbuf.rexp, xpos, ypos - p_l->height,
                        p_l->lbearing + p_l->rbearing,
                        p_l->height) != RectangleOut)
        {
/* Yes. String's rectangle is partially in region. Draw it */
            XDrawImageString(XtDisplay(w), dWin, fbuf.gc,
                        xpos, ypos, p_l->line, p_l->length);
        }
    }

/* Destroy current region and create a new "empty" one */
    XDestroyRegion(fbuf.rexp);
    fbuf.rexp = XCreateRegion();
}
/*-------------------------------------------------------------------*/
void scroll_text(Widget w, caddr_t client_data,
                XmScrollBarCallbackStruct *call_data)
{
    int slider_pos = call_data->value;
    if(file_not_loaded ¦ slider_pos == last_slider_pos) return;

    if(slider_pos > last_slider_pos)
    {
        scroll_lines(w, SCROLL_UP,
                        slider_pos - last_slider_pos);
    }
    else
    {
        scroll_lines(w, SCROLL_DOWN,
                        last_slider_pos - slider_pos);
    }
```

continues

Listing 7.3. continued

```c
/* Update the last slider position */
    last_slider_pos = slider_pos;
}
/*---------------------------------------------------------------*/
/* s c r o l l _ l i n e s
 *
 * Scroll the text display by a specified amount.
 */
static void scroll_lines(Widget w, int direction, int numlines)
{
    int i, ysrc, yclr, numpix = 0;
    D_LINE *p_l;

/* Figure out how many pixels to scroll */

    switch(direction)
    {
        case SCROLL_UP:
            for(i = 0, p_l = fbuf.lstart;
                i < numlines && p_l->next != NULL;
                i++, p_l = p_l->next) numpix += p_l->height;
            ysrc = numpix;
            yclr = fbuf.dheight - numpix;
            break;

        case SCROLL_DOWN:
            for(i = 0, p_l = fbuf.lstart;
                i < numlines && p_l->prev != NULL;
                i++, p_l = p_l->prev) numpix += p_l->height;
            ysrc = 0;
            yclr = 0;
            break;
    }

    if(numpix == 0)
    {
/* No need to scroll */
        XBell(XtDisplay(w), 0);
        return;
    }
/* Adjust first line to display */
    fbuf.lstart = p_l;

/* Copy area */
    XSetClipMask(XtDisplay(w), fbuf.gc, None);
    XCopyArea(XtDisplay(w), dWin, dWin, fbuf.gc,
              0, ysrc, fbuf.dwidth, fbuf.dheight - numpix,
              0, numpix - ysrc);

/* Clear new rectangle so that it is redrawn */
    XClearArea(XtDisplay(w), dWin, 0, yclr,
               fbuf.dwidth, numpix, True);
}
```

```
/*----------------------------------------------------------------*/
/* o p e n _ f i l e
 *
 * Display a "FileSelectionBox" and let user select the file
 * to be loaded for browsing
 */
void open_file(Widget w, caddr_t client_data,
                  XmAnyCallbackStruct *call_data)
{
    XmString  title, dir_mask;

/* Create dialog box, if not yet created */
    if(file_dialog == (Widget)0)
    {
        argcount = 0;
        XtSetArg(args[argcount], XmNdialogStyle,
                  XmDIALOG_MODELESS);                    argcount++;
        XtSetArg(args[argcount], XmNwidth, DWIDTH);   argcount++;
        XtSetArg(args[argcount], XmNheight, DHEIGHT); argcount++;
        file_dialog = XmCreateBulletinBoardDialog(
                            (Widget)client_data, "Select File",
                            args, argcount);

        title = XmStringLtoRCreate("Load...",
                                  XmSTRING_DEFAULT_CHARSET);
        dir_mask = XmStringLtoRCreate("*.c",
                                  XmSTRING_DEFAULT_CHARSET);
        argcount = 0;
        XtSetArg(args[argcount], XmNdirMask, dir_mask); argcount++;
        XtSetArg(args[argcount], XmNfilterLabelString, title);
                                                        argcount++;
        file_sel_box = XmCreateFileSelectionBox(file_dialog,
                                  "File Selection", args, argcount);

/* Add callbacks for the "OK" and "Cancel" buttons */
        XtAddCallback(file_sel_box, XmNcancelCallback, fs_cancel,
                      (caddr_t) file_dialog);
        XtAddCallback(file_sel_box, XmNokCallback, fs_ok,
                      (caddr_t) file_dialog);
        XmStringFree(title);
        XmStringFree(dir_mask);
        XtManageChild(file_sel_box);
    }
/* Display the dialog box */
    XtManageChild(file_dialog);
}
/*----------------------------------------------------------------*/
/* f s _ o k
 *
 * Callback for the "OK" button on the file selection box
 */
void fs_ok(Widget w, caddr_t client_data,
                  XmSelectionBoxCallbackStruct *call_data)
{
```

continues

Listing 7.3. continued

```
/* Get file name from user's selection */
    if(XmStringGetLtoR(call_data->value,
                        XmSTRING_DEFAULT_CHARSET, &file_name))
    {
        printf("File selected: %s\n", file_name);
/* Load the file */
        load_file(file_name);
        fbuf.lstart = fbuf.lines;
        apply_font(w);
        fbuf.rexp = XCreateRegion();
        resize_text(text_area, NULL, NULL);
/* Clear the display window so that text is displayed again */
        XClearArea(XtDisplay(w), dWin, 0, 0, 0, 0, True);
        XtFree(file_name);
    }
    else
    {
        printf("Nothing selected\n");
    }
    XtUnmanageChild((Widget)client_data);
}
/*-------------------------------------------------------------*/
/* f s _ c a n c e l
 *
 * Callback for the "Cancel" button in the file selection box
 */
void fs_cancel(Widget w, caddr_t client_data,
                    XmSelectionBoxCallbackStruct *call_data)
{
    XtUnmanageChild((Widget)client_data);
}
/*-------------------------------------------------------------*/
/* r e s i z e _ t e x t
 *
 * Callback to handle resizing of the text area
 */
void resize_text(Widget w, caddr_t client_data,
                    XmAnyCallbackStruct *call_data)
{
    int lines_visible, slider_size;

/* Determine the size of the text area */
    argcount = 0;
    XtSetArg(args[argcount], XmNheight, &fbuf.dheight);
                                            argcount++;
    XtSetArg(args[argcount], XmNwidth, &fbuf.dwidth);
                                            argcount++;
    XtGetValues(w, args, argcount);
```

```
/* Make sure scrollbar reflects size of the text display area */
    if(file_not_loaded) return;
    lines_visible = fbuf.dheight /
                    (fbuf.fstruct->ascent + fbuf.fstruct->descent);
    if(lines_visible > fbuf.count) lines_visible = fbuf.count;
    slider_size = lines_visible / fbuf.count;
    if(slider_size < 1) slider_size = 1;
    if(slider_size > fbuf.count) slider_size = fbuf.count;

    argcount = 0;
    XtSetArg(args[argcount], XmNminimum, 0);           argcount++;
    XtSetArg(args[argcount], XmNmaximum, fbuf.count); argcount++;
    XtSetArg(args[argcount], XmNincrement, 1);         argcount++;
    XtSetArg(args[argcount], XmNpageIncrement, lines_visible);
                                                       argcount++;
    XtSetArg(args[argcount], XmNsliderSize, slider_size);
                                                       argcount++;
    XtSetValues(vsbar, args, argcount);
}
```

Other Toolkit Features

The two sample programs, xmfigures and xmbrowse, illustrated how to mix Xlib functions with those from the OSF/Motif toolkit. However, there are several unique capabilities of the toolkit that we have not described. These include the idea of *work procedures* and *input callbacks*, described in this section.

WorkProcs

The Xt Intrinsics supports a special type of callback function known as a *WorkProc*, or work procedure, that is called whenever there are no events pending. This lets you perform some tasks in the background. Since normal event-handling by the Xt Intrinsics cannot proceed until the WorkProc returns, you should not include any time-consuming processing in a work procedure. Like other callbacks, you have to register a WorkProc. You do this with the XtAddWorkProc function (in Motif version 1.1 or later, you should use the XtAppAddWorkProc function for this purpose):

```
XtWorkProcId wp_id;

/* ANSI C prototype for the WorkProc */
Boolean do_work(caddr_t client_data);
```

```
    .
    .
    .
/* Register the WorkProc. "my_data" is a pointer or any
 * value that will fit into a pointer-sized variable
 */
wp_id = XtAddWorkProc(do_work, my_data);
```

The return value of the WorkProc function determines whether it
remains installed. If the function returns a True, it is removed after being called
once. You should return a False, if you want the function to be called
repeatedly.

At any time, you can remove a WorkProc by calling XtRemoveWorkProc
with the ID of the work procedure as the argument. This ID is returned by
XtAddWorkProc when you register the procedure. Thus, to remove the work
procedure do_work, identified by the ID wp_id, you have to call:

```
XtRemoveWorkProc(wp_id);
```

Input Callbacks

Sometimes you want to handle more than just the stream of X events. For
instance, you may have opened a connection to a network port and you want
to accept input from that port whenever there is something available. At other
times you want to go on processing X events. The Xt Intrinsics provide an
elegant way to do this. You can register an *input callback function* that will be
called whenever there is input available from a specified *file descriptor*. For
example, suppose you want to monitor stdin for any input and, when input
is available, read it and display it in a scrolled text window. The following
outline of a program shows how this might be done:

```
#include <stdio.h>

#include <X11/Intrinsic.h>
#include <X11/StringDefs.h>
#include <Xm/Xm.h>
#include <Xm/Text.h>

/* Our data structure to be passed to the input callback    */
typedef struct XINPUT_DATA
{
    FILE   *stream;   /* Identifies the stream             */
    Widget widget;    /* Widget where text will be displayed */
} XINPUT_DATA;

#define MAXCHR 255
```

```
/* Input callback's prototype */

void read_input(caddr_t client_data, int *fid, XtInputId *id);

void main(int argc, char **argv)
{
    XINPUT_DATA  xpinfo;
    Widget top_level, scrolled_text;
    .

    .
    .
/* Assume that a scrolled text window has been created to display
 * the characters received from "stdin" Use "XmCreateScrolledText"
 * to create such a widget. Also assume that the top_level widget
 * has been created
 */
    xpinfo.widget = scrolled_text;
    xpinfo.stream = stdin;

    XtAddInput(fileno(stdin), XtInputReadMask, read_input,
               &xpinfo);

/* Realize the widgets */
    XtRealizeWidget(top_level);

/* Start the main event-handling loop */
    XtMainLoop();
}
/*------------------------------------------------------------------*/
void read_input(caddr_t client_data, int *fid, XtInputId *id)
{
    int  insertion_point;
    char line[MAXCHR];
    XINPUT_DATA *p_xp = (XINPUT_DATA *)client_data;

    if(fgets(line, MAXCHR, p_xp->stream) == NULL)
    {
        perror("fgets");
        exit(1);
    }

/* Add line to scrolled text widget */

    insertion_point = XmTextGetInsertionPosition(p_xp->widget);
    XmTextReplace(p_xp->widget, insertion_point,
                  insertion_point, line);
}
```

Notice that the input callback enables you to monitor a file for available input without continuously trying to read from it.

Timeouts

Another useful facility of the Xt Intrinsics is the *timeout*, which you use to specify a function that will be called after a specified interval of time. You can use the XtAddTimeOut (XtAppAddTimeOut in Motif version 1.1 or later) function to specify a timeout callback that should be called after a certain number of milliseconds. You can pass one argument to this timeout callback function. The Xt Intrinsics calls this function only once. To create periodic timeouts, you have to call XtAddTimeOut inside the function with another timeout delay.

You can use timeouts to build a clock, for instance. Listing 7.4 shows a timer based on this timeouts. It gets the date and the time by executing the UNIX command date and displays the string in a Label widget. All the work is done in the update_time function.

Listing 7.4. A clock based on timeouts: `xmtime.c`.

```
/*---------------------------------------------------------------*/
/*  File: xmtime.c
 *
 *  Display time using timeouts.
 */
/*---------------------------------------------------------------*/
#include <stdio.h>

#include <X11/Intrinsic.h>
#include <X11/StringDefs.h>
#include <Xm/Xm.h>
#include <Xm/Label.h>

#define MAXCHR 80

void update_time(Widget w);
/*---------------------------------------------------------------*/
void main(int argc, char **argv)
{
    Widget      top_level, time_label;

/* Initialize the toolkit and create the top-level widget */
    top_level = XtInitialize(argv[0], "XMtime", NULL, 0,
                             &argc, argv);

/* Set up a Label widget to display the time */
    time_label = XmCreateLabel(top_level, "Time", NULL, 0);
    XtManageChild(time_label);
    update_time(time_label);

/* Realize the widgets */
    XtRealizeWidget(top_level);
```

```
/* Start the main event-handling loop */
    XtMainLoop();
}
/*------------------------------------------------------------------*/
/* u p d a t e _ t i m e
 *
 * Updates the time by invoking the UNIX "date" command
 * and reinstalls function using XtAddTimeOut
 */
void update_time(Widget w)
{
    FILE     *fp;
    char     line[MAXCHR];
    Arg      args[2];
    XmString xms;

/* Run "date" to get time */

    if((fp = popen("/bin/date", "r")) == NULL)
    {
        perror("popen");
        exit(1);
    }
    if(fgets(line, MAXCHR, fp) == NULL)
    {
        perror("fgets");
        exit(1);
    }
    pclose(fp);

/* Display the time in the label widget */
    xms = XmStringLtoRCreate(line, XmSTRING_DEFAULT_CHARSET);
    XtSetArg(args[0], XmNlabelString, xms);
    XtSetValues(w, args, 1);
    XmStringFree(xms);

/* Make sure function is called again in 10 seconds */
    XtAddTimeOut(10*1000, update_time, w);
}
```

7

Summary

Toolkits are indispensable for real-world X applications. They let you control the complexity of Xlib calls, handle the routine chores of building a user interface, and focus on the application-specific tasks. For the application-specific part, you have to rely on Xlib functions, especially the graphics and text drawing functions.

This chapter explains how to mix Xlib and toolkit calls for any Xt Intrinsics-based toolkit. It describes how to refer to a widget's window and its associated display. Also covered is the creation of graphics contexts for use by the Xlib drawing functions.

Two sample programs illustrate how to use the OSF/Motif toolkit to build applications. The `xmfigures` program illustrates the use of Xlib's graphics drawing functions, and `xmbrowse` is for browsing through text files. You can use these examples as starting points for developing similar applications.

Xt Intrinsics-based toolkits also provide several other techniques for performing tasks in an application. Apart from the normal callback functions, you can have work procedures that are called whenever there are no events pending. Input callbacks let you monitor if there is any data available from an open file, which, under UNIX, can be anything from a pipe to a network connection. For periodic calls to a function, you can use timeouts.

7

Part III

OSF/Motif Quick Reference

## Chapter 8

Motif Window Manager

Quick Reference

T his chapter describes the command-line options and resources for mwm, the Motif Window Manager. You will find a tutorial introduction to the Motif Window Manager in Chapter 3.

Command-Line Options

You can specify the following options when you start mwm:

`-display` *sys_name:m.n*
This causes mwm to manage screen n of display m on the system named sys_name. Consult Chapter 2 for more information on naming X displays. For example, to run mwm on screen 1 of display 0 on the system named mac08, you would enter

`mwm -display mac08:0.1&`

`-multiscreen`
If you use this option, mwm will manage the clients displaying output on all screens of a display. Another way to specify this option is through the resource named `multiscreen`.

-name *application_name*
This option gives a name under which resources for mwm will be found.

-screens *screen_name1 screen_name2 ...*
This assigns names to the screens that mwm is managing. You can use these names to specify resources for specific screens.

-xrm *resource_specification_string*
This option enables you to specify a resource through the command line. For example, you can specify that you want the keyboard focus to follow the pointer by running mwm as follows:

```
mwm -xrm "keyboardFocusPolicy: pointer"&
```

Resources

The Motif Window Manager uses three types of resources:

- *Component-specific resources:* These resources affect the appearance of the window frames, window manager menus, and icons. The color of the window frame is a resource of this type.

- *mwm-specific resources:* These are resources that affect the window manager but are not set separately for each component. The key and button bindings for mwm fall in this category.

- *Client-specific resources:* These resources affect one or more of the clients managed by mwm. For instance, the amount of decoration around the top-level window of a client can be controlled by setting the client-specific resource named clientDecoration.

Component-Specific Resources

This discussion lists the resources that affect all components of the Motif window manager. You can specify these resources with the following syntax:

Mwm*resource_name: resource_value

background   **class name:**   Background
Specifies the background color used in all components of mwm. You specify the color using any valid color name in the X color database (the file /usr/lib/X11/rgb.txt).

backgroundPixmap   **class name:** BackgroundPixmap
Specifies the background pixmap used to decorate the window frame of an *inactive* window (this refers to windows that do not have the input focus). The default pixmap depends on the visual supported by the display.

bottomShadowColor   **class name:** Foreground
This color is used in the lower and the right bevels of all window manager decorations. You can use any color name from the X color database (the file /usr/lib/X11/rgb.txt).

bottomShadowPixmap   **class name:** BottomShadowPixmap
Specifies the pixmap to be used in the lower and the right bevels of all window manager decorations.

fontList   **class name:** Font
Specifies the font to be used in all window manager decorations. The default is the fixed font.

foreground   **class name:** Foreground
This is the foreground color. The default value depends on the visual supported by the display.

saveUnder   **class name:** SaveUnder
If this resource is set to True, the window manager will use the "save-under" feature (the ability to save the contents of a window and redraw the contents later) of the X server when the window manager displays the window decorations. This resource takes effect only if the "save-under" feature is available in the X server. The default value of this resource is False.

topShadowColor   **class name:** Background
This is the color used in the top and left bevels of the window decorations. The default value depends on the visual supported by the display.

topShadowPixmap   **class name:** TopShadowPixmap
Specifies the pixmap to be used in the top and left bevels of the window decorations.

The resources listed in this section affect the window frame and icons. You can specify the resource for a specific component by using the following syntax:

Mwm*component*resource_name: resource_value

8

where *component* can take one of the following values:

client	indicates the window frames of all X clients
feedback	indicates the dialog boxes displayed by mwm
icon	refers to the icon box
menu	refers to the menus displayed by mwm

You can separately configure the title area of a client window. For this use the syntax:

```
Mwm*client*title*resource_name: resource_value
```

activeBackground   **class name:** Background
This resource specifies the background color used in the mwm decorations when a window is active (that means the window has input focus—all keystrokes go to the window). The default color depends on the type of visual supported by the X server.

active BackgroundPixmap   **class name:** ActiveBackgroundPixmap
Specifies the pixmap used as the background in the mwm decorations of an active window (that means the window has input focus—all keystrokes go to the window).

activeBottomShadowColor   **class name:** Foreground
This is the color of the lower and right bevels of the window decorations of an active window. The visual supported by the display determines the default color.

activeBottomShadowPixmap **class name:** BottomShadowPixmap
Pixmap used for the "bottom shadow" (the lower and right bevels of the decorations) of the active window.

activeForeground   **class name:** Foreground
Specifies the foreground color used for decorations on an active window—a window that has the input focus.

activeTopShadowColor   **class name:** Background
This color is used in the active window's "top shadow" (the upper and left bevels of the decorations).

activeTopShadowPixmap   **class name:** TopShadowPixmap
Pixmap used for the "top shadow" (the upper and left bevels of the decorations) of the active window.

8

mwm-Specific Resources

The resources listed in this section apply to the mwm application itself. The syntax for resource specification is

```
Mwm*resource_name: resource_value
```

autoKeyFocus   **class name:** AutoKeyFocus

This resource applies only when the keyboardFocusPolicy resource is set to Explicit. This resource controls what happens to the focus when the current active window is iconified. If the autoKeyFocus resource is True, the focus automatically goes to the window that previously had the focus.

autoRaiseDelay   **class name:** AutoRaiseDelay

If the focusAutoRaise resource is True and the keyboardFocusPolicy is set to pointer, the autoRaiseDelay resource comes into play. It specifies the number of milliseconds mwm should wait before raising a window (bringing the resource to the top of the stack of windows) once the window has received the input focus. The default value is 500 milliseconds.

bitmapDirectory   **class name:** BitmapDirectory

This resource specifies a directory to be searched by mwm to locate any bitmap needed by other mwm resources. The default setting of this resource is /usr/include/X11/bitmaps.

buttonBindings   **class name:** ButtonBindings

This resource specifies a set of button bindings (a table that assigns an action to a button-press) that augments the built-in button bindings of mwm. The value should be the name of a button binding from the mwm configuration file. The default value of the buttonBindings resource is NULL, which means the built-in bindings are the only ones available.

cleanText   **class name:** CleanText

If this resource is set to True, text appearing in a window's title and in mwm's dialogs is displayed with a clear background. The default value is False.

clientAutoPlace   **class name:** ClientAutoPlace

This resource affects how mwm tries to place a client's window on the screen. If clientAutoPlace is True, mwm positions each window with the upper left corner of the frame offset horizontally and vertically so that no two windows completely overlap. The default for clientAutoPlace is True.

8

colormapFocusPolicy　　　**class name:**　ColormapFocusPolicy

This resource controls the colormap focus—the window whose colormap is currently installed and used for displaying everything in a server. The colormapFocusPolicy resource can take one of the following three values:

> keyboard means the window with input focus has colormap focus
>
> pointer means the window with the pointer has the colormap focus
>
> explicit means that colormap has to be explicitly selected for a window

To allow explicit selection of colormap, assign a button or key to the function named f.focus_color. The default value of the colormapFocusPolicy is keyboard.

configFile　　　**class name:**　ConfigFile

This resource specifies the pathname of the mwm configuration file, which is a file with mwm resource settings, menu definitions, and button and key bindings. If the pathname specified by the configFile resource begins with a ~/, mwm considers that pathname to be absolute; otherwise, the path is assumed to be relative to the current directory. Here is how mwm uses this resource setting:

1. If the environment variable named LANG is set, mwm looks for the specified configuration file in the directory $HOME/$LANG (which means in a subdirectory of your login directory where the name of the subdirectory is specified by the LANG environment variable).

2. If the specified configuration file does not exist in $HOME/$LANG or if the LANG environment variable is not defined, mwm looks for that file in $HOME.

3. If you do not specify a configFile resource or if the specified file does not exist in one of the places listed in steps 1 and 2, mwm looks for a configuration file named .mwmrc. If the LANG environment variable is set, it looks for $HOME/$LANG/.mwmrc; otherwise, it looks for $HOME/.mwmrc.

4. If the .mwmrc file does not exist, mwm will look for a file named system.mwmrc—first in the directory /us/lib/X11/$LANG (provided the LANG environment variable is defined), then in /usr/lib/X11.

8

Typically, the workstation vendor would provide a file /usr/lib/X11/system.mwmrc with the default configuration for mwm. You can copy this file to your home directory under the name .mwmrc and modify it to suit your needs.

deiconifyKeyFocus   **class name:** DeiconifyKeyFocus

If this resource is set to True and keyboardFocusPolicy is explicit, a window receives input focus when it is *deiconified*—converted to normal size from an icon. The default value is True.

doubleClickTime   **class name:** DoubleClickTime

This resource specifies the maximum time in milliseconds that can elapse between two clicks that are to be interpreted by mwm as a double-click. The default value is 500 milliseconds.

enableWarp   **class name:** EnableWarp

If this resource is True, mwm will move the mouse pointer (*warp* it) to the center of the window being resized and moved through keyboard accelerators (key combinations that activate menu options without displaying the menu). If enableWarp is False, the pointer is left at its previous position. The default setting is True.

enforceKeyFocus   **class name:** EnforceKeyFocus

If this resource is True, mwm will set the input focus to a selected window even if it is a *globally active window* (a window that can be operated without setting focus to it). If the resource is False, input focus is not set to any globally active window (such as a scrollbar). This resource is by default True.

fadeNormalIcon   **class name:** FadeNormalIcon

If this resource is True, mwm will gray out an icon that has been normalized. The default setting is False.

frameBorderWidth   **class name:** FrameBorderWidth

This resource specifies the border width (in pixels) of the border of the window frame. This border width includes the three-dimensional shadows. The default value is 5 pixels.

iconAutoPlace   **class name:** IconAutoPlace

This resource controls where mwm places the icon for a window. If the resource is True (the default), mwm places all icons in a specific area of the screen determined by the iconPlacement resource. If this resource is False, the user can place the icons anywhere on the screen.

iconBoxGeometry   **class name:** IconBoxGeometry

This resource is a geometry specification for the icon box. For example, if you specify the value of 4x3+0-0, mwm will create a box

8

large enough to hold three rows of four icons across and position the box at the lower left corner of the screen. The default value for this resource is 6x1+0-0.

iconBoxName   **class name:**   IconBoxName
This resource is the name under which the resources for the icon box can be found. The default name is iconbox.

iconBoxSBDisplayPolicy   **class name:**   IconBoxSBDisplayPolicy
This resource controls which scrollbars are displayed for the iconbox. It can take three values:

> horizontal indicates that you want a single horizontal scrollbar.

> vertical is for a vertical scrollbar only.

> all means both horizontal and vertical scrollbars should be displayed.

The default is all.

iconBoxTitle   **class name:**   IconBoxTitle
This is a string to be displayed in the title of the icon box. The default name is Icons.

iconClick   **class name:**   IconClick
If this resource is True, the Window Menu of an icon is displayed and left visible when you click on the icon. The default setting is True.

iconDecoration   **class name:**   IconDecoration
This resource affects the amount of decoration on the icon box. The value of the resource can be a combination of the following values:

> label indicates that only the label (truncated to the width of the icon) is displayed.

> image means that only the image of the icon should be displayed.

> activelabel specifies that the complete label (not truncated) is shown when the icon is active. For icons appearing in the icon box, the default value of iconDecoration is image label. For icons displayed on the screen, the setting is image label activelabel.

iconImageMaximum   **class name:**   IconImageMaximum
This resource takes a value of the form *mxn*, where *m* and *n* specify the maximum width and height of an icon's image. The default is 50×50 (in pixels). The maximum allowed is 128×128.

iconImageMinimum   **class name:** IconImageMinimum

This resource takes a value of the form *mxn*, where *m* and *n* specify the minimum width and height of an icon's image. The default value for this resource is 16 × 16 (in pixels), which is also the minimum size supported by mwm.

iconPlacement   **class name:** IconPlacement

This resource specifies where mwm should place the icons. The value is a sequence of two keywords of the form

primary   secondary

where primary and secondary can take one of the following values:

   top means top-to-bottom placement

   bottom implies bottom-to-top layout

   left means left-to-right arrangement

   right is for right-to-left placement

The *primary* layout specifies where an icon is placed (in a row or a column) and in which direction. The *secondary* layout specifies where to place new rows or columns. The default value for iconPlacement is left bottom, which means that the icons are placed from left to right on the screen with the first row at the bottom, and the new rows are added in the bottom-to-top direction.

iconPlacementMargin   **class name:** IconPlacementMargin

This resource (a positive value) specifies the margin (in pixels) between the edge of the screen and the icons appearing at that edge of the screen. The default value is the same as the separation between the icons on the screen (this is determined by mwm so as to maximize the number of icons appearing in each row and column).

interactivePlacement   **class name:** InteractivePlacement

If this resource is True, mwm will prompt the user for the position of each new window. The user has to press the mouse button to indicate where the window should be placed. By default, this resource is False; thus, by default, mwm does not prompt the user for the window position.

keyBindings   **class name:** KeyBindings

This resource specifies a set of key bindings (a table that assigns an action to one or more keypresses) that replaces the built-in key bindings of mwm. The value should be the name of a key binding

8

from the mwm configuration file. The default value of the keyBindings resource is DefaultKeyBindings.

keyboardFocusPolicy   **class name:**   KeyboardFocusPolicy
This resource specifies how mwm should assign the input focus to a window (the window with the input focus receives the keystrokes entered by the user). This resource can take one of two values:

> explicit means the user indicates the focus window by pressing the first mouse button with the pointer in the window.

> pointer means the keyboard focus follows the mouse pointer.

The default setting for keyboardFocusPolicy is explicit.

limitResize   **class name:**   LimitResize
If this resource is True, the user cannot resize a window to have a size greater than the maximum size. This resource is True by default.

lowerOnIconify   **class name:**   LowerOnIconify
If this resource is True, mwm places a window's icon at the bottom of the stack when the window is reduced to an icon. This resource is False by default.

maximumMaximumSize   **class name:**   MaximumMaximumSize
This resource sets the upper limit on the maximum size that you can specify for a client window. For instance, if you set this resource to 800x600, client windows cannot be bigger than 800 × 600 pixels. The default value is twice the size of the screen.

moveThreshold   **class name:**   MoveThreshold
This resource controls how sensitive mwm is to *mouse drag* (moving the mouse with a button pressed down) operations. The value is interpreted as the number of pixels by which the mouse must move before mwm reacts to it. The default value is four pixels.

multiScreen   **class name:**   MultiScreen
If this resource is True, mwm controls windows displayed in all screens of a display. The default value is False, which means mwm manages only one screen by default.

8

passButtons   **class name:**   PassButtons
If this resource is True, mwm passes button-press events to the client even after the events are used for some window manager functions. The default value is False—mwm does not forward button-press events that it uses for window management functions.

passSelectButtons   **class name:** PassSelectButtons
This resource indicates whether a button-press that assigns input
focus to a window is passed as an event to that window. By default
this resource is True, which means that mwm passes the button-press
event to the window after giving the keyboard focus to that window. This resource applies only when keyboardFocusPolicy is
explicit, because this is the only case that requires you to transfer
input focus by clicking on a window.

positionIsFrame   **class name:** PositionIsFrame
This resource specifies how mwm interprets the information about a
client window's position as it appears in the WM_NORMALHINTS
property or in geometry specifications. If this resource is True, the
position is taken to be that of the frame placed around the client
window by mwm; otherwise, the position is that of the client window
alone. The default value is True.

positionOnScreen   **class name:** PositionOnScreen
If this resource is True, mwm will place a client window entirely
inside the screen. If the window's size exceeds the screen size, mwm
places the upper left corner of the window within the boundaries
of the screen. The default value is True.

quitTimeOut   **class name:** QuitTimeOut
This is the amount of time in milliseconds that mwm will wait for a
client to respond to a WM_SAVE_YOURSELF message. The client is
supposed to reply by updating the WM_COMMAND property. The default
value is 1000 milliseconds (1 second). This resource applies only to
those clients that have a WM_SAVE_YOURSELF atom but do not have a
WM_DELETE_WINDOW atom in the WM_PROTOCOLS property of their top-
level window.

raiseKeyFocus   **class name:** RaiseKeyFocus
If this resource is True and keyboardFocusPolicy is explicit, mwm
transfers the input focus to a window that has been raised by the
f.normalize_and_raise function. This resource is False by default.

resizeBorderWidth   **class name:** ResizeBorderWidth
This is the width (in pixels) of a window frame that allows the user
to resize the window by dragging the border. The default value is
10 pixels.

resizeCursors   **class name:** ResizeCursors
If this resource is True, the cursor changes shape (to indicate that
the resize operation is available) whenever the mouse pointer
enters the window frame.

8

screens   **class name:**   Screens
This resource is for assigning names to the screens that mwm will be
managing.

showFeedback   **class name:**   ShowFeedback
This resource specifies when mwm displays feedback information,
which includes dialog boxes and boxes displaying window size and
position during move and resize operations. The value of this
resource is a combination of one or more of the following names:

all, which shows all feedback information.

behavior, which uses feedback to confirm any changes in
behavior of mwm.

kill, which shows a dialog box when a SIGKILL signal is
received.

move, which shows position during moves.

none, which suppresses all feedback.

placement, which shows position and size during initial
placement of window.

quit, which shows a dialog box to confirm a request to quit mwm.

resize, which shows size when window is being resized.

restart, which shows a dialog box to confirm any attempt to
restart mwm.

The default for the showFeedback resource is all. You specify new
values for this resource in two ways:

- Enable selected feedbacks. For instance, if you want feedback
  during move and resize operations only, you can set this resource as follows:

```
Mwm*showFeedback: move resize
```

- Disable selected feedbacks. In this case, all but the specified
  feedbacks are shown. The syntax requires a minus sign to
  precede the first keyword. For example, if you want feedback in
  all cases except during move, resize, and placement, you would
  write

```
Mwm*showFeedback: -move placement resize
```

8

startupKeyFocus   **class name:** StartupKeyFocus
If this resource is True and keyboardFocusPolicy is set to explicit, mwm transfers input focus to a window when it is mapped. This resource is True by default.

transientDecoration   **class name:** TransientDecoration
This resource controls the amount of decoration that mwm places around a transient (temporary) window (identified by the WM TRANSIENT FOR property on the window). The syntax for specification is similar to that for the clientDecoration resource (shown under client-specific resources). The default value for this resource is menu title, which means that transient windows appear with a resizable window border and a title bar with the Window Menu button.

transientFunctions   **class name:** TransientFunctions
This resource specifies the window management functions that mwm allows for a transient (temporary) window (identified by the WM TRANSIENT FOR property on the window). The syntax for specification is similar to that for the clientFunctions resource (shown under client-specific resources). The default value for this resource is -maximize minimize, which means that mwm will apply the functions f.maximize and f.minimize to transient windows.

useIconBox   **class name:** UseIconBox
If this resource is True, mwm will place all icons in an icon box. If this resource is False, mwm places the icons on the root window. The default value is False.

wMenuButtonClick   **class name:** WMenuButtonClick
If this resource is True, mwm will display the Window Menu in response to a button click on the *Window Menu Button* and leave it displayed until another button click elsewhere. This resource value is True by default.

wMenuButtonClick2   **class name:** WMenuButtonClick2
If this resource is True, and the user double-clicks (clicks twice in rapid succession) on the Window Menu Button, mwm will invoke the f.kill function to remove the client window.

8

Client-Specific Resources

The resources listed in this section apply to a specified client application. You would specify these resources using the following syntax:

Mwm*`client_name_or_class`*`resource_name`: `resource_value`

where `client_name_or_class` identifies the client to which the resource applies. With the client-specific resources you can customize the behavior of mwm for individual clients. For example, you can make mwm display the bitmap `/usr/include/X11/bitmaps/terminal` as the icon for the xterm application by setting the client-specific resource iconImage as follows:

Mwm*xterm*iconImage: /usr/include/X11/bitmaps/terminal

clientDecoration   **class name:** ClientDecoration
This resource specifies the amount of decoration (buttons and frames) mwm applies to a client's top-level window. The value of this resource is a combination of one or more of the following names:

all, which includes all decorations listed below.

border, which displays the window border.

maximize, which adds the titlebar with the maximize button.

menu, which displays the titlebar with the Window Menu button.

minimize, which adds the titlebar with the minimize button.

resizeh, which shows the border with resize handles.

none, which suppresses all decorations.

title, which adds the titlebar and a border to the window.

The default for the clientDecorations resource is all. You specify new values for this resource in two ways:

- Enable selected decorations. For instance, if you want the xclock window to have a titlebar with a Window Menu and a resizable border only, you can set this resource as follows:

  Mwm*xclock*clientDecorations: menu resizeh

- Disable selected decorations. In this case, all but the specified decorations will appear. The syntax requires a minus sign to precede the first keyword. For example, if you want all the decorations except the maximize and minimize buttons, you would write

  Mwm*xclock*clientDecorations: -maximize minimize

clientFunctions   **class name:** ClientDecoration
This resource specifies which of the window management functions mwm applies to a client's window. The value of this resource is a combination of one or more of the following names:

all, which includes all functions listed below.

close, which refers to the f.kill function.

maximize, which refers to the f.maximize function.

minimize, which refers to the f.minimize function.

move, which refers to the f.move function.

none, which suppresses invocation of all functions.

resize, which refers to the f.resize function.

The default for the clientFunctions resource is all. You specify new values for this resource in two ways:

- Enable selected functions. For instance, if you want to invoke only the f.move and f.resize functions on the xclock window, you can set this resource as follows:

```
Mwm*xclock*clientFunctions: move resize
```

- Disable selected functions. In this case, all but the specified functions can be applied to a client's window. The syntax requires a minus sign to precede the first keyword. For example, if you want to apply all functions except f.maximize and f.minimize, you would write

```
Mwm*xclock*clientFunctions: -maximize minimize
```

focusAutoRaise　　　　　**class name:** FocusAutoRaise
If this resource is True, mwm raises a window to the top of the stacking order when the window receives the input focus. The default value depends on the keyboardFocusPolicy. If keyboardFocusPolicy is explicit, focusAutoRaise is True; otherwise, focusAutoRaise is False.

iconImage　　　　　**class name:** IconImage
This is the pathname of an X bitmap file that mwm will use as the icon for a client when the client's window is minimized. By default mwm displays a standard icon image for all applications. Note that the useClientIcon resource affects this resource. If useClientIcon is True, an image supplied by the client application (something that the programmer had set in that application) takes precedence over an icon specified by the user.

iconImageBackground　　　　　**class name:** Background
This is the background color for the icon image. The default value is the color specified by the resource Mwm*background or Mwm*icon*background.

8

iconImageBottomShadowColor   **class name:**   Foreground
This is the color used to create the bottom shadow of the icon image. The default value is the color specified by the resource Mwm*icon*bottomShadowColor.

iconImageBottomShadowPixmap   **class name:**   BottomShadowPixmap
This is the pixmap used for the bottom shadow of the icon image. The default value is the pixmap specified by the resource Mwm*icon*bottomShadowPixmap.

iconImageForeground   **class name:**   Foreground
This is the foreground color for the icon image. The default value is the color specified by the resource Mwm*foreground or Mwm*icon*foreground.

iconImageTopShadowColor   **class name:**   Background
This is the color used to create the top shadow of the icon image. The default value is the color specified by the resource Mwm*icon*topShadowColor.

iconImageTopShadowPixmap   **class name:**   TopShadowPixmap
This is the pixmap used for the top shadow of the icon image. The default value is the pixmap specified by the resource Mwm*icon*topShadowPixmap.

matteBackground   **class name:**   Background
This is the background color of the *matte* (a three-dimensional border between the client's window and the window frame added by mwm). This resource is used only if matteWidth is greater than zero. The default value is the color specified by the resource Mwm*background or Mwm*client*background.

matteBottomShadowColor   **class name:**   Foreground
This is the color used to create the bottom shadow of the matte. This resource is used only if matteWidth is greater than zero. The default value is the color specified by the resource Mwm*bottomShadowColor or Mwm*client*bottomShadowColor.

matteBottomShadowPixmap   **class name:**   BottomShadowPixmap
This is the pixmap used for the bottom shadow of the matte. This resource is used only if matteWidth is greater than zero. The default value is the color specified by the resource Mwm*bottomShadowPixmap or Mwm*client*bottomShadowPixmap.

8

matteForeground   **class name:**   Foreground
This is the foreground color of the matte. This resource is
used only if matteWidth is greater than zero. The default value
is the color specified by the resource Mwm*foreground or
Mwm*client*foreground.

matteTopShadowColor   **class name:**   Background
This is the color used to create the top shadow of the matte. This
resource is used only if matteWidth is greater than zero. The default
value is the color specified by the resource Mwm*topShadowColor or
Mwm*client*topShadowColor.

matteTopShadowPixmap   **class name:**   TopShadowPixmap
This is the pixmap used for the top shadow of the matte. This
resource is used only if matteWidth is greater than zero. The default
value is the color specified by the resource Mwm*topShadowPixmap or
Mwm*client*topShadowPixmap.

matteWidth   **class name:**   MatteWidth
This is the width of the matte in pixels. The default value is zero;
thus, no matte appears by default.

maximumClientSize   **class name:**   MaximumClientSize
This resource sets the size of the client's window when it is maximized. The window manager gets the default value for this resource from the WM_NORMAL_HINTS property. If this property is not
present, the maximized size is such that the window fills the screen.
If you do not specify the maximumClientSize resource, mwm uses the
value supplied in the maximumMaximumSize resource.

useClientIcon   **class name:**   UseClientIcon
If the useClientIcon resource is True, an image supplied by the
client application (something that the programmer had set in that
application) takes precedence over an icon specified by the user
through the imageIcon resource.

windowMenu   **class name:**   WindowMenu
This resource specifies the name of the menu to be displayed when
the Window Menu button is pressed. The value of the resource
must be the name of a menu defined in the mwm configuration file
(the file specified by the resource configFile). The default for
windowMenu is DefaultWindowMenu.

8

mwm **Configuration File**

The Motif window manager uses a supplementary configuration file for defining menus and button and key bindings. You can specify the name of this configuration file through the resource Mwm*configFile. For most users the configuration file will be the system-wide one, /usr/lib/X11/system.mwmrc, or the file .mwmrc in the user's login directory.

Menu Syntax

Definition of each menu has the following form:

```
Menu MenuName
{
    Label1      [Mnemonic1]    [Accelerator1]    function1
    Label2      [Mnemonic2]    [Accelerator2]    function2
                          .

                          .

    LabelN      [MnemonicN]    [AcceleratorN]    functionN
}
```

where the fields enclosed in square brackets ([ ]) are optional. Each line specifies an item in the menu. The label is normally a string without any double quotation marks. However, if the label contains embedded blank spaces, you have to use double quotation marks around the string. You can even display a bitmap as a label by providing the filename with an @ as prefix.

The mnemonic field is optional. Here, you can specify a single character (which must appear in the label) that will be a shortcut—the user presses the key to select that menu item. To specify the mnemonic, precede the character with an underscore. The mnemonics in the root menu example in Chapter 3 do not make sense, because that menu does not stay popped (and the shortcut key does not work while the mouse button is pressed). While a menu is visible, you can press the shortcut key to select that menu item.

The optional accelerator also specifies another way of accessing a menu item. The *accelerator* is the combination of a regular key pressed together with a special key (Alt or Meta key, or Ctrl, the Control key). Unlike the mnemonic key, it does not require you to make the menu visible. Thus, you can perform actions solely with the accelerator keystrokes.

The last required field, the function, specifies what happens when you release the mouse button while the pointer is in that item. The function names start with an f followed by a period. The functions are summarized in Table 8.2.

8

Because a large number of functions exist, you can customize almost everything in mwm. In the table, *selected window* means the window at the top of the stacking order—the one with which you are interacting.

Table 8.2. Functions to Define Action When a Menu Item Is Selected

Function Name	*Action*
f.beep	Causes a beeping sound.
f.circle_down	Moves the topmost window to the bottom of the stack of windows.
f.circle_up	The opposite of f.circle_down. It moves the window at the bottom to the top, thus making it visible.
f.exec	Executes a command using the shell (you can specify a shell by setting the SHELL environment variable; otherwise /bin/sh is used by default). A single exclamation point (!) can be substituted for f.exec.
f.focus_color	Installs the color map belonging to the current window.
f.focus_key	Changes the keyboard input focus to the current window.
f.kill	Kills the currently selected client.
f.lowe	Sends the selected window to the bottom of the stack of windows being displayed on the screen.
f.maximize	Displays the window using the entire screen or the maximum size allowed by the client that owns the window.
f.menu	Pops up the menu specified by the argument. For example, f.menu ClientsSubMenu will create a pop-up window and display the menu defined by ClientsSubMenu in it.
f.minimize	Reduces the selected window into an icon. The icon appears in the icon box, if there is one. Otherwise, the icon appears at the bottom of the screen.

continues

8

Table 8.2. continued

Function Name	Action
f.move	Changes the cursor to a cross with arrows at each end and enables you to interactively move the selected window. You can place the window at the selected position by clicking the mouse button.
f.next_cmap	Installs the next colormap from the list of colormaps associated with the window with the current colormap focus.
f.next_key	Sets the keyboard input focus to the next window in the stacking order.
f.nop	Displays a menu item that acts like a label— you click on it, but nothing happens.
f.normalize	Changes the size of the selected window to its default normal size.
f.normalize_and_raise	Changes the size of the selected window to its default normal size and raises it to the top of the stacking order.
f.pack_icons	Rearranges the icons in the icon box in a packed grid.
f.pass_keys	Works as a toggle to enable or disable the key bindings for the window manager. For example, suppose you have assigned Alt-4 (press the 4 key while you hold down the Alt key) to kill the window. If an application happens to need Alt-4, you can use f.pass_keys to disable its assigned binding.
f.post_wmenu	Posts the Window menu, which is the menu that appears when you press at the Window Menu button to the left of the title area in a window.
f.prev_cmap	The opposite of f.next_cmap. Installs the previous colormap in the list of color maps for the selected window.

8

Function Name	Action
`f.prev_key`	Switches the input focus to the previous window in the stacking order. This is the opposite of the `f.next_key`.
`f.quit_mwm`	Kills the OSF/Motif Window Manager `mwm`. This function does not always stop the X server. However, if you started the X server with `xinit` using a script that had `mwm` as the last foreground process, the X server will also exit.
`f.raise`	Brings the selected window to the top of the stack so that it is no longer obscured.
`f.raise_lower`	Raises the selected window to the top if it is obscured, otherwise, `f.raise_lower` sends the window to the bottom of the stacking order.
`f.refresh`	Redraws all windows currently on the screen.
`f.refresh_win`	Redraws the selected window.
`f.resize`	Changes the cursor and waits for the user to resize the selected window.
`f.restart`	Stops and immediately restarts `mwm`.
`f.send_msg`	Sends a message (indicated by a message number) to a client. This will only work with clients that follow certain rules (specifically, the message number has to appear in a property of type `_MOTIF_WM_MESSAGES` in the client's window).
`f.separator`	Draws a separator between menu items. The menu label is irrelevant for this function.
`f.set_behavior`	Restarts `mwm` with its default behavior.
`f.title`	Inserts the label as a title at this place in the menu.

8

Key Bindings

The key bindings are essentially a table that assigns an mwm function to a combination of keystrokes. The definition of a set of key bindings is similar to a menu definition and has the following form:

```
Keys KeyBindingName
{
  [Modifier1]<Key>key_name1    context1  function1
  [Modifier2]<Key>key_name2    context2  function2
                    .
                    .
                    .
  [ModifierN]<Key>key_nameN    contextN  functionN
}
```

The general syntax of each line is as follows:

```
key_specification context function
```

where *key* specifies the key combinations, *function* describes what action is taken, and *context* indicates when that action is taken. The key combination starts with one or more modifiers (Shift, Meta, Ctrl). Then comes the exact string <Key> followed by the name of a key to be pressed, together with the modifiers.

The context is a combination of one or more of the following keywords separated by vertical bars (¦):

app refers to the window of the client application (excluding the frame).

border is the window frame excluding the titlebar.

frame refers to the entire window frame including the title and the border.

icon refers to the icon of an application.

root refers to all the areas of the screen excluding windows and icons.

title means the titlebar.

window refers to a client's window including the frame.

As you can see, each keyword indicates an area of the screen. In other words, the action of the key takes place when the current active area is the one specified by the context keyword. For key bindings, the context is determined by the window that has the input focus.

8

Button Bindings

The button bindings are defined in the same way as the key bindings. The general form of a button binding is

```
Buttons ButtonBindingName
{
  Button_event_name1    context1    function1
  Button_event_name2    context2    function2
                 .
                 .
                 .
  Button_event_nameN    contextN    functionN
}
```

where the first entry in each line refers to the button event with which the action identified by the mwm function is associated. The context specifies where the pointer must be in order to perform the action assigned to that button event. The context keywords are the same as those used in defining key bindings.

The buttons are numbered one through five, and the names of the button events are as follows (this shows the events for Button 1; for other buttons replace 1 with the button number):

Btn1Down   Button 1 is pressed.

Btn1Up   Button 1 is released.

Btn1Click   Button 1 is "clicked" (pressed and released).

Btn1Click2   Button 1 "double-clicked" (clicked twice in rapid
                succession).

The location of the mouse pointer determines the context.

8

## Chapter 9

Motif Functions and

Widgets Quick Reference

T his chapter comprises reference entries for individual Motif functions and widgets. They are organized into two sections: the Motif functions, then the widgets. In each section, the entries are alphabetical. Each entry shows the syntax, any return value, and a short description of how each function or widget is used.

Motif Functions

The syntax of each entry in this section appears as an ANSI-standard prototype declaration of the function followed by a brief description of the function. Each argument is explained through a comment next to the argument.

XmActivateProtocol

```
void XmActivateProtocol(
    Widget shell,       /* Protocol is for this widget  */
    Atom    property,   /* Property containing protocol */
    Atom    protocol ); /* Protocol to be activated     */
```

Stores `protocol` in the specified `property` of the `shell`. Used for interclient communications. (Consult a book on X Window System programming for more information on properties and atoms.)

XmActivateWMProtocol

```
void XmActivateWMProtocol(
    Widget shell,       /* Protocol is for this widget  */
    Atom    protocol);  /* Protocol to be activated     */
```

Calls `XmActivateProtocol` with property set to the atom returned by interning `WM_PROTOCOLS`.

XmAddProtocolCallback

```
void XmAddProtocolCallback(
    Widget shell,        /* Protocol is for this widget        */
    Atom    property,    /* Property containing protocol       */
    Atom    protocol,    /* Register callback for this protocol */
    XtCallbackProc callback,    /* The callback function        */
    caddr_t        client_data); /* Data passed to callback     */
```

Calls `XmAddProtocols` to add the specified protocol to the `WM_PROTOCOLS` property and register `callback` as the function to be called when a message is received with that protocol.

XmAddProtocols

```
void XmAddProtocols(
    Widget    shell,      /* Protocols are for this widget */
    Atom    property,     /* Property containing protocols */
    Atom    *protocols,   /* Protocols to be registered    */
    Cardinal num_protocols); /* Number of protocols        */
```

Adds a set of protocols to the specified `shell`. You can activate any of these protocols by calling `XmActivateProtocol`.

XmAddTabGroup

```
void XmAddTabGroup(
    Widget widget);    /* Widget to be added to tab group */
```

Adds the specified widget to the list of tab groups associated with a hierarchy of widgets. A *tab group* is a collection of widgets such that, within that group, you can move the input focus from one widget to another by using the arrow keys. You can go from one tab group to another by pressing the tab key.

XmAddToPostFromList

```
void XmAddToPostFromList(
    Widget menu_pane,  /* An XmRowColumn widget (menu pane)   */
    Widget widget);    /* Add this to pane's "post from" list */
```

Adds widget to the XmNpostFromList resource of the XmRowColumn widget menu.

XmAddWMProtocolCallback

```
void XmAddWMProtocolCallback(
    Widget shell,             /* Protocol is for this widget */
    Atom   protocol, /* Register callback for this protocol */
    XtCallbackProc callback, /* The callback function      */
    caddr_t        client_data); /* Data passed to callback */
```

Calls XmAddProtocolCallback to add callback for the specified protocol stored in the WM_PROTOCOLS property.

XmAddWMProtocols

```
void XmAddWMProtocols(
    Widget    shell,       /* Protocols are for this widget */
    Atom      *protocols, /* Protocols to be registered     */
    Cardinal num_protocols); /* Number of protocols         */
```

Adds a set of protocols to the specified shell's WM_PROTOCOLS property. You can activate any of these protocols by calling XmActivateProtocol.

XmCascadeButtonGadgetHighlight

```
void XmCascadeButtonGadgetHighlight(
    Widget button,     /* Cascade button gadget to highlight */
    Boolean highlight); /* True (to highlight) or False      */
```

Changes the highlight attribute of the specified cascade button gadget. If highlight argument is True, a shadow is drawn around the gadget to highlight it.

XmCascadeButtonHighlight

```
void XmCascadeButtonHighlight(
    Widget button,     /* Cascade button widget to highlight */
    Boolean highlight); /* True (to highlight) or False      */
```

Changes the highlight attribute of the specified cascade button widget. If the `highlight` argument is True, the shadow highlight around the button's window is drawn.

XmClipboardCancelCopy

```
void XmClipboardCancelCopy(
    Display *display,   /* Identifies the X server        */
    Window  window,     /* Client application's window ID */
    long    item_id);   /* ID of data being copied        */
```

Cancels an ongoing copy (identified by `item_id`) to the clipboard and releases any temporary storage.

XmClipboardCopy

```
int XmClipboardCopy(
    Display *display,        /* Identifies the X server          */
    Window  window,          /* Client application's window ID    */
    long    item_id,         /* ID of data being copied           */
    char    *format name,    /* Format of data in buffer          */
    char    *buffer,     /* Data to be copied to the clipboard */
    unsigned long length,    /* Number of bytes in buffer         */
    int     private_id,  /* Private data stored with item_id   */
    int     *data_id );  /* Returned ID when buffer is NULL    */
```

Copies data in `buffer` to a temporary storage for later transfer to the clipboard. Returns `ClipboardSuccess` if all goes well, or `ClipboardLocked` if the clipboard is in use by another application. You must call `XmClipboardStartCopy` before calling `XmClipboardCopy`.

XmClipboardCopyByName

```
int XmClipboardCopyByName(
    Display *display,   /* Identifies the X server           */
    Window  window,     /* Client application's window ID     */
    int     data_id     /* ID of data item passed by name     */
    char    *buffer,        /* Data copied from this buffer      */
    unsigned long length,   /* Number of bytes in buffer         */
    int     private_id);    /* Private data stored with data_id */
```

Copies a data item passed by name. Returns `ClipboardSuccess` if all goes well or `ClipboardLocked` if the clipboard is being used by another application.

XmClipboardEndCopy

```
int XmClipboardEndCopy(
    Display *display,   /* Identifies the X server        */
    Window  window,     /* Client application's window ID */
    long    item_id);   /* ID of data being copied        */
```

Ends a copy to the clipboard by transferring data from temporary storage to the clipboard. Returns `ClipboardSuccess` if the operation succeeds or `ClipboardLocked` if the clipboard is being used by another application.

XmClipboardEndRetrieve

```
int XmClipboardEndRetrieve(
    Display *display,   /* Identifies the X server        */
    Window  window);    /* Client application's window ID */
```

Ends an incremental copy operation started by `XmClipboardStartRetrieve`. Returns `ClipboardSuccess` if all goes well, or `ClipboardLocked` if the clipboard is being used by another application.

XmClipboardInquireCount

```
int XmClipboardInquireCount(
    Display *display,   /* Identifies the X server          */
    Window  window,     /* Client application's window ID    */
    int     *num_format, /* Returns number of formats        */
    int     *max_length ); /* Returns maximum length of all */
                         /* format names in current item    */
```

On return, the number of formats for the current clipboard item will be in `num_format` and the maximum length of the format names in `max_length`. The function itself returns `ClipboardSuccess` if all goes well, or `ClipboardLocked` if the clipboard is in use by some other application.

XmClipboardInquireFormat

```
int XmClipboardInquireFormat(
    Display *display,   /* Identifies the X server          */
    Window  window,     /* Client application's window ID    */
    int     index,      /* Return format name with this index */
    char    *format_name, /* Format name is returned here    */
    unsigned long format_length, /* Bytes in format_name     */
    unsigned long *copied_length ); /* Bytes returned        */
```

Copies the format name specified by index to the buffer `format_name`, which has room for `format_length` bytes. On return, `*copied_length` is the number of bytes copied into `format_name`. Returns one of the following:

`ClipboardLocked`	if clipboard is locked by another application
`ClipboardNoData`	if the clipboard is empty
`ClipboardSuccess`	if the function succeeds
`ClipboardTruncate`	if `format_name` is not large enough for requested name

XmClipboardInquireLength

```
int XmClipboardInquireLength(
    Display *display,  /* Identifies the X server          */
    Window window,     /* Client application's window ID   */
    char    *format_name,   /* Name of data format         */
    unsigned long *length); /* Returns length of clipboard */
                            /* data item in bytes          */
```

On return, *length will be the length of data in the clipboard whose format is specified by format_name. This function returns one of the following:

ClipboardLocked   if clipboard is locked by another application
ClipboardNoData   if the clipboard is empty
ClipboardSuccess   if the function succeeds

XmClipboardInquirePendingItems

```
int XmClipboardInquirePendingItems(
    Display *display,  /* Identifies the X server          */
    Window window,     /* Client application's window ID   */
    int     index,     /* Return format name with this index */
    char    *format_name, /* Format name is returned here  */
    XmClipboardPendingList *item_list, /* Array where ID of */
                       /* pending data items is returned   */
    unsigned long    *num_item  /* On return, this holds the */
                       /* number of entries in item_list   */
```

Gets a list of pending items—these are data items passed to the clipboard by name, but not requested by any application. This function returns ClipboardSuccess if the function succeeds or ClipboardLocked to indicate that the clipboard is reserved for exclusive use by an application.

XmClipboardLock

```
int XmClipboardLock(
    Display *display,  /* This identifies the X server */
    Window window);    /* This application's window ID */
```

Locks the clipboard to prevent access by other applications. Use XmClipboardUnlock to release the clipboard. The clipboard is automatically locked between calls to XmClipboardStartCopy and XmClipboardEndCopy, as well as to XmClipboardStartRetrieve and XmClipboardEndRetrieve. XmClipboardLock returns ClipboardSuccess if the clipboard is successfully locked. If the clipboard is already locked by another application, this function returns ClipboardLocked.

9

XmClipboardRegisterFormat

```
int XmClipboardRegisterFormat(
    Display *display,      /* This identifies the X server     */
    char    *format_name  /* Name assigned to the new format   */
    unsigned long format_length); /* Length in bits 8,16,or 32 */
```

Registers a new data format with the X server and assigns it a name. This function returns one of the following:

ClipboardBadFormat   if name is NULL or length is not one of
                      8, 16, or 32

ClipboardLocked   if clipboard is locked by another application

ClipboardSuccess   if the function succeeds

XmClipboardRetrieve

```
int XmClipboardRetrieve(
    Display *display,   /* This identifies the X server     */
    Window  window,     /* This application's window ID     */
    char    *format_name, /* Format of clipboard data       */
    char    *buffer,    /* Clipboard data returned here     */
    unsigned long  length,   /* Size of buffer in bytes     */
    unsigned long  *num_bytes, /* On return, bytes copied */
    int     *private_id ); /* Returns private data if any */
```

Retrieves the current data item from the clipboard into buffer. Returns one of the following:

ClipboardLocked   if clipboard is locked by another application

ClipboardNoData   if the clipboard is empty

ClipboardSuccess   if the function succeeds

ClipboardTruncate if buffer is not large enough for requested data

XmClipboardStartCopy

```
int XmClipboardStartCopy(
    Display *display,     /* This identifies the X server */
    Window  window,       /* This application's window ID */
    XmString clip_label,  /* A label to describe the data */
    Time     timestamp,   /* Time of the initiating event */
    Widget   widget,      /* Widget with callback to       */
                          /* handle data passed by name    */
    VoidProc callback,    /* Function to call when          */
                          /* clipboard needs data           */
    long    *item_id);    /* On return, ID of data item    */
```

Sets up temporary storage areas and initializes the data structures to receive clipboard data. You must call this function before copying data to and from the clipboard. On return, item_id will be an identifier for the copy operation. You should use this item_id as argument in calls to functions such as XmClipboardCopy and XmClipboardEndCopy. XmClipboardStartCopy returns ClipboardSuccess if it succeeds or ClipboardLocked to indicate that the clipboard is already in use by another application.

XmClipboardStartRetrieve

```
int XmClipboardStartRetrieve(
    Display *display,    /* This identifies the X server */
    Window  window,      /* This application's window ID */
    Time    timestamp);  /* Time of the initiating event */
```

Locks the clipboard in preparation for data retrieval from the clipboard with a call to XmClipboardRetrieve. Returns ClipboardSuccess if all goes well or ClipboardLocked if the clipboard is already locked by another application.

XmClipboardUndoCopy

```
int XmClipboardUndoCopy(
    Display *display,   /* This identifies the X server */
    Window  window);    /* This application's window ID */
```

Deletes the last item placed in the clipboard. The item must have been placed by an application with the same display and window IDs. This function returns ClipboardSuccess if the undo operation is successful or ClipboardLocked if the clipboard is already in use.

XmClipboardUnlock

```
int XmClipboardUnlock(
    Display *display,        /* This identifies the X server   */
    Window  window,          /* This application's window ID    */
    Boolean unlock_all);     /* If True, all locks are removed */
```

Unlocks the clipboard. Normally each call to XmClipboardLock must be undone with a corresponding call to XmClipboardUnlock. However, a single call to XmClipboardUnlock suffices if you set the unlock_all argument to True.

XmClipboardWithdrawFormat

```
int XmClipboardWithdrawFormat(
    Display *display,   /* This identifies the X server   */
    Window  window,     /* This application's window ID    */
    int     data_id);   /* Identifies data item and format */
```

Sets the internal state of the clipboard to indicate that the application will no longer honor requests for the data identified by data_id. This function returns ClipboardSuccess if all goes well or ClipboardLocked if the clipboard is already in use.

XmCommandAppendValue

```
void XmCommandAppendValue(
    Widget   widget,   /* XmCommand widget affected by this   */
    XmString command); /* Append this string to command line */
```

Appends a string to the string being displayed in the command area of the XmCommand widget.

XmCommandError

```
void XmCommandError(
    Widget   widget,   /* XmCommand widget affected by this */
    XmString error);   /* Error message to be displayed     */
```

Displays the specified error message in the history area of the XmCommand widget.

XmCommandGetChild

```
Widget XmCommandGetChild(
    Widget        widget, /* XmCommand widget being queried */
    unsigned char child); /* Child widget ID to be returned */
```

Returns the widget ID of a child of the XmCommand widget. The child argument specifies the child whose ID is returned. It can take one of the following values: XmDIALOG_COMMAND_TEXT, XmDIALOG_PROMPT_LABEL, or Xm_DIALOG_HISTORY_LIST.

XmCommandSetValue

```
void XmCommandSetValue(
    Widget   widget,   /* Applies to this XmCommand widget */
    XmString command); /* This is the new command string   */
```

Displays command as the new string in the command area of the XmCommand widget.

XmConvertUnits

```
int XmConvertUnits(
    Widget widget,       /* Convert data for this widget */
    int    orientation,  /* XmHORIZONTAL or XmVERTICAL   */
    int    from_unit,    /* Unit of from_value          */
    int    from_value,   /* Data to be converted        */
    int    to_unit);     /* Convert to convert this unit */
```

Converts a value from one unit to another. The from_unit and to_unit arguments can be one of the following: XmPIXELS, Xm100TH_MILLIMETERS, Xm1000TH_INCHES, Xm100TH_POINTS, or Xm100TH_FONT_UNITS. If successful, this function returns the converted value; otherwise, it returns zero.

9

XmCreateArrowButton

```
Widget XmCreateArrowButton(
    Widget    parent,    /* ID of parent widget           */
    String    name,      /* Name of new widget            */
    ArgList   arglist,   /* Array of resource values      */
    Cardinal  nargs);    /* Number of arguments in arglist */
```

Creates an XmArrowButton widget as a child of the widget parent and returns the ID of the newly created widget. Consult the reference entry on the XmArrowButton widget for a list of its resources.

XmCreateArrowButtonGadget

```
Widget XmCreateArrowButtonGadget(
    Widget    parent,    /* ID of parent widget           */
    String    name,      /* Name of new widget            */
    ArgList   arglist,   /* Array of resource values      */
    Cardinal  nargs);    /* Number of arguments in arglist */
```

Creates an XmArrowButtonGadget as a child of the widget parent and returns the ID of the newly created widget. Consult the reference entry on XmArrowButtonGadget for a list of its resources.

XmCreateBulletinBoard

```
Widget XmCreateBulletinBoard(
    Widget    parent,    /* ID of parent widget           */
    String    name,      /* Name of new widget            */
    ArgList   arglist,   /* Array of resource values      */
    Cardinal  nargs);    /* Number of arguments in arglist */
```

Creates an XmBulletinBoard widget as a child of the widget parent and returns the ID of the newly created widget. Consult the reference entry of the XmBulletinBoard widget for a list of its resources.

XmCreateBulletinBoardDialog

```
Widget XmCreateBulletinBoardDialog(
    Widget    parent,    /* ID of parent widget           */
    String    name,      /* Name of new widget            */
    ArgList   arglist,   /* Array of resource values      */
    Cardinal  nargs);    /* Number of arguments in arglist */
```

Creates an XmDialogShell (as a child of parent) and an XmBulletinBoard widget as an unmanaged child of the XmDialogShell widget. This function returns the ID of the XmBulletinBoard widget. You can pop up the dialog by calling XtManage with the XmBulletinBoard's ID as an argument. Consult the reference entry of the XmDialogShell and XmBulletinBoard widgets for a list of their resources.

9

XmCreateCascadeButton

```
Widget XmCreateCascadeButton(
    Widget    parent,    /* ID of parent widget            */
    String    name,      /* Name of new widget             */
    ArgList   arglist,   /* Array of resource values       */
    Cardinal nargs);     /* Number of arguments in arglist */
```

Creates an XmCascadeButton widget as a child of the widget parent and returns the ID of the newly created widget. Consult the reference entry of the XmCascadeButton widget for a list of its resources.

XmCreateCascadeButtonGadget

```
Widget XmCreateCascadeButtonGadget(
    Widget    parent,    /* ID of parent widget            */
    String    name,      /* Name of new widget             */
    ArgList   arglist,   /* Array of resource values       */
    Cardinal nargs);     /* Number of arguments in arglist */
```

Creates an XmCascadeButtonGadget widget as a child of the widget parent and returns the ID of the newly created widget. Consult the reference entry of XmCascadeButtonGadget for a list of its resources.

XmCreateCommand

```
Widget XmCreateCommand(
    Widget    parent,    /* ID of parent widget            */
    String    name,      /* Name of new widget             */
    ArgList   arglist,   /* Array of resource values       */
    Cardinal nargs);     /* Number of arguments in arglist */
```

Creates an XmCommand widget as a child of the widget parent and returns the ID of the newly created widget. Consult the reference entry of the XmCommand widget for a list of its resources.

XmCreateDialogShell

```
Widget XmCreateDialogShell(
    Widget    parent,    /* ID of parent widget            */
    String    name,      /* Name of new widget             */
    ArgList   arglist,   /* Array of resource values       */
    Cardinal nargs);     /* Number of arguments in arglist */
```

Creates an XmDialogShell widget as a child of the widget parent and returns the ID of the newly created widget. Consult the reference entry of the XmDialogShell widget for a list of its resources.

XmCreateDrawButton

```
Widget XmCreateDrawButton(
    Widget   parent,   /* ID of parent widget          */
    String   name,     /* Name of new widget           */
    ArgList  arglist,  /* Array of resource values      */
    Cardinal nargs);   /* Number of arguments in arglist */
```

Creates an XmDrawnButton widget as a child of the widget parent and returns the ID of the newly created widget. Consult the reference entry of the XmDrawnButton widget for a list of its resources.

XmCreateDrawingArea

```
Widget XmCreateDrawingArea(
    Widget   parent,   /* ID of parent widget          */
    String   name,     /* Name of new widget           */
    ArgList  arglist,  /* Array of resource values      */
    Cardinal nargs);   /* Number of arguments in arglist */
```

Creates an XmDrawingArea widget as a child of the widget parent and returns the ID of the newly created widget. Consult the reference entry of the XmDrawingArea widget for a list of its resources.

XmCreateErrorDialog

```
Widget XmCreateErrorDialog(
    Widget   parent,   /* ID of parent widget          */
    String   name,     /* Name of new widget           */
    ArgList  arglist,  /* Array of resource values      */
    Cardinal nargs);   /* Number of arguments in arglist */
```

Creates an XmDialogShell widget (as a child of parent) and an XmMessageBox widget as an unmanaged child of the XmDialogShell widget. This function returns the ID of the XmMessageBox widget. You can pop up the dialog by calling XtManage with the XmMessageBox's ID as argument. The error dialog includes a symbol, a message, and three buttons labeled OK, Cancel, and Help. The default symbol is an octagon with a diagonal slash across it. Consult the reference entry of the XmDialogShell and XmMessageBox widgets for a list of their resources.

XmCreateFileSelectionBox

```
Widget XmCreateFileSelectionBox(
    Widget   parent,   /* ID of parent widget          */
    String   name,     /* Name of new widget           */
    ArgList  arglist,  /* Array of resource values      */
    Cardinal nargs);   /* Number of arguments in arglist */
```

Creates an `XmFileSelectionBox` widget as a child of the widget `parent` and returns the ID of the newly created widget. Consult the reference entry of the `XmFileSelectionBox` widget for a list of its resources.

XmCreateFileSelectionDialog

```
Widget XmCreateFileSelectionDialog(
    Widget    parent,    /* ID of parent widget          */
    String    name,      /* Name of new widget           */
    ArgList   arglist,   /* Array of resource values      */
    Cardinal  nargs);    /* Number of arguments in arglist */
```

Creates an `XmDialogShell` widget (as a child of `parent`) and an `XmFileSelectionBox` widget as an unmanaged child of the `XmDialogShell` widget. This function returns the ID of the `XmFileSelectionBox` widget. You can pop up the dialog by calling `XtManage` with the `XmFileSelectionBox`'s ID as argument. Consult the reference entry of the `XmDialogShell` and `XmFileSelectionBox` widgets for a list of their resources.

XmCreateForm

```
Widget XmCreateForm(
    Widget    parent,    /* ID of parent widget          */
    String    name,      /* Name of new widget           */
    ArgList   arglist,   /* Array of resource values      */
    Cardinal  nargs);    /* Number of arguments in arglist */
```

Creates an `XmForm` widget as a child of the widget `parent` and returns the ID of the newly created widget. Consult the reference entry of the `XmForm` widget for a list of its resources.

XmCreateFormDialog

```
Widget XmCreateFormDialog(
    Widget    parent,    /* ID of parent widget          */
    String    name,      /* Name of new widget           */
    ArgList   arglist,   /* Array of resource values      */
    Cardinal  nargs);    /* Number of arguments in arglist */
```

Creates an `XmDialogShell` widget (as a child of `parent`) and an `XmForm` widget as an unmanaged child of the `XmDialogShell` widget. This function returns the ID of the `XmForm` widget. You can pop up the dialog by calling `XtManage` with the `XmForm`'s ID as argument. Consult the reference entry of the `XmDialogShell` and `XmForm` widgets for a list of their resources.

XmCreateFrame

```
Widget XmCreateFrame(
    Widget    parent,    /* ID of parent widget           */
    String    name,      /* Name of new widget            */
    ArgList   arglist,   /* Array of resource values      */
    Cardinal nargs);     /* Number of arguments in arglist */
```

Creates an XmFrame widget as a child of the widget parent and returns the ID of the newly created widget. Consult the reference entry of the XmFrame widget for a list of its resources.

XmCreateInformationDialog

```
Widget XmCreateInformationDialog(
    Widget    parent,    /* ID of parent widget           */
    String    name,      /* Name of new widget            */
    ArgList   arglist,   /* Array of resource values      */
    Cardinal nargs);     /* Number of arguments in arglist */
```

Creates an XmDialogShell widget (as a child of parent) and an XmMessageBox widget as an unmanaged child of the XmDialogShell widget. This function returns the ID of the XmMessageBox widget. You can pop up the dialog by calling XtManage with the XmMessageBox's ID as argument. The information dialog includes a symbol, a message, and three buttons labeled OK, Cancel, and Help. The default symbol is a lowercase *i*. Consult the reference entry of the XmDialogShell and XmMessageBox widgets for a list of their resources.

XmCreateLabel

```
Widget XmCreateLabel(
    Widget    parent,    /* ID of parent widget           */
    String    name,      /* Name of new widget            */
    ArgList   arglist,   /* Array of resource values      */
    Cardinal nargs);     /* Number of arguments in arglist */
```

Creates an XmLabel widget as a child of parent and returns the ID of the newly created widget. Consult the reference entry of the XmLabel widget for a list of its resources.

XmCreateLabelGadget

```
Widget XmCreateLabelGadget(
    Widget    parent,    /* ID of parent widget           */
    String    name,      /* Name of new widget            */
    ArgList   arglist,   /* Array of resource values      */
    Cardinal nargs);     /* Number of arguments in arglist */
```

Creates an XmLabelGadget widget as a child of parent and returns the ID of the newly created widget. Consult the reference entry of XmLabelGadget for a list of its resources.

XmCreateList

```
Widget XmCreateList(
    Widget   parent,    /* ID of parent widget        */
    String   name,      /* Name of new widget         */
    ArgList  arglist,   /* Array of resource values   */
    Cardinal nargs);    /* Number of arguments in arglist */
```

Creates an XmList widget as a child of parent and returns the ID of the newly created widget. Consult the reference entry of the XmList widget for a list of its resources.

XmCreateMainWindow

```
Widget XmCreateMainWindow(
    Widget   parent,    /* ID of parent widget        */
    String   name,      /* Name of new widget         */
    ArgList  arglist,   /* Array of resource values   */
    Cardinal nargs);    /* Number of arguments in arglist */
```

Creates an XmMainWindow widget as a child of parent and returns the ID of the newly created widget. Consult the reference entry of the XmMainWindow widget for a list of its resources.

XmCreateMenuBar

```
Widget XmCreateMenuBar(
    Widget   parent,    /* ID of parent widget        */
    String   name,      /* Name of new widget         */
    ArgList  arglist,   /* Array of resource values   */
    Cardinal nargs);    /* Number of arguments in arglist */
```

Creates an XmRowColumn widget of type XmMENUBAR as a child of parent and returns the ID of the newly created widget. The newly created widget will only accept child widgets of type XmCascadeButton (or a subclass of XmCascadeButton). You can construct pull-down menus by inserting XmCascadeButtons as children of the menu bar. Consult the reference entry of the XmRowColumn widget for a list of its resources.

XmCreateMenuShell

```
Widget XmCreateMenuShell(
    Widget   parent,    /* ID of parent widget        */
    String   name,      /* Name of new widget         */
    ArgList  arglist,   /* Array of resource values   */
    Cardinal nargs);    /* Number of arguments in arglist */
```

Creates an XmMenuShell widget as a child of parent and returns the ID of the newly created widget. Consult the reference entry of the XmMenuShell widget for a list of its resources.

9

XmCreateMessageBox

```
Widget XmCreateMessageBox(
    Widget    parent,     /* ID of parent widget           */
    String    name,       /* Name of new widget            */
    ArgList   arglist,    /* Array of resource values       */
    Cardinal  nargs);     /* Number of arguments in arglist */
```

Creates an XmMessageBox widget as a child of parent and returns the ID of the newly created widget. The XmMessageBox widget includes a symbol, a message, and three push buttons whose default labels are OK, Cancel, and Help. By default, the message box does not have any symbol. Consult the reference entry of the XmMessageBox widget for a complete list of its resources.

XmCreateMessageDialog

```
Widget XmCreateMessageDialog(
    Widget    parent,     /* ID of parent widget           */
    String    name,       /* Name of new widget            */
    ArgList   arglist,    /* Array of resource values       */
    Cardinal  nargs);     /* Number of arguments in arglist */
```

Creates an XmDialogShell widget (as a child of parent) and an XmMessageBox widget as an unmanaged child of the XmDialogShell widget. This function returns the ID of the XmMessageBox widget. You can pop up the dialog by calling XtManage with the XmMessageBox's ID as argument. Consult the reference entry of the XmDialogShell and XmMessageBox widgets for a list of their resources.

XmCreateOptionMenu

```
Widget XmCreateOptionMenu(
    Widget    parent,     /* ID of parent widget           */
    String    name,       /* Name of new widget            */
    ArgList   arglist,    /* Array of resource values       */
    Cardinal  nargs);     /* Number of arguments in arglist */
```

Creates an XmRowColumn widget of type XmMENU_OPTION as a child of parent and returns the ID of the newly created widget. Consult the reference entry of the XmRowColumn widget for a list of its resources.

XmCreatePanedWindow

```
Widget XmCreatePanedWindow(
    Widget    parent,     /* ID of parent widget           */
    String    name,       /* Name of new widget            */
    ArgList   arglist,    /* Array of resource values       */
    Cardinal  nargs);     /* Number of arguments in arglist */
```

Creates an XmPanedWindow widget as a child of parent and returns the ID of the newly created widget. Consult the reference entry of the XmPanedWindow widget for a list of its resources.

9

XmCreatePopupMenu

```
Widget XmCreatePopupMenu(
    Widget    parent,    /* ID of parent widget           */
    String    name,      /* Name of new widget            */
    ArgList   arglist,   /* Array of resource values       */
    Cardinal  nargs);    /* Number of arguments in arglist */
```

Creates an XmMenuShell widget (as a child of parent) and an XmRowColumn widget of type XmMENU_POPUP as an unmanaged child of the XmMenuShell widget. This function returns the ID of the XmRowColumn widget. You can use the pop-up menu by first positioning it with the XmMenuPosition function and then managing the menu by calling XtManage with the XmRowColumn's ID as argument. Consult the reference entry of the XmRowColumn widget for a list of its resources.

XmCreatePromptDialog

```
Widget XmCreatePromptDialog(
    Widget    parent,    /* ID of parent widget           */
    String    name,      /* Name of new widget            */
    ArgList   arglist,   /* Array of resource values       */
    Cardinal  nargs);    /* Number of arguments in arglist */
```

Creates an XmDialogShell widget (as a child of parent) and an XmSelectionBox widget as an unmanaged child of the XmDialogShell widget. This function returns the ID of the XmSelectionBox widget. You can pop up the dialog by calling XtManage with the XmSelectionBox's ID as argument. Consult the reference entry of the XmDialogShell and XmSelectionBox widgets for a list of their resources.

XmCreatePulldownMenu

```
Widget XmCreatePulldownMenu(
    Widget    parent,    /* ID of parent widget           */
    String    name,      /* Name of new widget            */
    ArgList   arglist,   /* Array of resource values       */
    Cardinal  nargs);    /* Number of arguments in arglist */
```

Creates an XmMenuShell widget (as a child of parent) and an XmRowColumn widget of type XmMENU_PULLDOWN as an unmanaged child of the XmMenuShell widget. This function returns the ID of the XmRowColumn widget. Consult the reference entry of the XmRowColumn widget for a list of its resources.

XmCreatePushButton

```
Widget XmCreatePushButton(
    Widget    parent,    /* ID of parent widget           */
    String    name,      /* Name of new widget            */
    ArgList   arglist,   /* Array of resource values       */
    Cardinal  nargs);    /* Number of arguments in arglist */
```

Creates an XmPushButton widget as a child of parent and returns the ID of the newly created widget. Consult the reference entry of the XmPushButton widget for a list of its resources.

XmCreatePushButtonGadget

```
Widget XmCreatePushButtonGadget(
    Widget    parent,    /* ID of parent widget            */
    String    name,      /* Name of new widget             */
    ArgList   arglist,   /* Array of resource values        */
    Cardinal  nargs);    /* Number of arguments in arglist */
```

Creates an XmPushButtonGadget widget as a child of parent and returns the ID of the newly created widget. Consult the reference entry of XmPushButtonGadget for a list of its resources.

XmCreateQuestionDialog

```
Widget XmCreateQuestionDialog(
    Widget    parent,    /* ID of parent widget            */
    String    name,      /* Name of new widget             */
    ArgList   arglist,   /* Array of resource values        */
    Cardinal  nargs);    /* Number of arguments in arglist */
```

Creates an XmDialogShell widget (as a child of parent) and an XmMessageBox widget as an unmanaged child of the XmDialogShell widget. This function returns the ID of the XmMessageBox widget. You can pop up the dialog by calling XtManage with the XmMessageBox's ID as argument. The question dialog includes a symbol, a message, and three buttons labeled OK, Cancel, and Help. The default symbol is a question mark. Consult the reference entry of the XmDialogShell and XmMessageBox widgets for a list of their resources.

XmCreateRadioBox

```
Widget XmCreateRadioBox(
    Widget    parent,    /* ID of parent widget            */
    String    name,      /* Name of new widget             */
    ArgList   arglist,   /* Array of resource values        */
    Cardinal  nargs);    /* Number of arguments in arglist */
```

Creates an XmRowColumn widget of type XmWORK_AREA as a child of parent and returns the ID of the newly created widget. You would typically place a number of toggle buttons inside this XmRowColumn widget and use it as a "radio menu" to allow a selection from a set of choices. Consult the reference entry of the XmRowColumn widget for a list of its resources.

9

XmCreateRowColumn

```
Widget XmCreateRowColumn(
    Widget    parent,    /* ID of parent widget        */
    String    name,      /* Name of new widget         */
    ArgList   arglist,   /* Array of resource values   */
    Cardinal  nargs);    /* Number of arguments in arglist */
```

Creates an XmRowColumn widget as a child of parent and returns the ID of the newly created widget. The XmNrowColumnType resource specifies the type of XmRowColumn widget you want to create. If the XmNrowColumnType resource is unspecified, it will be of type XmWORK_AREA by default. Consult the reference entry of the XmRowColumn widget for a complete list of its resources.

XmCreateScale

```
Widget XmCreateScale(
    Widget    parent,    /* ID of parent widget        */
    String    name,      /* Name of new widget         */
    ArgList   arglist,   /* Array of resource values   */
    Cardinal  nargs);    /* Number of arguments in arglist */
```

Creates an XmScale widget as a child of parent and returns the ID of the newly created widget. Consult the reference entry of the XmScale widget for a list of its resources.

XmCreateScrollBar

```
Widget XmCreateScrollBar(
    Widget    parent,    /* ID of parent widget        */
    String    name,      /* Name of new widget         */
    ArgList   arglist,   /* Array of resource values   */
    Cardinal  nargs);    /* Number of arguments in arglist */
```

Creates an XmScrollbar widget as a child of parent and returns the ID of the newly created widget. Consult the reference entry of the XmScrollbar widget for a list of its resources.

XmCreateScrolledList

```
Widget XmCreateScrolledList(
    Widget    parent,    /* ID of parent widget        */
    String    name,      /* Name of new widget         */
    ArgList   arglist,   /* Array of resource values   */
    Cardinal  nargs);    /* Number of arguments in arglist */
```

Creates an XmScrolledWindow widget (as a child of parent) and an XmList widget as an unmanaged child of the XmScrolledWindow widget. This function returns the ID of the XmList widget. You can get the ID of the XmScrolledWindow by using the XtParent function with the XmList widget's ID as argument. Consult

9

the reference entry of the XmScrolledWindow and XmList widgets for a list of their resources.

XmCreateScrolledText

```
Widget XmCreateScrolledText(
    Widget   parent,    /* ID of parent widget            */
    String   name,      /* Name of new widget             */
    ArgList  arglist,   /* Array of resource values        */
    Cardinal nargs);    /* Number of arguments in arglist */
```

Creates an XmScrolledWindow widget (as a child of parent) and an XmText widget as an unmanaged child of the XmScrolledWindow widget. This function returns the ID of the XmText widget. You can get the ID of the XmScrolledWindow by using the XtParent function with the XmText widget's ID as argument. Consult the reference entry of the XmScrolledWindow and XmText widgets for a list of their resources.

XmCreateScrolledWindow

```
Widget XmCreateScrolledWindow(
    Widget   parent,    /* ID of parent widget            */
    String   name,      /* Name of new widget             */
    ArgList  arglist,   /* Array of resource values        */
    Cardinal nargs);    /* Number of arguments in arglist */
```

Creates an XmScrolledWindow widget as a child of parent and returns the ID of the newly created widget. Consult the reference entry of the XmScrolledWindow widget for a list of its resources.

XmCreateSelectionBox

```
Widget XmCreateSelectionBox(
    Widget   parent,    /* ID of parent widget            */
    String   name,      /* Name of new widget             */
    ArgList  arglist,   /* Array of resource values        */
    Cardinal nargs);    /* Number of arguments in arglist */
```

Creates an XmSelectionBox widget as a child of parent and returns the ID of the newly created widget. Consult the reference entry of the XmSelectionBox widget for a list of its resources.

XmCreateSelectionDialog

```
Widget XmCreateSelectionDialog(
    Widget   parent,    /* ID of parent widget            */
    String   name,      /* Name of new widget             */
    ArgList  arglist,   /* Array of resource values        */
    Cardinal nargs);    /* Number of arguments in arglist */
```

Creates an `XmDialogShell` widget (as a child of `parent`) and an `XmSelectionBox` widget as an unmanaged child of the `XmDialogShell` widget. This function returns the ID of the `XmSelectionBox` widget. You can pop up the dialog by calling `XtManage` with the `XmSelectionBox`'s ID as argument. Consult the reference entry of the `XmDialogShell` and `XmSelectionBox` widgets for a list of their resources.

XmCreateSeparator

```
Widget XmCreateSeparator(
    Widget   parent,    /* ID of parent widget         */
    String   name,      /* Name of new widget          */
    ArgList  arglist,   /* Array of resource values    */
    Cardinal nargs);    /* Number of arguments in arglist */
```

Creates an `XmSeparator` widget as a child of `parent` and returns the ID of the newly created widget. Consult the reference entry of the `XmSeparator` widget for a list of its resources.

XmCreateSeparatorGadget

```
Widget XmCreateSeparatorGadget(
    Widget   parent,    /* ID of parent widget         */
    String   name,      /* Name of new widget          */
    ArgList  arglist,   /* Array of resource values    */
    Cardinal nargs);    /* Number of arguments in arglist */
```

Creates an `XmSeparatorGadget` widget as a child of `parent` and returns the ID of the newly created widget. Consult the reference entry of `XmSeparatorGadget` for a list of its resources.

XmCreateSimpleCheckBox

```
Widget XmCreateSimpleCheckBox(
    Widget   parent,    /* ID of parent widget         */
    String   name,      /* Name of new widget          */
    ArgList  arglist,   /* Array of resource values    */
    Cardinal nargs);    /* Number of arguments in arglist */
```

Creates an `XmRowColumn` widget of type `XmWORK_AREA` as a child of `parent` and returns the ID of the newly created widget. This function also creates a number of `XmToggleButtonGadgets`, which you specify through the list of resources `arglist`. More specifically, you have to specify the following resources of the `XmRowColumn` widget: `XmNbuttons`, `XmNbuttonCount`, `XmNbuttonSet`, and `XmNsimpleCallback`. Additionally, this function sets the `XmNradioAlwaysOne` resource to `False`.

XmCreateSimpleMenuBar

```
Widget XmCreateSimpleMenuBar(
    Widget    parent,    /* ID of parent widget           */
    String    name,      /* Name of new widget            */
    ArgList   arglist,   /* Array of resource values      */
    Cardinal  nargs);    /* Number of arguments in arglist */
```

Creates an XmRowColumn widget of type XmMENU_BAR as a child of parent and returns the ID of the newly created widget. This function also creates a number of buttons whose style and callbacks you specify through the list of resources in arglist. More specifically, you have to specify the following resources of the XmRowColumn widget: XmNbuttonAccelerators, XmNbuttonAcceleratorText, XmNbuttonMnemonics, XmNbuttonMnemonicCharSets, XmNbuttons, XmNbuttonType, XmNbuttonCount, XmNbuttonSet, and XmNsimpleCallback.

XmCreateSimpleOptionMenu

```
Widget XmCreateSimpleOptionMenu(
    Widget    parent,    /* ID of parent widget           */
    String    name,      /* Name of new widget            */
    ArgList   arglist,   /* Array of resource values      */
    Cardinal  nargs);    /* Number of arguments in arglist */
```

Creates an XmRowColumn widget of type XmMENU_OPTION as a child of parent and returns the ID of the newly created widget. This function also creates a submenu with a number of XmPushButtonGadget children. To create the option menu, you have to specify the following resources of the XmRowColumn widget: XmNbuttonAccelerators, XmNbuttonAcceleratorText, XmNbuttonMnemonics, XmNbuttonMnemonicCharSets, XmNbuttons, XmNbuttonType, XmNbuttonCount, XmNbuttonSet, and XmNsimpleCallback. Additionally, you can use the XmNoptionLabel to set the label to be displayed to the left hand side of the option menu.

XmCreateSimplePopupMenu

```
Widget XmCreateSimplePopupMenu(
    Widget    parent,    /* ID of parent widget           */
    String    name,      /* Name of new widget            */
    ArgList   arglist,   /* Array of resource values      */
    Cardinal  nargs);    /* Number of arguments in arglist */
```

Creates an XmRowColumn widget of type XmMENU_POPUP as a child of parent and returns the ID of the newly created widget. This function also creates a number of buttons as children. You have to specify the button's parameters through the resources in arglist.

XmCreateSimplePulldownMenu

```
Widget XmCreateSimplePulldownMenu(
    Widget    parent,    /* ID of parent widget            */
    String    name,      /* Name of new widget             */
    ArgList   arglist,   /* Array of resource values       */
    Cardinal  nargs);    /* Number of arguments in arglist */
```

Creates an XmRowColumn widget of type XmMENU_PULLDOWN as a child of parent and returns the ID of the newly created widget. This function also creates a number of buttons as children. You have to specify the button's parameters through the resources in arglist. Additionally, you can attach the newly created pulldown menu to an XmCascadeButton or an XmCascadeButtonGadget whose ID you provide in the XmNpostFromButton resource of the XmRowColumn widget.

XmCreateSimpleRadioBox

```
Widget XmCreateSimpleRadioBox(
    Widget    parent,    /* ID of parent widget            */
    String    name,      /* Name of new widget             */
    ArgList   arglist,   /* Array of resource values       */
    Cardinal  nargs);    /* Number of arguments in arglist */
```

Creates an XmRowColumn widget of type XmWORK_AREA as a child of parent and returns the ID of the newly created widget. This function also creates a number of XmToggleButtonGadgets as children. You have to specify the toggle buttons through the resources in arglist.

XmCreateSimpleWorkArea

```
Widget XmCreateSimpleWorkArea(
    Widget    parent,    /* ID of parent widget            */
    String    name,      /* Name of new widget             */
    ArgList   arglist,   /* Array of resource values       */
    Cardinal  nargs);    /* Number of arguments in arglist */
```

Creates an XmRowColumn widget of type XmWORK_AREA as a child of parent and returns the ID of the newly created widget. This function also creates a number of XmPushButtonGadgets as children. You have to specify the push buttons through the resources in arglist.

XmCreateText

```
Widget XmCreateText(
    Widget    parent,    /* ID of parent widget            */
    String    name,      /* Name of new widget             */
    ArgList   arglist,   /* Array of resource values       */
    Cardinal  nargs);    /* Number of arguments in arglist */
```

9

Creates an XmText widget as a child of parent and returns the ID of the newly created widget. Consult the reference entry of the XmText widget for a list of its resources.

XmCreateTextField

```
Widget XmCreateTextField(
    Widget   parent,    /* ID of parent widget            */
    String   name,      /* Name of new widget             */
    ArgList  arglist,   /* Array of resource values       */
    Cardinal nargs);    /* Number of arguments in arglist */
```

Creates an XmTextField widget as a child of parent and returns the ID of the newly created widget. Consult the reference entry of the XmTextField widget for a list of its resources.

XmCreateToggleButton

```
Widget XmCreateToggleButton(
    Widget   parent,    /* ID of parent widget            */
    String   name,      /* Name of new widget             */
    ArgList  arglist,   /* Array of resource values       */
    Cardinal nargs);    /* Number of arguments in arglist */
```

Creates an XmToggleButton widget as a child of parent and returns the ID of the newly created widget. Consult the reference entry of the XmToggleButton widget for a list of its resources.

XmCreateToggleButtonGadget

```
Widget XmCreateToggleButtonGadget(
    Widget   parent,    /* ID of parent widget            */
    String   name,      /* Name of new widget             */
    ArgList  arglist,   /* Array of resource values       */
    Cardinal nargs);    /* Number of arguments in arglist */
```

Creates an XmToggleButtonGadget widget as a child of parent and returns the ID of the newly created widget. Consult the reference entry of XmToggleButtonGadget for a list of its resources.

XmCreateWarningDialog

```
Widget XmCreateWarningDialog(
    Widget   parent,    /* ID of parent widget            */
    String   name,      /* Name of new widget             */
    ArgList  arglist,   /* Array of resource values       */
    Cardinal nargs);    /* Number of arguments in arglist */
```

Creates an XmDialogShell widget (as a child of parent) and an XmMessageBox widget as an unmanaged child of the XmDialogShell widget. This function returns the ID of the XmMessageBox widget. You can pop up the dialog by calling

XtManage with the XmMessageBox's ID as argument. The warning dialog includes a symbol, a message, and three buttons labeled OK, Cancel, and Help. The default symbol is an exclamation mark. Consult the reference entry of the XmDialogShell and XmMessageBox widgets for a list of their resources.

XmCreateWorkArea

```
Widget XmCreateWorkArea(
    Widget    parent,   /* ID of parent widget         */
    String    name,     /* Name of new widget          */
    ArgList   arglist,  /* Array of resource values     */
    Cardinal  nargs);   /* Number of arguments in arglist */
```

Creates an XmRowColumn widget of type XmWORK_AREA as a child of parent and returns the ID of the newly created widget. You can achieve the same effect by calling XmCreateRowColumn with the XmNrowColumnType resource set to XmWORK_AREA.

XmCreateWorkingDialog

```
Widget XmCreateWorkingDialog(
    Widget    parent,   /* ID of parent widget         */
    String    name,     /* Name of new widget          */
    ArgList   arglist,  /* Array of resource values     */
    Cardinal  nargs);   /* Number of arguments in arglist */
```

Creates an XmDialogShell widget (as a child of parent) and an XmMessageBox widget as an unmanaged child of the XmDialogShell widget. This function returns the ID of the XmMessageBox widget. You can pop up the dialog by calling XtManage with the XmMessageBox's ID as argument. The working dialog includes a symbol, a message, and three buttons labeled OK, Cancel, and Help. The default symbol is an hourglass. Consult the reference entry of the XmDialogShell and XmMessageBox widgets for a list of their resources.

XmCvtCTToXmString

```
XmString XmCvtCTToXmString(
    char *text);         /* Convert this compound text */
```

Converts the specified compound text to an XmString type and returns the converted XmString.

XmCvtStringToUnitType

```
void XmCvtStringToUnitType(
    XmValuePtr  args,     /* Arguments to the converter  */
    Cardinal    nargs),   /* Number of arguments in args */
    XrmValue    *from,    /* Convert from this value and */
    XrmValue    *to);     /* return converted value here */
```

Converts a string to a unit type. You would not call this function directly; instead, install `XmCvtStringToUnitType` as a converter by calling the Xt Intrinsics function `XtAddConverter`.

XmCvtXmStringToCT

```
char* XmCvtXmStringToCT(
    XmString string);   /* Convert this to compound text */
```

Converts an `XmString` to a compound text and returns the resulting compound text.

XmDeactivateProtocol

```
void XmDeactivateProtocol(
    Widget shell,       /* Protocol is for this widget  */
    Atom    property,   /* Property containing protocol */
    Atom    protocol ); /* Protocol to be deactivated   */
```

Removes `protocol` from the specified `property` of the `shell`. Used for inter-client communications. (Consult a book on X Window System programming for more information on properties and atoms.)

XmDeactivateWMPProtocol

```
void XmDeactivateWMPProtocol(
    Widget shell,       /* Protocol is for this widget  */
    Atom    protocol);  /* Protocol to be activated     */
```

Calls `XmDeactivateProtocol` with property set to the atom returned by interning `WM_PROTOCOLS`.

XmDestroyPixmap

```
Boolean XmDestroyPixmap(
    Screen *screen,     /* Screen for which pixmap was cached */
    Pixmap pixmap);     /* Pixmap to be removed from cache    */
```

Removes the specified pixmap from Motif's pixmap cache. Returns `True` if all goes well or `False` if no such pixmap exists for the specified `Screen`.

XmFileSelectionBoxGetChild

```
Widget XmFileSelectionBoxGetChild(
    Widget widget, /* Query this FileSelectionBox widget */
    unsigned char child); /* Identifies the child whose  */
                          /* widget ID will be returned  */
```

Returns the ID of a child widget of an `XmFileSelectionBox` widget. You specify the child widget by setting the `child` argument to one of the following:

XmDIALOG_APPLY_BUTTON, XmDIALOG_CANCEL_BUTTON, XmDIALOG_DEFAULT_BUTTON, XmDIALOG_FILTER_LABEL, XmDIALOG_FILTER_TEXT, XmDIALOG_HELP_BUTTON, XmDIALOG_LIST, XmDIALOG_LIST_LABEL, XmDIALOG_OK_BUTTON, XmDIALOG_SELECTION_LABEL, or XmDIALOG_TEXT.

XmFileSelectionDoSearch

```
void XmFileSelectionDoSearch(
    Widget   widget, /* Affects this FileSelectionBox widget */
    XmString dirmask); /* New directory mask                  */
```

Copies the XmString dirmask into the XmNdirMask resource of the specified XmFileSelectionBox widget and updates the list of files to reflect the new directory search attribute. Nothing happens if dirmask is NULL.

XmFontListAdd

```
XmFontList XmFontListAdd(
    XmFontList      flist,   /* Add font to this list    */
    XFontStruct     *font,   /* Font being added to list */
    XmStringCharSet charset); /* Character set of the font */
```

Creates and returns a new font list by adding the specified font to an existing font list (flist). You can use the constant XmSTRING_DEFAULT_CHARSET for the charset argument.

XmFontListCreate

```
XmFontList XmFontListCreate(
    XFontStruct     *font,   /* Font used to create new list */
    XmStringCharSet charset); /* Character set of the font    */
```

Creates a new font list that contains the specified font. Returns the resulting XmFontList.

XmFontListFree

```
void XmFontListFree(
    XmFontList  flist); /* Font list to be freed */
```

Deallocates memory being used by the specified font list.

XmGetAtomName

```
String XmGetAtomName(
    Display *display,  /* Identifies the X server        */
    Atom    *atom);    /* Atom whose name will be returned */
```

Returns a string containing the name of a specified atom.

XmGetColors

```
XmColorData *XmGetColors(
    Screen   *screen,      /* Allocate colors for this screen */
    Colormap colormap,     /* Allocate from this colormap     */
    Pixel    background);  /* Based on this background color   */
```

Returns a pointer to an XmColorData structure that contains a reasonable set of foreground, background, and shadow colors for the specified screen, colormap, and background.

XmGetMenuCursor

```
Cursor XmGetMenuCursor(
    Display *display); /* Identifies the X server */
```

Returns the ID of the current menu cursor for the specified display. If the menu cursor is undefined, XmGetMenuCursor returns None.

XmGetPixmap

```
Pixmap XmGetPixmap(
    Screen *screen,       /* Locate pixmap for this screen   */
    char   *bm_name,      /* Bitmap name (cached or filename) */
    Pixel  foreground);   /* Foreground color for pixmap      */
    Pixel  background);   /* Background color for pixmap      */
```

Uses bm_name as the name of a bitmap to be used as the basis of a pixmap. If the pixmap already exists in Motif's pixmap cache, this function returns the Pixmap identifier. Otherwise, XmGetPixmap looks for a bitmap file using bm_name as the name. It searches for this file in the directories listed in the XBMLANGPATH environment variable. If XmGetPixmap cannot find the bitmap file and the pixmap is not in the cache, the function returns XmUNSPECIFIED_PIXMAP.

XmGetPostedFromWidget

```
Widget XmGetPostedFromWidget(
    Widget menu);         /* Menu (XmRowColumn) widget's ID */
```

Returns the ID of the widget that had posted the specified menu (a menu is created out of an XmRowColumn widget).

XmInstallImage

```
Boolean XmInstallImage(
    XImage *image,        /* Install this image             */
    char   *image_name);  /* Assign this name to the image */
```

Stores image in an image cache for later use in generating a pixmap. You can use image_name to refer to a pixmap based on this image. There are eight predefined images in Motif. You can refer to these images with the following names:

background	Solid background
25_foreground	25% foreground and 75% background
50_foreground	50% foreground and 50% background
75_foreground	75% foreground and 25% background
horizontal	Horizontal lines of alternating colors
vertical	Vertical lines of alternating colors
slant_left	Slanting lines of alternating colors
slant_right	Slanting lines of alternating colors

The XmInstallImage function returns True if it successfully installs the image or False if the image argument is NULL or if an image with the same name already exists in the image cache.

XmInternAtom

```
Atom XmInternAtom(
    Display *display,    /*Identifies the X server    */
    String  name,        /* Return atom of this name  */
    Boolean if_exists);  /* False = create atom if it */
                         /* does not already exist    */
```

Returns an atom corresponding to a specified name. If the atom does not exist, it is created only if the if_exists argument is False. If if_exists is True and the atom does not already exist, XmInternAtom will return None.

XmIsMotifWMRunning

```
Boolean XmIsMotifWMRunning(
    Widget shell); /* Is mwm running on this widget's screen? */
```

Returns True if the Motif Window Manager (mwm) is running on the screen where the specified shell widget appears.

XmListAddItem

```
void XmListAddItem(
    Widget   widget,      /* Add item to this XmList widget */
    XmString item,        /* Item being added to the list   */
    int      position);   /* Position where item is added   */
```

Adds an item to a specified XmList widget. The position indicates where the item is added. The position numbers start at 1 (for the first position). If position is zero, the item is added at the end of the list. If item matches an entry in the XmNselectedItems resource, item will appear as selected (in "reverse video" with the foreground and background colors swapped).

XmListAddItems

```
void XmListAddItems(
    Widget   widget,      /* Add items to this XmList widget */
    XmString *item_list,  /* Items being added to the list    */
    int      nitems,      /* Number of items in item_list     */
    int      position);   /* Position where items are added   */
```

Adds an array of items to a specified XmList widget. The position indicates where the items are added. The position starts at 1 (for the first position). If position is zero, the item is added at the end of the list.

XmListAddItemUnselected

```
void XmListAddItemUnselected(
    Widget   widget,      /* Add item to this XmList widget */
    XmString item,        /* Item being added to the list    */
    int      position);   /* Position where item is added    */
```

This function works like XmListAddItem, except that item will not appear selected.

XmListDeleteAllItems

```
void XmListDeleteAllItems(
    Widget   widget); /* Delete items from this XmList widget */
```

Deletes all items from the specified XmList widget.

XmListDeleteItem

```
void XmListDeleteItem(
    Widget   widget, /* Delete item from this XmList widget */
    XmString item);  /* Item being deleted from the list    */
```

Deletes an item from the specified XmList widget.

XmListDeleteItems

```
void XmListDeleteItems(
    Widget   widget,  /* Delete items from this XmList widget */
    XmString *items,  /* Items being deleted from the list    */
    int      nitems); /* Number of items in items array       */
```

Deletes an array of items from the specified XmList widget.

XmListDeleteItemsPos

```
void XmListDeleteItemsPos(
    Widget   widget, /* Delete items from this XmList widget */
    int      nitems, /* Number of items to delete            */
    int      pos);   /* Delete starting at this position     */
```

Deletes nitems items from the specified XmList widget starting with the item at position pos. Deletes only up to the end of the list.

XmListDeletePos

```
void XmListDeletePos(
    Widget    widget, /* Delete item from this XmList widget */
    int       pos);   /* Delete item at this position        */
```

Deletes the item at position pos from the specified XmList widget. If pos is zero, XmListDeletePos removes the last item in the list.

XmListDeselectAllItems

```
void XmListDeselectAllItems(
    Widget widget); /* Deselect all items from this widget */
```

Unhighlights all items in the specified XmList widget and removes them from the widget's list of selected items.

XmListDeselectItem

```
void XmListDeselectItem(
    Widget    widget, /* Deselect an item from this widget */
    XmString  item);  /* Item being deselected             */
```

Unhighlights an item from an XmList widget and removes the item from the widget's list of selected items.

XmListDeselectPos

```
void XmListDeselectPos(
    Widget    widget, /* Deselect item from this widget */
    int       pos);   /* Deselect item at this position */
```

Unhighlights the item at position pos from the specified XmList widget. If pos is zero, XmListDeletePos unhighlights the last item in the list. The deselected item is also removed from the XmList widget's list of selected items.

XmListGetMatchPos

```
Boolean XmListGetMatchPos(
    Widget    widget,  /* Search this XmList widget       */
    XmString  item,    /* Look for this item             */
    int       **pos,   /* Array of positions returned    */
    int       *count); /* Number of values in pos array  */
```

On return, the array pos will contain the positions where item was found in the currently selected items in the XmList widget. The number of matching items is returned in the variable whose address is in the last argument (count). The function returns True if the XmList has one or more selected items; otherwise, it returns False.

XmListGetSelectedPos

```
Boolean XmListGetSelectedPos(
    Widget   widget,  /* Query this XmList widget     */
    int      **pos,   /* Array of positions returned  */
    int      *count); /* Number of values in pos array */
```

On return, the array pos will have the positions of all currently selected items in the specified XmList widget. The variable count will contain the number of selected items. The function returns True if the XmList has one or more selected items; otherwise, it returns False.

XmListItemExists

```
Boolean XmListItemExists(
    Widget   widget, /* Check for item in this XmList widget */
    XmString item);  /* Check if this item exists           */
```

Returns True if item exists in the specified XmList widget and False if it does not.

XmListItemPos

```
int XmListItemPos(
    Widget   widget, /* Find position of item in this widget */
    XmString item);  /* Return position of this item         */
```

Returns the position of item in the XmList widget.

XmListReplaceItems

```
void XmListReplaceItems(
    Widget   widget,   /* Replace items in this widget    */
    XmString *oitems,  /* List of items to be replaced    */
    int      numitems, /* Number of items to be replaced  */
    XmString *nitems); /* List of replacement items       */
```

Replaces each item in oitems with a corresponding item in nitems.

XmListReplaceItemsPos

```
void XmListReplaceItemsPos(
    Widget   widget,  /* Replace items in this widget    */
    XmString *items,  /* List of replacement items       */
    int      nitems,  /* Number of items to be replaced  */
    int      pos);    /* Start replacing at this position */
```

Replaces items in the XmList widget starting at the position pos with items from the items array.

XmListSelectItems

```
void XmListSelectItems(
    Widget    widget,   /* Select item from this widget */
    XmString  item,     /* Highlight this item          */
    Boolean   notify);  /* True = selection callback    */
```

Highlights item in the specified XmList widget and adds it to the widget's list of selected items. If notify is True, a selection callback is generated.

XmListSelectPos

```
void XmListSelectPos(
    Widget    widget,   /* Select item from this widget   */
    int       pos,      /* Highlight item at this position */
    Boolean   notify);  /* True = selection callback       */
```

Highlights the item at position pos in the specified XmList widget and adds it to the widget's list of selected items. If notify is True, a selection callback is generated.

XmListSetBottomItem

```
void XmListSetBottomItem(
    Widget    widget,  /* Affects this XmList widget      */
    XmString  item);   /* Make this the last visible item */
```

Makes item the last visible item in the specified XmList widget.

XmListSetBottomPos

```
void XmListSetBottomPos(
    Widget widget,  /* Affects this XmList widget      */
    int    pos);    /* Make this the last visible item */
```

Makes the item at position pos the last visible item in the specified XmList widget.

XmListSetHorizPos

```
void XmListSetHorizPos(
    Widget widget,  /* Affects this XmList widget         */
    int    pos);    /* Set horizontal scroll bar to this */
```

Sets the horizontal scrollbar of the XmList widget to the position specified by pos.

XmListSetItem

```
void XmListSetItem(
    Widget widget,   /* Affects this XmList widget       */
    XmString item);  /* Make this the first visible item */
```

Makes item the first visible item in the specified XmList widget.

XmListSetPos

```
void XmListSetPos(
    Widget widget, /* Affects this XmList widget    */
    int    pos);   /* Make this the first visible item */
```

Makes the item at position pos the first visible item in the specified XmList widget.

XmMainWindowSep1

```
Widget XmMainWindowSep1(
    Widget widget); /* Query this XmMainWindow widget */
```

Returns the widget ID of the first XmSeparator widget in the specified XmMainWindow widget. This XmSeparator widget is located between the XmMenuBar and the XmCommand widget in the XmMainWindow widget.

XmMainWindowSep2

```
Widget XmMainWindowSep2(
    Widget widget); /* Query this XmMainWindow widget */
```

Returns the widget ID of the second XmSeparator widget in the specified XmMainWindow widget. This XmSeparator widget is located between the XmCommand widget and the XmScrolledWindow widget in the XmMainWindow widget.

XmMainWindowSetAeas

```
void XmMainWindowSetAreas(
    Widget widget,  /* These are for this MainWindow widget  */
    Widget menubar, /* The menu bar's widget ID              */
    Widget command, /* The command window's widget ID        */
    Widget hscroll, /* The horizontal scroll bar's widget ID */
    Widget vscroll, /* The vertical scroll bar's widget ID   */
    Widget work);   /* Widget ID of the work area            */
```

Sets the child widgets for a main window widget. Use NULL for components that you do not want to include in the main window.

XmMenuPosition

```
vid XmMenuPosition(
    Widget                  widget,  /* Position this pop-up menu */
    XButtonPressedEvent *event); /* Event passed to action     */
                                 /* procedure of the pop-up menu */
```

Positions a pop-up menu (an XmRowColumn widget of type XmMENU_POPUP) using the x_root and y_root values from a button-press event (see Chapter 11 for the definition of the XButtonPressedEvent structure).

9

XmMessageBoxGetChild

```
Widget XmMessageBoxGetChild(
    Widget          widget, /* XmMessageBox being queried    */
    unsigned char child); /* Child widget ID to be returned */
```

Returns the widget ID of a child of the `XmMessageBox` widget. The `child` argument specifies the child whose ID is returned. It can take one of the following values: `XmDIALOG_CANCEL_BUTTON`, `XmDIALOG_DEFAULT_BUTTON`, `XmDIALOG_HELP_BUTTON`, `XmDIALOG_MESSAGE_LABEL`, `XmDIALOG_OK_BUTTON`, `XmDIALOG_SEPARATOR`, or `Xm_DIALOG_SYMBOL_LABEL`.

XmOptionButtonGaget

```
Widget XmOptionButtonGadget(
    Widget option_menu); /* Query this Option menu widget */
```

Returns the ID of the `XmCascadeButtonGadget` created by the `XmCreateOptionMenu` function.

XmOptionLabelGadget

```
Widget XmOptionLabelGadget(
    Widget option_menu); /* Query this Option menu widget */
```

Returns the ID of the `XmLabelGadget` created by the `XmCreateOptionMenu` function.

XmRemoveFromPostFromList

```
void XmRemoveFromPostFromList(
    Widget menu, /* Modify this widget's "post from" list    */
    Widget w);   /* Remove this widget from "post from" list */
```

Removes the widget w from the `XmNpostFromList` of the specified pull-down menu (an `XmRowColumn` widget of type `XmMENU_PULLDOWN`).

XmRemoveProtocolCallback

```
void XmRemoveProtocolCallback(
    Widget shell,       /* Protocol is in this widget       */
    Atom   property,    /* Property containing protocol      */
    Atom   protocol,    /* Remove callback for this protocol */
    XtCallbackProc callback,  /* The callback function       */
    caddr_t        client_data); /* Data passed to callback */
```

Removes `callback` from the list of callbacks of the specified protocol.

XmRemoveProtocols

```
void XmRemoveProtocols(
    Widget    shell,       /* Remove protocols from widget  */
    Atom      property,    /* Property containing protocols */
    Atom      *protocols,  /* Protocols to be removed       */
    Cardinal num_protocols); /* Number of protocols         */
```

Removes a set of protocols from the specified shell.

XmRemoveTabGroup

```
void XmRemoveTabGroup(
    Widget widget);    /* Widget to be removed from tab group */
```

Removes the specified widget from the list of tab groups associated with a hierarchy of widgets. A *tab group* is a grouping of widgets within which you can move the input focus from one widget to another by using the arrow keys. You can go from one tab group to another by pressing the Tab key.

XmRemoveWMProtocolCallback

```
void XmRemoveWMProtocolCallback(
    Widget shell,     /* Remove protocol from this widget  */
    Atom   protocol, /* Remove callback for this protocol  */
    XtCallbackProc callback,     /* The callback function   */
    caddr_t        client_data); /* Data passed to callback */
```

Calls XmRemoveProtocolCallback to remove callback for the specified protocol stored in the WM_PROTOCOLS property.

XmRemoveWMProtocols

```
void XmRemoveWMProtocols(
    Widget    shell,       /* Protocols are in this widget */
    Atom      *protocols,  /* Protocols to be removed      */
    Cardinal num_protocols); /* Number of protocols        */
```

Removes a set of protocols from the specified shell's WM_PROTOCOLS property. This function calls XmRemoveProtocols with the property argument set to WM_PROTOCOLS.

XmResolvePartOffsets

```
void XmResolvePartOffsets(
    WidgetClass  wclass,  /* Offset records for this class */
    XmOffsetPtr *offset); /* List of offset resources      */
```

This function is meant for writing new widgets compatible with existing Motif widgets. A widget writer would call XmResolvePartOffsets during class initialization to install the specified offset resource list for the widget class wclass.

9

XmScaleGetValue

```
oid XmScaleGetValue(
    Widget widget,  /* Get slider pos. of this scale widget */
    int    *value); /* Current slider pos. returned here   */
```

On return, value will contain the current position of the slider of the specified XmScale widget.

XmScaleSetValue

```
oid XmScaleSetValue(
    Widget widget,  /* Set slider pos. of this scale widget */
    int    value);  /* This is the new slider position     */
```

Sets the current position of the slider of the specified XmScale widget to value.

XmScrollBarGetVaue

```
void XmScrollBarGetValue(
    Widget widget,  /* Get values for this scrollbar widget */
    int    *spos,   /* Current position of slider returned  */
    int    *ssize,  /* Current size of slider returned      */
    int    *bincr,  /* Button increment/decrement returned  */
    int    *pincr); /* Page increment/decrement returned    */
```

Accepts pointers to four int variables in which the function returns the current slider position, the slider's size, the amount of button increment, and the amount of page increment.

XmScrollBarSetValue

```
void XmScrollBarSetValue(
    Widget widget,  /* Get values for this scrollbar widget */
    int    spos,    /* New position of slider               */
    int    ssize,   /* New size of slider                   */
    int    bincr,   /* New button increment/decrement       */
    int    pincr);  /* New page increment/decrement         */
```

Sets four attributes of the specified XmScrollBar widget: the slider's position, slider's size, amount of button increment, and the amount of page increment.

XmScrolledWindowSetAreas

```
void XmScrolledWindowSetAreas(
    Widget widget,  /* Set children of this XmScrolledWindow */
    Widget hsbar,   /* The horizontal scrollbar's widget ID  */
    Widget vsbar,   /* The vertical scrollbar's widget ID    */
    Widget warea);  /* Widget ID of the work window          */
```

Sets up the standard children of an XmScrolledWindow widget. You can use a NULL for any child that you do not want to use.

XmSelectionBoxGetChild

```
Widget XmSelectionBoxGetChild(
    Widget widget, /* Query this XmSelectionBox widget  */
    unsigned char child); /* Identifies the child whose */
                          /* widget ID will be returned */
```

Returns the ID of a child widget of an XmSelectionBox widget. You have to indicate the child widget whose ID you want by setting the child argument to one of the following: XmDIALOG_APPLY_BUTTON, XmDIALOG_CANCEL_BUTTON, XmDIALOG_DEFAULT_BUTTON, XmDIALOG_HELP_BUTTON, XmDIALOG_LIST, XmDIALOG_LIST_LABEL, XmDIALOG_OK_BUTTON, XmDIALOG_SELECTION_LABEL, XmDIALOG_SEPARATOR, XmDIALOG_TEXT, or XmDIALOG_WORK_AREA.

XmSetFontUnit

```
void XmSetFontUnit(
    Display *display,  /* Identifies the X server     */
    int      fvalue);  /* font unit value to be used */
```

Sets the font unit value for an X server. This value is used in computing screen positions when a widget uses a resolution-independent, font-based unit to position text. By default, the font unit is the QUAD_WIDTH property of the font.

XmSetMenuCursor

```
void XmSetMenuCursor(
    Display *display,  /* Identifies the X server      */
    Cursor  cursor);   /* ID of cursor for Motif menus */
```

Sets the cursor to be displayed whenever the client application displays a Motif menu on the specified X server.

XmSetProtocolHooks

```
void XmSetProtocolHooks(
    Widget shell,      /* Protocol is in this widget         */
    Atom   property,   /* Property containing protocol       */
    Atom   protocol,   /* Set hook callbacks for this protocol */
    XtCallbackProc pre, /* The prehook callback function      */
    caddr_t predata,    /* Data passed to prehook callback    */
    XtCallbackProc post, /* The posthook callback function     */
    caddr_t postdata);  /* Data passed to posthook callback   */
```

Sets up callbacks to be called before (*prehook*) and after (*posthook*) a specified protocol message is received from the window manager.

XmSetWMProtocolHooks

```
void XmSetProtocolHooks(
    Widget shell,        /* Protocol is in this widget          */
    Atom    protocol,    /* Set hook callbacks for this protocol */
    XtCallbackProc pre,  /* The prehook callback function       */
    caddr_t predata,     /* Data passed to prehook callback     */
    XtCallbackProc post, /* The posthook callback function      */
    caddr_t postdata);   /* Data passed to posthook callback    */
```

Calls XmSetProtocolHooks with the property argument set to the WM_PROTOCOL atom.

XmStringBaseline

```
Dimension XmStringBaseline(
    XmFontList fontlist, /* Use the fonts in this list      */
    XmString   string);  /* Return "baseline" for this string */
```

Returns the number of pixels between the top of the character box and the baseline of the first line of text in string.

XmStringByteCompare

```
Boolean XmStringByteCompare(
    XmString s1,         /* Compare this compound string */
    XmString s2);        /* with this one                */
```

Returns True if s1 and s2 are identical byte-for-byte or False if the two strings differ in any byte.

XmStringCompare

```
Boolean XmStringCompare(
    XmString s1,         /* Compare this compound string */
    XmString s2);        /* with this one                */
```

Returns True if s1 and s2 have the same components (compound strings represented by the XmString data type include components such as text, direction, separators, and character set) or False if the two strings differ in any component.

XmStringConcat

```
XmString XmStringConcat(
    XmString s1,         /* Concatenate this compound string  */
    XmString s2);        /* with this one (s2 comes after s1) */
```

Concatenates s1 and s2 and returns the resulting compound string.

9

XmStringCopy

```
XmString XmStringCopy(
    XmString s);      /* Return a copy of this compound string */
```

Returns a copy of the compound string s.

XmStringCreate

```
XmString XmStringCreate(
    char           *text, /* Null-terminated C-style string */
    XmStringCharSet charset); /* Character set to use      */
```

Allocates storage for a compound string and initializes it with a specified null-terminated string text using the character set charset. Returns the newly created compound string. When you no longer need the compound string, you should free the storage used by that string by calling XmStringFree.

XmStringCreateLtoR

```
XmString XmStringCreateLtoR(
    char           *text, /* Null-terminated C-style string */
    XmStringCharSet charset); /* Character set to use      */
```

Allocates storage for a compound string and initializes it with a specified null-terminated string text using the character set charset. Replaces newline (\n) characters in text with separators in the compound string. Returns the newly created compound string. When you no longer need the compound string, you should free the storage used by that string by calling XmStringFree.

XmStringCreateSimple

```
XmString XmStringCreateSimple(
    Widget widget, /* Use language environment of this widget */
    char   *text); /* Null-terminated C-style string          */
```

Returns a compound string initialized with the specified text and based on the character set specified by resources of the widget. Use XmStringFree to deallocate the compound string when you no longer need it.

XmStringDirectionCreate

```
XmString XmStringDirectionCreate(
    XmStringDirection direction); /* Direction of XmString */
```

Creates a compound string with a direction component only and initializes that direction with the value provided in the function's argument. Two common values for the direction argument are XmSTRING_DIRECTION_L_TO_R and XmSTRING_DIRECTION_R_TO_L. Use XmStringFree to deallocate the compound string when you no longer need it.

XmStringDraw

```
void XmStringDraw(
     Display *display,       /* X server where string is drawn */
     Window  w,              /* Window where string is drawn   */
     XmFontList flist,       /* Use this font to draw string   */
     XmString   string,      /* Compound string being  drawn   */
     GC         gc,          /* Graphics context used to draw  */
                             /* the compound string            */
     Position   x,           /* Position of rectangle where    */
     Position   y,           /* text will appear               */
     Dimension  width,       /* Width (pixels) of rectangle    */
                             /* where text will be displayed   */
     unsigned char align,    /* one of: XmALIGNMENT_BEGINNING, */
                             /*         XmALIGNMENT_CENTER, or */
                             /*         XmALIGNMENT_END         */
     unsigned char dir,      /* Direction of text display      */
     XRectangle    *clip);   /* Clip against this rectangle or */
                             /* NULL if no clipping            */
```

Draws the compound string in a rectangle within a window using a specified graphics context.

XmStringDrawImage

```
void XmStringDrawImage(
     Display *display,       /* X server where string is drawn */
     Window  w,              /* Window where string is drawn   */
     XmFontList flist,       /* Use this font to draw string   */
     XmString   string,      /* Compound string being  drawn   */
     GC         gc,          /* Graphics context used to draw  */
                             /* the compound string            */
     Position   x,y,         /* Position of rectangle where    */
                             /* text will appear               */
     Dimension  width,       /* Width (pixels) of rectangle    */
                             /* where text will be displayed   */
     unsigned char align,    /* one of: XmALIGNMENT_BEGINNING, */
                             /*         XmALIGNMENT_CENTER, or */
                             /*         XmALIGNMENT_END         */
     unsigned char dir,      /* Direction of text display      */
     XRectangle    *clip);   /* Clip against this rectangle or */
                             /* NULL if no clipping            */
```

Draws the compound string in a rectangle within a window using a specified graphics context. Each character is drawn in foreground and then the background of the character cell is painted with the background color specified in the graphics context.

XmStringDrawUnderline

```
void XmStringDrawUnderline(
    Display *display,      /* X server where string is drawn */
    Window  w,             /* Window where string is drawn   */
    XmFontList flist,      /* Use this font to draw string   */
    XmString   string,     /* Compound string being drawn    */
    GC         gc,         /* Graphics context used to draw  */
                           /* the compound string            */
    Position   x,y,        /* Position of rectangle where    */
                           /* text will appear               */
    Dimension  width,      /* Width (pixels) of rectangle    */
                           /* where text will be displayed   */
    unsigned char align,   /* one of: XmALIGNMENT_BEGINNING, */
                           /*          XmALIGNMENT_CENTER, or */
                           /*          XmALIGNMENT_END        */
    unsigned char dir,     /* Direction of text display      */
    XRectangle    *clip,   /* Clip against this rectangle or */
                           /* NULL if no clipping            */
    XmString      uline);  /* Portion to be underlined       */
```

Draws the compound string in a rectangle within a window using a specified graphics context. Also underlines the substring indicated by the argument uline.

XmStringEmpty

```
Boolean XmStringEmpty(
    XmString s);           /* Is this compound string empty? */
```

Returns True if the text segments in the compound string s are all empty and False if they are not empty.

XmStringExtent

```
void XmStringExtent(
    XmFontList fontlist,   /* Use this font and char. set    */
    XmString   string,     /* Get extent of this string      */
    Dimension  *width,     /* Width of text extent returned  */
    Dimension  *height);   /* Height of text extent returned */
```

On return, the arguments width and height will hold the dimensions of the smallest rectangle capable of displaying the specified compound string in a particular font.

XmStringFree

```
void XmStringFree(
    XmString s);           /* Deallocate this compound string */
```

Releases the storage allocated for the compound string s.

9

XmStringFreeContext
```
void XmStringFreeContext(
    XmStringContext sc); /* Deallocate this string context */
```

Frees storage used for the string context sc.

XmStringGetLtoR
```
Boolean XmStringGetLtoR(
    XmString        s,       /* Search this compound string */
    XmStringCharset cset,    /* Use this character set       */
    char            **text); /* Look for this text in string */
```

Searches for any occurrence of text in the compound string s. If found, the function returns True and sets text to point to the matching text segment in s. Otherwise, the return value is False.

XmStringGetComponent
```
XmStringComponentType XmStringGetComponent(
    XmStringContext context,  /* Use this string context       */
    char            **text,   /* Returned pointer to text       */
    XmStringCharset *charset, /* Returned character set          */
    XmStringDirection *direction, /* Returned direction          */
    XmStringComponentType *tag, /* Tag for unknown component */
    Short *length,    /* Returned length of unknown component */
    char **value);    /* Returned value of unknown component  */
```

Returns information about the next component of a compound string identified by a context (see XmStringInitContext). The function returns the type of the next component and information about that component in an appropriate argument. The return value is one of the following:

XmSTRING_COMPONENT_CHARSET	Value returned in charset
XmSTRING_COMPONENT_DIRECTION	Value returned in direction
XmSTRING_COMPONENT_END	No more components in string
XmSTRING_COMPONENT_SEPARATOR	Next component is a separator
XmSTRING_COMPONENT_TEXT	Value returned in text (you have to free this string)
XmSTRING_COMPONENT_UNKNOWN	Type, length, and value returned

XmStringGetNextSegment
```
Boolean XmStringGetNextSegment(
    XmStringContext context,     /* Use this string context */
    char            **text,      /* Returned pointer to text */
    XmStringCharset *charset,    /* Returned character set   */
    XmStringDirection *direction, /* Returned direction      */
    Boolean *separator);         /* Returns True if separator */
```

Returns the text string, character set, and direction of the next segment of the compound string specified by context (see `XmStringInitContext`).

XmStringHasSubstring

```
Boolean XmStringHasSubstring(
    XmString string,      /* Search this compound string */
    XmString substring); /* for occurrences of this one */
```

Returns `True` if `substring` has one text segment and that segment is completely contained in one of the text segments of `string`. Otherwise, the function returns `False`.

XmStringHeight

```
Dimension XmStringHeight(
    XmFontList flist,  /* Use this font and character set */
    XmString   s);     /* and find height of this string  */
```

Returns the combined height (in pixels) of all the lines contained in the compound string s.

XmStringInitContext

```
Boolean XmStringInitContext(
    XmStringContext  *sc, /* Return a string context for    */
    XmString  s);         /* accessing this compound string */
```

Sets up a context for accessing the specified compound string. If all goes well, the function returns `True` and returns the context in sc. Otherwise, the function returns `False` to indicate failure.

XmStringLength

```
int XmStringLength(
    XmString s); /* Return length of this compound string */
```

Returns the length (in bytes) of the compound string s. A return value of zero indicates that the compound string s has an invalid structure.

XmStringLineCount

```
int XmStringLineCount(
    XmString s);        /* Return number of lines in s */
```

Returns the number of lines (one more than the number of separators) in the compound string s.

XmStringNConcat

```
XmString XmStringNConcat(
    XmString s1,      /* Concatenate this compound string */
    XmString s2,      /* with this one                     */
    int      n);      /* Number of bytes to concatenate    */
```

Returns a new compound string that is formed by concatenating n bytes of s2 to s1. You are responsible for deallocating the newly created XmString (by calling XmStringFree) when you no longer need it.

XmStringNCopy

```
XmString XmStringNCopy(
    XmString s,       /* Make a copy of this compound string */
    int      n);      /* Number of bytes to copy             */
```

Returns a new compound string that is formed by copying n bytes (includes tags, separators, and direction indicators) of s. Use XmStringFree to deallocate the newly created compound string when you no longer need it.

XmStringPeekNextComponent

```
XmStringComponentType XmStringPeekNextComponent(
    XmStringContext sc); /* Use this string context */
```

Returns the type of the next component of the compound string identified by the context sc (see XmStringInitContext). See the description of XmStringGetNextComponent for a list of the possible return values.

XmStringSegmentCreate

```
XmString XmStringSegmentCreate(
    char             *text, /* This is the text          */
    XmString         cset,  /* Use this character set     */
    XmStringDirection dir,  /* and this direction         */
    Boolean          sep);  /* True = add separator at end */
```

Assemble a compound string from a given set of components. Use XmStringFree to deallocate the newly created compound string when you no longer need it.

XmStringSeparatorCreate

```
XmString XmStringSeparatorCreate();
```

Returns a new compound string containing a single separator component.

XmStringwidth

```
Dimension XmStringwidth(
    XmFontList flist, /* Use this font and character set   */
    XmString   s);    /* Need width of this compound string */
```

Returns the width (in pixels) of the longest line in the compound string s.

XmTextClearSelection

```
void XmTextClearSelection(
    Widget widget, /* Clear selection on this XmText widget */
    Time   time);  /* Time of event that triggered this     */
```

Clears the primary selection in the specified XmText widget.

XmTextCopy

```
Boolean XmTextCopy(
    Widget w,    /* Copy selection from this XmText widget */
    Time   t);   /* Time of event triggering this request  */
```

Copies the primary selection from the specified XmText widget to the clipboard. Returns True if successful or False if the operation cannot be completed (because the selection is NULL or the widget does not own the selection).

XmTextCut

```
Boolean XmTextCut(
    Widget w,    /* Cut selection from this XmText widget */
    Time   t);   /* Time of event triggering this request */
```

Copies the primary selection from the specified XmText widget to the clipboard and then clears the selected text. Returns True if successful or False if operation cannot be completed (because the selection is NULL or the widget does not own the selection).

XmTextFieldClearSelection

```
void XmTextFieldClearSelection(
    Widget widget, /* Clear selection on this XmTextField */
    Time   time);  /* Time of event that triggered this   */
```

Clears the primary selection in the specified XmTextField widget.

XmTextFieldCut

```
Boolean XmTextFieldCut(
    Widget w,    /* Cut selection from this XmTextField    */
    Time   t);   /* Time of event triggering this request */
```

Copies the primary selection from the specified XmTextField widget to the clipboard and then clears the selected text. Returns True if successful, False if operation cannot be completed (because the selection is NULL or the widget does not own the selection).

XmTextFieldGetBaseline

```
int XmTextFieldGetBaseline(
    Widget w);      /* Return baseline of this XmTextField */
```

Returns the position of the baseline for the specified XmTextField widget (based on the first font in the font list).

XmTextFieldGetCursorPosition

```
XmTextFieldPosition XmTextFieldGetCursorPosition(
    Widget w);      /* Return cursor pos. of this XmTextField */
```

Returns the cursor position (where text will be inserted) for the specified XmTextField widget. The positions are numbered from zero upward, with zero denoting the first character.

XmTextFieldGetEditable

```
Boolean XmTextFieldGetEditable(
    Widget w);          /* Is this XmTextField editable? */
```

Returns the XmNeditable resource of the specified XmTextField widget. If this resource is True, the contents of the XmTextField can be edited.

XmTextFieldGetLastPosition

```
XmTextFieldPosition XmTextFieldGetLastPosition(
    Widget w);   /* Return last char. pos. of this XmTextField */
```

Returns the position of the last character in the specified XmTextField widget. The character positions are numbered from zero upward, with zero denoting the first character.

XmTextFieldGetMaxLength

```
int XmTextFieldGetMaxLength(
    Widget w);   /* Return maximum length of this XmTextField */
```

Returns the maximum number of characters that the specified XmTextField can store. This is the XmTextField widget's XmNmaxLength resource.

XmTextFieldGetSelection

```
char* XmTextFieldGetSelection(
    Widget w);          /* Return selection of this XmTextField */
```

Returns a pointer to a buffer containing the primary selection of the specified XmTextField widget or NULL if there is no selection in the widget. You are responsible for deallocating the storage to which the returned pointer points. Use XtFree to deallocate this buffer when you no longer need it.

XmTextFieldGetSelectionPosition

```
Boolean XmTextFieldGetSelectionPosition(
    Widget w,                /* Need selection of this XmTextField */
    XmTextFieldPosition *l,  /* Returns start of selection  */
    XmTextFieldPosition *r); /* Returns end of selection    */
```

Returns True if the specified XmTextField widget owns the primary collection. If it does, the arguments l and r will contain the starting and ending positions of the primary selection in the XmTextField widget. A False return value indicates that the XmTextField widget does not have the primary selection.

XmTextFieldGetString

```
char *XmTextFieldGetString(
    Widget w); /* Return string from this XmTextField */
```

Returns the string displayed in the specified XmTextField widget. You are responsible for releasing the storage allocated for the returned string. Use XtFree to free this storage when you no longer need the returned string.

XmTextFieldInsert

```
void XmTextFieldInsert(
    Widget widget,          /* Insert into this XmTextField */
    XmTextFieldPosition pos, /* Insert at this char. pos. */
    char *string);   /* Insert this null-terminated string */
```

Inserts a null-terminated string starting at a specified position in an XmTextField widget.

XmTextFieldPaste

```
Boolean XmTextFieldPaste(
    Widget w); /* Paste selection into this XmTextField */
```

Pastes the current selection from the clipboard into the specified XmTextField widget at the current position of the insertion cursor. Returns True if the paste operation is successful and False if the widget does not own the primary selection.

9

XmTextFieldPosToXY

```
Boolean XmTextFieldPosToXY(
    Widget widget,              /* Query this XmTextField */
    XmTextFieldPosition pos,    /* Character  position    */
    Position *x,                /* Returned x-y position  */
    Position *y);
```

Converts the character position pos into *x-y* coordinates with respect to the widget's upper left corner and returns the values in the arguments *x* and *y*.

XmTextFieldRemove

```
Boolean XmTextFieldRemove(
    Widget w); /* Delete selected text from this XmTextField */
```

Deletes the selected text (which constitutes the primary selection) from the specified XmTextField widget. This function returns True if the operation succeeds or False if the widget does not own the primary selection.

XmTextFieldReplace

```
void XmTextFieldReplace(
    Widget w, /* Modify contents of this XmTextField widget  */
    XmTextFieldPosition from, /* Start at this char position */
    XmTextFieldPosition to,   /* End at this char  position  */
    char *string);    /* Null-terminated replacement string */
```

Replaces the block of characters (in the XmTextField widget) between the positions from and to with the null-terminated string. You can insert the string at a character position by setting both from and to arguments to that character position.

XmTextFieldSetAddMode

```
Boolean XmTextFieldSetAddMode(
    Widget  widget, /* Affects this XmTextField widget */
    Boolean mode ); /* New value for the "add mode"    */
```

Returns the current setting of the XmTextField widget's "add mode" and sets the add mode to the Boolean value in the mode argument. If the add mode is True, you can move the cursor within the XmTextField without altering the primary selection.

XmTextFieldSetCursorPosition

```
void XmTextFieldSetCursorPosition(
    Widget w, /* Set cursor position of this XmTextField */
    XmTextFieldPosition pos); /* Position cursor here    */
```

Positions the insertion cursor at the character position pos in a specified XmTextField widget.

XmTextFieldSetEditable

```
void XmTextFieldSetEditable(
    Widget  w,     /* Alter "editability" of this XmTextField */
    Boolean edit); /* New value for the XmNeditable resource */
```

Sets the XmNeditable resource of the specified XmTextField widget with the value given in the edit argument. When the XmNeditable resource is True, the user can edit the contents of the XmTextField widget.

XmTextFieldSetHighlight

```
void XmTextFieldSetHighlight(
    Widget  w,     /* Set highlight for this XmTextField */
    XmTextFieldPosition left,  /* Starting position   */
    XmTextFieldPosition right, /* Ending position     */
    XmHighlightMode mode);     /* One of: XmNORMAL,
                XmSELECTED, or XmSECONDARY_SELECTED  */
```

Sets the highlighting of the block of characters between the character positions left and right. If mode is XmNORMAL, the text is not highlighted. If mode is XmSELECTED, the selected characters appear in "reverse video" (with foreground and background colors swapped). If the mode argument is XmSECONDARY_SELECTED, the characters between left and right are underlined.

XmTextFieldSetMaxLength

```
void XmTextFieldSetMaxLength(
    Widget  w,     /* Set max length for this XmTextField */
    int     nchar); /* Allow up to these many characters   */
```

Sets the XmNmaxLength resource of the specified XmTextField widget. This resource specifies the maximum number of characters that the XmTextField widget can hold.

XmTextFieldSetSelection

```
void XmTextFieldSetSelection(
    Widget  w,     /* Set selection from this XmTextField */
    XmTextFieldPosition start, /* Starting position   */
    XmTextFieldPosition end,   /* Ending position     */
    Time time);       * Timestamp of triggering event */
```

Sets the characters between positions start and end in the specified XmTextField widget as the current primary selection.

XmTextFieldSetString

```
void XmTextFieldSetString(
    Widget  w,   /* Set the text of this XmTextField */
    char  *s); /* to this null-terminated string   */
```

Sets the text string of the specified XmTextField widget to the null-terminated string s.

XmTextFieldShowPosition

```
void XmTextFieldShowPosition(
    Widget w,              /* Affects this XmTextField  widget */
    XmTextFieldPosition pos); /* Display text starting here */
```

Displays the text starting at the character position pos.

XmTextFieldXYToPos

```
XmTextFieldPosition XmTextFieldXYToPos(
    Widget   w,    /* For this XmTextField widget       */
    Position x,y); /* Return char pos for this x-y coord. */
```

Returns the character position corresponding to the *x-y* coordinate (with respect to the upper left corner of the widget).

XmTextGetBaseline

```
int XmTextGetBaseline(
    Widget w); /* Return baseline of this XmText widget */
```

Returns the position of the baseline for the specified XmText widget (based on the first font in the font list).

XmTextGetCursorPosition

```
XmTextPosition XmTextGetCursorPosition(
    Widget w); /* Return cursor position of this XmText */
```

Returns the cursor position (where text will be inserted) for the specified XmText widget. The positions are numbered from zero onwards with zero denoting the first character.

XmTextGetEditable

```
Boolean XmTextGetEditable(
    Widget w); /* Return edit permission of this XmText */
```

Returns the XmNeditable resource of the specified XmText widget. If this resource is True, the contents of the XmText widget can be edited.

XmTextGetLastPosition

```
XmTextPosition XmTextGetLastPosition(
    Widget w);/* Return last char. pos of this XmText */
```

Returns the position of the last character in the specified XmText widget. The character positions are numbered from zero upward, with zero denoting the first character.

XmTextGetMaxLength

```
int XmTextGetMaxLength(
    Widget w);      /* Return max length of this XmText */
```

Returns the maximum number of characters that the specified XmText can store. This is the XmText widget's XmNmaxLength resource.

XmTextGetSelection

```
char* XmTextGetSelection(
    Widget w); /* Return selection of this XmText */
```

Returns a pointer to a buffer containing the primary selection of the specified XmText widget or NULL if there is no selection in the widget. You are responsible for deallocating the storage to which the returned pointer points. Use XtFree to deallocate this buffer when you no longer need it.

XmTextGetSelectionPosition

```
Boolean XmTextGetSelectionPosition(
    Widget w,             /* Need selection of this XmText */
    XmTextPosition *l,  /* Returns start of selection    */
    XmTextPosition *r); /* Returns end of selection      */
```

Returns True if the specified XmText widget owns the primary collection. If it does, the arguments l and r will contain the starting and ending positions of the primary selection in the XmText widget. A False return value indicates that the XmText widget does not have the primary selection.

XmTextGetSource

```
XmTextSource XmTextGetSource(
    Widget w); /* Return text source of this XmText widget */
```

Returns the text source of this XmText widget. Two or more XmText widgets may share a text source so that when the user edits the text in one widget, the changes are reflected in the others.

XmTextGetString

```
char  *XmTextGetString(
    Widget w); /* Return string from this XmText widget */
```

Returns the string displayed in the specified XmText widget. You are responsible for releasing the storage allocated for the returned string. Use XtFree to free this storage when you no longer need the returned string.

XmTextGetTopCharacter

```
XmTextPosition XmTextGetTopCharacter(
    Widget w); /* Return pos of first char in XmText widget */
```

Returns the position of the first character displayed in the specified XmText widget.

XmTextInsert

```
void XmTextInsert(
    Widget widget,      /* Insert into this XmText widget */
    XmTextPosition pos, /* Insert at this char. position  */
    char *string);  /* Insert this null-terminated string */
```

Inserts a null-terminated string starting at a specified position in an XmText widget.

XmTextPaste

```
Boolean XmTextPaste(
    Widget w); /* Paste selection into this XmText widget */
```

Pastes the current selection from the clipboard into the specified XmText widget at the current position of the insertion cursor. Returns True if the paste operation is successful and False if the widget does not own the primary selection.

XmTextPosToXY

```
Boolean XmTextPosToXY(
    Widget widget,      /* For this XmText widget        */
    XmTextPosition pos, /* Character  position to convert */
    Position *x,        /* Returned x-y coordinate       */
    Position *y);
```

Converts the character position pos into *x-y* coordinates with respect to the widget's upper left corner and returns the values in the arguments *x* and *y*.

XmTextRemove

```
Boolean XmTextRemove(
    Widget w);      /* Delete selected text from this XmText */
```

Deletes the selected text (which constitutes the primary selection) from the specified XmText widget. This function returns True if the operation succeeds

9

and False if the primary selection is NULL or if the widget does not own the primary selection.

XmTextReplace

```
void XmTextReplace(
    Widget w,       /* Modify contents of this XmText widget */
    XmTextPosition from, /* Start at this char position     */
    XmTextPosition to,   /* End at this char  position      */
    char *string); /* Null-terminated replacement string    */
```

Replaces the block of characters (in the XmText widget) between the positions from and to with the null-terminated string. You can insert the string at a specific character position by setting both from and to arguments to that character position.

XmTextScroll

```
Boolean XmTextScroll(
    Widget w,       /* Scroll text in this XmText widget */
    int    nlines); /* Scroll by these many lines        */
```

Scrolls the text in the specified XmText widget by a number of lines. If nlines is positive, the text scrolls up. If nlines is negative, the text scrolls down.

XmTextSetAddMode

```
Boolean XmTextSetAddMode(
    Widget  widget, /* Affects this XmText widget  */
    Boolean mode ); /* New value for the "add mode" */
```

Returns the current setting of the XmText widget's "add mode" and sets the add mode to the Boolean value in the mode argument. If the add mode is True, you can move the cursor within the XmText without altering the primary selection.

XmTextSetCursorPosition

```
void XmTextSetCursorPosition(
    Widget w,             /* Set cursor position of this XmText */
    XmTextPosition pos); /* Position cursor here               */
```

Positions the insertion cursor at the character position pos in a specified XmText widget.

XmTextSetEditable

```
void XmTextSetEditable(
    Widget  w,     /* Alter "editability" of this XmText  */
    Boolean edit); /* New value for the XmNeditable resource */
```

9

Sets the XmNeditable resource of the specified XmText widget with the value given in the edit argument. When the XmNeditable resource is True, the user can edit the contents of the XmText widget.

XmTextSetHighlight

```
void XmTextSetHighlight(
    Widget w,                /* Set highlight for this XmText */
    XmTextPosition left,    /* Starting position */
    XmTextPosition right,   /* Ending position   */
    XmHighlightMode mode); /* One of: XmNORMAL,
            XmSELECTED, or XmSECONDARY_SELECTED */
```

Sets the highlighting of the block of characters between the character positions left and right. If mode is XmNORMAL, the text is not highlighted. If mode is XmSELECTED, the selected characters appear in "reverse video" (with foreground and background colors swapped). If the mode argument is XmSECONDARY_SELECTED, the characters between left and right are underlined.

XmTextSetMaxLength

```
void XmTextSetMaxLength(
    Widget w,          /* Set max length of this XmText widget */
    int    nchar);     /* Allow up to these many characters    */
```

Sets the XmNmaxLength resource of the specified XmText widget. This resource specifies the maximum number of characters that the XmText widget can hold.

XmTextSetSelection

```
void XmTextSetSelection(
    Widget w,              /* Set selection from this XmText */
    XmTextPosition start, /* Starting position             */
    XmTextPosition end,   /* Ending position               */
    Time time);           /* Timestamp of triggering event */
```

Sets the characters between positions start and end in the specified XmText widget as the current primary selection.

XmTextSetSource

```
void XmTextSetSource(
    Widget w,    /* Set text source for this XmText widget */
    XmTextSource   src,   /* New text source for widget    */
    XmTextPosition top,   /* Char pos displayed at top     */
    XmTextPosition cpos); /* Insertion cursor position     */
```

Sets a text source for the specified XmText widget. Two or more XmText widgets may share a text source so that when the user edits the text in one widget, the changes are reflected in the others.

9

XmTextSetString

```
void XmTextSetString(
    Widget w,      /* Set the text of this XmText widget */
    char *s);      /* to this null-terminated string      */
```

Sets the text string of the specified XmText widget to the null-terminated string s.

XmTextSetTopCharacter

```
void XmTextSetTopCharacter(
    Widget w, /* Set the "top" char. for this XmText widget */
    XmTextPosition pos); /* Display this char in widget      */
```

Displays the character at position pos as the first character in the specified XmText widget.

XmTextShowPosition

```
void XmTextShowPosition(
    Widget w,              /* Affects this XmText widget */
    XmTextPosition pos); /* Display text starting here */
```

Displays the text starting at the character position pos.

XmTextXYToPos

```
XmTextPosition XmTextXYToPos(
    Widget   w,    /* For this XmText widget              */
    Position x,y); /* Return char pos for this x-y coord. */
```

Returns the character position corresponding to the *x-y* coordinate (with respect to the upper left corner of the widget).

XmToggleButtonGadgetGetState

```
Boolean XmToggleButtonGadgetGetState(
    Widget g); /* Return state of this toggle button gadget */
```

Returns the current state (True if "on" and False if "off") of the specified XmToggleButtonGadget.

XmToggleButtonGadgetSetState

```
void XmToggleButtonGadgetSetState(
    Widget   g,      /* Set state of this toggle button gadget */
    Boolean state,   /* New state of toggle button gadget      */
    Boolean notify); /* True = call XmNvalueChangedCallback */
```

Sets the state of the specified XmToggleButtonGadget from the value given in the state argument (True means "on" and False means "off"). If the notify argument is True, the callbacks listed in the gadget's XmNvalueChangedCallback are called.

XmToggleButtonGetState

```
Boolean XmToggleButtonGetState(
    Widget w); /* Return state of this toggle button widget */
```

Returns the current state (True if "on" and False if "off") of the specified XmToggleButton widget.

XmToggleButtonSetState

```
void XmToggleButtonSetState(
    Widget  w,  /* Set state of this toggle button widget */
    Boolean state,   /* New state of toggle button widget */
    Boolean notify); /* True=call XmNvalueChangedCallback */
```

Sets the state of the specified XmToggleButton widget from the value given in the state argument (True means "on" and False means "off"). If the notify argument is True, the callbacks listed in the gadget's XmNvalueChangedCallback are called.

XmTrackingLocate

```
Widget XmTrackingLocate(
    Widget  w,  /* Use this widget for a modal interaction */
    Cursor  c,  /* Use this cursor during the interaction */
    Boolean restrict); /* True=confine cursor to widget w  */
```

Takes over exclusive control of ("grabs") the pointer and returns ID of the widget where the user clicks Button 1 of the mouse pointing device. A NULL return value signifies that the window where the user clicked the mouse is not a part of the application.

XmUninstallImage

```
Boolean XmUninstallImage(
    XImage *image); /* Remove this image from image cache */
```

Removes the specified image from the image cache. Returns True if successful and False if the image argument is NULL or if image is not present in the image cache.

XmUpdateDisplay

```
void XmUpdateDisplay(
    Widget w); /* Update display used by this widget */
```

9

Send all pending expose events to the X server associated with the specified widget. You can call `XmUpdateDisplay` before starting a time-consuming operation. This ensures that the display appears up to date while the application performs the lengthy operation.

Motif Widgets

This section includes reference entries for the Motif widgets, arranged alphabetically. For each widget, you will find the class name, the class pointer, and the class from which it inherits. Each widget's resources are listed in a tabular form. The resource table shows the name, type, and default value of each resource. The letters in the last column mean the following:

- If a `C` is present, you can set that particular resource at the time of creation through an argument list.

- An `S` means you can use `XtSetValues` to set that resource.

- A `G` implies that you can retrieve its value using `XtGetValues`.

- A `*` for a default value indicates that default is determined at runtime.

The symbols appearing in the resource table are defined in the header file `<Xm/Xm.h>`.

A word about the resources: A widget inherits the resources of its superclass (the class from which it inherits); the superclass, in turn, inherits the resources of its superclass; and so on. The resource table of each widget shows only the new resources for that class. To learn about all the resources that the widget can have, you have to follow the inheritance hierarchy all the way up to the `Core` class, which is at the root of the inheritance hierarchy. To do this, start with the class name shown here in the *Inherits from:* field and continue following the inheritance hierarchy. For example, if you do this for the `ApplicationShell` class, you will get the following inheritance hierarchy (read → as "inherits from"):

`ApplicationShell→TopLevelShell→VendorShell→WMShell→Shell →Composite→Core`

ApplicationShell

class name: `ApplicationShell`   class pointer: `applicationShell-WidgetClass`

include file: `<X11/Shell.h>`   inherits from: `TopLevelShell`

The `ApplicationShell` widget provides the main top-level window for an application.

Name	Type	Default	Set/Get
XmNargc	int	NULL	CSG
XmNargv	String*	NULL	CSG

Composite

class name: Composite   class pointer: compositeWidgetClass

include file: <Xm/Xm.h>   inherits from: Core

Composite widgets act as containers for other widgets. A Composite widget takes care of the overall management of its children from creation to destruction. This includes mapping and unmapping the children and the physical arrangement of the managed children.

Name	Type	Default	Set/Get
XmNinsertPosition	XtOrderProc	NULL	CSG

Constraint

class name: Constraint   class pointer: constraintWidgetClass

include file: <Xm/Xm.h>   inherits from: Composite

A Constraint widget attaches additional resources to its children. This class defines no new resources.

Core

class name: Core   class pointer: widgetClass

include file: <Xm/Xm.h>   inherits from: None

Xt Intrinsics defines Core as the basis of all widgets in the toolkit. The resources in the Core class are important because they are available in every widget in the toolkit.

Name	Type	Default	Set/Get
XmNaccelerators	XtTranslations	NULL	CSG
XmNancestorSensitive	Boolean	True	G
XmNbackground	Pixel	White	CSG
XmNbackgroundPixmap	Pixmap	XmUNSPECIFIED_PIXMAP	CSG
XmNborderColor	Pixel	Black	CSG

continues

9

continued

Name	Type	Default	Set/Get
XmNborderPixmap	Pixmap	XmUNSPECIFIED_PIXMAP	CSG
XmNborderWidth	Dimension	1	CSG
XmNcolormap	Colormap	XtCopyFromParentC	G
XmNdepth	int	XtCopyFromParent	C G
XmNdestroyCallback	XtCallbackList	NULL	C
XmNheight	Dimension	0	CSG
XmNmappedWhenManaged	Boolean	True	CSG
XmNscreen	Pointer	XtCopyScreen	C G
XmNsensitive	Boolean	True	CSG
XmNtranslations	XtTranslationsc	NULL	CSG
XmNwidth	Dimension	0	CSG
XmNx	Position	0	CSG
XmNy	Position	0	CSG

Object

class name: `Object`   class pointer: `objectClass`

include file: `<Xm/Xm.h>`   inherits from: None

The `Object` class serves as a building block for other widget classes. You never have to create an instance of the `Object` class.

Name	Type	Default	Set/Get
XmNdestroyCallback	XtCallbackList	NULL	C

OverrideShell

class name: `OverrideShell`   class pointer: `overrideShellWidgetClass`

include file: `<X11/Shell.h>`   inherits from: `Shell`

Widgets of this class are used to create windows (such as pop-up menu windows) that bypass the window manager. `OverrideShell` widgets do not define any new resource.

RectObj

class name: `RectObj`   class pointer: `rectObjClass`

include file: `<Xm/Xm.h>`   inherits from: `Object`

Like the `Object` class, `RectObj` serves as a building block for other widget classes. You never have to create an instance of the `RectObj` class.

Name	Type	Default	Set/Get
XmNancestorSensitive	Boolean	*	CSG
XmNborderWidth	Dimension	1	CSG
XmNheight	Dimension	0	CSG
XmNsensitive	Boolean	True	CSG
XmNwidth	Dimension	0	CSG
XmNx	Position	0	CSG
XmNy	Position	0	CSG

Shell

class name: `Shell`   class pointer: `shellWidgetClass`

include file: `<X11/Shell.h>`   inherits from: `Composite`

A `Shell` is a top-level widget with one managed child. This class takes care of interactions with the window manager.

Name	Type	Default	Set/Get
XmNallowShellResize	Boolean	False	C G
XmNcreatePopupChildProc	XmCreatePopupChildProc	NULL	CSG
XmNgeometry	String	NULL	CSG
XmNoverrideRedirect	Boolean	False	CSG
XmNpopdownCallback	XtCallbackList	NULL	C
XmNpopupCallback	XtCallbackList	NULL	C
XmNsaveUnder	Boolean	False	CSG
XmNVisual	Visual	XtCopyFromParent	CSG

TopLevelShell

class name: `TopLevelShell`   class pointer: `topLevelShellWidgetClass`

include file: `<X11/Shell.h>`   inherits from: `VendorShell`

The `TopLevelShell` class provides the normal top-level windows for an application.

Name	Type	Default	Set/Get
XmNiconic	Boolean	False	CSG
XmNiconName	String	NULL	CSG
XmNiconNameEncoding	Atom	XA_STRING	CSG

TransientShell

class name: TransientShell   class pointer: transientShellWidgetClass

include file: <X11/Shell.h>   inherits from: VendorShell

The TransientShell class provides windows that can be manipulated by the window manager but cannot be iconified.

Name	Type	Default	Set/Get
XmNtransientFor	Widget	NULL	CSG

VendorShell

class name: VendorShell   class pointer: vendorShellWidgetClass

include file: <X11/Shell.h>   inherits from: WMShell

The VendorShell class is the basis for all shell widgets that are visible to the window manager. The XmNshellUnitType resource is worth noting. It determines the unit to be used for interpreting the resources that specify geometry (size and position). You can specify the unit with one of the constants: XmPIXELS, Xm100TH_MILLIMETERS, Xm1000TH_INCHES, Xm100TH_POINTS, or Xm100TH_FONT_UNIT, defined in the header file <Xm/Xm.h>. The default setting of XmPIXELS indicates that everything is specified in pixels. To specify really device-independent units, you can use Xm100TH_MILLIMETERS for one hundredth of a millimeter, Xm1000TH_INCHES for one thousandth of an inch, Xm100TH_POINTS for one hundredth of a point where a point is 1/72 inch. Use Xm100TH_FONT_UNIT to indicate that all dimensions are in terms of one hundredth of a font's unit, which is taken from the font's QUAD_WIDTH property. You can also explicitly set the font unit with the XmSetFontUnits function.

Name	Type	Default	Set/Get
XmNdefaultFontList	XmFontList	*	C
XmNdeleteResponse	unsigned char	XmDESTROY	CSG
XmNkeyboardFocusPolicy	unsigned char	XmEXPLICIT	CSG
XmNmwmDecorations	int	-1	CSG
XmNmwmFunctions	int	-1	CSG
XmNmwmInputMode	int	-1	CSG

Name	Type	Default	Set/Get
XmNmwmMenu	String	NULL	CSG
XmNshellUnitType	unsigned char	XmPIXELS	CSG

WMShell

class name: WMShell   **class pointer:** wmShellWidgetClass

include file: <X11/Shell.h>   **inherits from:** Shell

The WMShell class takes care of interactions with the window manager.

Name	Type	Default	Set/Get
XmNbaseHeight	int	-1	CSG
XmNbaseWidth	int	-1	CSG
XmNheightInc	int	-1	CSG
XmNiconMask	Pixmap	NULL	CSG
XmNiconPixmap	Pixmap	NULL	CSG
XmNiconWindow	Window	NULL	CSG
XmNiconX	int	-1	CSG
XmNiconY	int	-1	CSG
XmNinitalState	int	1	CSG
XmNinput	Boolean	True	CSG
XmNmaxAspectX	int	-1	CSG
XmNmaxAspectY	int	-1	CSG
XmNminAspectX	int	-1	CSG
XmNminAspectY	int	-1	CSG
XmNmaxHeight	int	-1	CSG
XmNmaxWidth	int	-1	CSG
XmNminHeight	int	-1	CSG
XmNminWidth	int	-1	CSG
XmNtitle	char*	NULL	CSG
XmNtitleEncoding	Atom	XA_STRING	CSG
XmNtransient	Boolean	False	CSG
XmNwaitForWm	Boolean	True	CSG
XmNwidthInc	int	-1	CSG
XmNwindowGroup	Window	None	CSG
XmNwinGravity	int	-1	CSG
XmNwmTimeOut	int	5000 (milliseconds)	CSG

XmArrowButton

class name: XmArrowButton   class pointer: xmArrowButtonWidgetClass

include file: <Xm/ArrowB.h>   inherits from: XmPrimitive

The XmArrowButton class displays an arrow (you specify the direction) in a window. The arrow has a shadow around it to give it a three-dimensional look.

Name	Type	Default	Set/Get
XmNactivateCallback	XtCallbackList	NULL	C
XmNarmCallback	XtCallbackList	NULL	C
XmNarrowDirection	unsigned char	XmARROW_UP	CSG
XmNdisarmCallback	XtCallbackList	NULL	C
XmNmultiClick	XmMultiClick	XmMULTICLICK_KEEP	CSG

XmArrowButtonGadget

class name: XmArrowButtonGadget   class pointer: xmArrowButtonGadgetClass

include file: <Xm/ArrowBG.h>   inherits from: XmGadget

The XmArrowButtonGadget class behaves like the XmArrowButton class except that it does not use a window to display the arrow.

Name	Type	Default	Set/Get
XmNactivateCallback	XtCallbackList	NULL	C
XmNarmCallback	XtCallbackList	NULL	C
XmNarrowDirection	unsigned char	XmARROW_UP	CSG
XmNdisarmCallback	XtCallbackList	NULL	C
XmNmultiClick	XmMultiClick	XmMULTICLICK_KEEP	CSG

XmBulletinBoard

class name: XmBulletinBoard   class pointer: xmBulletinBoardWidgetClass

include file: <Xm/BulletinB.h> inherits from: XmManager

XmBulletinBoard is a general-purpose container widget that serves as the base widget for most dialog widgets. The XmNBulletinBoard widget does not enforce any particular position or size on its children.

Name	Type	Default	Set/Get
XmNallowOverlap	Boolean	True	CSG
XmNautoUnmanage	Boolean	True	CSG
XmNbuttonFontList	XmFontList	NULL	CSG
XmNcancelButton	Widget	NULL	SG
XmNdefaultButton	Widget	NULL	SG
XmNdialogStyle	unsigned char	*	CSG
XmNdialogTitle	XmString	NULL	CSG
XmNfocusCallback	XtCallbackList	NULL	C
XmNlabelFontList	XmFontList	NULL	CSG
XmNmapCallback	XtCallbackList	NULL	C
XmNmarginHeight	Dimension	10	CSG
XmNmarginWidth	Dimension	10	CSG
XmNnoResize	Boolean	False	CSG
XmNresizePolicy	unsigned char	XmRESIZE_ANY	CSG
XmNshadowType	unsigned char	XmSHADOW_OUT	CSG
XmNstringDirection	XmStringDirection	XmSTRING_DIRECTION_L_TO_R	CSG
XmNtextFontList	XmFontList	NULL	CSG
XmNtextTranslations	XtTranslations	NULL	C
XmNunmapCallback	XtCallbackList	NULL	C

XmCascadeButton

class name: XmCascadeButton   class pointer: xmCascadeButtonWidgetClass

include file: <Xm/CascadeB.h> inherits from: XmLabel

The XmCascadeButton widget accepts a pull-down menu attached to it as a submenu. The pull-down menu is displayed when the XmCascadeButton widget is activated.

Name	Type	Default	Set/Get
XmNactivateCallback	XtCallbackList	NULL	C
XmNcascadePixmap	Pixmap	"menu-cascade"	CSG
XmNcascadingCallback	XtCallbackList	NULL	C
XmNmappingDelay	int	100 (milliseconds)	CSG
XmNsubmenuId	Widget	0	CSG

XmCascadeButtonGadget

class name: `XmCascadeButton`   class pointer: `xmCascadeButtonGadgetClass`

include file: `<Xm/CascadeBG.h>`   inherits from: `XmLabelGadget`

The `XmCascadeButtonGadget` is a gadget (a gadget is a widget without a window) that performs the same function as `XmCascadeButton` widget.

Name	Type	Default	Set/Get
XmNactivateCallback	XtCallbackList	NULL	C
XmNcascadePixmap	Pixmap	"menu-cascade"	CSG
XmNcascadingCallback	XtCallbackList	NULL	C
XmNmappingDelay	int	100 (milliseconds)	CSG
XmNsubmenuId	Widget	0	CSG

XmCommand

class name: `XmCommand`   class pointer: `xmCommandWidgetClass`

include file: `<Xm/Command.h>`   inherits from: `XmSelectionBox`

The `XmCommand` widget is meant for accepting commands from the user. It includes a text field for entering the commands, a prompt, and a scrollable history of past commands.

Name	Type	Default	Set/Get
XmNcommand	XmString	NULL	CSG
XmNcommandChangedCallback	XtCallbackList	NULL	C
XmNcommandEnteredCallback	XtCallbackList	NULL	C
XmNhistoryItems	XmStringTable	NULL	CSG
XmNhistoryItemCount	int	0	CSG
XmNhistoryMaxItems	int	100	CSG
XmNhistoryVisibleItemCount	int	8	CSG
XmNpromptString	XmString	">"	CSG

XmDialogShell

class name: `XmDialogShell`   class pointer: `xmDialogShellWidgetClass`

include file: `<Xm/DialogS.h>`   inherits from: `TransientShell`

The `XmDialogShell` widget is the basis for most pop-up dialogs. This class does not define any new resources.

XmDrawingArea

class name: `XmDrawingArea`   class pointer: `xmDrawingAreaWidgetClass`

include file: `<Xm/DrawingA.h>`   inherits from: `XmManager`

The `XmDrawingArea` widget provides an empty window in which you can draw graphics or text (by calling appropriate Xlib functions).

Name	Type	Default	Set/Get
XmNexposeCallback	XtCallbackList	NULL	C
XmNinputCallback	XtCallbackList	NULL	C
XmNmarginHeight	Dimension	10	CSG
XmNmarginWidth	Dimension	10	CSG
XmNresizeCallback	XtCallbackList	NULL	C
XmNresizePolicy	unsigned char	XmRESIZE_ANY	CSG

XmDrawnButton

class name: `XmDrawnButton`   class pointer: `xmDrawnButtonWidgetClass`

include file: `<Xm/DrawnB.h>`   inherits from: `XmLabel`

The `XmDrawingArea` widget provides an empty window in which you can draw graphics or text (by calling appropriate Xlib functions).

Name	Type	Default	Set/Get
XmNactivateCallback	XtCallbackList	NULL	C
XmNarmCallback	XtCallbackList	NULL	C
XmNdisarmCallback	XtCallbackList	NULL	C
XmNexposeCallback	XtCallbackList	NULL	C
XmNmultiClick	XmMultiClick	XmMULTICLICK_DISCARD	CSG
XmNpushButtonEnabled	Boolean	False	CSG
XmNresizeCallback	XtCallbackList	NULL	C
XmNshadowType	unsigned char	XmSHADOW_ETCHED_IN	CSG

XmFileSelectionBox

class name: `XmFileSelectionBox` class pointer: `xmFileSelectionBoxWidgetClass`

include file: `<Xm/FileSB.h>`   inherits from: `XmSelectionBox`

The `XmFileSelectionBox` widget lets the user browse through directories, view the files in a directory, and pick a file.

9

Name	Type	Default	Set/Get
XmNdirListItemCount	int	0	CSG
XmNdirListItems	XmStringList	NULL	CSG
XmNdirListLabelString	XmString	"Directories"	CSG
XmNdirMask	XmString	"*"	CSG
XmNfileSearchProc	XtProc	a built-in function	CSG
XmNfileTypeMask	unsigned char	XmREGULAR_FILE	CSG
XmNfilterLabelString	XmString	"FileFilter"	CSG
XmNfilterTextString	XmString	*	CSG
XmNlistUpdated	Boolean	True	CSG

XmForm

class name: XmForm   class pointer: xmFormWidgetClass

include file: <Xm/Form.h>   inherits from: XmBulletinBoard

The XmForm widget is a container widget that you use to specify a layout for its children. The layout is specified by attaching child widgets to each other, to the XmForm widget, or to a relative position within the XmForm widget.

Name	Type	Default	Set/Get
XmNbottomAttachment	unsigned char	XmATTACH_NONE	CSG
XmNbottomOffset	int	0	CSG
XmNbottomPosition	int	0	CSG
XmNbottomWidget	Widget	NULL	CSG
XmNfractionBase	int	100	CSG
XmNhorizontalSpacing	int	0	CSG
XmNleftAttachment	unsigned char	XmATTACH_NONE	CSG
XmNleftOffset	int	0	CSG
XmNleftPosition	int	0	CSG
XmNleftWidget	Widget	NULL	CSG
XmNresizable	Boolean	True	CSG
XmNrightAttachment	unsigned char	XmATTACH_NONE	CSG
XmNrightOffset	int	0	CSG
XmNrightPosition	int	0	CSG
XmNrightWidget	Widget	NULL	CSG
XmNrubberPositioning	Boolean	False	CSG
XmNtopAttachment	unsigned char	XmATTACH_NONE	CSG

Name	Type	Default	Set/Get
XmNtopOffset	int	0	CSG
XmNtopPosition	int	0	CSG
XmNtopWidget	Widget	NULL	CSG
XmNverticalSpacing	int	0	CSG

XmFrame

class name: XmFrame   class pointer: xmFrameWidgetClass

include file: <Xm/Frame.h>   inherits from: XmManager

The XmFrame widget provides a frame (with a three-dimensional look) around a single child widget.

Name	Type	Default	Set/Get
XmNmarginHeight	Dimension	0	CSG
XmNmarginWidth	Dimension	0	CSG
XmNshadowType	unsigned char	XmSHADOW_ETCHED_IN	CSG

XmGadget

class name: XmGadget   class pointer: xmGadgetClass

include file: <Xm/Gadget.h>   inherits from: RectObj

The XmGadget class is the basis for all gadgets (a gadget is a widget that does not have a window of its own and displays itself in its parent's window). You never have to create an instance of XmGadget class, but you should know about the resources defined for this class because all gadgets inherit them. The XmNunitType resource is similar to the XmNshellUnitType resource of the VendorShell widget. Consult the reference entry for VendorShell widget for a description of this resource.

Name	Type	Default	Set/Get
XmNhelpCallback	XtCallbackList	NULL	C
XmNhighlightOnEnter	Boolean	False	CSG
XmNhighlightThickness	Dimension	2	CSG
XmNnavigationType	XmNavigationType	*	CSG
XmNshadowThickness	Dimension	2	CSG
XmNtraversalOn	Boolean	True	CSG
XmNunitType	unsigned char	XmPIXELS	CSG
XmNuserData	caddr_t	NULL	CSG

9

XmLabel

class name: `XmLabel`   class pointer: `xmLabelWidgetClass`

include file: `<Xm/Label.h>`   inherits from: `XmPrimitive`

The `XmLabel` widget displays text or pixmap in a window. The text is a compound string (of type `XmString`).

Name	Type	Default	Set/Get
XmNaccelerator	String	NULL	CSG
XmNacceleratorText	XmString	NULL	CSG
eXmNalignment	unsigned char	XmALIGNMENT_CENTER	CSG
XmNfontList	XmFontList	"Fixed"	CSG
XmNlabelInsensitivePixmap	Pixmap	XmUNSPECIFIED_PIXMAP	CSG
XmNlabelPixmap	Pixmap	XmUNSPECIFIED_PIXMAP	CSG
XmNlabelString	XmString	NULL	CSG
XmNlabelType	unsigned char	XmSTRING	CSG
XmNmarginBottom	Dimension	0	CSG
XmNmarginHeight	Dimension	2	CSG
XmNmarginLeft	Dimension	0	CSG
XmNmarginRight	Dimension	0	CSG
XmNmarginTop	Dimension	0	CSG
XmNmarginWidth	Dimension	2	CSG
XmNmnemonic	char	'\0'	CSG
XmNmnemonicCharSet	String	"ISO8859-1"	CSG
XmNrecomputeSize	Boolean	True	CSG
XmNstringDirection	XmStringDirection	XmSTRING_DIRECTION_L_TO_R	CSG

XmLabelGadget

class name: `XmLabelGadget`   class pointer: `xmLabelGadgetClass`

include file: `<Xm/LabelG.h>`   inherits from: `XmGadget`

The `XmLabelGadget` is a gadget version of the `XmLabel` widget. It behaves like an `XmLabel` widget, except that an `XmLabelGadget` does not have its own window.

9

Name	Type	Default	Set/Get
XmNaccelerator	String	NULL	CSG
XmNacceleratorText	XmString	NULL	CSG
XmNalignment	unsigned char	XmALIGNMENT_CENTER	CSG
XmNfontList	XmFontList	"Fixed"	CSG
XmNlabelInsensitivePixmap	Pixmap	XmUNSPECIFIED_PIXMAP	CSG
XmNlabelPixmap	Pixmap	XmUNSPECIFIED_PIXMAP	CSG
XmNlabelString	XmString	NULL	CSG
XmNlabelType	unsigned char	XmSTRING	CSG
XmNmarginBottom	Dimension	0	CSG
XmNmarginHeight	Dimension	2	CSG
XmNmarginLeft	Dimension	0	CSG
XmNmarginRight	Dimension	0	CSG
XmNmarginTop	Dimension	0	CSG
XmNmarginWidth	Dimension	2	CSG
XmNmnemonic	char	'\0'	CSG
XmNmnemonicCharSet	String	"ISO8859-1"	CSG
XmNrecomputeSize	Boolean	True	CSG
XmNstringDirection	XmStringDirection	XmSTRING_DIRECTION_L_TO_R	CSG

XmList

class name: XmList   class pointer: xmListWidgetClass

include file: <Xm/List.h>   inherits from: XmPrimitive

The XmList widget displays a number of items in a window and lets the user select one or more items from the list of items.

Name	Type	Default	Set/Get
XmNautomaticSelection	Boolean	False	CSG
XmNbrowseSelectionCallback	XtCallbackList	NULL	C
XmNdefaultActionCallback	XtCallbackList	NULL	C
XmNdoubleClickInterval	int	250 (milliseconds)	CSG
XmNextendedSelectionCallback	XtCallbackList	NULL	C

continues

continued

Name	Type	Default	Set/Get
XmNfontList	XmFontList	NULL	CSG
XmNhorizontalScrollBar	Widget	NULL	CSG
XmNitemCount	int	0	CSG
XmNitems	XmStringTable	NULL	CSG
XmNlistMarginHeight	Dimension	0	CSG
XmNlistMarginWidth	Dimension	0	CSG
XmNlistSizePolicy	unsigned char	XmVARIABLE	CSG
XmNlistSpacing	Dimension	0	CSG
XmNmultipleSelectionCallback	XtCallbackList	NULL	C
XmNscrollBarDisplayPolicy	unsigned char	XmAS_NEEDED	CSG
XmNscrollBarPlacement	unsigned char	XmBOTTOM_RIGHT	CSG
XmNscrolledWindowMsrginHeight	Dimension	0	CSG
XmNscrolledWindowMsrginWidth	Dimension	0	CSG
XmNselectedItemCount	int	0	CSG
XmNselectedItems	XmStringTable	NULL	CSG
XmNselectionPolicy	unsigned char	XmBROWSE_SELECT	CSG
XmNsingleSelectionCallback	XtCallbackList	NULL	C
XmNspacing	Dimension	4	CSG
XmNstringDirection	unsigned char	XmSTRING_DIRECTION_L_TO_R	CSG
XmNtopItemPosition	int	1	CSG
XmNverticalScrollBar	Widget	NULL	CSG
XmvisibleItemCount	int	1	CSG

XmMainWindow

class name: XmMainWindow   class pointer: xmMainWindowWidgetClass

include file: <Xm/MainW.h>   inherits from: XmScrolledWindow

The XmMainWindow class provides a standard layout for the main window of an application. The XmMainWindow widget can manage a combination of a menubar, an XmCommand widget, an XmDrawingArea widget, and scrollbars.

Name	Type	Default	Set/Get
XmNcommandWindow	Widget	NULL	CSG
XmNcommandWindowLocation	XmCommandWindowLocation	XmCOMMAND_ABOVE_WORKSPACE	CSG
XmNmainWindowMarginHeight	Dimension	0	CSG
XmNmainWindowMarginWidth	Dimension	0	CSG
XmNmenuBar	Widget	NULL	CSG
XmNmessageWindow	Widget	NULL	CSG
XmNshowSeparator	Boolean	False	CSG

XmManager

class name: `XmManager`   class pointer: `xmManagerWidgetClass`

include file: `<Xm/Xm.h>`   inherits from: `Constraint`

The `XmManager` widget is the basis for all widgets that manage the layout of several child widgets. You never have to create an instance of `XmManager` class, but you should know about the resources defined for this class because many widgets inherit them. The purpose of the `XmNunitType` resource is the same as that of the `XmNshellUnitType` resource of the `VendorShell` widget. Consult the reference entry for `VendorShell` widget for a description of that resource.

Name	Type	Default	Set/Get
XmNbottomShadowColor	Pixel	*	CSG
XmNbottomShadowPixmap	Pixmap	XmUNSPECIFIED_PIXMAP	CSG
XmNforeground	Pixel	*	CSG
XmNhelpCallback	XtCallbackList	NULL	C
XmNhighlightColor	Pixel	Black	CSG
XmNhighlightPixmap	Pixmap	*	CSG
XmNnavigationType	XmNavigationType	XmTAB_GROUP	CSG
XmNshadowThickness	Dimension	0	CSG
XmNtopShadowColor	Pixel	*	CSG
XmNtopShadowPixmap	Pixmap	XmUNSPECIFIED_PIXMAP	CSG
XmNunitType	unsigned char	XmPIXELS	CSG
XmNuserData	caddr_t	NULL	CSG

9

XmMenuShell

class name: XmMenuShell   class pointer: xmMenuShellWidgetClass

include file: <Xm/MenuShell.h>   inherits from: OverrideShell

The XmMenuShell class serves as the basis of pop-up and pull-down menus whose windows bypass the window manager. When writing Motif programs, you do not have to directly create instances of XmMenuShell. Instead, you would use convenience functions such as XmCreatePopupMenu or XmCreatePulldownMenu that create the XmMenuShell widgets.

Name	Type	Default	Set/Get
XmNdefaultfontList	XmFontList	*	CSG

XmMessageBox

class name: XmMessageBox   class pointer: xmMessageBoxWidgetClass

include file: <Xm/MessageB.h>   inherits from: XmBulletinBoard

The XmMessageBox widget is used to display a message in a window. The widget can contain a message symbol (a pixmap), a message, and up to three standard push-buttons labeled OK, Cancel, and Help. You can change these labels.

Name	Type	Default	Set/Get
XmNcancelCallback	XtCallbackList	NULL	C
XmNcancelLabelString	XmString	"Cancel"	CSG
XmNdefaultButtonType	unsigned char	XmDIALOG_OK_BUTTON	CSG
XmNdialogType	unsigned char	XmDIALOG_MESSAGE	CSG
XmNhelpLabelString	XmString	"Help"	CSG
XmNmessageAlignment	unsigned char	XmALIGNMENT_BEGINNING	CSG
XmNmessageString	XmString	NULL	CSG
XmNminimizeButton	Boolean	False	CS
XmNokCallback	XtCallbackList	NULL	C
XmNokLabelString	XmString	"OK"	CSG
XmNsymbolPixmap	Pixmap	*	CSG

XmPanedWindow

class name: XmPanedWindow   class pointer: xmPanedWindowWidgetClass

include file: <Xm/PanedW.h>   inherits from: XmManager

XmPanedWindow is a manager widget that lays out its children in vertical panes. The child widgets appear in top-to-bottom order with the first child appearing at the top.

Name	Type	Default	Set/Get
XmNallowResize	Boolean	False	CSG
XmNmarginHeight	Dmenion	3	CSG
XmNmarginWidth	Dimension	3	CSG
XmpaneMaximum	int	1000	CSG
XmNpaneMinimum	int	1	CSG
XmNrefigureMode	Boolean	True	CSG
XmNsashHeight	Dimension	10	CSG
XmNsashIndent	Position	-10	CSG
XmNsashShadowThickness	int	2	CSG
XmNsashWidth	Dimension	10	CSG
XmNseparatorOn	Boolean	True	CSG
XmNskipAdjust	Boolea	False	CSG
XmNspacing	int	8	CSG

XmPrimitive

class name: XmPrimitive class pointer: xmPrimitiveWidgetClass

include file: <Xm/Xm.h> inherits from: Core

All stand-alone widgets (such as XmLabel, XmList, and XmPushButton) in the Motif toolkit inherit from the XmPrimitive class. This class contains the resources that are used to control the three-dimensional look of Motif widgets. You never directly create an instance of the XmPrimitive class, but you should know about the resources defined for this class because many widgets inherit them. The purpose of the XmNunitType resource is the same as that of the XmNshellUnitType resource of the VendorShell widget. Consult the reference entry for VendorShell widget for a description of that resource.

Name	Type	Default	Set/Get
XmNbottomShadowColor	Pixel	*	CSG
XmNbottomShadowPixap	Pixmap	XmUNSPECIFIED_PIXMAP	CSG
XmNforeground	Pixel	*	CSG
XmNhelpCallback	XtCallbackList	NULL	C

continues

continued

Name	Type	Default	Set/Get
XmNhighlightColor	Pixel	Black	CSG
XmNhighlightOnEnter	Boolean	False	CSG
XmNhighlightPixmap	Pixmap	XmUNSPECIFIED_PIXMAP	CSG
XmNhighlightThickness	XmRShort	0	CSG
XmNnavigationType	XmNavigarionType	*	CSG
XmNshadowThickness	Dimension	2	CS
XmNtopShadowColor	Pixel	*	CSG
XmNtopShadowPixmap	Pixmap	XmUNSPECIFIED_PIXMAP	CSG
XmNtraversalOn	Boolean	False	CSG
XmNunitType	unsigned char	XmPIXELS	CSG
XmNuserData	caddr_t	NULL	CSG

XmPushButton

class name: XmPushButton   class pointer: xmPushButtonWidgetClass

include file: <Xm/PushB.h>   inherits from: XmLbel

XmPushButton widget displays a text label or a pixmap in a window. You can optionally set up callbacks that the XmPushButton widget will call when the user presses the mouse button with the pointer inside the "button" window. Thus the user can issue a command by clicking on a button.

Name	Type	Default	Set/Get
XmNactivateCallback	XtCallbackList	NULL	C
XmNarmCallback	XtCallbackList	NULL	C
XmNarmColor	Pixel	*	CSG
XmNarmPixmap	Pixmap	XmUNSPECIFIED_PIXMAP	CSG
XmNdefaultButtonShadow	ThicknessDimension	0	CSG
XmNdisarmCallback	XtCallbackList	NULL	C
XmNfillOnArm	Boolean	True	CSG
XmNmultiClick	XmMultiClick	XmMULTICLICK_DISCARD	CSG
XmNshowAsDefault	Dimension	0	CSG

XmPushButtonGadget

class name: XmPushButtonGadget   class pointer: xmushButtonGadgetClass

include file: <Xm/PushBG.h>   inherits from: XmGadget

9

`XmPushButtonGadget` is similar to `XmPushButton` widget, except that `XmPushButtonGadget` does not have its own window (because it is a gadget) and displays the button in its parent's window.

Name	*Type*	*Default*	*Set/Get*
XmNactivateCallback	XtCallackist	NULL	C
XmNarmCallback	XtCallbackList	NULL	C
XmNarmColor	Pixel	*	CSG
XmNarmPixmap	Pixmap	XmUNSPECIFIED_PIXMAP	CSG
XmNdefaultButtonShadowThickness	Dimension	0	CSG
XmNdisarmCallback	XtCallbackList	NULL	C
XmNfillOnArm	Boolean	True	CSG
XmNmultiClick	XmMultiClick	XmMULTICLICK_DISCARD	CSG
XmNshowAsDefault	Dimension	0	CSG

XmRowColumn

class name: `XmowColumn`   class pointer: `xmRowColumnWidgetClass`

include file: `<Xm/RowColumn.h>`   inherits from: `XmManager`

The `XmRowColumn` widget arranges its children in rows and columns. You can use this widget in menubars and menu panes.

Name	*Type*	*Default*	*Set/Get*
XmNadjustLast	Boolean	True	CSG
XmNadjustMargin	Boolean	True	CSG
XmNbuttonAccelerators	StringTable	NULL	C
XmNbutoncceleratorText	XmStringTable	NULL	C
XmNbuttonCount	int	0	C
XmNbuttonMnemonicCharSets	XmStringCharSetTable	NULL	C
XmNbuttonMnemonics	KeySymTable	NULL	C G
XmNbuttons	XmStringTable	NULL	C
XmNbuttonSet	int	0	C
XmNbuttonType	XmButtonTypeTable	NULL	C
XmNentryAlignment	unsigned char	*	CSG
XmNentryBorder	Dimension	*	CSG
XmNentryCallback	XtCallbackList	NULL	C
XmNentryClass	WidgetClass	*	CSG

continues

9

continued

Name	Type	Default	Set/Get
XmNisAligned	Boolean	True	CSG
XmNisHomogeneous	Boolean	*	CSG
mNlabelString	XmString	NULL	C
XmNmapCallback	XtCallbackList	NULL	C
XmNmarginHeight	Dimension	*	CSG
XmNmarginWidth	Dimension	3	CSG
XmNmenuAccelerator	String	*	CSG
XmNmenuHelpWidget	Widget	NULL	CSG
XmNmenuHistory	Widget	NULL	CSG
XmNmenuCursor	String	"arrow"	C
XmNmnemonic	XmMnemonic	*	CSG
XmNmnemonicCharSet	String	"ISO8859-1"	CSG
XmNnumColumns	short	*	CSG
XmNoptionLabel	XmString	NULL	C G
XmNorientation	unsigned char		CSG
XmNpacking	unsigned char	*	CSG
XmNpopupEnabled	Boolean	True	CSG
XmNpostFromButton	int	0	C
XmNpostFromCount	int	0	CSG
XmNpostFromList	WidgetList	NULL	CSG
XmNradioAlwaysOne	Boolean	True	CSG
XmNradioBehavior	Boolean	False	CSG
XmNresizeHeight	Boolean	True	CSG
XmNresizeWidth	Boolean	True	CSG
XmNrowColumnType	unsigned char	XmWORK_AREA	C G
XmNshadowThickness	Dimension	0	CSG
XmNsimpleCallback	XtCallbackList	NULL	C
XmNspacing	Dimension	*	CSG
XmNsubMenuId	Widget	NULL	CSG
XmNunmapCallback	XtCallbackList	NULL	C
XmNwhichButton	unsigned int	*	CSG

9

XmScale

class name: XmScale   class pointer: xmScaleWidgetClass

includeFile: <Xm/Scale.h>   inherits from: XmManager

The XmScale widget displays a scale with a range of values from which the user can specify a value by moving the slider within the scale.

Name	Type	Default	Set/Get
XmNdecimalPoint	short	0	CSG
XmNdragCallback	XtCallbackList	NULL	C
XmNfontList	XmFontList	NULL	CSG
XmNhghlghtOnEnter	Boolean	False	CSG
XmNhighlightThickness	Dimension	2	CSG
XmNmaximum	int	100	CSG
XmNminimum	int	0	CSG
XmNorientation	unsigned char	XmVERTICAL	CSG
XmNprocessingDirection	unsigned char	*	CSG
XmNscaleHeight	Dimension	0	CSG
XmNscaleMultiple	int	1	CSG
XmNscaleWidth	Dimension	0	CSG
XmNshowValue	Boolea	False	CSG
XmNtitleString	XmString	NULL	CSG
XmNtraversalOn	Boolean	False	CSG
XmNvalue	int	0	CSG
XmNvalueChangedCallback	XtCallbackList	NULL	C

XmScrollBar

class name: XmScrollBar   class pointer: xmScrollBarWidgetClass

include file: <Xm/ScrollB.h>   inherits from: XmPrimitive

The XmScrollBar widget displays a scrollbar. You can set up callbacks to scroll the contents of the work area appropriately when the user presses on various parts of the scrollbar.

9

Name	Type	Default	Set/Get
XmNdecrementCallback	XtCallbackList	NULL	C
XmNdagCllback	XtCallbackList	NULL	C
XmNincrement	int	1	CSG
XmNincrementCallback	XtCallbackList	NULL	C
XmNinitialDelay	int	250 (milliseconds)	CSG
XmNmaximum	int	0	CSG
XmNminimum	int	0	CSG
XmNorientation	unsigned char	XmVERTICAL	CSG
XmNpagedecrementCallback	XtCallbackList	NULL	C
XmNpageIncrement	int	10	CSG
XmNpageincrementCallback	XtCallbackList	NULL	C
XmNprocessingDirection	unsigned char	*	CSG
XmNrepeatDelay	int	50	CS
XmNshowArrows	Boolean	True	CSG
XmNsliderSize	int	10	CSG
XmNtoBottomCallback	XtCallbackList	NULL	C
XmNtoTopCallback	XtCallbackList	NULL	C
XmNtroughColr	Pixel	*	CSG
XmNvalue	int	0	CSG
XmNvalueChangedCallback	XtCallbackList	NULL	C

XmScrolledWindow

class name: `XmScrolledWindow`   class pointer: `xmScrolledWindowWidgetClass`

include file: `<Xm/ScrolledW.h>`   inherits from: `XmManager`

The `XmScrolledWindow` widget manages a work area and two scrollbars (vertical and horizontal).

Name	Type	Default	Set/Get
XmNclipWindow	Widget	NULL	G
XmNhorizontalScrollBar	Widget	NULL	CSG
XmNscrollBarDisplayPolicy	unsigned char	XmSTATIC	C
XmNscrollBarPlacement	unsigned char	XmBOTTOM_RIGHT	CSG
XmNscrolledWindowMarginHeight	Dimension	0	CSG
XmNscrolledWindowMarginWidth	Dimension	0	CSG

Name	Type	Default	Set/Get
XmNscrollingPolicy	unsigned char	XmAPPLICATION_DEFINED	CSG
XmNspacing	int	4	CSG
XmNverticalScrollBar	Widget	NULL	CSG
XmNvisualPolicy	unsigned char	XmVARIABLE	C G
XmNworkWindow	Widget	NULL	CSG

9

XmSelectionBox

class name: `XmSelectinBox`   class pointer: `xmSelectionBoxWidgetClass`

include file: `<Xm/SelectioB.h>`   inherits from: `XmBulletinBoard`

The `XmSelectionBox` widget enables users to select one item from a list of items. This widget manages an `XmList` widget, an area for text entry, and three buttons labeled OK, Cancel, and Help. A button labeled `Apply` is also available. You can change these labels by setting appropriate resources.

Name	Type	Default	Set/Get
XmNapplyCallback	XtCallbackList	NULL	C
XmNapplyLabelString	XmStrin	"Apply"	CSG
XmNcancelCallback	XtCallbackList	NULL	C
XmNcancelLabelString	XmString	"Cancel"	CSG
XmNdialogType	unsigned char	*	C G
XmNhelpLabelString	XmString	"Help"	CSG
XmNlistItemCount	int	0	CSG
XmNListItems	XmStringList	NULL	CSG
XmNlistLabelString	XmString	NULL	CSG
XmNlistVisibleItemCount	int	8	CSG
XmNminimizeButton	Boolean	False	CSG
XmNmustMatch	Boolean	False	CSG
XmNnoMatchCallback	XtCallackList	NULL	C
XmNokCallback	XtCallbackList	NULL	C
XmNokLabelString	XmString	"OK"	CSG
XmNselectionLabelString	XmString	Selection"	CSG
XmNtextAccelerators	XtTranslations	(predefined)	C
XmNtextColumns	int	20	CSG
XmNtextString	XmString	NULL	CSG

9

XmSeparator

class name: `XmSeparator`   class pointer: `xmSeparatorWidgetClass`

include file: `<Xm/Separator.h>`   inherit from: `XmPrimitive`

The `XmSeparator` widget can display a horizontal or vertical line with a three-dimensional look. You can use `XmSeparator` widgets as separators in lists and menu panes.

Name	Type	Default	Set/Get
XmNmargin	Dimension	0	CSG
XmNorientation	unsigned char	XHORZONTAL	CSG
XmNseparatorType	unsigned char	XmSHADOW_ETCHED_IN	CSG

XmSeparatorGadget

class name: `XmSeparatorGadget`   class pointer: `xmSeparatorGadgetClass`

include file: `<Xm/SeparatoG.h>`   inherits from: `XmGadget`

The `XmSeparatorGadget` is a gadget version of the `XmSeparator` widget.

Name	Type	Default	Set/Get
XmNmargin	Dimension	0	CSG
XmNorientation	unsigned char	XmHORIZONTAL	CSG
XmNseparatorType	unsigned char	XmSHADOW_ETCHED_IN	CSG

XmText

class name: `XText`   class pointer: `xmTextWidgetClass`

include file: `<Xm/Text.h>`   inherits from: `XmPrimitive`

The `XmText` widget acts as a single-line or multiline text editor.

Name	Type	Default	Set/Get
XmNactivateCallback	XtCallbackList	NULL	C
XmNautoShowCursorPosition	Boolean	True	CSG
XmNblinkRate	int	500 (milliseconds)	CSG
XmNcolumns	short	20	CSG
XmNcursorPosition	XmTextPosiion	0	CSG
XmNcursorPositionVisible	Boolean	True	CSG
XmNeditable	Boolean	True	CSG

Name	Type	Default	Set/Get
XmNeditMode	int	XmSINGLE_LINE_EDIT	CSG
XmNfocusCallback	XtCallbackList	NULL	C
XmNfontList	XmFontList	NULL	CSG
XmNgainPrimaryCallback	XtCallbackList	NULL	C
XmNlosePrimaryCallback	XtCallbackList	NULL	C
XmNlosingFocusCallback	XtCallbackList	NULL	C
XmNmarginHeight	Dimension	3	CG
XmNmarginWidth	Dimension	3	CSG
XmNmaxLength	int	MAXINT	CSG
XmNmodifyVerifyCallback	XtCallbackList	NULL	C
XmNmotionVerifyCallback	XtCallbackList	NULL	C
XmNpendingDelete	Boolean	True	CSG
XmNresizeHeight	Boolean	False	CSG
XmNresizeWidth	Boolean	False	CSG
XmNrows	int	1	CSG
XmNscrollHorizontal	Boolean	True	C G
XmNcrollLeftSide	Boolean	False	C G
XmNscrollTopSide	Boolean	False	C G
XmNscrollVertical	Boolean	True	C G
XmNselectionArray	Pointer	default array	CSG
XmNselectionArrayCount	int	4	CSG
XmNselectThreshold	int	5	CSG
XmNsource	XmTextSource	default source	CSG
XmNtopCharacter	XmTextPosition	0	CSG
XmNvalue	String	" "	CSG
XmNvalueChangedCallback	XtCallbackList	NULL	C
XmNverifyBell	Boolean	True	CSG
XmNwordWrap	Boolean	False	CSG

XmTextField

class name: XmTextFeld   class pointer: xmTextWidgetClass

include file: <Xm/TextF.h>   inherits from: XmPrimitive

The XmText widget provides a single-line editable text field.

9

Name	Type	Default	Set/Get
XmNactivateCallback	XtCallbackList	NULL	C
XmNblinkRate	int	500 (milliseconds)	CSG
XmNcolumns	short	20	CSG
XmNcursorPosition	XmTextPosition	0	CS
XmNcursorPositionVisible	Boolan	True	CSG
XmNeditable	Boolean	True	CSG
XmNfontList	XmFontList	NULL	CSG
XmNgainPrimaryCallback	XtCallbackList	NULL	C
XmNlosePrimaryCallback	XtCallbackList	NULL	C
XmNlosingFocusCallback	XtCallbackList	NULL	C
XmNmarginHeight	Dimension	3	CSG
XmNmarginWidth	Dimension	3	CSG
XmNmaxLength	int	MAXINT	CSG
XmNmodifyVerifyCallback	XtCalbackList	NULL	C
XmNmotionVerifyCallback	XtCallbackList	NULL	C
XmNpendingDelete	Boolean	True	CSG
XmNresizeWidth	Boolean	False	CSG
XmNselectionArray	Pointer	default arra	CSG
XmNselectionArrayCount	int	4	CSG
XmNselectThreshold	int	5	CSG
XmNsource	XmTextSource	default source	CSG
XmNvalue	String	" "	CSG
XNvalueChangedCallback	XtCallbackList	NULL	C
XmNverifyBell	Boolean	True	CSG

XmToggleButton

class name: XmToggleButton   class pointer: xmToggleButtonWidgetClass

include file: <Xm/ToggleB.h>   inherits from: XmLabel

The XmToggleButton widget is used to select one or more of a fixed set of
selections that are displayed as buttons that can be toggled on or off.

Name	Type	Default	Set/Get
XmNarmCallback	XtCallbackList	NULL	C
XmNdisarmCallback	XtCallbackList	NULL	C
XmNillOnSelect	Boolean	True	CSG
XmNindicatorOn	Boolean	True	CSG
XmNindicatorSize	Dimension	XmINVALID_DIMENSION	CSG
XmNindicatorType	unsiged char	*	CSG
XmNselectColor	Pixel	*	CSG
XmNselectInsensitivePixmap	Pixmap	XmUNSPECIFIED_PIXMAP	CSG
XmNselectPixmap	Pixmap	XmUNSPECIFIED_PIXMAP	CSG
XmNset	Boolean	False	CSG
XmNspacing	Dimension	4	CSG
XmNvalueChangedCallback	XtCallbackList	NULL	C
XmNvisibleWhenOff	Boolean	*	CSG

XmToggleButtonGadget

class name: XmToggleButtonGadget　　　class pointer: xmToggleButtonGadgetClass

include file: <Xm/ToggleBG.h>　　　inherits from: XmGadget

The XmToggleButtonGadget is the gadget version of the XmToggleButton widget.

Name	Type	Default	Set/Get
XmNarmCallback	XtCallbackList	NULL	C
XmNdisarmCallback	XtCallbackList	NULL	C
XmNfillOnSelect	Boolean	True	CSG
XmNindicatorOn	Booean	True	CSG
XmNindicatorSize	Dimension	XmINVALID_DIMENSION	CSG
XmNindicatorType	unsigned char	*	CSG
XmNselectColor	Pixel	*	CSG
XmNselectInsensitivePixmap	Pixmap	XmUNSPECIFIED_PIXMAP	CSG
XmNselectPixmap	Pixmap	XmUNSPECIFIED_PIXMAP	CSG
XmNset	Boolean	False	CS
XmNspacing	Dimension	4	CSG
XmNvalueChangedCallback	XtCallbackList	NULL	C
XmNvisibleWhenOff	Boolean	*	CSG

9

Motif Callback Structures

In Xt Intrinsics-based toolkits such as Motif, a callback function has three arguments:

First argument: The ID of the widget for which the callback is registered.

Second argument: In this argument, the callback receives a pointer that you have to provide when you register the calback. Through this pointer you can pass to the callback function any information you deem necessary for your application.

Third argument: This argument is a pointer to a *callback structure*—a Motif data structure that usually includes information on the event that caused the callback and any other information about the widget that will help you perform the appropriate action in the callback.

This section shows the data structures for a number of callback structures. The XmAnyCallbackStruct is the most common callback structure, but many widgets have special structures to convey information specific to those widgets.

XmAnyCallbackStruct
Defined in: <Xm/Xm.h>

```
typedef struct
{
    int     reason;
    XEvent  *event;
} XmAnyCallbackStruct;
```

XmCommandCallbackStruct
Defined in: <Xm/Xm.h>

```
typedef struct
{
    int       reason;
    XEvent    *event;
    XmString  value;
    int       length;
} XmCommandCallbackStruct;
```

9

XmDrawingAreaCallbackStruct

Defined in: `<Xm/Xm.h>`

```
typedef struct
{
    int     reason;
    XEvent  *event;
    Window  window;
} XmDrawingAreaCallbackStruct;
```

XmDrawnButtonCallbackStruct

Defined in: `<Xm/Xm.h>`

```
typedef struct
{
    int     reason;
    XEvent  *event;
    Window  window;
} XmDrawnButtonCallbackStruct;
```

XmFileSelectionBoxCallbackStruct

Defined in: `<Xm/Xm.h>`

```
typedef struct
{
    int       reason;
    XEvent    *event;
    XmString  value;
    int       length;
    XmString  mask;
    int       mask_length;
} XmFileSelectionBoxCallbackStruct;
```

XmFontList
XmFontListRec

Defined in: `<Xm/Xm.h>`

```
typedef struct
{
    XFontStruct     *font;
    XmStringCharSet charset;
} XmFontListRec, *XmFontList;
```

XmListCallbackStruct

Defined in: <Xm/Xm.h>

```
typedef struct
{
    int       reason;
    XEvent    *event;
    XmString  item;
    int       item_length;
    int       item_position;
    XmString  *selected_items;
    int       selected_item_count;
    int       selection_type;
} XmListCallbackStruct;
```

XmRowColumnCallbackStruct

Defined in: <Xm/Xm.h>

```
typedef struct
{
    int       reason;
    XEvent    *event;
    Widget    widget;
    char      *data;
    char      *callbackstruct;
} XmRowColumnCallbackStruct;
```

XmScaleCallbackStruct

Defined in: <Xm/Xm.h>

```
typedef struct
{
    int reason;
    XEvent * event;
    int value;
} XmScaleCallbackStruct;
```

9

XmScrollBarCallbackStruct
Defined in: <Xm/Xm.h>

```
typedef struct
{
    int     reason;
    XEvent *event;
    int     value;
    int     pixel;
} XmScrollBarCallbackStruct;
```

XmSelectionBoxCallbackStruct
Defined in: <Xm/Xm.h>

```
typedef struct
{
    int reason;
    XEvent    *event;
    XmString   value;
    int        length;
} XmSelectionBoxCallbackStruct;
```

XmToggleButtonCallbackStruct
Defined in: <Xm/Xm.h>

```
typedef struct
{
    int     reason;
    XEvent *event;
    int     set;
} XmToggleButtonCallbackStruct;
```

10

Xt Intrinsics Quick Reference

T his chapter is designed to serve as a quick reference guide to the Xt Intrinsics—the foundation on which toolkits like Motif are built. It provides summary descriptions of the Xt Intrinsics functions, and it lists the form of callbacks, event handlers, and other functions that you have to define when programming with the Xt Intrinsics. You will also find the definitions of some commonly used Xt Intrinsic data types. The material in this quick reference guide conforms to the Xt Intrinsics that accompany X Window System, Version 11, Release 4 (X11R4).

The function prototypes shown in this chapter will help you recall the calling syntax of a function, but the short description does not tell you fully how to use that function. For detailed information on the Xt Intrinsics functions, consult Paul J. Asente or Ralph R. Swick, *X Window System Toolkit*, Digital Press, 1990, 1002 pages.

Xt Intrinsics Functions

The Xt Intrinsics functions for X11R4 are shown in ANSI standard prototype format. Each argument is explained through a comment next to the argument. A brief description of the function follows each prototype declaration. Some functions from the X11R3 Xt Intrinsics are superseded by others in X11R4 version of the Intrinsics. A comment on the first line of the function's declaration (see XtAddActions, for instance) tells you which function to use in X11R4.

XtAddActions

```
void XtAddActions(          /* Superseded by XtAppAddActions */
    XtActionList actions,      /* Action name and procedure */
    Cardinal     num_actions); /* Number of actions in list */
```

Registers an action table with the translation manager. An action table binds a name to a function to be called when that action's name appears in the translation resource of the application.

XtAddCallback

```
void XtAddCallback(
    Widget         widget,        /* Callback for this widget */
    const String   callback_name, /* Name of callback list    */
    XtCallbackProc callback,      /* The callback function    */
    XtPointer      client_data);  /* 2nd argument to callback */
```

Adds a callback function to the named callback list of a widget.

XtAddCallbacks

```
void XtAddCallbacks(
    Widget         widget,        /* Callbacks for this widget  */
    const String   callback_name, /* Name of callback list      */
    XtCallbackList callbacks);    /* List of callback functions */
                                  /* A NULL marks list's end    */
```

Adds several callback functions to the named callback list of a widget.

XtAddConverter

```
void XtAddConverter(        /* Superseded by XtSetTypeConverter */
    const String     from_type,    /* Convert from this type */
    const String     to_type,      /* to this data type      */
    XtConverter      converter,    /* Function that converts */
    XtConvertArgList convert_args, /* Arguments to function  */
    Cardinal         nargs);       /* Number of arguments    */
```

Registers a function that can convert values from from_type to to_type.

XtAddEventHandler

```
void XtAddEventHandler(
    Widget         widget,        /* Register for this widget */
    EventMask      eventMask,     /* To handle these events   */
    Boolean        nonmaskable,   /* For nonmaskable events?  */
    XtEventHandler proc,          /* The event handler        */
    XtPointer      client_data);  /* Data for the handler     */
```

Registers an event handler that is called when events matching eventMask occur in the widget.

XtAddExposureToRegion

```
void XtAddExposureToRegion(
    XEvent*  event,    /* Expose or GraphicsExpose event   */
    Region   region);  /* Region to which rectangle is added */
```

Adds the "exposed" rectangle from the specified Expose or GraphicsExpose event to the specified region.

XtAddGrab

```
void XtAddGrab(
    Widget   widget,          /* Widget to be made modal       */
    Boolean  exclusive,       /* True = send all events to widget */
    Boolean  spring_loaded);  /* True = popped up by button-press */
```

Redirects user's inputs to a specified widget.

XtAddInput

```
XtInputId XtAddInput(            /* Superseded by XtAppAddInput */
    int                 source,     /* File descriptor         */
    XtPointer           condition,  /* When event generated   */
    XtInputCallbackProc proc,       /* Callback function       */
    XtPointer           client_data); /* Data for callback     */
```

Adds a file as a source of input events for the default application context. Returns the descriptor for the new input source.

XtAddRawEventHandler

```
void XtAddRawEventHandler(
    Widget          widget,       /* Handler for this widget  */
    EventMask       eventMask,    /* Handler for this event   */
    Boolean         nonmaskable,  /* For nonmaskable event    */
    XtEventHandler  proc,         /* Function to handle event */
    XtPointer       client_data); /* Data for event handler   */
```

Registers an event handler for the widget without selecting the specified event.

XtAddTimeOut

```
XtIntervalId XtAddTimeOut(  /* Superseded by XtAppAddTimeOut */
    unsigned long       interval,     /* Milliseconds        */
    XtTimerCallbackProc proc,         /* Callback function   */
    XtPointer           client_data); /* Data for callback   */
```

Sets up a function that is called when the specified time interval has elapsed. The function is called only once. You can activate the callback function repeatedly by setting up a new time-out in the time-out callback function (by calling XtAddTimeOut again).

10

XtAddWorkProc

```
XtWorkProcId XtAddWorkProc( /* Superseded by XtAppAddWorkProc */
    XtWorkProc  proc,          /* The "work procedure"          */
    XtPointer   client_data); /* Pointer passed to WorkProc     */
```

Sets up a *WorkProc*—a function to be called when the application is waiting for input.

XtAppAddActionHook

```
XtActionHookId XtAppAddActionHook(
    XtAppContext     app,          /* Use hook in this context */
    XtActionHookProc proc,         /* The hook function        */
    XtPointer        client_data); /* Data passed to "proc"    */
```

Sets up a function to be called just before an action is about to be performed by the translation manager. Returns an identifier for the registered "action hook." You can use this identifier as an argument to XtRemoveActionHook to remove the function.

XtAppAddActions

```
void XtAppAddActions(
    XtAppContext app,          /* Use in this context   */
    XtActionList actions,      /* List of actions       */
    Cardinal     num_actions); /* Number of actions     */
```

Registers a list of actions with the translation manager for use in the specified application context.

XtAppAddConverter

```
void XtAppAddConverter( /* Superseded by XtAppSetTypeConverter */
    XtAppContext     app,           /* Use in this context      */
    const String     from_type,     /* Convert from this type   */
    const String     to_type,       /* to this type             */
    XtConverter      converter,      /* Function that converts   */
    XtConvertArgList convert_args,  /* Arguments to function    */
    Cardinal         nargs);         /* Number of arguments      */
```

Registers a function for converting between two data types. The function is used in the specified application context.

XtAppAddInput

```
XtInputId XtAppAddInput(
    XtAppContext        app,          /* Use in this context  */
    int                 source,       /* File descriptor      */
    XtPointer           condition,    /* What types of inputs? */
    XtInputCallbackProc proc,         /* The callback function */
    XtPointer           client_data); /* Argument to callback  */
```

Adds a callback function that will be called whenever there is input from the specified input source.

XtAppAddTimeOut

```
XtIntervalId XtAppAddTimeOut(
    XtAppContext        app,          /* For this application */
    unsigned long       interval,     /* In milliseconds      */
    XtTimerCallbackProc proc,         /* Call this function   */
    XtPointer           client_data); /* Pass this to proc    */
```

Sets up a function to be called after a specified number of milliseconds. After the function is called, the time-out is removed.

XtAppAddWorkProc

```
XtWorkProcId XtAppAddWorkProc(
    XtAppContext app,          /* For this context */
    XtWorkProc   proc,         /* "work" function  */
    XtPointer    client_data); /* Pass this to proc */
```

Sets up a *work procedure*—a function to be called when the application would otherwise wait for input.

XtAppCreateShell

```
Widget XtAppCreateShell(
    const String name,          /* Name of application     */
    const String class,         /* Class name of application */
    WidgetClass  widget_class,  /* Class of top-level shell */
    Display*     display,       /* Connect to this X server */
    ArgList      args,          /* List of arguments       */
    Cardinal     nargs);        /* Number of arguments     */
```

Creates the top-level shell for an application and returns its widget ID.

10

10

XtAppError

```
void XtAppError(
    XtAppContext   app,       /* For this application context */
    const String   message); /* Report this error message    */
```

Calls the error-handling function of the specified application context and passes it the error message.

XtAppErrorMsg

```
void XtAppErrorMsg(
    XtAppContext app,       /* Application context           */
    const String name,      /* Error name                    */
    const String type,      /* Error type                    */
    const String class,     /* Resource class                */
    const String default,   /* Default error message         */
    String*      params,    /* Values for error message      */
    Cardinal*    nparams); /* Number of values in "params" */
```

Calls an error handler with arguments to help locate an error message and display the message.

XtAppGetErrorDatabase

```
XrmDatabase *XtAppGetErrorDatabase(
    XtAppContext    app);    /* Application context */
```

Returns the current error database.

XtAppGetErrorDatabaseText

```
void XtAppGetErrorDatabaseText(
    XtAppContext app,       /* Application context            */
    const String name,      /* Descriptive name of error      */
    const String type,      /* Error type                     */
    const String class,     /* Resource class                 */
    const String default,   /* Default error message          */
    String       buffer,    /* Buffer for returned message    */
    int          nbytes,    /* Buffer size                    */
    XrmDatabase  database); /* Use this error database        */
```

In buffer, this function returns the error message corresponding to the specified error.

XtAppGetSelectionTimeout

```
unsigned int XtAppGetSelectionTimeout(
    XtAppContext    app);   /* Application context         */
```

Returns the selection time-out value (in milliseconds).

XtAppInitialize

```
Widget XtAppInitialize(
    XtAppContext*    app_context_return, /* Returned context  */
    const String     application_class,  /* Appl. class name  */
    XrmOptionDescList options,            /* Command-line opt. */
    Cardinal         noptions,            /* Number of options */
    Cardinal*        argc_in_out,
    String*          argv_in_out,
    const String*    fallback_resources, /* Resources         */
    ArgList          args,                /* Arguments         */
    Cardinal         nargs);              /* Num. of arguments */
```

Initializes the Xt Intrinsics, creates an application context, opens a connection to the X server identified by the DISPLAY environment variable, and creates a top-level shell. When the function returns, the app_context_return argument will have the application context. This function returns the ID of the newly created application shell widget.

XtAppMainLoop

```
void XtAppMainLoop(
    XtAppContext app);
```

Starts processing events for the specified application context. This is equivalent to calling XtAppNextEvent followed by a call to XtDispatchEvent.

XtAppNextEvent

```
void XtAppNextEvent(
    XtAppContext app,
    XEvent*      event); /* Event information returned here */
```

This function provides the next event for the specified application context. The information is returned in the XEvent structure whose address is in the event argument.

XtAppPeekEvent

```
Boolean XtAppPeekEvent(
    XtAppContext app,
    XEvent*      event); /* Event information returned here */
```

Returns True if there is an event for the specified application context and provides information for the event in the XEvent structure whose address you pass in the event argument.

XtAppPending

```
XtInputMask XtAppPending(
    XtAppContext app);
```

Returns a bit mask indicating the type of pending events for the specified application context. A zero return value indicates that there are no pending events. The returned bit mask will be a bitwise OR of the following constants: XtIMXEvent (the XtIM prefix stands for Xt Input Mask), XtIMTime, and XtIMAlternateInput.

XtAppProcessEvent

```
void XtAppProcessEvent(
    XtAppContext app,
    XtInputMask  mask); /* Identifies event to process */
```

Processes an event from the source specified by the mask, which can be one of the following:

> XtAlternateInput, which refers to an alternate input (set up by XtAppAddInput)

> XtIMTime, which refers to a time-out event (set up by XtAppAddTimeOut)

> XtIMXEvent, which refers to a normal X event

XtAppReleaseCacheRefs

```
void XtAppReleaseCacheRefs(
    XtAppContext app,
    XtICacheRef  *refs); /* Release these cache entries */
```

Decrements the reference count for the cache entries listed in the array refs. The cache IDs in refs are values previously returned by XtAppAddConverter.

XtAppSetErrorHandler

```
XtErrorHandler XtAppSetErrorHandler(
    XtAppContext    app,
    XtErrorHandler eproc); /* New handler for fatal errors */
```

Sets up eproc as the function to be called when a fatal error occurs for the specified application context. This function returns the previously installed error handler which, in most cases, would be the default error handler called _XtDefaultError. On UNIX systems, the default error handler prints a message on stderr and terminates the application.

XtAppSetErrorMsgHandler

```
XtAppSetErrorMsgHandler(
    XtAppContext        app,
    XtErrorMsgHandler eproc); /* New handler for fatal errors */
```

Installs eproc as the handler for fatal errors and returns the previously installed handler. The default handler is _XtDefaultErrorMsg which calls XtGetErrorDatabaseText to construct an error message and passes that message to XtAppError.

XtAppSetFallbackResources

```
void XtAppSetFallbackResources(
XtAppContext    app,
    const String* defaults); /* Default values of resources */
```

Sets up the resource specifications in the defaults array as the default values for the resources applicable to that application context.

XtAppSetSelectionTimeout

```
void XtAppSetSelectionTimeout(
    XtAppContext    app,
    unsigned long    timeout); /* Time in milliseconds */
```

Sets the selection time-out value (in milliseconds) for the specified application context. This is the time within which an application must respond to a selection event from another application. The default value comes from the application's selectionTimeout resource. If this resource is undefined the selection time-out is set to 5000 milliseconds (5 seconds).

10

10

XtAppSetTypeConverter

```
void XtAppSetTypeConverter(
    XtAppContext     app,
    const String     from_type,      /* Convert from this type  */
    const String     to_type,        /* to this type            */
    XtTypeConverter  converter,      /* Function that converts  */
    XtConvertArgList convert_args,   /* Arguments for function   */
    Cardinal         nargs,          /* Number of arguments     */
    XtCacheType      cache_type,     /* Indicates how to share  */
                                     /* this resource           */
    XtDestructor     destructor);    /* Function to be called   */
                                     /* before freeing resource */
```

Sets up a function to be called when a resource has to be converted from from_type to to_type. These types are identified by constants such as XtRColor, XtRPixel, and XtRString, which are defined in the file <X11/StringDefs.h>. The cache_type argument can take one of the following values:

XtCacheAll to share among all applications displaying at an X server.

XtCacheByDisplay is like XtCacheAll, but destructor is called when the display is closed by calling XtCloseDisplay.

XtCacheNone means do not share (in other words, no need to save in cache).

XtCacheRefCount means share, but destroy when no application uses resource.

XtAppSetWarningHandler

```
XtErrorHandler XtAppSetWarningHandler(
    XtAppContext  app,
    XtErrorHandler  wproc); /* New handler for warnings */
```

Sets up wproc as the function to be called to handle warnings (nonfatal errors) and returns the previously installed warning handler.

XtAppSetWarningMsgHandler

```
XtErrorMsgHandler XtAppSetWarningMsgHandler(
    XtAppContext      app,
    XtErrorMsgHandler wproc); /* Handler for warnings */
```

Installs wproc as the function to be called to handle warnings (nonfatal errors) and returns the previously installed warning handler.

10

XtAppWarning

```
void XtAppWarning(
    XtAppContext app,
    const String message); /* Report this warning message */
```

Calls the default warning handler with a message to be reported.

XtAppWarningMsg

```
void XtAppWarningMsg(
    XtAppContext app,       /* Application context        */
    const String name,      /* Descriptive name of warning */
    const String type,      /* Error type                 */
    const String class,     /* Resource class             */
    const String default,   /* Default warning message    */
    String*      params,    /* Values for warning message */
    Cardinal*    nparams);  /* Number of values in "params" */
```

Calls the nonfatal error handler with arguments to help locate a warning message and display the message.

XtAugmentTranslations

```
void XtAugmentTranslations(
    Widget         w,     /* Alter this widget's translations */
    XtTranslations new);  /* Merge in this translation table  */
```

Merges a set of new translations into the existing translation table of the specified widget. A *translation table* specifies what function should be called when an event or a sequence of events occurs in a widget.

XtBuildEventMask

```
EventMask XtBuildEventMask(
    Widget w); /* Return event mask for this widget */
```

Returns the event mask for the specified widget. The event mask indicates what type of events the widget accepts.

XtCallAcceptFocus

```
Boolean XtCallAcceptFocus(
    Widget w, /* Call widget's "accept_focus" function */
    Time*  t); /* Timestamp of the triggering event     */
```

Calls the accept_focus procedure of the specified widget. This function returns False if the widget's accept_focus function is NULL. Otherwise, XtCallAcceptFocus returns the same value returned by the widget's accept_focus function.

10

XtCallActionProc

```
void XtCallActionProc(
    Widget       widget,    /* Call this widget's action func. */
    const String action,    /* Invoke action with this name    */
    XEvent*      event,     /* Event passed to action routine  */
    String*      params,    /* Parameters passed to action     */
    Cardinal     nparams);  /* Number of parameters in params  */
```

Calls the action procedure bound to an action of a specified name.

XtCallbackExclusive

```
void XtCallbackExclusive(
    Widget    widget,       /* Use this widget's callbacks     */
    XtPointer client_data,  /* Map this pop-up shell           */
    XtPointer call_data);   /* Not used, okay to specify NULL  */
```

Maps a pop-up shell from a widget's callback list. The client_data argument specifies the shell to be mapped. This function does its job by calling XtPopup with the grab_kind argument set to XtGrabExclusive. This is a modal pop-up; all inputs go the specified shell's widgets only.

XtCallbackNone

```
void XtCallbackNone(
    Widget    widget,       /* Use this widget's callbacks     */
    XtPointer client_data,  /* Map this pop-up shell           */
    XtPointer call_data);   /* Not used, okay to specify NULL  */
```

Maps a pop-up shell from a widget's callback list. The client_data argument specifies the shell to be mapped. This function does its job by calling XtPopup with the grab_kind argument set to XtGrabNone. In this case, user input is not restricted (a nonmodal pop-up).

XtCallbackNonexclusive

```
void XtCallbackNonexclusive(
    Widget    widget,       /* Use this widget's callbacks    */
    XtPointer client_data,  /* Map this pop-up shell          */
    XtPointer call_data);   /* Not used, ok to specify NULL   */
```

Pops up a shell widget from a widget's callback list. The client_data argument specifies the shell to be mapped. This function does its job by calling XtPopup with the grab_kind argument set to XtGrabNonexclusive.

XtCallbackPopdown

```
void XtCallbackPopdown(
    Widget    widget,        /* Widget activating pop-down  */
    XtPointer client_data,  /* Pointer to an XtPopdownID    */
    XtPointer call_data);   /* Not used, ok to specify NULL */
```

Pops down the shell identified by the shell_widget field of the XtPopdownID structure whose address is in the client_data argument of the function.

10

XtCallbackReleaseCacheRef

```
void XtCallbackReleaseCacheRef(
    Widget    widget,        /* Affects this widget's cache  */
    XtPointer client_data,  /* Pointer to a XtCacheRef       */
    XtPointer call_data);   /* Not used, ok to specify NULL */
```

Decrements the reference count for the cache entry identified by the XtCacheRef structure whose address is in the client_data argument.

XtCallbackReleaseCacheRefList

```
void XtCallbackReleaseCacheRefList(
    Widget    widget,        /* Affects this widget's cache  */
    XtPointer client_data,  /* Pointer to a XtCacheRef*      */
    XtPointer call_data);   /* Not used, ok to specify NULL */
```

Decrements the reference count for the cache entries identified by the null-terminated list of XtCacheRef structures whose address is in the client_data argument.

XtCallCallbackList

```
void XtCallCallbackList(
    Widget    widget,        /* Call this widget's callbacks */
    XtCallbackList cblist,   /* Call this list of callbacks  */
    XtPointer      cbdata); /* Data passed to each callback */
```

Calls the callback functions listed in the argument cblist.

XtCallCallbacks

```
void XtCallCallbacks(
    Widget    widget,        /* Call this widget's callbacks */
    const String cbname,     /* Name of callback list        */
    XtPointer      cbdata); /* Data passed to each callback */
```

Calls the callbacks in the named list of callbacks for the specified widget.

XtCallConverter

```
Boolean XtCallConverter(
    Display*         display,                /* Identifies X server */
    XtTypeConverter  converter,              /* Conversion function */
    XrmValuePtr      args,                   /* Arguments for func. */
    Cardinal         nargs,                  /* Number of arguments */
    XrmValuePtr      from,                   /* Convert this value  */
    XrmValuePtr      to_return,              /* Returned value      */
    XtCacheRef*      cache_ref_return);      /* Returned cache ID   */
```

Explicitly calls a conversion function to convert a resource from one type to another and return a cache ID for the converted resource.

XtCalloc

```
char *XtCalloc(
    Cardinal nelements,  /* Storage for these many elements */
    Cardinal elem_size); /* each of this size (bytes)       */
```

Allocates storage for an array of elements and initializes the storage to zero. Returns a pointer to the newly allocated storage. Calls XtAppErrorMsg if memory allocation fails.

XtClass

```
WidgetClass XtClass(
    Widget w); /* Return this widget's "widget class" */
```

Returns a pointer to a widget's class structure.

XtCloseDisplay

```
void XtCloseDisplay(
    Display* display); /* Connection to be closed */
```

Closes the connection to the X server identified by display.

XtConfigureWidget

```
void XtConfigureWidget(
Widget    w               /* Configure this widget      */
    Position  x,          /* New position of widget     */
    Position  y,
    Dimension width,      /* New width of widget        */
    Dimension height,     /* New height of widget       */
    Dimension bdwidth);   /* New border width (pixels)  */
```

Moves and resizes the specified widget.

XtConvert

```
void XtConvert(        /* Superseded by XtConvertAndStore */
    Widget        widget,    /* Resource for this widget */
    const String from_type,  /* Convert from this type   */
    XrmValue*    from,       /* Convert this value       */
    const String to_type,    /* Convert to this type     */
    XrmValue*    to_return); /* Returned value           */
```

Converts a resource from one type to another.

XtConvertAndStore

```
Boolean XtConvertAndStore(
    Widget        widget,    /* Resource for this widget */
    const String from_type,  /* Convert from this type   */
    XrmValue*    from,       /* Convert this value       */
    const String to_type,    /* Convert to this type     */
    XrmValue*    to_return); /* Returned value           */
```

Converts a resource from one type to another. Returns True if conversion is successful and False otherwise.

XtConvertCase

```
void XtConvertCase(
    Display* display,        /* Identifies the X server   */
    KeySym   keysym,         /* Convert this keysym       */
    KeySym*  lower_return,   /* Returns lowercase version */
    KeySym*  upper_return);  /* Returns uppercase version */
```

Converts the specified keysym into lowercase and uppercase and returns these values in the arguments lower_return and upper_return.

XtCreateApplicationContext

```
XtAppContext XtCreateApplicationContext(void);
```

Creates and returns an application context.

XtCreateApplicationShell

```
Widget XtCreateApplicationShell(
                    /* Superseded by XtAppCreateShell */
    const String name,    /* Not used (call with NULL)      */
    WidgetClass  wclass, /* Widget's class                 */
    ArgList      args,   /* Arguments with resource values */
    Cardinal     nargs); /* Number of arguments in args    */
```

Creates a top-level shell widget and returns its ID. This function has been superseded by XtAppCreateShell in X11R4.

10

XtCreateManagedWidget

```
Widget XtCreateManagedWidget(
     const String name,    /* Name of the new widget      */
     WidgetClass  wclass,  /* Widget's class              */
     Widget       parent,  /* Create as child of this widget */
     ArgList      args,    /* Arguments with resource values */
     Cardinal     nargs);  /* Number of arguments in args */
```

Creates and manages a widget and returns the ID of the newly created widget.

XtCreatePopupShell

```
Widget XtCreatePopupShell(
     const String name,    /* Name of the new widget      */
     WidgetClass  wclass,  /* Widget's class              */
     Widget       parent,  /* Create as child of this widget */
     ArgList      args,    /* Arguments with resource values */
     Cardinal     nargs);  /* Number of arguments in args */
```

Creates a pop-up shell widget as a child of a specified widget and returns the ID of the newly created widget.

XtCreateWidget

```
Widget XtCreateWidget(
     const String name,    /* Name of the new widget      */
     WidgetClass  wclass,  /* Widget's class              */
     Widget       parent,  /* Create as child of this widget */
     ArgList      args,    /* Arguments with resource values */
     Cardinal     nargs);  /* Number of arguments in args */
```

Creates a widget and returns the ID of the newly created widget.

XtCreateWindow

```
void XtCreateWindow(
     Widget   widget,  /* Create window for this widget */
     unsigned class,   /* Class of window: InputOutput, */
                       /* InputOnly, CopyFromParent     */
     Visual   visual,  /* Visual type of window         */
     XtValueMask vm,   /* Indicates attributes to use   */
     XSetWindowAttributes xswa); /* Window attributes   */
```

Creates a widget's window. You normally need not call this function directly. The `realize` procedure of a widget calls this function to create the widget's window.

XtDatabase

```
XrmDatabase XtDatabase(
    Display* d); /* Return resource database for this server */
```

Returns the resource manager database associated with a particular X server.

XtDestroyApplicationContext

```
void XtDestroyApplicationContext(
    XtAppContext app); /* Destroy this application context */
```

Destroys the specified application context and closes its connection to the X server.

XtDestroyGC

```
void XtDestroyGC( /* Superseded by XtReleaseGC        */
    GC gc);        /* Graphics context to be destroyed */
```

Destroys a graphics context when it is no longer needed.

XtDestroyWidget

```
void XtDestroyWidget(
    Widget w); /* Destroy this widget */
```

Destroys the specified widget.

XtDirectConvert

```
void XtDirectConvert(  /* Superseded by XtCallConverter */
    XtConverter converter,  /* Function that converts  */
    XrmValuePtr args,       /* Arguments to converter  */
    Cardinal    nargs,      /* Number of arguments     */
    XrmValuePtr from,       /* Convert from this value  */
    XrmValue*   to_return); /* Returns converted value */
```

Converts a resource from one type to another. Starting with X11R4, you should call XtCallConverter to do this conversion.

XtDisownSelection

```
void XtDisownSelection(
    Widget widget,     /* Widget that is giving up ownership */
    Atom   selection, /* Selection being disowned          */
    Time   time);      /* Time when selection is given up    */
```

Indicates that the specified widget is giving up ownership of a selection.

XtDispatchEvent

```
Boolean XtDispatchEvent(
    XEvent* event); /* Event being dispatched */
```

Sends the event to the appropriate event handler.

XtDisplay

```
Display *XtDisplay(
    Widget w);  /* Return display for this widget */
```

Returns the X server connection ID for the specified widget.

XtDisplayInitialize

```
void XtDisplayInitialize(
    XtAppContext       app,      /* Application context     */
    Display*           display,  /* Connect to this server  */
    const String       name,     /* Name of application     */
    const String       class,    /* Class name of appl.     */
    XrmOptionDescRec*  options,  /* Acceptable options      */
    Cardinal           noptions, /* Elements in "options"   */
    Cardinal*          argc,     /* Number of cmd.-line args */
    char**             argv);    /* Command-line options    */
```

Initializes the connection to an X server and adds the connection to the specified application context.

XtDisplayOfObject

```
Display *XtDisplayOfObject(
    Widget w); /* Return display for this widget */
```

Returns the display pointer for a widget.

XtDisplayStringConversionWarning

```
void XtDisplayStringConversionWarning(
    Display*      dpy,      /* Display pointer              */
    const String  from,     /* Attempted to convert this    */
    const String  to_type); /* Tried conversion to this type */
```

Calls XtAppWarningMsg to issue a warning message when an attempted conversion fails.

XtDisplayToApplicationContext

```
XtAppContext XtDisplayToApplicationContext(Display* dpy);
```

Returns the application context in which the display is initialized.

XtError

```
void XtError(           /* Superseded by XtAppError        */
    const String msg); /* Error message passed to handler */
```

Calls the current fatal error handler with the specified error message.

XtErrorMsg

```
void XtErrorMsg(          /* Superseded by XtAppErrorMsg */
    const String name,    /* Error name                 */
    const String type,    /* Error type                 */
    const String class,   /* Resource class             */
    const String default, /* Default error message      */
    String*      params,  /* Values for error message   */
    Cardinal*    nparams); /* Number of values in "params" */
```

Calls an error handler with arguments to help locate an error message and display the message.

XtFindFile

```
String XtFindFile(
    const String     path,   /* List of pathnames        */
    Substitution     subst,  /* List of substitutions    */
    Cardinal         nsubst, /* Number of substitutions  */
    XtFilePredicate pfunc); /* Function to evaluate names */
```

Searches for a file using substitutions in a path list. Returns a filename, if the function pfunc declares one to be suitable. Please consult the book on Xt Intrinsics by Paul Asente and Ralph Swick (see the beginning of this chapter for details) for further information.

XtFree

```
void XtFree(
    char* ptr); /* Deallocate this memory */
```

Frees a block of memory allocated by a toolkit function.

XtGetActionKeysym

```
KeySym XtGetActionKeysym(
    XEvent*    ev,          /* Event passed to action proc */
    Modifiers* mod_return); /* Modifiers returned here      */
```

Returns the keysym and modifiers of an event in the translation table that matches the keyboard event specified by the ev argument.

XtGetApplicationNameAndClass

```
void XtGetApplicationNameAndClass(
    Display* display,       /* Identifies the X server      */
    String*  name_return,   /* Instance name returned here */
    String*  class_return); /* Class name returned here     */
```

Returns the instance name and the class name of the application. These are the same values that were passed to XtDisplayInitialize. You should not free the strings that are returned.

XtGetApplicationResources

```
void XtGetApplicationResources(
    Widget        widget,    /* Get resources for this     */
    XtPointer     base,      /* Where to write resources */
    XtResourceList resources, /* Resources to get           */
    Cardinal      nresource, /* Number of resources        */
    ArgList       args,      /* Command-line arguments     */
    Cardinal      nargs);    /* Number of arguments        */
```

Loads resources from the resource database associated with the specified widget's display.

XtGetConstraintResourceList

```
void XtGetConstraintResourceList(
    WidgetClass     wclass,      /* Resources for this class */
    XtResourceList* res_return,  /* Returned resource list   */
    Cardinal*     numres_return); /* Number of resources      */
```

Returns the resources for a particular widget class. The resource list is returned in res_return.

XtGetErrorDatabase

```
XrmDatabase *XtGetErrorDatabase(void);
                    /* Superseded by XtAppGetErrorDatabase */
```

Returns the error database.

XtGetErrorDatabaseText

```
void XtGetErrorDatabaseText(
        /* Superseded by XtAppGetErrorDatabaseText */
    const String name,    /* Name of error          */
    const String type,    /* Type of error          */
    const String class,   /* Resource class of error */
    const String default, /* Default error message  */
    String       buffer,  /* Returned error message */
    int          nbytes); /* Size of buffer in bytes */
```

Retrieves an error message from the error database.

XtGetGC

```
GC XtGetGC(
    Widget     widget,  /* Widget used to locate GC     */
    XtGCMask   gcvmask, /* Bitmask indicates desired values */
    XGCValues* values); /* GC values returned here      */
```

Returns selected graphics attributes in the values structure. The bitmask gcvmask indicates which attributes of the graphics context should be returned.

XtGetKeysymTable

```
KeySym* XtGetKeysymTable(
    Display* dpy,       /* Get table for this X server whose */
    KeyCode* min_keycode_return,  /* Minimum valid keycode  */
    int*     keysyms_per_keycode_return); /* A return value */
```

Returns a pointer to the X server's keycode-to-keysym mapping table.

XtGetMultiClickTime

```
int XtGetMultiClickTime(
    Display* dpy);
```

Returns the multiclick time in milliseconds for the specified X server.

XtGetResourceList

```
void XtGetResourceList(
    WidgetClass      wclass,       /* Resources for this class */
    XtResourceList* res_return,    /* Returned resource list   */
    Cardinal*       numres_return); /* Number of resources     */
```

Returns the resources for a particular widget class. The resource list is returned in res_return. When you are done with this list, call XtFree to deallocate it.

XtGetSelectionRequest

```
XSelectionRequestEvent *XtGetSelectionRequest(
    Widget      widget,    /* Widget owning selection       */
    Atom        selection, /* Selection being processed     */
    XtRequestId req_id);   /* ID for incremental conversion */
```

Returns the SelectionRequest event that triggered a call to the convert selection procedure of the widget. You generally need not call this function directly.

XtGetSelectionTimeout

```
unsigned int XtGetSelectionTimeout(void);
        /* Superseded by XtAppGetSelectionTimeout */
```

Returns the selection time-out value (in milliseconds).

XtGetSelectionValue

```
void XtGetSelectionValue(
    Widget      widget,    /* Widget requesting selection   */
    Atom        selection, /* Get this selection            */
    Atom        target,    /* Convert to this type          */
    XtSelectionCallbackProc callback, /* Procedure to be    */
                           /* called after getting selection */
    XtPointer client_data, /* Data passed to callback       */
    Time        time);     /* Timestamp of triggering event */
```

Retrieves the specified selection in a single transfer.

XtGetSelectionValueIncremental

```
void XtGetSelectionValueIncremental(
    Widget      widget,    /* Widget requesting selection   */
    Atom        selection, /* Get this selection            */
    Atom        target,    /* Convert to this type          */
    XtSelectionCallbackProc callback, /* Procedure to be    */
                           /* called after getting selection */
    XtPointer client_data, /* Data passed to callback       */
    Time        time);     /* Timestamp of triggering event */
```

Retrieves the specified selection using incremental transfer.

XtGetSelectionValues

```
void XtGetSelectionValues(
    Widget    widget,         /* Widget requesting selection   */
    Atom      selection,      /* Get from this selection       */
    Atom      *targets,       /* Convert to these types        */
    int       count,          /* Number of atoms in targets    */
    XtSelectionCallbackProc callback, /* Procedure to be       */
                              /* called after getting selection */
    XtPointer *client_data,   /* List of data for the callback */
    Time      time);          /* Timestamp of triggering event */
```

The effect of calling XtGetSelectionValues is identical to calling XtGetSelectionValue once for each target type in the targets array.

XtGetSelectionValuesIncremental

```
void XtGetSelectionValuesIncremental(
    Widget    widget,         /* Widget requesting selection   */
    Atom      selection,      /* Get from this selection       */
    Atom      *targets,       /* Convert to these types        */
    int       count,          /* Number of atoms in targets    */
    XtSelectionCallbackProc callback, /* Procedure to be       */
                              /* called after getting selection */
    XtPointer *client_data,   /* List of data for the callback */
    Time      time);          /* Timestamp of triggering event */
```

The effect of calling XtGetSelectionValuesIncremental is identical to calling XtGetSelectionValueIncremental once for each target type in the targets array.

XtGetSubresources

```
void XtGetSubresources(
    Widget        widget,   /* Subpart of this widget       */
    XtPointer     base,     /* Write resources here         */
    const String  name,     /* Name of subpart              */
    const String  class,    /* Class of subpart             */
    XtResourceList res,     /* Resource list of subpart     */
    Cardinal      nres,     /* Number of resources          */
    ArgList       args,     /* Resource specifications      */
    Cardinal      nargs);   /* Number of entries in args    */
```

Gets the resources for the subpart of a widget.

10

10

XtGetSubvalues

```
void XtGetSubvalues(
    XtPointer     base,     /* Write resources here      */
    XtResourceList res,     /* Resource list of subpart  */
    Cardinal      nres,     /* Number of resources       */
    ArgList       args,     /* Resource specifications   */
    Cardinal      nargs);   /* Number of entries in args */
```

Gets values of resources that are not associated with a widget (that is why there is no widget ID in the argument list).

XtGetValues

```
void XtGetValues(
    Widget  widget, /* Get this widget's resources */
    ArgList args,   /* Resource specifications     */
    Cardinal nargs); /* Number of entries in args  */
```

Retrieves a widget's resources. You specify the resources to be retrieved in the argument list args.

XtGrabButton

```
void XtGrabButton(
    Widget        widget,      /* Widget where grab occurs       */
    int           button,      /* Button to grab                 */
    Modifiers     modifiers,   /* Allowable modifier keys        */
    Boolean       own_events,  /* True=report events normally    */
    unsigned int  event_mask,  /* Report these events            */
    int           ptr_mode,    /* GrabModeSync or GrabModeAsync  */
    int           kbd_mode,    /* GrabModeSync or GrabModeAsync  */
    Window        cwin,        /* Confining window for pointer   */
    Cursor        cursor);     /* Cursor shown during grab       */
```

Passively grabs a specified pointer button. Grabbing implies that events are sent to one client only. A passive grab becomes active only when the user presses the button and key combination specified in the call to XtGrabButton.

XtGrabKey

```
void XtGrabKey(
    Widget    widget,       /* Widget where grab occurs       */
    KeyCode   keycode,      /* Key being grabbed              */
    Modifiers modifiers,    /* Allowable modifier keys        */
    Boolean   own_events,   /* True = report events normally  */
    int       ptr_mode,     /* GrabModeSync or GrabModeAsync  */
    int       kbd_mode);    /* GrabModeSync or GrabModeAsync  */
```

Passively grabs a single key on the keyboard.

XtGrabKeyboard

```
int XtGrabKeyboard(
    Widget    widget,      /* Widget where grab occurs    */
    Boolean   own_events,  /* True = report events normally */
    int       ptr_mode,    /* GrabModeSync or GrabModeAsync */
    int       kbd_mode,    /* GrabModeSync or GrabModeAsync */
    Time      time);       /* Timestamp or CurrentTime    */
```

Actively grabs the keyboard. Returns `GrabNotViewable` if the widget is not realized. An active grab starts as soon as the client calls the functions `XtGrabKeyboard` or `XtGrabPointer`.

XtGrabPointer

```
int XtGrabPointer(
    Widget    widget,          /* Widget where grab occurs    */
    Boolean   own_events,      /* True=report events normally */
    unsigned int event_mask,   /* Report these events         */
    int       ptr_mode,        /* GrabModeSync or GrabModeAsync */
    int       kbd_mode,        /* GrabModeSync or GrabModeAsync */
    Window    cwin,            /* Confining window for pointer */
    Cursor    cursor,          /* Cursor shown during grab    */
    Time      time);           /* Timestamp or CurrentTime    */
```

Actively grabs the pointer. Returns `GrabNotViewable` if the widget is not realized.

XtHasCallbacks

```
XtCallbackStatus XtHasCallbacks(
    Widget    w,        /* Search this widget's callback list */
    const String callback_name); /* Name of list to check */
```

Checks whether a widget has the specified callback list. The function returns one of the following values:

> `XtCallbackHasNoList` if there is no such callback list

> `XtCallbackHasNone` if the callback list exists but is empty

> `XtCallbackHasSome` if the callback list exists and has at least one entry

XtInitialize

```
Widget XtInitialize(                  /* Superseded by XtAppInitialize */
    const String      name,           /* Name of application */
    const String      class,          /* Class name of appl. */
    XrmOptionDescRec* options,        /* Acceptable options  */
```

```
Cardinal          noptions,  /* Elements in "options"        */
Cardinal*         argc,      /* Number of cmd.-line args     */
char**            argv);     /* Command-line options         */
```

Initializes the Xt Intrinsics, creates a default application context, and sets up connection the X server identified by the DISPLAY environment variable. Then, XtInitialize calls XtAppCreateShell to create a top-level shell widget and returns the widget ID.

XtInitializeWidgetClass

```
void XtInitializeWidgetClass(
    WidgetClass wclass);
```

Initializes a widget class.

XtInsertEventHandler

```
void XtInsertEventHandler(
    Widget        w, /* Register handler for this widget      */
    EventMask     eventMask,   /* Handler for this event       */
    Boolean       nonmaskable, /* True = for nonmaskable events */
    XtEventHandler proc,       /* The event handler            */
    XtPointer     client_data, /* Data passed to handler       */
    XtListPosition position);  /* Position of handler in list  */
```

Inserts an event handler at a specified position in the list of handlers for the widget.

XtInsertRawEventHandler

```
void XtInsertRawEventHandler(
    Widget        w, /* Register handler for this widget      */
    EventMask     eventMask,   /* Handler for this event       */
    Boolean       nonmaskable, /* True = for nonmaskable events */
    XtEventHandler proc,       /* The event handler            */
    XtPointer     client_data, /* Data passed to handler       */
    XtListPosition position);  /* Position of handler in list  */
```

Inserts an event handler at a specified position in the list of handlers for the widget. Unlike XtInsertEventHandler, XtInsertRawEventHandler does not modify the widget's event mask and does not solicit events from the X server by calling the Xlib function XSelectInput.

XtInstallAccelerators

```
void XtInstallAccelerators(
    Widget destination, /* Install on this widget by */
    Widget source);     /* copying from this one     */
```

Augments the accelerators in the destination widget with those from the source widget.

XtInstallAllAccelerators

```
void XtInstallAllAccelerators(
    Widget destination, /* Install on this widget by */
    Widget source);     /* copying from this one    */
```

Augments the accelerators in the destination widget with those from the source widget and all of the descendants of source.

XtIsApplicationShell

```
Boolean XtIsApplicationShell(widget);
```

This macro returns True if widget is of class ApplicationShell or is derived from an ApplicationShell.

XtIsComposite

```
Boolean XtIsComposite(Widget w);
```

Returns True if widget is of class Composite or is derived from a Composite.

XtIsConstraint

```
Boolean XtIsConstraint(Widget w);
```

Returns True if widget is of class Constraint or is derived from a Constraint.

XtIsManaged

```
Boolean XtIsManaged(Widget rectobj);
```

Returns True if widget is currently managed.

XtIsObject

```
Boolean XtIsObject(Widget object);
```

Returns True if widget is of class Object or is derived from an Object.

XtIsOverrideShell

```
Boolean XtIsOverrideShell(Widget w);
```

Returns True if widget is of class OverrideShell or is derived from an OverrideShell.

10

XtIsRealized

```
Boolean XtIsRealized(Widget widget);
```

Returns True if widget is currently realized.

XtIsRectObj

```
Boolean XtIsRectObj(Widget object);
```

Returns True if widget is of class RectObj or is derived from a RectObj.

XtIsSensitive

```
Boolean XtIsSensitive(Widget widget);
```

Returns True if widget is currently sensitive. When a widget is *sensitive*, user input events are dispatched to it.

XtIsShell

```
Boolean XtIsShell(Widget w);
```

Returns True if widget is of class Shell or is derived from a Shell.

XtIsSubclass

```
Boolean XtIsSubclass(
    Widget      widget,  /* Is this widget */
    WidgetClass wclass); /* of this class? */
```

Returns True if the specified widget is of class wclass or if the widget is an instance of a subclass of wclass.

XtIsTopLevelShell

```
Boolean XtIsTopLevelShell(Widget widget);
```

Returns True if widget is of class TopLevelShell or is an instance of a subclass of TopLevelShell.

XtIsTransientShell

```
Boolean XtIsTransientShell(Widget widget);
```

Returns True if widget is of class TransientShell or is an instance of a subclass of TransientShell.

XtIsVendorShell

```
Boolean XtIsVendorShell(Widget widget);
```

Returns True if widget is of class VendorShell or is an instance of a subclass of VendorShell.

XtIsWidget

```
Boolean XtIsWidget(Widget object);
```

Returns True if widget is of class Core or is an instance of any subclass of Core.

XtIsWMShell

```
Boolean XtIsWMShell(Widget widget);
```

Returns True if widget is of class WMShell or is an instance of a subclass of WMShell.

XtKeysymToKeycodeList

```
void XtKeysymToKeycodeList(
    Display*   display,  /* Search key mapping of this server  */
    KeySym     keysym,            /* Look for this keysym       */
    KeyCode**  keycodes_return,   /* Returned keycode list      */
    Cardinal*  keycount_return);  /* Number of keycodes in list */
```

In keycode_return, this function returns all the keycodes that have the specified keysym in the keyboard mapping table. You have to free the memory allocated for the keycode list by calling XtFree.

XtLastTimestampProcessed

```
Time XtLastTimestampProcessed(
    Display* dpy);  /* Identifies the X server */
```

Returns the time stamp for the most recent event (with a time stamp) received from the specified X server. The return value is zero if no event containing a time stamp has yet arrived from the server.

XtMainLoop

```
void XtMainLoop(void);   /* Superseded by XtAppMainLoop */
```

Starts the main event-processing loop of the application. You must call XtInitialize before calling XtMainLoop. Starting with X11R4, you should use XtAppMainLoop in place of XtMainLoop.

10

XtMakeGeometryRequest

```
XtGeometryResult XtMakeGeometryRequest(
    Widget            widget,        /* Change this widget */
    XtWidgetGeometry* request,       /* Requested geometry */
    XtWidgetGeometry* reply_return); /* Final geometry     */
```

Requests the parent of widget to change widget's geometry.

XtMakeResizeRequest

```
XtGeometryResult XtMakeResizeRequest(
    Widget      widget,         /* Resize this widget    */
    Dimension   width,          /* Desired width         */
    Dimension   height,         /* Desired height        */
    Dimension*  replyWidth,     /* Width after resizing  */
    Dimension*  replyHeight);   /* Height after resizing */
```

Requests the parent of widget to resize widget.

XtMalloc

```
char *XtMalloc(
    Cardinal numbytes); /* Number of bytes to allocate */
```

Allocates a specified number of bytes of storage and returns a pointer to the newly allocated storage. Calls the error handler if the memory allocation fails.

XtManageChild

```
void XtManageChild(Widget child);
```

Manages (resizes and positions) the specified child widget.

XtMapWidget

```
void XtMapWidget(Widget widget);
```

Maps the specified widget's window.

XtMenuPopdown

```
void XtMenuPopdown(Widget shell);
```

Pops down a menu shell widget.

XtMenuPopup

```
void XtMenuPopup(Widget shell);
```

Pops up a menu shell widget.

XtMergeArgLists

```
ArgList XtMergeArgLists(
    ArgList   args1,    /* First argument list        */
    Cardinal  nargs1,   /* Number of entries in args1 */
    ArgList   args2,    /* Second argument list       */
    Cardinal  nargs2);  /* Number of entries in args2 */
```

Appends the argument lists args1 and args2 and returns a pointer to the combined list. Does not check for duplicates. When you no longer need the merged list, you should free its storage by calling XtFree.

XtName

```
String XtName(Widget object);
```

Returns the name of object.

XtNameToWidget

```
Widget XtNameToWidget(
    Widget        root,  /* Start of search hierarchy   */
    const String  name); /* Look for a widget of this name */
```

Searches for a widget with a specific name in a hierarchy and returns the widget's ID if it finds one. If there is no such widget in the hierarchy, XtNameToWidget returns NULL.

XtNew

```
#define XtNew(type) \
    ((type *) XtMalloc((unsigned) sizeof(type)))
```

This macro allocates storage of a specific type by calling XtMalloc.

XtNewString

```
String XtNewString(String str);
```

Allocates enough storage to hold str and then copies str into that storage.

10

XtNextEvent

```
void XtNextEvent(        /* Superseded by XtAppNextEvent */
    XEvent* event);
```

Returns the next event from the queue of the default application context.

XtNumber

```
#define XtNumber(arr) \
    ((Cardinal) (sizeof(arr)/sizeof(arr[0])))
```

This macro returns the size of an array.

XtOffset

```
Cardinal XtOffset(p_type,field);
```

This macro returns the byte offset of a field within a structure. The p_type argument is a pointer to the structure and `field` is the name of a field in that structure.

XtOffsetOf

```
Cardinal XtOffset(p_type,field);
```

This macro is similar to `XtOffset`, but more portable than `XtOffset`. It also returns the byte offset of a field within a structure. The p_type argument is a pointer to the structure and `field` is the name of a field in that structure.

XtOpenDisplay

```
Display *XtOpenDisplay(
    XtAppContext      app,       /* Application context     */
    const String      dname,     /* Name of X server or NULL */
    const String      name,      /* Name of application     */
    const String      class,     /* Class name of appl.     */
    XrmOptionDescRec* options,    /* Acceptable options      */
    Cardinal          noptions,  /* Elements in "options"   */
    Cardinal*         argc,      /* Number of cmd.-line args */
    String*           argv);     /* Command-line arguments  */
```

Opens a connection with an X server and adds the connection to the specified application context. Returns a pointer to the `Display` structure that identifies the connection to this X server.

XtOverrideTranslations

```
void XtOverrideTranslations(
    Widget          w,    /* Alter this widget's translations */
    XtTranslations new); /* Merge in these translations      */
```

Merges in a set of translations with a widget's existing translations. If new has a translation that already exists in the widget, the old one is overwritten by the new version.

XtOwnSelection

```
Boolean XtOwnSelection(
    Widget  widget,    /* Widget that wants to own selection  */
    Atom    selection, /* Selection it wants to own           */
    Time    time,      /* Timestamp of triggering event       */
    XtConvertSelectionProc convert, /* Function to call when   */
                       /* selection is requested by others    */
    XtLoseSelectionProc lose,  /* Call when ownership is lost  */
    XtSelectionDoneProc done); /* Call after a successful      */
                       /* transfer of selection               */
```

Indicates that the specified widget wants ownership of a selection. Returns True if the widget receives ownership; otherwise returns False.

XtOwnSelectionIncremental

```
Boolean XtOwnSelectionIncremental(
    Widget  widget,    /* Widget that wants to own selection  */
    Atom    selection, /* Selection it wants to own           */
    Time    time,      /* Timestamp of triggering event       */
    XtConvertSelectionIncrProc convert, /* Function to call    */
                  /* when selection is requested by others    */
    XtLoseSelectionIncrProc lose,  /* Function to call         */
                           /* when ownership is lost           */
    XtSelectionDoneIncrProc  done, /* Function to call         */
                           /* when transfer is done            */
    XtCancelConvertSelectionProc cancel, /* Function to call   */
                           /* if transfer is aborted           */
    XtPointer client_data);   /* Data passed to each callback  */
```

Indicates that the specified widget wants ownership of a selection and that the widget wants to provide the selection incrementally. Returns True if the widget receives ownership; otherwise, returns False.

XtParent

```
Widget XtParent(Widget widget);
```

Returns ID of a widget's parent.

XtParseAcceleratorTable

```
XtAccelerators XtParseAcceleratorTable(
    const String source); /* Accelerator table to be parsed */
```

Parses the specified accelerator table and returns a pointer to an internal parsed representation of the table.

XtParseTranslationTable

```
XtTranslations XtParseTranslationTable(
    const String source); /* Translation table to be parsed */
```

Parses the specified translation table and returns a pointer to an internal parsed representation of the table.

XtPeekEvent

```
Boolean XtPeekEvent( /* Superseded by XtAppPeekEvent */
    XEvent* ev);     /* Returned event                */
```

If the event queue of the default application context is not empty, this function returns True and provides information about the first event in the queue through the ev argument. If the event queue is empty, this function waits for an event.

XtPending

```
XtInputMask XtPending(void); /* Superseded by XtAppPending */
```

Returns a nonzero value if there are events (from any source such as the X server or another input) waiting for the default application context.

XtPopdown

```
void XtPopdown(Widget widget);
```

Unmaps a pop-up shell widget.

XtPopup

```
void XtPopup(
    Widget    w,        /* Maps this pop-up shell widget    */
    XtGrabKind grab);   /* Controls handling of input events */
```

Pops up a shell widget.

XtPopupSpringLoaded

```
void XtPopupSpringLoaded(Widget widget);
```

Maps a spring-loaded pop-up shell widget.

XtProcessEvent

```
void XtProcessEvent(     /* Superseded by XtAppProcessEvent */
    XtInputMask  mask);  /* Identifies event to process     */
```

Processes an event from the source specified by the `mask`, which can be one of the following:

> `XtAlternateInput`, which refers to an alternate input (set up by `XtAddInput`)

> `XtIMTime`, which refers to a time-out event (set up by `XtAddTimeOut`)

> `XtImXEvent`, which refers to a normal X event

XtQueryGeometry

```
XtGeometryResult XtQueryGeometry(
    Widget            widget,  /* Query this widget        */
    XtWidgetGeometry* intended, /* Planned geometry changes */
    XtWidgetGeometry* reply_return); /* Preferred geometry  */
```

Retrieves a widget's preferred geometry. Usually called by a parent widget to determine the preferred geometry of a child.

XtRealizeWidget

```
void XtRealizeWidget(Widget widget);
```

Creates a window for the widget.

10

XtRealloc

```
char *XtRealloc(
    char*    ptr,   /* Resize this block of memory */
    Cardinal num);  /* New size of the block      */
```

Resizes a block of memory whose address is in ptr to hold at least num bytes. The block of memory may be moved if necessary. If ptr is NULL, XtRealloc allocates a new block.

XtRegisterCaseConverter

```
void XtRegisterCaseConverter(
    Display*  dpy,    /* Identifies X server           */
    XtCaseProc proc,  /* This is the converter function */
    KeySym    start,  /* Handle keysyms between start  */
    KeySym    stop);  /* and stop                      */
```

Registers a converter for translating keysyms to upper- and lowercase.

XtRegisterGrabAction

```
void XtRegisterGrabAction(
    XtActionProc action_proc, /* Function for grab processing  */
    Boolean      own_events,  /* True = report events normally */
    unsigned int event_mask,  /* Report these events           */
    int          ptr_mode,    /* GrabModeSync or GrabModeAsync  */
    int          kbd_mode);   /* GrabModeSync or GrabModeAsync  */
```

Sets up a function to be called when a specified grab occurs in a widget.

XtReleaseGC

```
void XtReleaseGC(
    Widget w,   /* Determines GC's display */
    GC     gc); /* GC to be released       */
```

Frees up a shared graphics context (GC) when it is no longer needed.

XtRemoveActionHook

```
void XtRemoveActionHook(
    XtActionHookId id); /* Hook procedure to be removed */
```

Removes the specified action hook procedure.

XtRemoveAllCallbacks

```
void XtRemoveAllCallbacks(
    Widget      widget,          /* Affected widget      */
    const String callback_name); /* Name of callback list */
```

Removes all callback functions from the specified callback list of the widget.

XtRemoveCallback

```
void XtRemoveCallback(
    Widget         widget,        /* Affected widget        */
    const String   callback_name, /* Name of callback list  */
    XtCallbackProc callback,      /* Remove this callback    */
    XtPointer      client_data);  /* Data for that callback */
```

Removes a specific callback from a widget's callback list.

XtRemoveCallbacks

```
void XtRemoveCallbacks(
    Widget        widget,         /* Affected widget         */
    const String  callback_name,  /* Name of callback list   */
    XtCallbackList callbacks);    /* List of callbacks to remove */
```

Removes a number of callbacks registered for the callback named callback_name.

XtRemoveEventHandler

```
void XtRemoveEventHandler(
    Widget         widget,        /* Remove from this widget */
    EventMask      eventMask,     /* To handle these events  */
    Boolean        nonmaskable,   /* For non-maskable events? */
    XtEventHandler proc,          /* The event handler       */
    XtPointer      client_data);  /* Data for the handler    */
```

Removes an event handler meant for processing events matching eventMask.

XtRemoveGrab

```
void XtRemoveGrab(Widget widget);
```

Removes a grab (exclusive input redirection to a widget) for the specified widget.

10

XtRemoveInput

```
void XtRemoveInput(
    XtInputId id); /* ID of input source from XtAppAddInput */
```

Stops accepting input from an alternate input source identified by id.

XtRemoveRawEventHandler

```
void XtRemoveRawEventHandler(
    Widget          widget,        /* Remove from this widget   */
    EventMask       eventMask,     /* To handle these events    */
    Boolean         nonmaskable,   /* For nonmaskable events?   */
    XtEventHandler proc,           /* The event handler         */
    XtPointer       client_data); /* Data for the handler      */
```

Removes an event handler that was set up for events matching eventMask. This function is like XtRemoveEventHandler except that it does not affect the widget's event mask and it does not call the Xlib function XSelectInput.

XtRemoveTimeOut

```
void XtRemoveTimeOut(
    XtIntervalId timer); /* ID returned by XtAppAddTimeOut */
```

Removes a time-out before it has occurred.

XtRemoveWorkProc

```
void  XtRemoveWorkProc(
    XtWorkProcId id); /* ID returned when WorkProc was added */
```

Removes a work procedure registered earlier by calling XtAppAddWorkProc.

XtResolvePathname

```
String XtResolvePathname(
    Display*        dpy,      /* Identifies the X server     */
    const String    type,     /* Type substituted into path */
    const String    fname,    /* Filename part of path       */
    const String    suffix,   /* Suffix part of path         */
    const String    path,     /* List of pathnames           */
    Substitution    subst,    /* List of substitutions       */
    Cardinal        nsubst,   /* Number of substitutions     */
    XtFilePredicate pfunc);  /* Function to evaluate names */
```

Searches for a file using substitutions in a path list. Returns a filename, if the function pfunc declares one to be suitable. Please consult the book on Xt

Intrinsics by Paul Asente and Ralph Swick (see the beginning of this chapter for details) for further information. This function calls XtFindFile with the following substitutions:

%L refers to the language specification of the X server.

%N refers to the fname argument (application's class if fname is NULL).

%S refers to suffix argument.

%T refers to the type argument.

%c refers to the "codeset" portion of the xnlLanguage resource.

%l refers to the language portion of the xnlLanguage resource.

%t refers to the territory portion of the xnlLanguage resource.

XtScreen

```
Screen *XtScreen(Widget widget);
```

Returns the Screen pointer of a widget.

XtScreenOfObject

```
Screen *XtScreenOfObject(Widget object);
```

Behaves the same as XtScreen when object is a descendant of the Core class. However, if object is of class Object, this function returns the Screen pointer for the nearest ancestor of object that is a widget.

XtSetArg

```
#define XtSetArg(arg, n, d) \
    ((void)((arg).name = (n), (arg).value = (XtArgVal) ))
```

This macro sets up the name-value pair in an Arg structure. XtSetArg is commonly used to set up the argument list for widgets.

XtSetErrorHandler

```
void XtSetErrorHandler( /* Superseded by XtAppSetErrorHandler */
    XtErrorHandler handler) /* New handler for fatal errors    */
```

Registers function to be called when fatal errors occur in the Xt Intrinsics library.

XtSetErrorMsgHandler

```
void XtSetErrorMsgHandler(
            /* Superseded by XtAppSetErrorMsgHandler */
    XtErrorMsgHandler handler); /* New error handler */
```

Registers a handler for fatal errors.

XtSetKeyboardFocus

```
void XtSetKeyboardFocus(
    Widget subtree, /* Set keyboard focus for this hierarchy */
    Widget descendant); /* Widget to receive keyboard events */
```

Redirects keyboard input to the descendant widget.

XtSetKeyTranslator

```
void XtSetKeyTranslator(
    Display* dpy,   /* Register for this X server       */
    XtKeyProc proc); /* Function that will translate keys */
```

Registers a function that will translate keystrokes for the specified X server.

XtSetMappedWhenManaged

```
void XtSetMappedWhenManaged(
    Widget  widget,              /* Affects this widget     */
    Boolean mappedWhenManaged); /* New mapped_when_managed */
```

Sets the mapped_when_managed attribute of the widget. If mapped_when_managed is True, the widget is mapped as soon as it is realized and managed.

XtSetMultiClickTime

```
void XtSetMultiClickTime(
    Display* dpy,              /* Set for this X server */
    int      milliseconds); /* New multiclick time   */
```

Sets the time interval that controls the interpretation of consecutive events. For example, the Xt Intrinsics will consider two successive button-press events as a double-click only if the time interval between their occurrences is less than the multiclick time.

XtSetSelectionTimeout

```
void XtSetSelectionTimeout(
                /* Superseded by XtAppSetSelectionTimeout */
    unsigned long timeout); /* New timeout in milliseconds */
```

Sets the selection time-out value for the default application context.

XtSetSensitive

```
void XtSetSensitive(
    Widget   widget,      /* Set sensitivity of this widget */
    Boolean sensitive);   /* New value for the sensitivity  */
```

Sets the sensitivity of a widget. Only sensitive widgets receive input events.

XtSetSubvalues

```
void XtSetSubvalues(
    XtPointer      base,    /* Retrieve resources from this */
    XtResourceList res,     /* Resource list of subpart     */
    Cardinal       nres,    /* Number of resources          */
    ArgList        args,    /* Resource specifications       */
    Cardinal       nargs);  /* Number of entries in args     */
```

Sets values of resources that are not associated with a widget.

XtSetTypeConverter

```
void XtSetTypeConverter(
    const String     from_type,     /* Convert from this type */
    const String     to_type,       /* to this type           */
    XtTypeConverter  converter,     /* Function that converts */
    XtConvertArgList convert_args,  /* Arguments for function */
    Cardinal         nargs,         /* Number of arguments    */
    XtCacheType      cache_type,    /* Indicates how to share */
                                    /* this resource          */
    XtDestructor     destructor);   /* Function to be called   */
                                    /* before freeing resource */
```

Sets up a function to be called when a resource has to be converted from from_type to to_type. These types are identified by constants such as XtRColor, XtRPixel, and XtRString which are defined in the file <X11/StringDefs.h>. The cache_type argument can take one of the following values:

XtCacheAll to share among all applications displaying at an X server

XtCacheByDisplay, which is like XtCacheAll, but destructor is called when the display is closed by calling XtCloseDisplay

XtCacheNone, which means do not share (in other words, no need to save in cache)

XtCacheRefCount, which means share, but destroy when no application uses resource

10

XtSetValues

```
void XtSetValues(
    Widget   widget, /* Get this widget's resources */
    ArgList  args,   /* Resource specifications    */
    Cardinal nargs); /* Number of entries in args  */
```

Sets a widget's resources. You specify the resources to be modified in the argument list args.

XtSetWarningHandler

```
void XtSetWarningHandler(
                    /* Superseded by XtAppSetWarningHandler */
    XtErrorHandler handler); /* New nonfatal error handler */
```

Registers a function to be called when nonfatal errors occur in the Xt Intrinsics library.

XtSetWarningMsgHandler

```
void XtSetWarningMsgHandler(
                    /* Superseded by XtAppSetWarningMsgHandler */
    XtErrorMsgHandler handler); /* New nonfatal error handler */
```

Registers a function to be called when nonfatal errors occur in the Xt Intrinsics library.

XtSetWMColormapWindows

```
void XtSetWMColormapWindows(
    Widget   widget, /* Store WM_COLORMAP_WINDOWS property */
                     /* on this window                    */
    Widget*  list,   /* List of widgets whose windows will */
                     /* be listed in the property          */
    Cardinal count); /* Number of widgets in list          */
```

Stores a list of windows in the WM_COLORMAP_WINDOWS property of widget. Standard-conforming (ICCCM) window managers should install the colormap for a window in the list when that window receives the colormap focus.

XtStringConversionWarning

```
void XtStringConversionWarning(
    const String from,     /* Attempted to convert this     */
    const String to_type); /* Tried conversion to this type */
```

Issues a warning message when an attempted conversion fails.

XtSuperclass

```
WidgetClass XtSuperclass(Widget object);
```

Returns ID of widget's super class (the class from which widget's class is derived).

XtToolkitInitialize

```
void XtToolkitInitialize(void);
```

Initializes the Xt Intrinsics library.

XtTranslateCoords

```
void XtTranslateCoords(
    Widget     widget, /* Coordinates in this widget        */
    Position   x,      /* Coordinates to be translated from */
    Position   y,      /* widget frame to root window       */
    Position*  rootx,  /* x-y coordinates in root window's  */
    Position*  rooty); /* coordinates frame                 */
```

Translates the point (x,y) from the widget's coordinate frame to the root window's coordinates and returns the converted coordinates in rootx and rooty.

XtTranslateKeycode

```
void XtTranslateKeycode(
    Display*   dpy,               /* Identifies X server  */
    KeyCode    keycode,           /* Translate this keycode */
    Modifiers  modifiers,         /* Value of modifiers   */
    Modifiers* modifiers_return,  /* Modifiers examined   */
    KeySym*    keysym_return);    /* Returned keysym      */
```

Translates a keycode to a keysym by calling the currently registered key translator.

XtUngrabButton

```
void XtUngrabButton(
    Widget       widget,    /* Grab is on this widget */
    unsigned int button,    /* For this mouse button  */
    Modifiers    modifiers); /* With these modifiers   */
```

Ends a passive button grab.

10

XtUngrabKey

```
void XtUngrabKey(
    Widget    widget,    /* Grab is on this widget */
    KeyCode   keycode,   /* For this key           */
    Modifiers modifiers); /* With these modifiers   */
```

Ends a passive key grab.

XtUngrabKeyboard

```
void XtUngrabKeyboard(
    Widget widget, /* Grab is on this widget   */
    Time   time);  /* Timestamp or CurrentTime */
```

Ends an active keyboard grab.

XtUngrabPointer

```
void XtUngrabPointer(
    Widget widget, /* Grab is on this widget   */
    Time   time);  /* Timestamp or CurrentTime */
```

Ends an active button grab.

XtUninstallTranslations

```
void XtUninstallTranslations(Widget widget);
```

Removes the translations for the specified widget.

XtUnmanageChild

```
void XtUnmanageChild(Widget widget);
```

Removes the specified child widget from its parent's list of managed children.

XtUnmanageChildren

```
void XtUnmanageChildren(
    WidgetList widget,    /* Widgets to unmanage */
    Cardinal   nwidgets); /* Number of widgets   */
```

Removes the specified child widgets from the parent's list of managed children.

XtUnmapWidget

```
void XtUnmapWidget(Widget widget);
```

Unmaps a widget's window.

XtUnrealizeWidget

```
void XtUnrealizeWidget(Widget widget);
```

Destroys the windows of the specified widget and its children.

XtVaAppCreateShell

```
Widget XtVaAppCreateShell(
    const String    name ,
    const String    class ,
    WidgetClass     widget_class ,
    Display*        display ,
    ...);
```

Behaves the same as `XtAppCreateShell`, except that the resource arguments are replaced with a variable-length argument list whose end is indicated by a NULL.

XtVaAppInitialize

```
Widget XtVaAppInitialize(
    XtAppContext*     app_context_return ,
    const String      application_class ,
    XrmOptionDescList options ,
    Cardinal          num_options ,
    Cardinal*         argc_in_out ,
    String*           argv_in_out ,
    const String*     fallback_resources ,
    ...);
```

Behaves the same as `XtAppInitialize`, except that the resource arguments are replaced with a variable-length argument list whose end is indicated by a NULL.

XtVaCreateArgsList

```
XtVarArgsList XtVaCreateArgsList(
    XtPointer  unused, ...);
```

Creates a variable-length argument list and returns a pointer to the newly created structure.

XtVaCreateManagedWidget

```
Widget XtVaCreateManagedWidget(
    const String name,
    WidgetClass  widget_class,
    Widget       parent,
    ...);
```

Behaves the same as `XtCreateManagedWidget`, except that the resource arguments are replaced with a variable-length argument list whose end is indicated by a NULL.

XtVaCreatePopupShell

```
Widget XtVaCreatePopupShell(
    const String    name ,
    WidgetClass     widgetClass,
    Widget          parent,
    ...);
```

Behaves the same as XtCreatePopupShell, except that the resource arguments are replaced with a variable-length argument list whose end is indicated by a NULL.

XtVaCreateWidget

```
Widget XtVaCreateWidget(
    const String    name ,
    WidgetClass     widget,
    Widget          parent,
    ...);
```

Behaves the same as XtCreateWidget, except that the resource arguments are replaced with a variable-length argument list whose end is indicated by a NULL.

XtVaGetApplicationResources

```
void XtVaGetApplicationResources(
    Widget          widget,
    XtPointer       base,
    XtResourceList  resources,
    Cardinal        num_resources,
    ...);
```

Behaves the same as XtGetApplicationResources, except that the resource arguments are replaced with a variable-length argument list whose end is indicated by a NULL.

XtVaGetSubresources

```
void XtVaGetSubresources(
    Widget          widget,
    XtPointer       base,
    const String    name,
    const String    class,
    XtResourceList  resources,
    Cardinal        num_resources,
    ...);
```

Behaves the same as XtGetSubresources, except that the resource arguments are replaced with a variable-length argument list whose end is indicated by a NULL.

XtVaGetSubvalues

```
void XtVaGetSubvalues(
    XtPointer        base,
    XtResourceList   resources,
    Cardinal         num_resources,
    ...);
```

Behaves the same as XtGetSubvalues, except that the resource arguments are replaced with a variable-length argument list whose end is indicated by a NULL.

XtVaGetValues

```
void XtVaGetValues(
    Widget    widget,
    ...);
```

Behaves the same as XtGetValues, except that the resource arguments are replaced with a variable-length argument list whose end is indicated by a NULL.

XtVaSetSubvalues

```
void XtVaSetSubvalues(
    XtPointer      base,
    XtResourceList resources,
    Cardinal       num_resources,
    ...);
```

Behaves the same as XtSetSubvalues, except that the resource arguments are replaced with a variable-length argument list whose end is indicated by a NULL.

XtVaSetValues

```
void XtVaSetValues(
    Widget    widget,
    ...);
```

Behaves the same as XtSetValues, except that the resource arguments are replaced with a variable-length argument list whose end is indicated by a NULL.

10

XtWarning

```
void XtWarning(   /* Superseded by XtAppWarning */
    const String message); /* Warning message  */
```

Calls the current nonfatal error handler and passes a message to it.

XtWarningMsg

```
void XtWarningMsg(        /* Superseded by XtAppWarningMsg */
    const String name,    /* Descriptive name of warning  */
    const String type,    /* Error type                   */
    const String class,   /* Resource class               */
    const String default, /* Default warning message      */
    String*      params,  /* Values for warning message   */
    Cardinal*    nparams); /* Number of values in "params"  */
```

Calls the nonfatal error handler with arguments to help locate a warning message and display the message.

XtWidgetToApplicationContext

```
XtAppContext XtWidgetToApplicationContext(Widget widget);
```

Returns the application context for a widget.

XtWindow

```
Window XtWindow(Widget widget);
```

Returns the window ID of a widget.

XtWindowOfObject

```
Window XtWindowOfObject(Widget object);
```

Returns the window ID if object is a widget. If it is not, this function returns the window ID of the nearest ancestor of object that is a widget.

XtWindowToWidget

```
Widget XtWindowToWidget(
    Display* display, /* X server which displays this window */
    Window   window); /* Return widget for this window       */
```

Returns the widget ID for a window.

Xt Intrinsics Data Types

This section provides an alphabetic listing of some data types used in the Xt Intrinsics. In some cases, the exact definition of the data type is not shown because those details are supposed to be hidden from the programmers. However, you can always look at the header file for the definition of these types.

Arg

Defined in: `<X11/Intrinsic.h>`

```
typedef struct
{
    String      name;
    XtArgVal      value;
} Arg, *ArgList;
```

Boolean

Defined in: `<X11/Intrinsic.h>`

This is an integer data type that takes the values TRUE or FALSE.

Cardinal

Defined in: `<X11/Intrinsic.h>`

This is an unsigned integer data type that, at a minimum, takes the values in the range 0 to 65,536. This data type is used for counting.

Dimension

Defined in: `<X11/Intrinsic.h>`

This represents a data type whose inner details are supposed to be hidden from the programmer.

EventMask

Defined in: `<X11/Intrinsic.h>`

```
typedef unsigned long EventMask;
```

Modifiers

Defined in: <X11/Intrinsic.h>

```
typedef unsigned int Modifiers;
```

Opaque

Defined in: <X11/Intrinsic.h>

This is an unsigned integer data type that, at a minimum, takes the values in the range 0 to 65,536. It is used to specify width and height of windows.

Pixel

Defined in: <X11/Intrinsic.h>

```
typedef unsigned long Pixel;
```

Position

Defined in: <X11/Intrinsic.h>

This is a signed integer data type that, at a minimum, takes the values in the range –32,767 to 32,767. It is used to specify the position of windows.

String

Defined in: <X11/Intrinsic.h>

```
typedef char* String;
```

Substitution, SubstitutionRec

Defined in: <X11/Intrinsic.h>

```
typedef struct
{
    char    match;
    String substitution;
} SubstitutionRec, *Substitution;
```

Widget

Defined in: <X11/Intrinsic.h>

A data type that is used as a "handle" to a widget. It is a pointer to a data structure that represents a widget.

WidgetClass

Defined in: <X11/Intrinsic.h>

A pointer to a widget's class data structure.

WidgetList

Defined in: <X11/Intrinsic.h>

```
typedef Widget *WidgetList;
```

XtAccelerators

Defined in: <X11/Intrinsic.h>

A pointer to an internal accelerator table.

XtActionHookId

Defined in: <X11/Intrinsic.h>

```
typedef Opaque XtActionHookId;
```

XtActionHookProc

Defined in: <X11/Intrinsic.h>

```
typedef void (*XtActionHookProc)(
    Widget     w,
    XtPointer  client_data,
    String     action_name,
    XEvent*    event,
    String*    params,
    Cardinal*  num_params);
```

XtActionList

Defined in: <X11/Intrinsic.h>

```
typedef struct _XtActionsRec *XtActionList;
```

XtActionProc

Defined in: <X11/Intrinsic.h>

```
typedef void (*XtActionProc)(
Widget    widget,
    XEvent*    event,
    String*    params,
    Cardinal* num_params);
```

XtActionsRec

Defined in: <X11/Intrinsic.h>

```
typedef struct _XtActionsRec
{
    String          string;
    XtActionProc proc;
} XtActionsRec;
```

XtAddressMode

Defined in: <X11/Intrinsic.h>

```
typedef enum
{
/* address mode          parameter representation */
/* -----------          ----------------------- */
    XtAddress,           /* Address               */
    XtBaseOffset,        /* Offset                */
    XtImmediate,         /* Constant              */
    XtResourceString,    /* Resource name string  */
    XtResourceQuark,     /* Resource name quark   */
    XtWidgetBaseOffset,  /* Offset from ancestor  */
    XtProcedureArg       /* Procedure to invoke   */
} XtAddressMode;
```

XtAppContext

Defined in: <X11/Intrinsic.h>

A pointer to an internal data structure representing an application context.

XtArgVal

Defined in: <X11/Intrinsic.h>

A system-dependent data type large enough to hold a Cardinal, Dimension, Position, or XtPointer.

XtBoundActions

Defined in: <X11/Intrinsic.h>

```
typedef XtActionProc* XtBoundActions;
```

XtCacheRef

Defined in: <X11/Intrinsic.h>

```
typedef Opaque XtCacheRef;
```

XtCacheType

Defined in: <X11/Intrinsic.h>

```
typedef int XtCacheType;
```

XtCallbackList

Defined in: <X11/Intrinsic.h>

```
typedef struct _XtCallbackRec
{
    XtCallbackProc callback;
    XtPointer      client_data;
} XtCallbackRec,    *XtCallbackList;
```

XtCallbackProc

Defined in: <X11/Intrinsic.h>

```
typedef void (*XtCallbackProc)(
    Widget     widget,
    XtPointer client_data, /* Data registered by client */
    XtPointer call_data);  /* Callback-specific data    */
```

XtCallbackStatus

Defined in: <X11/Intrinsic.h>

```
typedef enum
{
    XtCallbackNoList,
    XtCallbackHasNone,
    XtCallbackHasSome
} XtCallbackStatus;
```

10

10

XtCancelConvertSelectionProc

Defined in: `<X11/Intrinsic.h>`

```
typedef void (*XtCancelConvertSelectionProc)(
    Widget      widget,
    Atom*       selection,
    Atom*       target,
    XtRequestId*  receiver_id,
    XtPointer   client_data);
```

XtCaseProc

Defined in: `<X11/Intrinsic.h>`

```
typedef void (*XtCaseProc)(
    Display* display,
    KeySym   keysym,
    KeySym*  lower_return,
    KeySym*  upper_return);
```

XtConvertArgList

Defined in: `<X11/Intrinsic.h>`

```
typedef struct
{
    XtAddressMode   address_mode;
    XtPointer       address_id;
    Cardinal        size;
} XtConvertArgRec, *XtConvertArgList;
```

XtConvertArgProc

Defined in: `<X11/Intrinsic.h>`

```
typedef void (*XtConvertArgProc)(
    Widget      widget,
    Cardinal*   size,
    XrmValue*   value);
```

XtConvertArgRec

Defined in: `<X11/Intrinsic.h>`

```
typedef struct
{
    XtAddressMode   address_mode;
    XtPointer       address_id;
    Cardinal        size;
} XtConvertArgRec, *XtConvertArgList;
```

XtConverter

Defined in: <X11/Intrinsic.h>

```
typedef void (*XtConverter)(
    XrmValue*      args,
    Cardinal*      num_args,
    XrmValue*      from,
    XrmValue*      to);
```

XtConvertSelectionIncrProc

Defined in: <X11/Intrinsic.h>

```
typedef Boolean (*XtConvertSelectionIncrProc)(
    Widget           widget,
    Atom*            selection,
    Atom*            target,
    Atom*            type,
    XtPointer*       value,
    unsigned         long*    length,
    int*             format,
    unsigned long*   max_length,
    XtPointer        client_data,
    XtRequestId*     receiver_id);
```

XtConvertSelectionProc

Defined in: <X11/Intrinsic.h>

```
typedef Boolean (*XtConvertSelectionProc)(
    Widget           widget,
    Atom*            selection,
    Atom*            target,
    Atom*            type_return,
    XtPointer*       value_return,
    unsigned long*   length_return,
    int*             format_return);
```

XtDestructor

Defined in: <X11/Intrinsic.h>

```
typedef void (*XtDestructor)(
    XtAppContext app,
    XrmValue*    to,
    XtPointer    converter_data,
    XrmValue*    args,
    Cardinal*    num_args);
```

10

XtErrorHandler

Defined in: <X11/Intrinsic.h>

```
typedef void (*XtErrorHandler)(String msg);
```

XtErrorMsgHandler

Defined in: <X11/Intrinsic.h>

```
typedef void (*XtErrorMsgHandler)(
    String     name,
    String     type,
    String     class,
    String     default,
    String*    params,
    Cardinal*  num_params);
```

XtEventHandler

Defined in: <X11/Intrinsic.h>

```
typedef void (*XtEventHandler)(
    Widget     widget,
    XtPointer  client_data,
    XEvent*    event,
    Boolean*   continue_to_dispatch);
```

XtFilePredicate

Defined in: <X11/Intrinsic.h>

```
typedef Boolean (*XtFilePredicate)(String filename);
```

XtGCMask

Defined in: <X11/Intrinsic.h>

```
typedef unsigned long XtGCMask;
```

XtGeometryMask

Defined in: <X11/Intrinsic.h>

```
typedef unsigned int XtGeometryMask;
```

XtGeometryResult

Defined in: <X11/Intrinsic.h>

```
typedef enum   {
    XtGeometryYes,      /* Geometry request accepted    */
    XtGeometryNo,       /* Geometry request denied      */
    XtGeometryAlmost,   /* Request denied, but willing  */
                        /* to accept next try           */
    XtGeometryDone      /* Request accepted and done    */
} XtGeometryResult;
```

XtGrabKind

Defined in: <X11/Intrinsic.h>

```
typedef enum
{
    XtGrabNone,
    XtGrabNonexclusive,
    XtGrabExclusive
} XtGrabKind;
```

XtInputCallbackProc

Defined in: <X11/Intrinsic.h>

```
typedef void (*XtInputCallbackProc)(
    XtPointer    client_data,
    int*         source,
    XtInputId*   id);
```

XtInputId

Defined in: <X11/Intrinsic.h>

```
typedef unsigned long XtInputId;
```

XtInputMask

Defined in: <X11/Intrinsic.h>

```
typedef unsigned long XtInputMask;
```

10

XtIntervalId

Defined in: <X11/Intrinsic.h>

```
typedef unsigned long XtIntervalId;
```

XtKeyProc

Defined in: <X11/Intrinsic.h>

```
typedef void (*XtKeyProc)(
    Display*    dpy,
    int         keycode,
    Modifiers   modifiers,
    Modifiers*  modifiers_return,
    KeySym*     keysym_return);
```

XtListPosition

Defined in: <X11/Intrinsic.h>

```
typedef enum {XtListHead, XtListTail} XtListPosition;
```

XtLoseSelectionIncrProc

Defined in: <X11/Intrinsic.h>

```
typedef void (*XtLoseSelectionIncrProc)(
    Widget     widget,
    Atom*      selection,
    XtPointer  client_data);
```

XtLoseSelectionProc

Defined in: <X11/Intrinsic.h>

```
typedef void (*XtLoseSelectionProc)(
    Widget   widget,
    Atom*    selection);
```

XtPointer

Defined in: <X11/Intrinsic.h>

A data type large enough to contain a pointer to any function, any struct, and any one of the data types char, int, or long.

XtPopdownID

Defined in: <X11/Intrinsic.h>

```
typedef struct
{
    Widget   shell_widget;
    Widget   enable_widget;
} XtPopdownIDRec, *XtPopdownID;
```

10

XtRequestID

Defined in: <X11/Intrinsic.h>

```
typedef XtPointer XtRequestId;
```

XtResource, XtResourceList

Defined in: <X11/Intrinsic.h>

```
typedef struct _XtResource {
    String    resource_name;    /* Resource name                  */
    String    resource_class;   /* Resource class                 */
    String    resource_type;    /* Desired representation type    */
    Cardinal  resource_size;    /* Bytes in that representation   */
    Cardinal  resource_offset;  /* Store resource value at this   */
                                /* offset from base of struct     */
    String    default_type;     /* Default representation type    */
    XtPointer default_addr;     /* Address of default resource    */
} XtResource, *XtResourceList;
```

XtResourceDefaultProc

Defined in: <X11/Intrinsic.h>

```
typedef void (*XtResourceDefaultProc)(
    Widget      widget,
    int         offset,
    XrmValue*   value);
```

XtSelectionCallbackProc

Defined in: <X11/Intrinsic.h>

```
typedef void (*XtSelectionCallbackProc)(
    Widget          widget,
    XtPointer       client_data,
    Atom*           selection,
    Atom*           type,
    XtPointer       value,
    unsigned long*  length,
    int*            format);
```

XtSelectionDoneIncrProc

Defined in: <X11/Intrinsic.h>

```
typedef void (*XtSelectionDoneIncrProc)(
    Widget       widget,
    Atom*        selection,
    Atom*        target,
    XtRequestId* receiver_id,
    XtPointer    client_data);
```

XtSelectionDoneProc

Defined in: <X11/Intrinsic.h>

```
typedef void (*XtSelectionDoneProc)(
    Widget  widget,
    Atom*   selection,
    Atom*   target);
```

XtTimerCallbackProc

Defined in: <X11/Intrinsic.h>

```
typedef void (*XtTimerCallbackProc)(
    XtPointer     client_data,
    XtIntervalId* id);
```

XtTranslations

Defined in: <X11/Intrinsic.h>

A pointer to an internal translation table.

XtTypeConverter

Defined in: <X11/Intrinsic.h>

```
typedef Boolean (*XtTypeConverter)(
    Display*   dpy,
    XrmValue*  args,
    Cardinal*  num_args,
    XrmValue*  from,
    XrmValue*  to,
    XtPointer* converter_data);
```

XtValueMask

Defined in: <X11/Intrinsic.h>

```
typedef unsigned long XtValueMask;
```

XtWidgetGeometry

Defined in: <X11/Intrinsic.h>

```
typedef struct
{
    XtGeometryMask request_mode;
    Position    x, y;
    Dimension   width, height, border_width;
    Widget      sibling;
    int         stack_mode; /* One of: Above, Below, TopIf,   */
                            /* BottomIf, Opposite, DontChange */
} XtWidgetGeometry;
```

XtWorkProc

Defined in: <X11/Intrinsic.h>

```
typedef Boolean (*XtWorkProc)(
    XtPointer client_data); /* Application registered data */
```

XtWorkProcId

Defined in: <X11/Intrinsic.h>

```
typedef unsigned long XtWorkProcId;
```

10

X Events Quick Reference

Summary of X Events

X provides for a large number of events, as summarized in Table 11.1, to handle everything from mouse and keyboard to messages from other X clients. The types of events, shown in the first column of Table 11.1, are defined in the include file <X11/X.h>. Note that you do not have to explicitly include this file, because toolkit header files already include it.

The X server never sends unsolicited events to an application. Table 11.1 shows 33 events, but X applications are not required to process all of them, thus avoiding the overhead of unnecessary event handling code. Xlib-based applications usually call the function XSelectInput to indicate the events that it wants to receive (in Motif programs, you would use XtAddEventHandler to specify a function to be called in response to an event). This approach of selective reporting of events is good for the server also, because it relieves the server of the necessity to keep track of all events for all clients.

One exception to the rule of selective reporting: the MappingNotify event, generated when the meaning of keys are changed, is automatically sent to all X clients.

11

The 33 X events shown in Table 11.1 can be broadly grouped into seven categories:

• **Mouse Events**: The server generates these events when the user presses a mouse button or moves the mouse. X applications trying to provide a *point-and-click* graphical interface usually accept and handle these events.

• **Keyboard Events**: These events are generated when the user presses or releases any key on the keyboard. They are delivered to an application only if a window owned by the application has the input focus. Usually, the window manager decides how the focus is transferred from one window to another. There are two common models: one is to click on a window to type in it (used by the Macintosh and Microsoft Windows), the other is to give the focus to the window containing the mouse pointer. In Motif, the keyboardFocusPolicy resource of the Motif window manager determines how the focus is determined (see Chapters 3 and 8 for details).

• **Expose Events**: Of all X events, the Expose event is the most crucial—applications draw in their windows in response to this event. Almost all X applications request and process this event. The GraphicsExpose and NoExpose events have to do with copying from one part of a window or a pixmap to another. They allow applications to handle the case in which the source of the copy operation is obscured by another window and the contents of the obscured area is unavailable for copying.

• **Colormap Notification Event**: The server generates the ColorMapNotify event whenever an application changes the colormap associated with a window or installs a new colormap.

• **Interclient Communication Events**: These events send information from one X application to another. The concepts of *property* and *selection* are used for this purpose.

• **Window State Notification Events**: The server generates these events whenever a window is moved or resized, or its place in the stacking order is altered. These events are useful for keeping track of changes in the layout of windows on the screen. Typically, window managers use these events for this purpose. Your application can use them too, if you want to alter the size and position of the subwindows when the user resizes the topmost window.

- **Window Structure Control Events**: These events are almost exclusively used by window managers to intercept an application's attempt to change the layout of its windows. For example, by monitoring the MapRequest event, the window manager can tell when an application maps its topmost window. When this happens, the window manager can add its own frame to the window and place it at an appropriate location on the screen.

Table 11.1. List of 33 X Events

Event Type	When Generated
Mouse Events	
ButtonPress	A mouse button is pressed with pointer in the window
ButtonRelease	A mouse button is released with pointer in the window
EnterNotify	Mouse pointer enters the window
LeaveNotify	Mouse pointer leaves the window
MotionNotify	The mouse is moved
Keyboard Events	
FocusIn	Window receives input focus (all subsequent keyboard events will come to the window)
FocusOut	Window loses input focus
KeyMapNotify	After an EnterNotify or FocusIn event occurs (to inform application of the state of the keys after these events)
KeyPress	A key is pressed (when window has focus)
KeyRelease	A key is released (when window has focus)
MappingNotify	The keyboard is reconfigured (the mapping of a key to a string is changed)
Expose Events	
Expose	Previously obscured window or part of window becomes visible

continues

11

Table 11.1. continued

Event Type	When Generated
GraphicsExpose	During graphics copy operations, parts of the source image is obscured (means the copied image is not complete)
NoExpose	Graphics copy is successfully completed

Colormap Notification Event

ColormapNotify	Window's colormap is changed

Interclient Communication Events

ClientMessage	Another client sends a message using the XSendEvent function
PropertyNotify	A property associated with the window has changed
SelectionClear	Window loses ownership of selection
SelectionNotify	A selection has been successfully converted
SelectionRequest	A selection needs conversion

Window State Notification Events

CirculateNotify	Window is raised or lowered in the stacking order
ConfigureNotify	Window is moved, resized, or its position in the stacking order has changed
CreateNotify	Window is created
DestroyNotify	Window is destroyed
GravityNotify	Window is moved because its parent's size changed
MapNotify	Window is mapped
ReparentNotify	Window's parent changed
UnmapNotify	Window is unmapped
VisibilityNotify	Window's visibility changed (became visible or invisible)

Windows Structure Control Events

CirculateRequest	Request received to raise or lower the window in the stacking order (used by window managers)

Event Type	When Generated
ConfigureRequest	Request received to move, resize, or restack window (used by window managers)
MapRequest	Window about to be mapped (used by window manager)
ResizeRequest	Request received to resize window (used by window managers)

Event Masks

Table 11.2 shows the event masks for selecting specific X events. When programming with the Motif toolkit, you have to use the event mask when registering an event handler by calling XtAddEventHandler (see Chapter 6 for a description of this function).

Table 11.2. Names of Event Masks Corresponding to the X Events

Event Type	Name of Event Mask in X.b
ButtonPress	ButtonPressMask
ButtonRelease	ButtonReleaseMask
CirculateNotify	StructureNotifyMask, SubstructureNotifyMask
CirculateRequest	SubstructureRedirectMask
ClientMessage[1]	—
ColormapNotify	ColormapChangeMask
ConfigureNotify	StructureNotifyMask, SubstructureNotifyMask
ConfigureRequest	SubstructureRedirectMask
CreateNotify	SubstructureNotifyMask
DestroyNotify	StructureNotifyMask, SubstructureNotifyMask
EnterNotify	EnterWindowMask
Expose	ExposureMask
FocusIn	FocusChangeMask
FocusOut	FocusChangeMask
GraphicsExpose	ExposureMask
GravityNotify	StructureNotifyMask, SubstructureNotifyMask
KeyMapNotify	KeymapStateMask

continues

Table 11.2. continued

Event Type	Name of Event Mask in X.h
KeyPress	KeyPressMask
KeyRelease	KeyReleaseMask
LeaveNotify	LeaveWindowMask
MapNotify	StructureNotifyMask, SubstructureNotifyMask
MappingNotify[1]	—
MapRequest	SubstructureRedirectMask
MotionNotify	ButtonMotionMask, Button1MotionMask, Button2MotionMask, Button3MotionMask, Button4MotionMask, Button5MotionMask, PointerMotionMask, PointerMotionHintMask
NoExpose	ExposureMask
PropertyNotify	PropertyChangeMask
ReparentNotify	StructureNotifyMask, SubstructureNotifyMask
ResizeRequest	ResizeRedirectMask
SelectionClear[1]	—
SelectionNotify[1]	—
SelectionRequest[1]	—
UnmapNotify	StructureNotifyMask, SubstructureNotifyMask
VisibilityNotify	VisibilityChangeMask

[1]*No event mask is available to control selection of this event.*

The XEvent Union

When an event is reported by the X server, the program must be able to find out the type of the event and, depending on the type, other relevant information describing the event. For example, if the event reports a mouse button-press, you may want to know which button and the location of the mouse pointer at the time of the button-press. Because of the diversity of events in X, the information necessary to describe one class of events (say, mouse events) differs significantly from that needed by another (say, keyboard events). Thus, a number of different data structures are used to describe the events. Since a common format is needed to report all events, a C union of these data structures is used to hold the information. The header file <X11/Xlib.h> defines this union named XEvent as follows:

```
typedef union _XEvent
{
    int                     type;    /* Event's type comes first */
    XAnyEvent               xany;
    XKeyEvent               xkey;
    XButtonEvent            xbutton;
    XMotionEvent            xmotion;
    XCrossingEvent          xcrossing;
    XFocusChangeEvent       xfocus;
    XExposeEvent            xexpose;
    XGraphicsExposeEvent    xgraphicsexpose;
    XNoExposeEvent          xnoexpose;
    XVisibilityEvent        xvisibility;
    XCreateWindowEvent      xcreatewindow;
    XDestroyWindowEvent     xdestroywindow;
    XUnmapEvent             xunmap;
    XMapEvent               xmap;
    XMapRequestEvent        xmaprequest;
    XReparentEvent          xreparent;
    XConfigureEvent         xconfigure;
    XGravityEvent           xgravity;
    XResizeRequestEvent     xresizerequest;
    XConfigureRequestEvent  xconfigurerequest;
    XCirculateEvent         xcirculate;
    XCirculateRequestEvent  xcirculaterequest;
    XPropertyEvent          xproperty;
    XSelectionClearEvent    xselectionclear;
    XSelectionRequestEvent  xselectionrequest;
    XSelectionEvent         xselection;
    XColormapEvent          xcolormap;
    XClientMessageEvent     xclient;
    XMappingEvent           xmapping;
    XErrorEvent             xerror;
    XKeymapEvent            xkeymap;
    long                    pad[24];
} XEvent;
```

As you can see, the data type XEvent is defined as the union of a large number of different data structures. You will encounter the structures for the common events later in this chapter.

The XAnyEvent Structure

The simplest event data structure is XAnyEvent, which is defined as follows:

```
typedef struct
{
```

```
int          type;        /* The event type                */
unsigned long serial;     /* Number of last processed event */
Bool         send_event;  /* True = event is from SendEvent */
Display      *display;    /* Identifies the reporting server */
Window       window;      /* Window requesting this event  */
} XAnyEvent;
```

The fields appearing in the XAnyEvent structure happen to be the first five entries in every event's data structure. The type field tells you the kind of event being reported. The X server keeps track of the sequence of protocol requests it has processed so far and reports the sequence number of the last processed request in the serial field.

The next field, send_event, describes how the event originated. In X, you can send a simulated event to a window. For example, even when there is no keypress, you can prepare an event structure for a keypress event and send it to a window using the XSendEvent function. The server indicates such events by setting the send_event flag in the event structure to True. If the event was generated by the server, send_event will be zero (False).

The display field identifies the server from which the event arrived. The next field is the window that had requested this type of event. The window hierarchy determines which window receives an event.

ButtonPress and ButtonRelease Events

These events are generated whenever the user presses or releases a mouse button. The data structure for XButtonEvent is defined as follows:

```
typedef struct
{
    int          type;        /* Type of event                */
    unsigned long serial;     /* Last processed request no.   */
    Bool         send_event;  /* True if from SendEvent       */
    Display      *display;    /* This display sent event      */
    Window       window;      /* Reported to this window      */
    Window       root;        /* Root window                  */
    Window       subwindow;   /* Pointer is in this child     */
    Time         time;        /* Timestamp in milliseconds    */
    int          x, y;        /* Position in event window     */
    int          x_root, y_root; /* Position relative to root */
    unsigned int state;       /* State of key and buttons     */
    unsigned int button;      /* Which button is involved?    */
    Bool         same_screen; /* True=grab on same screen     */
} XButtonEvent;
```

CirculateNotify and
CirculateRequest Events

These events are generated when the stacking order of the windows is changed. The CirculateRequest event is generated when the X server receives a request to rearrange the windows. The server sends the CirculateNotify event after the windows are restacked. The information for these events are in the xcirculate and xcirculaterequest members of the XEvent union. These members are structures of type XCirculateEvent and XCirculateRequestEvent respectively and are defined in <X11/Xlib.h> as follows:

```
typedef struct
{
    int             type;         /* Type of event = CirculateNotify */
    unsigned long   serial;       /* Last processed request number   */
    Bool            send_event;   /* True = if from a SendEvent      */
    Display         *display;     /* This display sent the event     */
    Window          event;        /* Window to receive the event     */
    Window          window;       /* Window that was restacked       */
    int             place;        /* One of: PlaceOnTop,             */
                                  /*          PlaceOnBottom          */
} XCirculateEvent;

typedef struct
{
    int             type;         /* CirculateRequest                */
    unsigned long   serial;       /* Last processed request number   */
    Bool            send_event;   /* True = if from a SendEvent      */
    Display         *display;     /* This display sent the event     */
    Window          parent;       /* Parent of window restacked      */
    Window          window;       /* Window that was restacked       */
    int             place;        /* One of: PlaceOnTop,             */
                                  /*          PlaceOnBottom          */
} XCirculateRequestEvent;
```

ClientMessage Event

If you write two cooperating applications that need to coordinate their actions, you can do so by sending ClientMessage events. Because X applications do their work in response to events, it is convenient to communicate with other clients through an event. You send ClientMessage events by calling the XSendEvent function.

In Xt Intrinsics, you can add event-handlers (see Chapter 6) for ClientMessage events by specifying the constant NoEventMask as the second argument to the XtAddEventHandler function like this:

```
Widget w;
void    msg_handler();

XtAddEventHandler(w, NoEventMask, TRUE, msg_handler, NULL);
```

where msg_handler is the function called when any nonmaskable event is received for the widget w. Since there are other nonmaskable events such as SelectionClear, SelectionNotify, and SelectionRequest, the msg_handler function should first make sure that the event type is ClientMessage before processing the event.

Unlike other X events that deal with user inputs and repainting of windows, the ClientMessage event is meant to transmit a small amount of information from one client to another. The data for the ClientMessage event is in the xclient field of the XEvent union. This field is an XClientMessageEvent structure, defined in <X11/Xlib.h> as follows:

```
typedef struct
{
    int           type;         /* Type of event = ClientMessage */
    unsigned long serial;       /* Last processed request number */
    Bool          send_event;   /* Always True for ClientMessage */
    Display       *display;     /* This display sent event        */
    Window        window;       /* Window to receive the event    */
    Atom          message_type; /* Atom for message type          */
    int           format;       /* Data format: 8, 16, or 32      */
    union                       /* You can pass up to 20 bytes     */
    {                           /* using ClientMessage events      */
        char  b[20];            /* Data when format is  8          */
        short s[10];            /* Data when format is 16          */
        long  l[5];             /* Data when format is 32          */
    } data;
} XClientMessageEvent;
```

ColormapNotify Event

The X server generates a ColormapNotify event when the colormap attribute of a window changes or when a new colormap is installed. The information for this event is in the xcolormap member of the XEvent union. The xcolormap member is a structure of type XColormapEvent, declared as follows in <X11/Xlib.h> (note the conditional declaration to accomodate the needs of C++ programmers—in C++, new is a reserved keyword):

```
typedef struct
{
    int          type;        /* EnterNotify or LeaveNotify    */
    unsigned long serial;     /* Last processed request number */
    Bool         send_event;  /* True = if from a SendEvent    */
    Display      *display;     /* Display where event occurred  */
    Window       window;      /* Window whose colormap changed */
    Colormap     colormap;    /* Colormap ID or None           */
#if defined(__cplusplus) || defined(c_plusplus)
    Bool c_new;                /* Cannot use "new" in C++       */
#else
    Bool new;                  /* True means colormap changed   */
#endif
    int state;                 /* One of: ColormapInstalled,    */
                               /*         ColormapUninstalled   */
} XColormapEvent;
```

11

ConfigureNotify and ConfigureRequest Events

The X server sends these events when a window is reconfigured—when its size, position, border width, or stacking order changes (ConfigureNotify) or is about to be changed (ConfigureRequest). The relevant information is in the xconfigure and xconfigurerequest members of the XEvent union. These members are structures of type XConfigureEvent and XConfigureRequestEvent, which are declared as follows:

```
typedef struct
{
    int          type;        /* ConfigureNotify               */
    unsigned long serial;     /* Last processed request number */
    Bool         send_event;  /* True = if from a SendEvent    */
    Display      *display;     /* Display where event occurred  */
    Window       event;       /* Window to which event reported */
    Window       window;      /* Window that was reconfigured   */
    int          x, y;        /* New position in parent's frame */
    int          width,       /* New width of window            */
                 height;      /* New height of window           */
    int          border_width;/* New border width of window     */
    Window       above;       /* Set to: Sibling or None        */
    Bool         override_redirect; /* If True, window manager
                                   will not intervene with the
                                   reconfiguration of this window */
} XConfigureEvent;
```

```
typedef struct
{
    int           type;          /* ConfigureNotify                  */
    unsigned long serial;        /* Last processed request number    */
    Bool          send_event;    /* True = if from a SendEvent        */
    Display       *display;      /* Display where event occurred      */
    Window        parent;        /* Parent of "window"                */
    Window        window;        /* Window to be reconfigured         */
    int           x, y;          /* New position in parent's frame    */
    int           width,         /* New width of window               */
                  height;        /* New height of window              */
    int           border_width;  /* New border width of window        */
    Window        above;         /* Set to: Sibling or None           */
    int           detail;        /* One of: Above, Below, TopIf,      */
                                 /*         BottomIf, Opposite        */
    unsigned long value_mask;    /* Indicates the type of changes     */
} XConfigureRequestEvent;
```

CreateNotify Event

The X server reports the CreateNotify event when a window is created. The relevant information of this event is in an XCreateWindowEvent structure, declared as follows:

```
typedef struct
{
    int           type;          /* CreateNotify                     */
    unsigned long serial;        /* Last processed request number    */
    Bool          send_event;    /* True = if from a SendEvent        */
    Display       *display;      /* Display where event occurred      */
    Window        parent;        /* Parent of "window"                */
    Window        window;        /* ID of window that was created     */
    int           x, y;          /* Location in parent's frame        */
    int           width, height; /* Size of window                    */
    int           border_width;  /* Border width in pixels            */
    Bool          override_redirect; /* If True, window manager
                                 will not intervene with the
                                 creation of this window           */
} XCreateWindowEvent;
```

DestroyNotify Event

The X server can send a DestroyNotify event to any client that requests information about windows being destroyed. The information for this event is in the xdestroywindow member of the XEvent union. The xdestroywindow member is an XDestroyWindowEvent structure, which is declared in <X11/Xlib.h> as follows:

```
typedef struct
{
    int             type;        /* DestroyNotify                */
    unsigned long   serial;      /* Last processed request number */
    Bool            send_event;  /* True = if from a SendEvent   */
    Display         *display;    /* Display where event occurred */
    Window          event;       /* Window to which event reported */
    Window          window;      /* ID of window being destroyed  */
} XDestroyWindowEvent;
```

EnterNotify and LeaveNotify Events

The X server reports the information for EnterNotify and LeaveNotify events in the field named xcrossing in the XEvent union. This is an XCrossingEvent data structure, defined in <X11/Xlib.h> as:

```
typedef struct
{
    int             type;        /* EnterNotify or LeaveNotify   */
    unsigned long   serial;      /* Last processed request number */
    Bool            send_event;  /* True = if from a SendEvent   */
    Display         *display;    /* Display where event occurred */
    Window          window;      /* Window to which event reported */
    Window          root;        /* Root window in that screen   */
    Window          subwindow;   /* Child window involved in event */
    Time            time;        /* Time in milliseconds         */
    int             x, y;        /* Final position in event window */
    int             x_root,      /* Pointer's final position in  */
                    y_root;      /* root window's coordinate frame */
    int             mode;        /* One of the three constants:   */
                                 /* NotifyNormal, NotifyGrab,     */
                                 /* NotifyUngrab                 */
    int             detail;      /* One of the five constants:    */
                                 /* NotifyAncestor, NotifyVirtual, */
                                 /* NotifyInferior, NotifyNonLinear, */
                                 /* NotifyNonLinearVirtual        */
```

11

```
    Bool           same_screen;/* Pointer/window in same screen? */
    Bool           focus;       /* Input focus on this window?    */
    unsigned int   state;       /* State of key and buttons       */
} XCrossingEvent;
```

Expose Event

Expose events are generated by the server whenever any of your application's windows need redrawing. This can happen when the window is first mapped, when an obscuring window is moved, or when you clear an area of a window by calling XClearArea.

In most applications, all drawing occurs in reponse to Expose events. This is because you cannot draw in a window until it is ready and there is no good way of knowing when it is ready. However, when you receive an Expose event for a window, you can be sure that it is ready for use.

When parts of a window need redrawing, the X server generates an Expose event for every rectangular region that was exposed. When you retrieve an Expose event, the relevant information is in an XExposeEvent data structure (accessed as the member xexpose of the XEvent union):

```
typedef struct
{
    int            type;        /* Event's type                   */
    unsigned long  serial;      /* Last processed request number  */
    Bool           send_event;  /* True means from a SendEvent    */
    Display        *display;     /* Display where event occurred   */
    Window         window;      /* Window that needs redrawing    */
    int            x, y;        /* Origin and dimensions of the   */
    int            width,       /* rectangle that has been        */
                   height;      /* "exposed"                      */
    int            count;       /* Number of expose events to come */
} XExposeEvent;
```

The members x, y, width, and height identify the rectangle whose contents are lost and have to be redrawn. The last member of the structure, count, tells you how many more expose events for the same window are yet to arrive. Knowing this, you can devise a simple strategy of handling Expose events.

Wait for the expose event with count equal to zero. Then, clear the entire window and redraw everything in the window. In other words, you are ignoring the information about the specific parts that need refreshing and simply updating the whole window.

Handling Expose events on count zero works well for simple drawings, but for complex drawings, it is better to make use of the information on the rectangle that needs redrawing. One method is to use a region. You can use XUnionRectWithRegion to add all the rectangles in a region. Set the clipping mask of the drawing GC with XSetRegion. Then redraw when the Expose event with count zero arrives. For maximum efficiency, your application's drawing function must be smart enough to draw only within the regions. Since the server clips against the region, there is no harm in drawing everything, but that sends unnecessary graphics requests and wastes time.

FocusIn and FocusOut Events

11

The FocusIn and FocusOut events are generated when the keyboard input focus changes. The structure for this event type is declared as follows:

```
typedef struct
{
    int            type;        /* FocusIn or FocusOut         */
    unsigned long serial;       /* Last processed request number */
    Bool           send_event;  /* True = if from a SendEvent   */
    Display        *display;     /* Display where event occurred */
    Window         window;       /* Window to which event reported */
    int            mode;         /* One of the three constants:
                                    NotifyNormal, NotifyGrab,
                                    NotifyUngrab                 */
    int            detail;       /* One of the five constants:
                                    NotifyAncestor, NotifyVirtual,
                                    NotifyInferior, NotifyNonLinear,
                                    NotifyNonLinearVirtual        */
} XFocusChangeEvent;
```

GraphicsExpose and NoExpose Events

These events are sent if a source area is obscured during copy operations initiated with calls to the Xlib functions XCopyArea or XCopyPlane. These events are sent only if the graphics_exposures member of the graphics context (GC) is set to True. When this flag is set, the X server generates a NoExpose event whenever a graphics operation that might have produced a GraphicsExpose event does not produce any. The structures for this event are XGraphicsExposeEvent and XNoExposeEvent which are declared as follows:

```
typedef struct
{
    int            type;         /* Event's type = GraphicsExpose  */
    unsigned long serial;        /* Last processed request number  */
    Bool           send_event;   /* True means from a SendEvent     */
    Display        *display;      /* Display where event occurred    */
    Drawable       drawable;      /* Destination of copy operation   */
    int            x, y;          /* Origin and dimensions of the    */
    int            width,         /* rectangle that has been          */
                   height;        /* "exposed"  (in pixels)           */
    int            count;         /* Number of expose events to come */
    int major_code;              /* one of: CopyArea or CopyPlane    */
    int minor_code;              /* Reserved for extensions           */
} XGraphicsExposeEvent;

typedef struct
{
    int            type;         /* Event's type = GraphicsExpose */
    unsigned long serial;        /* Last processed request number */
    Bool           send_event;   /* True means from a SendEvent    */
    Display        *display;      /* Display where event occurred   */
    Drawable       drawable;      /* Destination of copy operation  */
    int major_code;              /* one of: CopyArea or CopyPlane  */
    int minor_code;              /* Reserved for extensions         */
} XNoExposeEvent;
```

GravityNotify Event

The X server generates this event when a window is moved because of a change in the size of its parent. The XGravityEvent contains information for this event:

```
typedef struct
{
    int            type;         /* GravityNotify                    */
    unsigned long serial;        /* Last processed request number   */
    Bool           send_event;   /* True = if from a SendEvent       */
    Display        *display;      /* Display where event occurred     */
    Window         event;         /* Window to which event reported   */
    Window         window;        /* ID of window that was moved      */
    int            x, y;          /* New coordinates of window        */
} XGravityEvent;
```

KeymapNotify Event

The X server generates a KeymapNotify event (during an EnterWindow or FocusIn event) whenever there is a change in the state of the keyboard—the condition of each key in the keyboard. The structure for this event is defined as follows:

```
typedef struct
{
    int         type;          /* KeymapNotify                    */
    unsigned long serial;      /* Last processed request number */
    Bool        send_event;    /* True = if from a SendEvent      */
    Display     *display;      /* Display where event occurred   */
    Window      window;        /* "window" member of latest
                                  FocusIn or EnterNotify event   */
    char        key_vector[32]; /* A 256-bit mask, each
                                   representing status of a key  */
} XKeymapEvent;
```

11

KeyPress and KeyRelease Events

KeyPress and KeyRelease are generated when any key is pressed or released. You will find information about these events in the xkey member of the XEvent union. xkey is an XKeyEvent structure, which is declared in <X11/Xlib.h> as follows:

```
typedef struct
{
    int         type;          /* Event's type                    */
    unsigned long serial;      /* Last processed request number */
    Bool        send_event;    /* True = if from a SendEvent      */
    Display     *display;      /* Display where event occurred   */
    Window      window;        /* Window to which event reported */
    Window      root;          /* Root window in that screen      */
    Window      subwindow;     /* Child window involved in event */
    Time        time;          /* Time in milliseconds            */
    int         x, y;          /* Position in event window        */
    int         x_root,        /* Pointer's position in the       */
                y_root;        /* root window's coordinate frame */
    unsigned int state;        /* State of key and buttons        */
    unsigned int keycode;      /* detail */
    Bool        same_screen;   /* Pointer/window in same screen? */
} XKeyEvent;
```

MapNotify and UnmapNotify Events

The X server sends MapNotify and UnmapNotify events to an interested client whenever a window is mapped (made visible) or unmapped. The structures for the events are as follows:

```
typedef struct
{
    int             type;       /* Event's type = MapNotify      */
    unsigned long serial;       /* Last processed request number */
    Bool            send_event; /* True = if from a SendEvent     */
    Display         *display;   /* Display where event occurred   */
    Window          event;      /* Window to which event reported */
    Window          window;     /* ID of window that was mapped    */
    Bool            override_redirect; /* If True, window manager
                                  will not intervene with the
                                  creation of this window          */
} XMapEvent;

typedef struct
{
    int             type;       /* Event's type = UnmapNotify     */
    unsigned long serial;       /* Last processed request number */
    Bool            send_event; /* True = if from a SendEvent     */
    Display         *display;   /* Display where event occurred   */
    Window          event;      /* Window to which event reported */
    Window          window;     /* Window that was unmapped        */
    Bool            from_configure; /* True if event was generated
                                  because parent's win_gravity
                                  was set to UnmapGravity           */
} XUnmapEvent;
```

MappingNotify Event

The X server manages the translation of keycodes to keysym (symbolic name for a key). Applications can change this mapping by calling the function XChangeKeyboardMapping. An application should not do this on its own, but the user may run a utility program such as xmodmap to alter the mapping of one or more keys. When this happens, all X client applications will receive a MappingNotify event (you cannot mask this event). Future mappings of keycodes to keysyms will work properly as long as your application calls XRefreshKeyboardMapping each time it receives a MappingNotify event. The event itself is reported in the following structure:

```
typedef struct
{
    int           type;         /* Event's type                 */
    unsigned long serial;       /* Last processed request number */
    Bool          send_event;   /* True = if from a SendEvent    */
    Display       *display;      /* Display where event occurred  */
    Window        window;       /* Unused                        */
    int           request;      /* One of: MappingModifier,
                                   MappingKeyboard, MappingPointer */
    int           first_keycode; /* First keycode altered        */
    int           count;        /* Number of keycodes changed    */
} XMappingEvent;
```

MapRequest Event

This event is generated just before a window is mapped. Window managers can use this to detect when a new window is made visible on the display. Information for this event appears in a structure as follows:

```
typedef struct
{
    int           type;         /* MapRequest                    */
    unsigned long serial;       /* Last processed request number */
    Bool          send_event;   /* True = if from a SendEvent    */
    Display       *display;      /* Display where event occurred  */
    Window        parent;       /* Parent of "window"            */
    Window        window;       /* Window to be mapped           */
} XMapRequestEvent;
```

MotionNotify Event

The X server generates a MotionNotify event when the user moves the mouse pointer. The XMotionEvent contains information for this event.

```
typedef struct
{
    int           type;         /* Event's type                  */
    unsigned long serial;       /* Last processed request number */
    Bool          send_event;   /* True = if from a SendEvent     */
    Display       *display;      /* Display where event occurred   */
    Window        window;       /* Window to which event reported */
    Window        root;         /* Root window in that screen     */
    Window        subwindow;    /* Child window involved in event */
```

11

```
        Time          time;         /* Time in milliseconds          */
        int           x, y;         /* Position in event window      */
        int           x_root,       /* Pointer's position in the     */
                      y_root;       /* root window's coordinate frame */
        unsigned int  state;        /* State of key and buttons      */
        char          is_hint;      /* NotifyNormal or NotifyHint     */
        Bool          same_screen;  /* Pointer/window in same screen? */
} XMotionEvent;
```

PropertyNotify Event

The X server generates a PropertyNotify event when a property (see Chapter 8) of a window is changed (a property is a value with a name associated with a window). You can request this event by using the PropertyChangeMask event mask. The data associated with the PropertyNotify event is in the xproperty field of the XEvent union. This field is an XPropertyEvent structure, defined in <X11/Xlib.h> as follows:

```
typedef struct
{
        int           type;       /* Type of event = PropertyNotify */
        unsigned long serial;     /* Last processed request number   */
        Bool          send_event; /* True if from SendEvent          */
        Display       *display;   /* This display sent event         */
        Window        window;     /* Window whose property changed   */
        Atom          atom;       /* Name of property involved        */
        Time          time;       /* Time when property changed       */
        int           state;      /* One of: PropertyNewValue or      */
                                  /*          PropertyDelete          */
} XPropertyEvent;
```

ReparentNotify Event

This event is generated when a window's parent is changed. The information is reported in an XReparentEvent structure, declared as follows:

```
typedef struct
{
        int           type;       /* ReparentNotify                  */
        unsigned long serial;     /* Last processed request number   */
        Bool          send_event; /* True = if from a SendEvent       */
        Display       *display;   /* Display where event occurred     */
        Window        event;      /* Event sent to this window        */
```

```
    Window        window;     /* Window that was reparented  */
    Window        parent;     /* New parent of "window"      */
    int           x, y;       /* Location in new parent      */
    Bool          override_redirect; /* If True, window manager
                                        will not intervene with the
                                        reparenting             */
} XReparentEvent;
```

ResizeRequest Event

The server generates a ResizeRequest event when a window's size is about to be changed. The information for this event is reported in a XResizeRequestEvent structure, declared as follows:

```
typedef struct
{
    int           type;        /* ResizeRequest              */
    unsigned long serial;      /* Last processed request number */
    Bool          send_event;  /* True = if from a SendEvent  */
    Display       *display;    /* Display where event occurred */
    Window        window;      /* Window to be resized        */
    int           width, height; /* New size of window        */
} XResizeRequestEvent;
```

Selection Events

There are three events for coordinating the exchange of data through selections: SelectionClear, SelectionRequest, and SelectionNotify. Applications do not have to solicit these events—they are sent automatically.

The X server sends a SelectionClear event to the current owner of a selection whenever the owner of the selection changes. The information for this event is in the xselectionclear field of the XEvent union. The xselectionclear field in this union is an XSelectionClearEvent structure, defined in <X11/Xlib.h> as follows:

```
typedef struct
{
    int           type;        /* Type of event = SelectionClear */
    unsigned long serial;      /* Last processed request number */
    Bool          send_event;  /* True if from SendEvent      */
    Display       *display;    /* This displays sent event    */
    Window        window;      /* Window losing ownership     */
```

```
      Atom         selection;  /* Name of selection involved   */
      Time         time;       /* Time when ownership was lost  */
} XSelectionClearEvent;
```

When an application wants to receive the data corresponding to a selection, it calls the XConvertSelection function, which causes a SelectionRequest event to be sent to the current owner of the selection. The xselectionrequest field in the XEvent union contains information on this event. The event data structure is defined in <X11/Xlib.h> as follows:

```
typedef struct
{
      int          type;        /* Type of event = SelectionRequest*/
      unsigned long serial;     /* Last processed request number  */
      Bool         send_event;  /* True if from SendEvent          */
      Display      *display;     /* This display sent event         */
      Window       owner;       /* Window that owns the selection  */
      Window       requestor;   /* Window requesting data          */
      Atom         selection;   /* Name of selection involved      */
      Atom         target;      /* Data should be converted to     */
                                /* this type by the owner          */
      Atom         property;    /* Selection's owner should copy   */
                                /* data to this property           */
      Time         time;        /* Time when selection requested   */
} XSelectionRequestEvent;
```

When a selection's owner receives the SelectionRequest event, it should convert the data to the type specified by the target atom in the event and copy the converted data to the specified property on the requesting window. After that, the owner sends a SelectionNotify event to the requesting window to indicate the result of the request. The information for the SelectionNotify event is in the xselection field of the XEvent union. This field is a structure of type XSelectionEvent, defined in <X11/Xlib.h> as follows:

```
typedef struct
{
      int          type;        /* Type of event = SelectionNotify */
      unsigned long serial;     /* Last processed request number  */
      Bool         send_event;  /* True if from SendEvent          */
      Display      *display;     /* This display sent event         */
      Window       requestor;   /* Window that had requested data  */
      Atom         selection;   /* Name of selection involved      */
      Atom         target;      /* Data type of value in property  */
      Atom         property;    /* Property where data has been    */
                                /* placed. "None" means failure    */
      Time         time;        /* Time when data stored           */
} XSelectionEvent;
```

VisibilityNotify Event

The X server generates a VisibilityNotify event whenever there is a change in the visibility of a window. You can select this event using the mask named VisibilityChangeMask. The event is reported in the following structure:

```
typedef struct
{
    int           type;        /* VisibilityNotify                    */
    unsigned long serial;      /* Last processed request number       */
    Bool          send_event;  /* True = if from a SendEvent           */
    Display       *display;    /* Display where event occurred         */
    Window        window;      /* Window whose visibility changed */
    int           state;       /* One of: VisibilityUnobscured,
                                  VisibilityPartiallyObscured,
                                  VisibilityFullyObscured              */
} XVisibilityEvent;
```

11

Index

G

H

I

K

X

Find The Latest Technology
And Most Up-To-Date Information
In Hayden Books

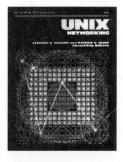

Mastering Turbo Debugger
Tom Swan

This book is for accomplished IBM PC MS-DOS programmers who have mastered Pascal, C, or assembly language and who need useful guidelines for quickly finding and fixing the bugs in their code.

700 pages, 73/8 x 91/4, $29.95 USA
0-672-48454-4

UNIX Networking
Stephen G. Kochan and Patrick H. Wood, Editors

This book provides a comprehensive look at the major aspects of networking in the UNIX system. It's a must for both computer professionals and students with a basic understanding of programming and networking.

600 pages, 73/8 x 91/4, $29.95 USA
0-672-48440-4

SAMS

Motif Functions